Recent Trends in Blockchain for Information Systems Security and Privacy

Recent Trends in Blockchain for Information Systems Security and Privacy

Edited by
Amit Kumar Tyagi and Ajith Abraham

CRC Press
Taylor & Francis Group
Boca Raton   London

CRC Press is an imprint of the
Taylor & Francis Group, an **informa** business

First edition published 2022
by CRC Press
6000 Broken Sound Parkway NW, Suite 300, Boca Raton, FL 33487–2742

and by CRC Press
2 Park Square, Milton Park, Abingdon, Oxon, OX14 4RN

ISBN: 978-0-36768-943-8 (hbk)
ISBN: 978-0-36768-955-1 (pbk)
ISBN: 978-1-00313-973-7 (ebk)

DOI: 10.1201/9781003139737

Typeset in Times
by Apex CoVantage, LLC

Contents

Preface

Blockchain technology as an emerging distributed, decentralized architecture and computing paradigm, which has accelerated the development/application of the cloud/fog/edge computing, artificial intelligence, cyberphysical systems, social networking, crowdsourcing and crowdsensing, 5G, trust management, finance, and other many useful sectors. Nowadays, blockchain technology uses are in information systems to keep information secure and private, but many threats and vulnerabilities have been faced in the past decade on blockchain, like 51% attacks, double spending attacks, etc. The popularity and rapid development of blockchain brings many technical and regulatory challenges for research and academic communities. The main goal of this book is to encourage both researchers and practitioners to share and exchange their experiences and recent studies between academia and industry.

In summary, this book provides the reader with the most up-to-date knowledge of blockchain in mainstream areas of security and privacy in the decentralized domain, which is timely and essential (this is due to the fact that distributed and P2P [peer-to-peer] applications are increasing day by day, and attackers adopt new mechanisms to threaten the security and privacy of the users in those environments). This book provides a detailed explanation of security and privacy aspects with respect to blockchain for information systems, and we assure the reader that this book will be more helpful for students, researchers, and scientists to clear their doubts regarding blockchain uses in information systems. Also, this book will provide a complete detail from origin of blockchain to till this smart era (including security and privacy issues, where almost applications/sectors use digital devices), i.e. uses in many applications for reducing corruption and building trust in people or society (via P2P networking).

Finally, researchers will be able to select their research problems (to do their research) from future research directions sections from our included section in this book. In conclusion, we want to thank our God, family members, teachers, friends, and last but not least, all our authors from the bottom of our hearts (including the publisher) for helping us complete this book before the deadline.

Really, kudos to all.

—Amit Kumar Tyagi,
—Ajit Abraham

Acknowledgments

First of all, we would like to extend our gratitude to our family members, friends, and supervisors, who stood with us as advisors in completing this book. Also, we would like to thank our Almighty "God" who gave us the ability to complete this project. We also thank CRC Press for providing continuous support during this COVID 19 pandemic, and our colleagues at the college/university and others outside the college/university who have provided their support.

Also, we thank our Respected Madam Prof. G Aghila and our Respected Sir Prof. N Sreenath for giving their valuable inputs and helping us in completing this book.

—Amit Kumar Tyagi
—Ajith Abraham

Editors

Amit Kumar Tyagi is Assistant Professor (Senior Grade), and Senior Researcher at Vellore Institute of Technology (VIT), Chennai Campus, India. He earned his PhD in 2018 from Pondicherry Central University, India. He joined the Lord Krishna College of Engineering, Ghaziabad (LKCE) from 2009–2010 and 2012–2013. He was Assistant Professor and Head Researcher at Lingaya's Vidyapeeth (formerly known as Lingaya's University), Faridabad, Haryana, India from 2018 to 2019. Dr. Tyagi's current research focuses on machine learning with big data, blockchain technology, data science, cyberphysical systems, smart and secure computing and privacy. He contributed to several projects such as "AARIN" and "P3-Block" to address some of the open issues related to the privacy breaches in vehicular applications (such as parking) and medical cyberphysical systems (MCPS). He has also published more than 8 patents in the area of deep learning, Internet of Things, cyberphysical systems and computer vision. Recently, he was awarded best paper award for "A Novel Feature Extractor Based on the Modified Approach of Histogram of oriented Gradient", ICCSA 2020, Italy. He is a regular member of the ACM, IEEE, MIRLabs, Ramanujan Mathematical Society, Cryptology Research Society, and Universal Scientific Education and Research Network, CSI, and ISTE.

Ajith Abraham is Director of Machine Intelligence Research Labs (MIR Labs), a not-for-profit scientific network for innovation and research excellence connecting industry and academia. As an investigator and co-investigator, he has won research grants worth over US$100 million from Australia, USA, EU, Italy, Czech Republic, France, Malaysia, and China. His research focuses on real world problems in the fields of machine intelligence, cyberphysical systems, Internet of Things, network security, sensor networks, web intelligence, web services, and data mining. He is Chair of the IEEE Systems Man and Cybernetics Society Technical Committee on Soft Computing. He is editor-in-chief of *Engineering Applications of Artificial Intelligence* (EAAI) and serves/served on the editorial board of several international journals. He earned his Ph.D. in computer science from Monash University, Melbourne, Australia.

Contributors

Amrutha Ann Aby
Sree Chitra Thirunal College of Engineering
Trivandrum, India

Deepshikha Agarwal
Department of Computer Science and Engineering
Amity University
Lucknow, India

Anjalikrishna U. R.
Sree Chitra Thirunal College of Engineering
Trivandrum, India

Aswathy S. U.
Department of Computer Science
Jyothi Engineering College
Thrissur, India

Bindu V
Sree Chitra Thirunal College of Engineering
Trivandrum, India

Aswani Kumar Cherukuri
School of Information Technology & Engineering
Vellore Institute of Technology
Vellore, India

Meenu Gupta
Department of Computer Science and Engineering
Chandigarh University
Punjab, India

Neeraja James
Department of Computer Science
Jyothi Engineering College
Thrissur, India

Annapurna Jonnalagadda
School of Computer Science & Engineering
Vellore Institute of Technology
Vellore, India

Blesmi Rose Joseph
Department of Computer Science
Jyothi Engineering College
Thrissur, India

Geeta Kakarla
Sreenidhi Institute of Science and Technology
Hyderabad, India

Shirisha Kakarla
Sreenidhi Institute of Science and Technology
Hyderabad, India

Anu Kesari
Sree Chitra Thirunal College of Engineering
Trivandrum, India

Kiruba K
Department of Computer Science and Engineering
IFET College of Engineering
Villupuram, India

Kumar Krishen
University of Houston
Houston, TX

Tanmay Kulkarni
School of Computer Science Engineering
Vellore Institute of Technology
Chennai, India

Shabnam Kumari
Department of Computer Science
Faculty of Science and Humanities
SRM Institute of Science and Technology
Chennai, India

Leema Roselin G
Department of Computer Science and Engineering
IFET College of Engineering
Villupuram, India

Maheswari R
School of Computer Science Engineering
Vellore Institute of Technology
Chennai, India

Manjubala P
Department of Computer Science and Engineering
IFET College of Engineering
Villupuram, India

Raghuram Nadipalli
Department of Computer Science and Engineering
Sri Chandrasekharendra Saraswathi Viswa
    Mahavidyalaya University
Kanchipuram, India

D. Narsinga Rao
Directorate of Economics and Statistics (DES)
Govt. of Telangana State, India

Shivam Narula
School of Computer Science & Engineering
Vellore Institute of Technology
Vellore, India

Chirag Paunwala
Department of Electronics and Communication
Sarvajanik College of Engineering and
    Technology, affiliated to Gujarat Technological
    University
Ahmedabad, India

Mita Paunwala
Department of Electronics and Communication
C K Pithawala College of Engineering and
    Technology, affiliated to Gujarat Technological
    University
Ahmedabad, India

Rajmohan R
Department of Computer Science and Engineering
IFET College of Engineering
Villupuram, India

S. Ramamoorthy
Department of Computer Science and Engineering
SRM IST
Chennai, India

G. Rekha
Department of Computer Science and Engineering
Koneru Lakshmaiah Education Foundation
Guntur, India

Dhanya Sabu
Sree Chitra Thirunal College of Engineering
Trivandrum, India

Saranya P
School of Computer Science Engineering
Vellore Institute of Technology
Chennai, India

S. Selvi
Department of Computer Science and Engineering
Erode Sengunthar Engineering College
Erode, India

Shyam Mohan J. S.
Department of Computer Science and Engineering
Sri Chandrasekharendra Saraswathi Viswa
    Mahavidyalaya University
Kanchipuram, India

Kathiravan Srinivasan
School of Information Technology & Engineering
Vellore Institute of Technology
Vellore, India

Sruti C R
School of Management Studies
Sathyabama Institute of Science and Technology
Chennai, India

Divya Stephen
Department of Computer Science
Jyothi Engineering College
Thrissur, India

Ciza Thomas
Directorate of Technical Education
Government of Kerala
Trivandrum, India

Khushboo Tripathi
Department of Computer Science and Engineering
Amity University
Haryana, India

Amit Kumar Tyagi
School of Computer Science and Engineering
Vellore Institute of Technology
Chennai, India

S Umamaheswari
School of Management Studies
Sathyabama Institute of Science and Technology
Chennai, India

Usharani S
Department of Computer Science and Engineering
IFET College of Engineering
Villupuram, India

Chetanya Ved
Department of Information Technology
Bharati Vidyapeeth College of Engineering
Delhi, India

Narasimha Krishna Amruth Vemuganti
Department of Computer Science and Engineering
Sri Chandrasekharendra Saraswathi Viswa
    Mahavidyalaya University
Kanchipuram, India

Vankadara Naga Venkata Kuladeep
Department of Computer Science and Engineering
Sri Chandrasekharendra Saraswathi Viswa
    Mahavidyalaya University
Kanchipuram, India

M. Vimala Devi
Department of Computer Science and Engineering
K.S.R. Institute for Engineering and Technology
Tiruchengode, India

Aarohi Vora
Department of Electronics and Communication
Gujarat Technological University
Ahmedabad, India

Varun Wahi
School of Information Technology & Engineering
Vellore Institute of Technology
Vellore, India

TRACK 1

Blockchain
Background and Importance

Fundamentals of Blockchain and Distributed Ledger Technology (DLT)

Leema Roselin G, Rajmohan R,
Usharani S, Kiruba K, Manjubala P

Contents

1.1 INTRODUCTION OF BLOCKCHAIN AND DISTRIBUTED LEDGER TECHNOLOGY (DLT)

Blockchain-based distributed ledger technology (DLT) has a range of possible uses outside the limited world of digital currency and cryptocurrencies that was first implemented as the underlying infrastructure of the cryptocurrency Bitcoin. For example, DLT might have uses in capital markets for cross-border transfers, financial market infrastructure, and security registries.

However, DLT's future implementations are not confined to the financial industry [1][2]. DLT is presently being explored by using trustworthy partners to verify flows and trends to promote digital identity goods or to create untampered, decentralized records of the distribution of goods and services through a supply chain [1][3]. Usually, DLT advocates emphasize a range of possible benefits over conventional unified ledgers and some other kinds of collaborative ledgers, like decentralization, deregulation, better transparency and easy accountability, speed and productivity improvements, cost savings, and modernization and fully programmability. That said, technology continues to improve and faces new threats and challenges, which are often yet to be addressed.

Scalability, interoperability, organizational protection and cyber security, identity authentication, data privacy, transaction conflicts and redress mechanisms, and difficulties in establishing a regulatory and legal system for DLT implementations are the most widely cited technical, regulatory, and legal challenges relevant to DLT, which may bring significant changes in the functions and obligations of DLT implementation. Significant costs related to the transfer of current long-standing IT processes, operating structures and policy structures to DLT-based architecture are another problem, especially applicable to the field of financial market infrastructure. Many industry analysts note that DLT implementations would likely launch in places without many legacy automation investments, like financial transactions and syndicated lending in the financial industry, because of these challenges. It is possible to open/permitless or permit distributed ledger structures, and there are basic variations between these two forms that relate to somewhat different risk profiles. There is no centralized controller who manages access to the network in permissionless networks. A database server with the appropriate program is all that is required to enter the network and connect transaction history. Members of the network are preselected on registered networks by the controller or administrator of that same ledger, who manages access to the network and enforces the guidelines of the ledger.

DLT led to a special and increasingly developing approach to data storage and distribution across various data sources or ledgers. Such technology enables the capturing, sharing, and synchronization of transactions and data through a global network of separate network members. A "blockchain" is a special kind of data structure in certain distributed ledgers that stores and transmits information in packages called "blocks" in a digital "chain" that are linked to each other. Blockchains use cryptographic and algorithmic techniques in an irreversible fashion to store and sync data throughout network. Distributed ledgers (DLs) are really a particular application of the wider "public ledgers" category which is simply represented as a shared data record across multiple parties. For instance, a new cryptocurrency transaction will be registered and distributed in a block of data to a network, which is first authenticated by members of the network and then connected in an append-only manner, to an existing block, thereby forming a blockchain. Even as linear chain expands as new blocks are inserted, each network member does not retrospectively modify older blocks. Note that blockchain technology is not inherently used by all distributed ledgers, and blockchain technology might be used in different ways instead.

Blockchain arranges data in blocks, which are used primarily for square calculation in chains. Blockchain square tests the "Internet import" building block and alters contact tracking and peer-to-peer sharing, but it is not a requirement for a centrally organized body. "Value" means any records of ownership of plus such as money, shares, and land titles and, together, data such as identification, health data, and various personal details. Both forms have advantages and drawbacks that vary considerably in different usage cases. Registered programs, for example, are better at addressing identity authentication and data protection problems, but they involve a central access control authority that provides a possible target for cyberattacks. It is also likely that approved structures could more conveniently integrate into current legislative and regulatory processes and administrative arrangements. To a degree, however, authorized DLs eliminate core advantages of the most important invention of DLT. This is because free permissionless DLs are accomplished through protection and system integrity by cryptography and algorithmic approaches ensuring that confidential network members are empowered to implement the ledger's consistency without the use of entry barriers or trust among members.

The majority of DLT's research and development efforts are currently dedicated to upgrading financial systems and procedures, and there is tremendous scope for this commitment to be leveraged for the good of developed countries by development organizations. With that being said, the technology is still at an initial phase of development, but there is still a ways to go before it will be possible to realize its full potential, particularly with regard to privacy, stability, interoperability, scalability, and regulatory and legal issues. It is not always an optimal strategy for development organizations to wait for "perfect" DLT solutions, though. Provided DLT's ability to structure responses to growth problems in the finance industry and even beyond, the World Bank Group is able to track and form trends closely and, where necessary, promote their healthy implementation while ensuring institutional independence with respect to private sector actors. It needs not only analysis, and moreover legitimate experiments and trials, to grasp DLT's true potential for growth goals.

The use of DLT to help meet growth goals in the finance industry includes the development and successful promotion of vital accompanying components in addition to the development of the technology itself. Significant among these are user-friendly architecture of the mobile interface, money management, and functionality, a solid system for the safety of financial users, interoperability with conventional payments and financial institutions and infrastructure, and efficient regulation.

1.2 WORKS OF DISTRIBUTED LEDGER TECHNOLOGY

Distributed ledger technology falls on the back of numerous Internet-enabled (peer-to-peer [P2P]) applications, such as email, music distribution or other shared folders, and electronic mail. Internet-based asset ownership transactions, however, have been difficult for a long time, as this involves verifying that a resource is only exchanged by its rightful owner and guaranteeing that the resource cannot be transmitted multiple times, i.e. without double spending. Anything of worth may be the commodity at issue. DLT led to a fundamental and quickly changing approach to data recording and sharing across different data stores (ledgers), each of which has the very same data records and is stored and managed collectively by a distributed computer server network known as nodes. Another means of conversing of DLT is based on it being essentially a hierarchical database with some particular properties. Blockchain, a specialized version of DLT, utilizes cryptographic and algorithmic approaches to construct and validate a constantly expanding, append-only data system that serves the purpose of a blockchain and serves the purpose of a ledger, a chain of so-called "transaction blocks." New database additions are introduced by a member (node) who generates a new "data block" containing, for example, many transaction documents.

Knowledge concerning this new block of data is then transmitted across the whole network, as shown in Figure 1.1, containing encrypted information such that transaction specifics are also not publicly disclosed, as per a predefined analytic confirmation process ("consensus mechanism"), all network members jointly decide the legitimacy of the block. Only after authentication will all participants add their respective ledgers to the new block. Each update to the database is repeated throughout the overall infrastructure by this process, and each member of the network has a complete, duplicate copy of the original ledger at a certain time. That methodology could be used to document transactions in a digital way on any

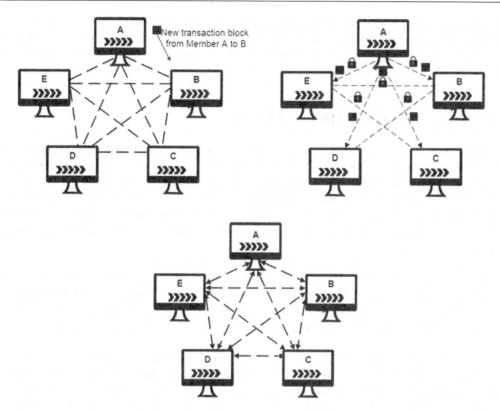

FIGURE 1.1 Data block transaction in DLT systems.

commodity that can be depicted. A modification of the characteristic of the commodity or a transition of ownership may be a sale.

1. DLT systems based on blockchain occur as a result of an append-only data chain "blocks." They are changes made to the database started by a few of the representatives nodes who is creating a new one "block" of data that contains several records of transactions [4].
2. Information is then shared throughout the entire system about this new block of data containing encrypted information so that transaction information is not revealed to the public [4].
3. The validity of the block is collectively evaluated by all network participants as per the pre-defined algorithmic evaluation technique "consensus mechanism" [4]. After evaluation, all individuals add their corresponding ledgers to the new block. Every other alteration to that same ledger is imitated all around the existing system through this mechanism, and each node on the network has a complete equivalent replica ledger at any time. Two key features for DLT-based network are: (i) capacity to digitally archive, monitor, and share "information" between multiple self-interested financial institutions with no need for a centralized record that is peer-to-peer without any need for counterparty trust, and (ii) ensuring that there is no "double spending."

1.2.1 Primary Attributes of DLT

For a number of years, there have been individual ledgers of layered privileges that are exchanged, read, and updated by just a network for verified users, but the idea of a decentralized, shared, and irreversible ledger was first understood via DLT. Three characteristics of DLT which are commonly considered essential to the technology are the distributed design of a ledger, its system of consensus, and its cryptographic frameworks. It also should be stressed that not a single, well-defined technique is DLT. Instead, currently, a multitude of blockchain technology and distributed ledger technology are involved or under production, and their architectures and accurate implementations differ based on the aims of the developers and the intent and level of development of the DL.

1.2.2 The Ledger's Dispersed Design

A structured mechanism that involves confidence throughout the team members has always been record-keeping. The most interesting development of DLT would be that, depending on the form of DL, power and over ledger doesn't really lie with any single person but is with many or all network members. This also sets it apart from the other technical innovations that are widely found with current public ledgers, such as cloud storage or data replication. This implies, in particular, that no single network entity can change previous data entry throughout the DL ledger, and that no single individual can authorize new changes to the directory.

A global consensus system is instead used to verify new data entries which are applied to a block-chain and therefore create new entries throughout the ledger. Only one edition of the ledger is avail-able at all times, and each network member has a complete up-to-date link to the original ledger. Each regional addition to that same ledger is spread to all nodes by a network member. Upon authentication; the latest transaction is applied to all applicable ledgers, ensuring continuity of data across the whole network.

This distributed function of DLT helps interested participants in an independent P2P network to gather validated data, such as transaction information, without depending on a trustworthy central party, in their respective ledgers. The elimination of the core party will speed up and eventually reduce costs and inefficiencies related to the maintenance of a ledger and resulting reconciliations. It can also greatly improve protection, as the whole network no longer has a single attack target. To corrupt the chief, an attacker needs to take control of the majority of the servers on the network, which would not undermine the credibility of the system by corrupting one or more members. However, additional attack surfaces may be caused by privacy issues in the application levels placed on top of the DL. Layer vulnerabilities will cause DL device users failure, even though the core technology stays safe and stable.

1.3 THEORETICAL CONTRIBUTIONS
TO BLOCKCHAIN AND DLT

These results add to the literature on technology, as well as the marketing strategy, particularly creativity of the business model.

1.3.1 Contribution to Business Model Literature

The results add in two respects to literature on the business model. Current research recognizes that the blockchain ability is to modify existing models and cause radically new products and services in sepa-rate branches without coping empirically with how this transition happens. This research examines this phenomenon empirically. The taxonomy strengthens the interpretation of market models through how blockchain operates. It can be a language which promotes a structured explanation of business models in blockchain. The taxonomy also reveals potential for creativity in the business model, without making its complexity too plain. In addition, the five idealized business strategy architectures allow better explaining the effect of cryptocurrency on business practices. The trends indicate potential options to build a business model using blockchain technologies.

Project experiments operate as a testing technique of strictness, pertinence, and cycles in design. These periods are further characterized by recommendations for case surveys, the creation of taxonomies, and cluster analysis. Case studies offer a generalized cross-sectional study of the methodological foundations. The creation of taxonomy then offers a structured approach to scientific and philosophical analysis. Cluster analysis finally means that trends are built to be robust. We draw upon all three layers of market models: real-world (cases), organizational models (taxonomies), and models. Therefore, the business model framework uses its full potential.

On the basis of these approaches, we demonstrate how unique business models and models that take the current knowledge base into account and maintain realistic validity are routinely drawn up. In summary, we first give first a common language for blockchain new business models mostly as a framework for future testing, classification, viewing, and review. Second, our broadly applicable research methodology reveals how to build a business model classification system for a certain area of operation and how to recognize business model trends. We are also contributing to business model research, as well as the increasing variety of business classifications focused on business models.

1.3.2 Positive Contribution to Blockchain Works of Literature

Blockchain technology literature primarily focuses on technical issues and neglects their business importance. In comparison, recent research lacks longitudinal study about how technological blockchain transforms market models. Including modern studies into blockchain and also its implementations, this review includes latest advances in practice to expand blockchain literature. We improve our understanding of the effect of blockchain technologies on business practices and business valuation through analytical and concept-based creation of a taxonomy business strategy and the extraction of five archetype designs for decentralized business strategies.

The taxonomy shows essential aspects in which organizations using blockchain technologies can be identified and analyzed. The measurements include both strategies and components of business models of blockchain solutions. The trends often demonstrate concrete instances of how blockchain technologies can be leveraged for industry. By researching decentralized business strategies, this member an opportunity up a business viewpoint on the innovation body of knowledge on Bitcoin blockchain. Distributed restricted technology as a creative way of data management and upgrading inside and across entities has gained growing attention. DLT/core blockchain's functions are linked to its distributed character independently from other databases. Different parties retain several versions of the headline, including format files by consensus without a third party need. Data can be generated by the DLT/blockchain:

- Permanent record: The data applied to the blockchain is technically inalterable, stable, and protected for the existence of its ledger with the consensus of all members on its contents.
- Decentralization: Nodes were capable of communicating directly, even without an intermediary. That requires the right to initiate direct transfers of data or digitized properties.
- Lack of one party's unified power: Multiple members vote on improvements to the chief or improvements to the governance system.
- New management and data sharing opportunities: These resources are gained by allowing participants to store and view diverse types of data. These frameworks together have a clear and verifiable transaction record. This helps DLT/blockchain to boost the performance, confidence, and data reconciliation of participants in the leaderboard. Although the finance industry consistently shows broad emerging trends in DLT/blockchain, its use in schooling, the artistic sector, the food industry, and agriculture have also been explored.

1.4 EVALUATION OF BLOCKCHAIN PROBLEMS AND OPPORTUNITIES

In an attempt to comprehend the wider DLT/blockchain technologies environment and the significance that guidelines can play in their creation and application, it is crucial to understand DLT/blockchain's challenges with regard to market development and technology adoption by end-users, as well as governance and implementation.

The prospective position of standards to benefit DLT/blockchain are the established fields where guidelines could—to different degrees—theoretically resolve difficulties and could support creativity, development, and competition in the DLT/blockchain ecosystem [5]:

- Specifications could play a significant role in maintaining interoperability between various Distributed Ledger Technology (DLT)/blockchain/DLT applications and, in doing just that, could mitigate the possibility of such a decentralized environment.
- Using guidelines to create a greater agreement on consistent terms and language could enhance awareness of the technologies and positively impact the market.
- Defining specifications to fix protection and stability and DLT/blockchain-related privacy and data processing issues could lead to creating trust in the technologies.
- Standards can play a significant role in data security management which inspire end user interest in technology.

The collection is a wide variety of topics that the DLT/blockchain group will discuss and investigate more. The literary analysis and interviews indicate that the role played by the standards involves a proactive measure to the immediate and near future production of the standards. It is still too premature to consider the criteria relating to the DLT/blockchain technological aspects. While the majority of interviewees acknowledged that standards play a role in defining and improving DLT/blockchain over the longer run, some also believed that extra time could be taken to allow a more knowledgeable approach to determine which facets and uses of the technology should then be given priority. In Figure 1.2, our goals are outlined and the relative timelines for the future creation of criteria in respect to all these areas are roughly shown. Again, our research shows that while there is agreement on the general value of blockchain's growth support requirements, opinions vary in regards to future standardization areas and schedules for the creation and application of standards. Our research shows that blockchain's prospects are extensive, but it also faces many obstacles.

The standard areas have the opportunity to play a role in promoting technologies, such as to allow the growth and acceptance of DLT/blockchain and for its market room to be developed—but the timing for implementation and adoption of standards is important, as is usually the case for new technologies. Early intervention may risk ensuring stakeholders engaging in policies that may not be more efficient, and innovation in the longer term is inevitably stifled. The traditional technology strategy risks missed opportunities to maximize technology gains. Although this is a field of accelerated transition and uncertainty, steps should be taken to recognize the current situation and the drivers and sectors involved.

1.4.1 Main DLT/Blockchain Challenges and Opportunities

Inadequate transparency and contradictory terminological interpretation, together with the presumed nascent technologies of DLT/blockchain, raise obstacles for broader acceptance of DLT/blockchain. The possible costs associated with initial execution, the perceived risks related to early DLT/blockchain deployment, and the likelihood of disruption to current practices could pose big problems for organizations [5]. The lack of clarification regarding technical enhancements relative to current solutions will

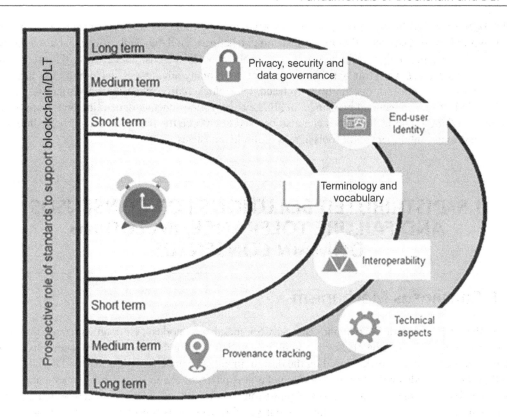

FIGURE 1.2 Specifications of areas in DLT/blockchain and potential timeline predictor.

hamper the company's adoption. The wider economic influence of the system in the mid- to long term is not readily established in the lack of broad DLT/blockchain acceptance. Owing to the emerging existence of technology, the regulation of DLT/blockchain networks is lacking in transparency.

The existing regulatory structures that will be applicable to DLT/blockchain and the improvements that may be expected for broader DLT/blockchain acceptance across industries remain unclear. The existence of several non-interoperable implementations of DLT/blockchain may contribute to a fractured environment, which could limit broad acceptance.

There are major challenges to possible security vulnerabilities and privacy issues, particularly if DLT/blockchain technologies are being entrusted to consumers. Protection of data privacy and maintaining robust encryption protocols are viewed as critical obstacles for broader DLT/blockchain adoption. Blockchain systems' distributed design and a need for additional processing capacity could contribute to high energy use and related costs. The constitutional compliance of DLT/blockchain technology, mainly related to the notion of clarification with reference to the meaning and execution of intelligent contracts through DLT/blockchain, remains a key obstacle.

1.4.2 Opportunities and Possibilities

DLT/blockchain technologies have the ability to offer substantial performance and cost reductions for companies and end consumers by automating procedures and minimizing the need for more third-party intermediation [5]. The implementation of DLT/blockchain technology could theoretically allow new sources of revenue for companies. The development of the DLT/blockchain ecosystem could contribute to the emergence of new economic and business models; for example, new modes of cooperation and cryptocurrencies.

DLT/decentralized blockchain's existence and the absence of a central source of the problem could still encourage more resilient and stable transaction structures. DLT/blockchain is capable of motivating users by managing their own knowledge and is able to boost the customer trust in the execution of transactions. DLT/blockchain transfers are permanent, with many advantages, including the transparent audit trail and the decrease in susceptibility to fraud. DLT/blockchain could allow cost-effective and efficient digital identity management by using a public key encryption scheme, depending on the application situation. DLT/blockchain technologies can also be used to enforce the framework underlying intelligent contracts and to use intelligent audit tools across multiple industries.

1.5 DISTRIBUTED SOLUTIONS FOR CONSENSUS AND FAILURE TOLERANCE, INCLUDING DOMAIN CONSENSUS

1.5.1 Consensus Mechanism

The distributed existence of DL demands that network members ("nodes") enter an understanding on the authenticity of new information entries in compliance with a set of guidelines. This is accomplished by a consensus process that may differ based on the design, intent, and underlying asset of the DL's algorithm. In a DL, all of the nodes will usually recommend a new payment to the ledger, but implementations do propose specific functions for entities, whereby just some nodes can recommend an inclusion of a transaction. To assess whether or not a given transaction is genuine, a consensus process must be applied using a particular cryptographical framework for authentication specified for such a DL. The consensus process is often essential when communicating with disputes between several concurrent entries—when separate transactions on the same asset are suggested by various nodes, for instance. This system guarantees that transactions are properly sequenced and avoids takeover by bad actors. The consensus and sequence mechanism guard against the previously mentioned issue of double spending. The blockchain technology uses "working proof" to create trust on a shared global network, which was first created as a spamming measure.

A "proof of work" protocol is mandatory in trying to generate a new transaction to the blockchain, which requires the inclusion of a new collection of data in the chain directory. This is a challenging, but easy to check, estimation problem. The timestamp is produced by the repeated use of one-way cryptographic hashes until a sequence of numbers is produced which satisfies a predefined but arbitrary requirement: specifically, that same number of digits in the Bitcoin network.

Resolving this "proof of work" problem is an incredibly challenging task, as there are no alternatives and only a small possibility of achieving the requisite proof of work—and without a large volume of expensive computational resources is required of any device in the network. The Bitcoin mechanism is optimized to generate correct evidence each ten minutes and also to ensure that the application with the higher complexity rating is recognized as valid if both are produced in exactly the same period. Any miner who generates credible data on the Bitcoin network is awarded Bitcoins as a financial reward for upholding system security.

The large scale of an open, non-permitted device is therefore vital to its protection. Network integrity directly requires a lot of device nodes which are encouraged to correctly verify any updates to the ledger and to achieve a consensus throughout the network by providing data accuracy. The proof of working costs network members greatly to sustain the DL, which would be appropriate only for networks of distrusted members. According to an estimate, the required electricity would surpass the current global electricity demand if Bitcoin community had to expand to the current rate of use of current payment networks such as Visa and MasterCard. However, for Bitcoin blockchain, this issue is most pronounced.

The DLT method used among ether, a digital currency newly launched from Ethereum, demands substantially less computational power. Permissioned blockchains usually don't need complicated "work evidence," since network members are preselected and trusted, as a consensus framework for verifying transactions. Other consensus processes exist, such as a proof of engagement that honors seniors through computer power and includes proof of payment of an estate.

1.5.2 Distributed Ledger

The distributed functionality of DLT enables self-interested P2P network users to independently record validated data without depending on even a trustworthy central group in a shared directory. The replacement of a key group will speed up the preservation of the headline and further reconciliation expense and inefficiency. It can also improve security, since a single attack point in the whole network is no longer possible. Authorized programs can more easily integrate into current legal and regulatory processes and arrangements. However, DLs who are allowed to some extent will take advantage of DLT's most significant developments, including the absence of a central party.

1.5.3 Centralized Ledger

As shown in Figure 1.3, both parties merge their territorial databases with a nationally managed and regulated electronic ledger from a confident central group [4].

FIGURE 1.3 Centralized ledger.

1.5.4 Distributed Ledger (Permissionless)

A complete and latest copy is available in any node in a P2P network. The network member communicates to all nodes any suggested local inclusion to its directory. Collectively, nodes verify the shift using a consensus algorithm [4]. Once certification is approved, all the respective ledgers will be added to ensure data integrity across the network. Figure 1.4 illustrates a permissionless distributed ledger.

1.5.5 Distributed Ledger (Permissioned)

Nodes require the authorization of a central authority from a licensed framework to reach the network and alter the repository, as shown in Figure 1.5. Identity checking can provide access controls. In the sense of distributed networks, the consensus on fault tolerance has been thoroughly discussed. Through control of information dissemination in the network of the components distributed, a consensus fault-tolerant algorithm ensures that all components rely on shared data values and carry out a certain way to proceed, despite the existence of flawed components and unstable communication links, in reaction to a request [4]. This promise of consensus is important for a distributed system to operate normally. As an output system, a blockchain system uses a consensus technique to ensure that all network nodes agree on a single transaction history chain, as malfunctioning and malicious nodes adversely affect them.

1.5.6 Fault-Tolerant Consensus in a Distributed System

While physically isolated, all elements of a distributed system aim to accomplish a shared purpose. In the simplest terms, consensus implies that these elements come to an agreement on certain validity of data.

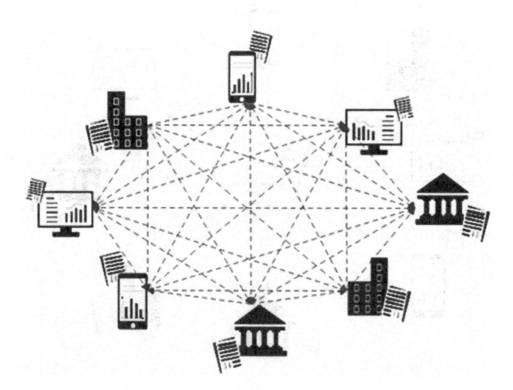

FIGURE 1.4 Distributed ledger (permissionless).

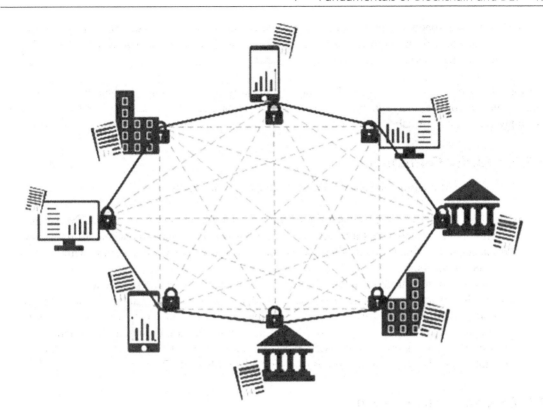

FIGURE 1.5   Distributed ledger (permissioned).

The machine elements and their contact networks in an individual system are vulnerable to unexpected failures and detrimental consequences. This section addresses the consensus topic of message-passing systems [6] where two forms of component failures exist: crash and Byzantine failure. Those part failures in distributed computation can be accepted in two practice consensus algorithms.

1.5.7 The System Model

In a distributed system, there are three main consensus factors: network synchrony, component failures, and the consensus algorithm [7].

1.5.7.1 Network Synchrony

Network synchrony in the distributed system is a fundamental principle. It determines how well the device elements are organized. Before any protocol construction or performance measurement, we need to have the network synchronization state. Three network synchronization requirements occur in particular:

- Synchronous: Part operations are rounded. The central clock synchronization service also makes it possible. Both components carry out the same form of operations in each round.
- Asynchronous: Portion processes are uncoordinated. This is frequently the product of no clock sync service or part clocks drifting. Each part shall not be bound by any laws of teamwork and shall execute an opportunity of its own routine. The distribution of messages or a higher limit on message transmission between components is not assured.

- Partly synchronous: component activities are not synchronized, but message propagation time is at the upper limit. In other words, the transmission of messages is guaranteed, which might not be in due course.

For most functional distributed networks, that's the networking state. Thus, presume that the device is indeed simultaneous or partly synchronous in most application areas. The voting mechanism in a national assembly, for instance, is called synchronous, whereas the Bitcoin community is partly synchronous.

1.5.7.2 Faulty Component

A part is defective if it has a flaw that prevents it from running normally.

- Crash failures: The device suddenly fails to work and doesnot restart. Consider two types of dysfunctional activities that a component might have. The other components will understand the accident and timely change their local choices. The part behaves unilaterally without absolute requirements.
- Byzantine failures: It may send conflicting signals or actually remain passive to the other elements. It will appear natural external sources and are not suspected by anyone in the network's history. In the case of Byzantine malfunction, the device mechanism is always misused or the malicious actor is exploited. If several Byzantine components are present in the system, it will disrupt the network even more. Byzantine fault is assumed to be the worst case for flaws of modules, and the crash failure with Byzantine faults is also considered.

1.5.7.3 Consensus Protocol

A consensus protocol specifies a collection of rules for passing and processing messages to achieve agreement on a shared topic across all interconnected resources [7]. A message-passing law governs how far a component communicates and switches messages, although a rule specifies how a component in the face of those messages changes its internal status. In general, when all no-fault components come to an understanding on the same issue, they thus conclude that the consensus is achieved. The intensity of a consensus mechanism from the security point of view will generally be calculated by the amount of damaged components tolerated. Specifically, the crash-fault tolerance to a consensus protocol can withstand at minimum of one crash failure (CFT). Often, if only one Byzantine error could be accepted by a consensus protocol, it is termed as accommodating Byzantine failure (BFT). The BFT consensus was obviously a CFT due to the extreme inclusive interaction between Byzantine failures and crash failures. In addition, compromise is not feasible for even one crash failure in an asynchronous framework [7][8]. The majority of this chapter focuses on Byzantine error tolerance in synchronous or partly synchronous networks of consensus protocols.

1.6 TRADEOFFS FOR BLOCKCHAIN SCALABILITY

One of the most common reasons for Bitcoin's slow adoption is its scalability. The fact is that, in comparison to traditional central communication and technologies like Visa or AWS, cryptocurrency networks are mostly lent out. For instance, in the region of 15 operations per second, Ethereum can execute transactions—and Bitcoin is much slower. On the other hand, blockchain networks offer unique features that cannot be accomplished easily with centralized techniques, such as digital format scarcity and unstopping.

If developers continue to experience and iterate new implementations of these assets within decentralized apps, common platforms tackle scalability and transaction limitations. In this sense, the blockchain scalability of software engineers and end customers is generally shown as a significant barrier of additional blockchain deployment. The group has put a lot of work into designing scalability approaches at Layer 2 and migrating current frameworks to quicker consensus structures in response to these scalability problems in blockchain.

Developers who research the decentralized model to construct on should definitely inspect their desires and the platform architecture priorities they chose into account. The degrees of decentralization, as well as programmability you need, are two critical compromises to ensure the optimal interoperability for the software. Not every application has to be as decentralized as possible or programmable.

1.6.1 The Top Two Tradeoffs to Blockchain Scalability: Level of Decentralization

For those not familiar with the popular blockchain trilemma, it says that only two of these three parameters can be designed when designing a decentralized protocol: scalability, security and decentralization, as shown in Figure 1.6. The assumption is that it is impossible to achieve all three of them at the same time. In my experience, the most important cases of usage of blockchains apply to storage and transfer of value, such that any major security sacrifice seems to be non-starter.

The major aspect behind the circularity is that it ties decentralization to scalability. Scalability can be quickly accomplished if decentralization is sacrificed. In a centralized system, for example, typical AWS implementations achieve a high degree of scalability, but the main characteristics that render blockchains fascinating—that is, digital format scarcities coupled with disability—vanish into this implementation model. Any ventures benefit from this partnership. Please take the EOS example. There are 21 block-generating nodes within the EOS framework. This is much less than Bitcoin and Ethereum. EOS produces a much higher transaction performance than Ethereum and or Bitcoin by being more centralized. The 21 nodes are not completely centralized, and they are more centralized than most of the other centralized exchanges. EOS's purpose is to be distributed to preserve intact another very interesting blockchain artifact, but centralized to achieve considerably greater efficiency than efficient blockchain networks. What degree of decentralization would your use case need to be asked for as a DApp designer? How are you concerned about your submission being censored? Most elevated applications will need enhanced decentralization; it may not be necessary for others.

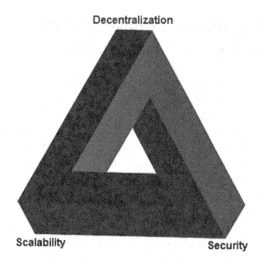

FIGURE 1.6 The blockchain trilemma.

1.6.2 Level of Programmability

At least as essential as decentralization is the extent of programmability provided by a Bitcoin blockchain. The main question is: what are the applications that will allow you to accomplish your goals, and what rationale in the chain? I will look at a variety of apps that need to be coded at one side of the spectrum with distribute products and services apps, but at the other side of the spectrum, starting from the money and wealth movement scenario. The breadth of the programming generated by a blockchain network is at least as critical as decentralization. The key question is: which applications will help you achieve your objectives and what justification in the chain? I'm looking at a number of applications which have to be programmed from one side to another with apps that deliver goods and services, but from the income and capital transfer situation to any of the side of the continuum.

Scalability of the network also declines by applying smart contract technology to Turing. With smart Turings, you just want a gas definition to calculate the efficiency of the deal, which adds costs and running costs to the application and results in deterministic behavior. You would allow intelligent contracts to save arbitrary states or information on the line, which indicates that the blockchain consensus nodes have more charges and storage requirements. For all platform contracts, most intelligent contract platforms feature a single, single-pack virtual machine, which may potentially be used as a scaling constraint. All of these issues decrease Turing-wide smart contract platforms' scalability and capacity, Scalability of Opposite technology (i.e., centralized), Algorand and Ethereum Scalability Spectrum.

1.6.3 Algorand Prioritized Performance over Turing-Complete Programmability

Algorand is a highly efficient blockchain of the next generation focused on the profitability and investment side of the architecture continuum and extremely decentralized. It achieves high efficiency and transaction performance by concentrating on and performing well on currency, assets, and transfer of assets. Algorand's latest language of scripting, TEAL, is purposely incomplete in order to discourage gas costs, random storage, and endless loops, together with Turing's full smart contract framework. There are unique choices that permit the economical, asset, and transition scenarios to achieve high efficiency. That is why technologies that help certain applications that need high throughput, such as Tether and Securitize, could be used in Algorand.

1.6.4 Ethereum Prioritized Turing-Complete Programmability over Performance

Ethereum, in comparison, is the most popular total smart contracting network. At the cost of throughput and scalability, Ethereum positions programmability first. Ethereum's scalability difficulties are induced by arbitrarily complicated logical output and the arbitrarily broad storage of clever contracts. Storage and logic are calculated by gas charges, and the number of intelligent contracts has risen over time. The underlying blockchain at the Ethereum total node requires over 100 GB of storage and rises (skipping archive nodes for now). Ethereum also has a small portion of Algorand's scalability from the viewpoint of payment per second, as well as storage of nodes.

Fortunately, whatever you get is potential for the Ethereum virtual environment to communicate random, intellectual contract reasoning. And since all programs work in a same virtual environment, one can able to make much improvement across numerous contracts in DeFi. As DApp programmers, it is worth considering what elements of an application must be de-centralized and if smart contract terms are actually necessary to construct your application. A complete smart contract platform provides all the online logic expressions, although frequently at the cost of performance and scalability.

1.6.5 Choosing the Right Platform for Your Application

Scalability is crucial in deciding where to construct the underlying platform. Those scalability problems lead eventually to high transaction charges, even though the program itself does not need to raise the running cost as a product that may also render certain use cases commercially impractical. When choosing a platform for your use case, you must carefully account for your depictions and programming level.

In an implementation case that only involves an ERC-20 agreement with Ethereum, and does not need interoperability with the other intelligent Ethereum contracts, a glance at frameworks that are designed for this situation could be meaningful, such as Algorand. At Ethereum, you could spend a lot more without understanding the advantage of increased programming.

1.6.6 Tradeoffs between Distributed Ledger Technology Characteristics

DLT offers a highly open, supplemental database managed in an unregulated environment by physically distributable storage and processing machines (nodes). DLT pledges to make partnerships between individuals and/or organizations more productive and open based on qualities inherent in this area, including tampering and censor resistance and democratization of information. Also as result, a growing number of DLT applications in different fields, including the supply chain, finance, and healthcare, are being developed.

DLT is used, for instance, to prevent tampering with the data storage system in the supply chain distribution system that is distributed through several nodes of the collaborative entities in the supply chain. Implementations utilize distributed headings as a standard architecture which, for example, makes data storage simple and efficient, data-driven processing (e.g. for digital asset transfers), and business processes automation feasible. Every application in DLT is based on a certain DLT framework that is specified as a structured DLT definition specification. Despite DLT's encouraging advantages, previous DLT implementations demonstrate crucial dependence on DLT features that lead to tradeoffs, i.e. enhancing one DLT feature correlating with some other DLT feature. For example, a balance occurs between availability and accuracy in distributed ledgers. By raising the number of repeats of the ledger, a dealer can achieve a high availability.

As a result, the distributed ledger network of nodes tends to increase; however, that tends to diminish accuracy due to higher message spread delays. During DLT, no one-size-fits-all DLT architecture for applications will be available, provided the prevalent tradeoffs between DLT features. Instead, DLT designs will satisfy basic specifications but poorly meet certain specifications frequently associated with inconveniences emerging from the tradeoffs inherent in DLT. It is also very difficult to choose acceptable DLT principles for implementation and quantify possible disadvantages for the respective DLT application. It is also more important to make deliberate and rational decisions for a DLT system to establish successful DLT implementations, because technological variations between DLT designs inhibit the transfer of data among distributed ledger technology. The viability of software in this sense refers to the potential to run over a long time, with future modifications or enhancements and consequent upgrades being considered.

A thorough study of correlations among DLT specifications and the subsequent tradeoffs is necessary in order to understand the exchange between DLT features and their effect on DLT applications' viability. While DLT research has evolved during the last decade, similar DLT research characteristically focuses mainly on considering the significance of characteristics. In comparison, study of DLT features and their dependency is widely dispersed throughout disciplines and requires reprocessing so as to provide an understanding of the dependencies within DLT properties and the resulting compromises that restrict the utility of DLT designs.

DLT characteristics are only sparse in scale. An incentive structure is needed in shared DLT designs, since validating entities should be encouraged to share computing resources. The compensation framework

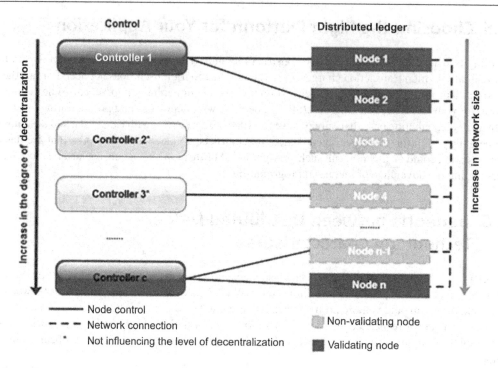

FIGURE 1.7   Degree of decentralization for distributed ledger.

lays out a recompense structure for nodes participating in blocks and transactions development and/or confirmation, consensus discovery, and maintenance. The presence of entities in a distributed network is called mining. Validation nodes are therefore often pointed to as mining. For example, if they would be the first to build a legitimate new block in a Bitcoin network, validating nodes earn a sum of coins. These reward structures are specifically applicable to distributed ledgers, and thus enable a high level of decentralization with nodes of unknown network controllers. Assuming that all nodes function on equal terms, the distributed level of decentralization determines the number of individual validation node controllers who have the capacity to handle more than the average nodes divided by total number of DLT nodes. The degree of decentralization for a distributed ledger is then defined by two dimensions, namely the number of individual node validates and the numbers of authenticating nodes.

If the nodes that have been authenticated increase and the remaining nodes are managed by the same administrator, the amount of decentralization reduces, provided that this controller has a disproportionate effect on the agreement and credibility of the distributed ledger. On the other hand, when independently managed nodes connect nodes that are at maximum average computational services only of the distributed ledger, the level of decentralization is improved. The extent of decentralization is calculated by the number of independent node controls within a distributed ledger (e.g. an entity or individual). Figure 1.7 illustrates that the total degree of decentralization for the distributed ledger increases the number of autonomous controllers running validating nodes.

1.7 BLOCKCHAIN CONSENSUS ALGORITHM

A method whereby all of the blockchain system members mutually agree to the required state of the published ledger is the easiest solution to a consensus mechanism on blockchain. The Bitcoin network will

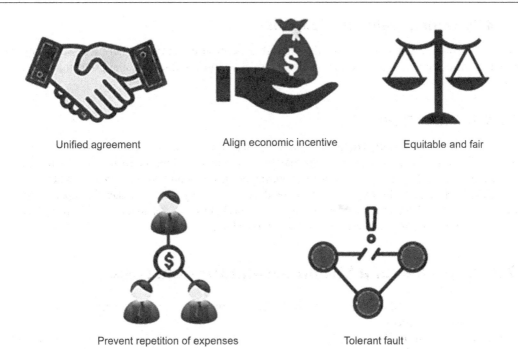

Unified agreement   Align economic incentive   Equitable and fair

Prevent repetition of expenses   Tolerant fault

FIGURE 1.8   Strategies of blockchain mechanism.

achieve consistency and morality between the different nodes while preserving environmental security through a consensus process. This is why it is one of the key components of every program development guide and implementation in the field of blockchain's digital currency.

1.7.1 Strategies of Blockchain Mechanism

Figure 1.8 displays the strategies of blockchain mechanism.

1.7.1.1 Unified Agreement

Unified agreement is one of the principal aims of consensus processes. In contrast to centralized systems, in which confidence in power is needed, people can even work autonomously without creating confidence in each other. The protocols incorporated inside the blockchain distributed network ensure that the data involved with the procedure is truthful and accurate.

1.7.1.2 Align Economic Incentives

In building an autonomous and confidence-building structure, it is important to balance the priorities of network members.

In this case, the underlying blockchain framework would honor good actions and discipline the poor actors. It also means that economic benefits are regulated.

1.7.1.3 Equitable and Fair

Mechanisms of consensus encourage us to interact and use the same fundamentals in the network. This justifies the blockchain system's free software and decentralization assets.

1.7.1.4 Prevent Repetition of Expenses

Consensus methods are based on particular algorithms to ensure that the publicly accessible ledger verifies and validates only such transactions. This addresses the typical double-dollar problem, that is, double the digital money issue.

1.7.1.5 Tolerant Fault

The consensus approach is often defined by ensuring that perhaps the blockchain is error resistant, stable, and secure. That is, except in accidents and challenges, the managed mechanism will operate forever.

There is already wealth of consensus mechanisms in the community of blockchain, and even more are entering the marketplace. This requires that any production company and passionate developer in blockchain know the factors that characterize a successful consensus mechanism, as well as the future impact of a bad one.

Let's start with what is a positive thing about blockchain.

1.7.2 Properties of a Strong System for Consensus

1. Safe: All nodes will generate results which are true under the rules of the protocol in a successful consensus process.
2. Inclusive: A strong framework for consensus means that every node of the network contributes throughout the voting process.
3. Participatory: The strong consensus models are used as a mechanism for consensus whereby all nodes communicate and contribute to the updating of the blockchain database.
4. Egalitarian: Another feature of a strong mechanism is that each vote obtained from the node gives equal importance and weight.

1.7.3 Consensus Blockchain Algorithms Popular in the Enterprise

Figure 1.9 illustrates the consensus blockchain algorithms popular in the enterprise.

1.7.3.1 Proof of Work (PoW)

Proof of work itself is blockchain's oldest consensus tool. It is also called mining, whereby miners are called the participating nodes [9].

The miners must solve complicated mathematical puzzles using extensive computational power in this control mechanism. The new tools used include graphics processing unit (GPU) mining operations, central processing unit (CPU) mining operations, application-specific integrated circuit (ASIC) mining operations and field-programmable gate array (FPGA) mining operations. Being the one who solves the problem the first time will be awarded a block.

1.7.3.2 Proof of Stake (PoS)

Proof of stakes is the simple alternative to the PoW consensus protocol which respects the environment [9]. The block creators are not really miners in this blockchain system, but act as validators. They get a chance to build a block that saves resources and reduces time overall. But they have to spend a certain large sum of money or acquire a majority stake to become another validator.

1.7.3.2.1 Delegated Proof of Stake (DPoS)

The stakeholders stake each coin and voting for just a number of delegates for delegates to the assigned proof of stake, in such a way that the more investment they spend, the more weight. For instance, if

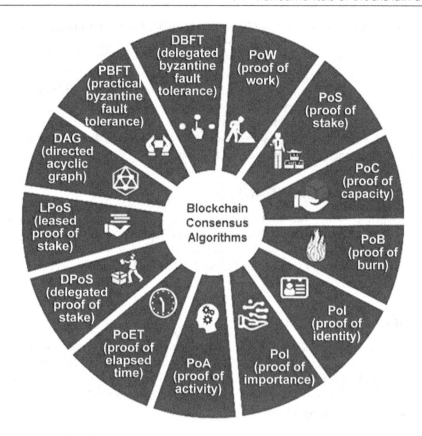

FIGURE 1.9   Consensus blockchain algorithms popular in the enterprise.

consumer A invests a delegate ten coins and user B spends five coins, A's votes will get a greater weight than B's. Delegates are often compensated by purchase costs or certain quantities of coins. DPoS is among the fastest underlying blockchain models and is commonly accepted as a democracy, because of another direct risk voting mechanism [9].

1.7.3.2.2 Leased Proof of Stake (LPoS)
LPoS is an updated version of the Waves network consensus framework for PoS.

Contrary to the standard PoS method in which each node has a certain cryptocurrency right to the next blockchain, this consensus algorithm helps users to rent those balances to complete nodes.

But if one leases the greater sum to the entire network, it is more likely that the next block will be created. In addition, the leaser is paid a processing cost percentage, which is received by the entire node. This PoS version is an effective and secure choice for public cryptocurrencies growth.

1.7.3.3 Byzantine Fault Tolerance (BFT)

The Byzantine failure resistance is used, as its name implies, to dealing with Byzantine faults: a situation in which players in the system have to compromise on an appropriate strategy to prevent a disastrous systemic failure; however, some of them would be questionable. The BFT consensus paradigm is primarily PBFT and DBFT in the cryptocurrency arena.

1.7.3.3.1 Practical Byzantine Fault Tolerance (PBFT)
PBFT is a compact algorithm which addresses the problems of the Byzantine general failure by encouraging users to validate their messages by executing a computer to determine the authenticity of a message.

The group then tells other nodes that its vote is eventually made. The final decision is based on the decisions made by the other nodes.

1.7.3.3.2 Delegated Byzantine Fault Tolerance (DBFT)
The Byzantine Delegate Fault Tolerance System was introduced by NEO and is identical to DPoS. Here, too, the owners of the NEO token are given the chance to vote in favor. The speaker generates a new block for a confirmation from the transaction. It also sends a resolution to the elected delegates responsible for supervising and monitoring all transactions on the network. This delegate should share and evaluate their ideas to validate the correctness of the speaker and their integrity.

1.7.3.4 Direct Acyclic Graph (DAG)

Another simple but primary consensus model blockchain that any organization operating with blockchain in the mobile app creation needs to know is DAG. Each node itself practices to be the "miners" in this form of underlying blockchain protocol. Now the corresponding charge is reduced to zero if miners were eliminated and payments checked by consumers themselves. Transactions between two nearest nodes are simpler to verify, which makes the entire operation easier, quicker, and safer.

1.7.3.5 Proof of Capacity (PoC)

In the mechanism of proof of capability (PoC), solutions are stored in electronic storage facilities such as hard drives for any complicated mathematical puzzle. Users may use certain hard drives to generate blocks in order to make blocks more likely to be produced by others that are faster to determine the solutions. Plotting is the process that follows. Burstcoin and SpaceMint are indeed the two cryptocurrency that are based on PoC's consensus protocol.

1.7.3.6 Proof of Burn (PoB)

Considered as an alternative to PoS and PoW approaches in terms of power consumption, the consensus model PoB is based on the idea of allowing the digital cryptocurrency coins to be "burned" or "ruined," which often enables miners to write blocks proportionately to their currency. The more coins they burn, the greater the chances that they will be able to successfully mine the next block. However, to burn coin, they really must give this to the account where the block cannot be checked. Throughout the context of distributed agreement, this is commonly used. The Slim coin is the best example of this system of consensus.

1.7.3.7 Proof of Identity (PoI)

The PoI concept is the same as that of the accepted identification. It is indeed a cryptographic verification for a private user key connected to each transaction. Each user defined can build and maintain a database that can be submitted in the network to others.

This blockchain consensus model guarantees that the data generated are genuine and integral. Therefore, the launch of clever cities is a smart choice.

1.7.3.8 Proof of Activity (PoA)

PoA is essentially a hybrid method developed by converging PoW and PoS models of blockchain consensus. In PoA mechanisms, miners compete early on with special hardware and electro-energy to overcome a cryptographic puzzle, as in PoW. Even then, the chains they meet only include the name and the compensation transaction of the block winner. The process flips to PoS in this regard. The validators search and validate the block accuracy. The validator switches on a complete block unless the block has been tested several times. That indicates that open transfers are operations that are integrated finally in the discovered containers block.

1.7.3.9 Proof of Elapsed Time (PoET)

Intel implemented PoET with the purpose of solving cryptographic puzzles in the PoW mechanism, taking into account that a miner knows the block by the processor architecture, as well as the quantities of mining operations. The theory is that the chances for a greater fraction of the participants should be spread and raised equally. Thus, any node involved will be asked to attend the following mining process for certain duration. It is asked to give a block to the participant with the shortest stop time. Simultaneously, each node often has its own waiting period to reach sleep mode.

1.7.3.10 Proof of Importance (PoI)

PoI is a deviation in the PoS protocol adopted by NEM, which takes account of the position of owners and evaluators by its operations. However, it does not rely entirely on the scale and potential of the shares of these parties; there are several other considerations such as prestige, balance, and number of transactions. PoI-based networks are costly to attack and reward users for contributing to protection of the network. This shared knowledge may help distinguish the complex consensus protocols from blockchain.

1.7.4 The DLT Consensus Ecosystem

A DLT/blockchain is a linear, sequential, and chained database structure, distributed across a network of peer-to-peer networks that store and group transactions into new chains. Networking partners (peers) enter distributed agreements on the validity and ordering of the contract. Blocks are a transaction data structure and a header with a relation through a hash to the original data. Nowadays, blockchain networks belong more commonly to a broad family called distributed ledger networks. Many DLTs are implemented, but some of them have the very same consensus structure, which enables the temperature tolerance of certain solutions. In this post, I want to provide a high degree, but full, outline of the numerous consensus mechanisms within DLTs without the intention of providing a ranking.

1.7.5 Byzantine Fault Tolerance

It is really the stability of a computer system with a tolerance to faults, particularly distributed computer systems, in which components fail and knowledge about the failed component is imperfect. The phrase applies to the issue of the Byzantine commanders, in which players must agree to a coordinated plan to prevent the collapse of the catastrophe scheme. This definition is central to DLT/blockchain, as a distributed environment or untrustworthy node will cause disturbance or total system collapse if the fundamental system architecture integrates its decisions/proposals for new transactions and blocks. Therefore, to maintain stability and security in the transaction stored, it is necessary to define and separate these nodes, but this process is usually accomplished through a consensus process.

1.7.6 Distributed Computing Consensus

Consensus is a programming problem. It requires finding consensus between varieties of processes which are distributed. Consensus is introduced in the DLT in order to attain fault tolerance structures by including many nodes that are expected to agree on planned transactions or a particular outcome. This decision is deemed definitive until they make a shared decision, and cannot be overturned.

1.7.7 Consistency Availability Partition Tolerance (CAP)

In theory, CAP theorem, often known as Brewer's computer theorem, states that as more than 2 in 3 guarantees cannot be given concurrently by a data store that is distributed.

- **Consistency** (C): Each read gets the new writing or mistake.
- **Availability** (A): Any submission receives an answer (no error), without a promise that it includes the latest written material.
- **Partition tolerance** (P): The device is still running as the network among nodes deletes (or delays) an undefined number of messages.

1.7.8 Permissioned/Private DLTs

Because the variety of interventions of consensus is gradually increasing, let's start with the kind of consensus protocol that targets private/permitted projects in particular. Any user will access the network as both an end-user and a node in permission-free environments, and there are no relations of confidence between nodes, which significantly reduce the frequency of transaction confirmation. These environments typically produce different kinds of consensus algorithm vs. approved environments in which gatekeepers must allow nodes and/or users to access the network.

1.8 BLOCKCHAIN EXTENSIONS AND CONSTRAINTS

In conventional systems, blockchain technology gives consumers certain benefits that are not available. Blockchain was the first completely distributed and autonomous framework to retain a trustworthy chief. This enables a system to maintain track of its past and to rest assured that a malicious attacker is not able to change that history for their own gain. Bitcoin was initially planned to replace existing payment mechanisms, but it cannot do so by itself. Blockchain technology has drawbacks, and blockchain extensions to reduce or remove them have been developed.

1.8.1 Constraints

The layout of blockchains is very unique. Given the need for synchronization of the network and for validating all transactions by the network, transactions cannot be added to a distributed directory on an ongoing basis. Transactions are now grouped into blocks that are applied at regular intervals to the distributed directory. This architecture reduces the blockchain solution's speed and power. On the blockchain, there is a substantial limit to how many transfers are applied to the distributed chief. Usually, blockchains have a goal block rate, which their consensus algorithm enforces on a certain level. For example, Bitcoin has a 10-minute block rate, meaning there may be a long wait because of the three-block rule before a transaction can be considered trustworthy. This is detrimental when compared to credit cards, where "slow" purchases take place in one minute. There is still a difficulty with optimum bandwidth for blockchains in order to secure many blockchains, in addition to fixed size; they also have a set limit block size for denial of service attacks. Blockchain can only handle multiple transactions over time with set block sizes generated at fixed times, and this capability is therefore much smaller than that offered by the credit card system.

1.8.2 Extensions

In order to overcome these issues, some distributed ledger systems have abandoned the data system blockchain. For example, the guided acyclic graph (DAG), which improves its system throughput and capability dramatically, is an underlying data structure. Some blockchains allow minor protocol tweaks for boosting the transfer speed and reliability, and several blockchains have started to leverage blockchain extensions to further overcome these challenges while preserving the initial blockchain architecture.

1.8.3 Sidechains

Sidechains are mainly intended to expand network capability by discharging transactions into an independent blockchain. There are many different sidechain implementations, but atypical one is to "peg" the sidechain to something like a blockchain parent. With stuck blocks, a user may submit tokens to an "output address" on a blockchain and the same number of tokens to the sidechain. Pegs are two-way, meaning that the user can revert at will to the initial blockchain. The expansion of the ability for the initial blockchain is one advantage of sidechains.

The system's overall capacity is improved as transactions conducted in the sidechain are not registered in the main blockchain blocks. Sidechains may even be used to fix the parent blockchain's unique weaknesses. For instance, sidechain could see an improvement in transaction speed faster than parent chain. Instead of that, sidechains will expand the system's capacities, such as the Rootstock sidechain, which plans to add intelligent contracts to Bitcoin functions.

The key safety feature of sidechains has been that the sidechain is an entirely different mechanism than main chain. This requires a diverse pool of miners, owners, etc., to secure consensus. Such a hack may otherwise control the consistency of its connection to the main chain, as well as the willingness of its users to turn back and forth.

1.8.4 Channels of State

The state channel is yet another blockchain extension which has generated a lot of news. Perhaps the most popular state channel device is the Lightning Network, mostly on Bitcoin blockchain, but some state channel implementation operates under various names on other blockchains. State channels serve as just a second-level mechanism that is supported by a conventional implementation of blockchain. State network seems to be a direct link among blockchain users. They set up a channel and use a conventional blockchain transaction, which decides the balance of the channel. The payments are made only after a channel is formed by making mutually signed claims concerning the value balance in the channel.

The channel could be shut down at any moment, or the most recent balances statement is used to make another blockchain transaction, which would put the right amount of cryptocurrency on each blockchain participant's account. Processing time, interoperability, and anonymity are the key advantages of state networks. Transactions involve only the participants in the channel and can be done almost instantly, but it might not be possible to produce a payment if a channel gets too unbalanced. That's where the state channels' network could be very useful because transactions can be re-equaled through different paths or switched between unconnected parties. The primary safety concern of government networks would be that payments are facilitated but not registered on the blockchain. Global channel transfers are the recipient's private enterprise, as well as the blockchain has to be assured in validity in all transactions. Point-to-point design of state channels, however, defends against double spending attacks, as it is specific to a certain platform and it cannot be utilized to access and carry out transactions on other channels.

1.8.5 The Universe of Distributed Ledger

The purpose of this series was to implement blockchain technology with an emphasis on blockchain protection. Many distributed ledger implementations have various data structures and security features. Blockchain may also be expanded by external devices communicating by application programming interfaces (APIs) or intelligent agreements. It is important to take account of all available infrastructure and related security concerns when planning a distributed ledger approach.

1.9 EMERGING BLOCKCHAIN APPLICATIONS: BEST-FIT APPLICATION SCENARIOS AND MODELS

The best in terms of blockchain technology implementations for blockchain technology were planned to explore reliability, immutability, and transparency. A blockchain system of transactions reported secretly and which cannot be changed or abused, does not have a superior participant.

Blockchain networks ought in general to fix those sore points only with the specific subject scenarios by converting an untrustworthy ecosystem into a creditworthy blockchain environment. A blockchain framework can also be built as a distributed ledger as an infrastructural ecosystem of blocks that are distributed not only in all its modern architecture, but also in other its data and operating rights. There are a variety of decentralized peer entities in the ledger of the ecosystem. The ecosystem members are peer bodies with equal rights. The data from ecosystem documents are private and independent, meaning that the members can be used and received. Tens of thousands of blockchain technology-based software programs have been established for storage, finance, smart contracts, data API, to provide service-level or data-level or business-level infrastructure, notarization, asset dealing, bank clearing, e-commerce, social communication, and the Internet of Things.

1.9.1 Cryptomonetary and Payment Blockchains

It is Bitcoin's cryptocurrency that provides acceptance and stability for blockchain technology, as blockchains offer Bitcoin's safe, accessible, and decentralized transaction platform [10].

For this time, the various ICO (initial coin offering) systems prevailed worldwide. The majority of the blockchain concepts are evolving from the blockchain, and even if few of them succeed and Bitcoin is illegally in some countries, cryptocurrency and payment firms continue to appear among the most common applications. Figure 1.10 shows the five blockchain enterprise concerns.

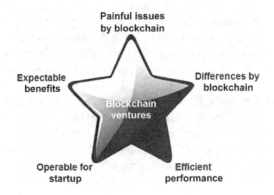

FIGURE 1.10 Five blockchain enterprise concerns.

1.9.2 Product Monitoring Blockchains

The best method of religious behavior monitoring is to use blockchain technologies. In order to minimize prescription drug fraud, a blockchain-based technology was proposed in the health sector to incorporate medical knowledge and the dental industry. The blockchain helps address issues that are often kept without complete patient control by private data collectors. Blockchains can monitor transactional information effectively and confidentially at each level of the process [10][11]. Several Internet of things (IoT) implementations have been placed on the market for commercial blockchains.

1.9.3 Supply Chain Blockchains

The supply chain is the most suitable place for blockchains, since several businesses situated in the supply chain need another likely to default system to cooperate [10][12]. The ecosystem blockchain can be built to ensure that the supply chain participants receive safe, creditworthy, and full information to prevent deception. For medium-sized and small enterprises, the reliable statistics are beneficial in delivering financial services, a challenging topic in conventional sectors. The finance agency will include creditworthy purchasing orders with funds for small vendors and service providers.

As Figure 1.11 demonstrates, the information can be found on several blockchain financing projects for the supply chain [10][13]. In addition, with intelligent contracts, blockchains are able to make trades and collaborative among a supplier's chain more stable and trustworthy. Intelligent agreements could be used to write and automatically conduct the whole transaction in transparent, safe, and cost-effective manner. For instance, a blockchain-based production credit mechanism for the purpose of controlling business-to-business cooperation between socialized manufacturing tools is proposed.

1.9.4 Blockchains for Business Applications

Blockchains can apply in many business fields, but as previously described, most businesses have struggled. The key to a workable blockchain technology is a viable application scenario. The scenarios must be

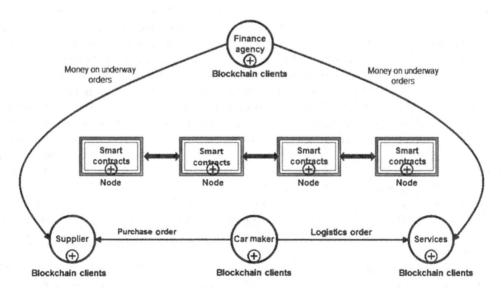

FIGURE 1.11 A blockchain ecosystem for car supply chain.

drawn up in order to test the special characteristics of blockchain and to follow invented market principles in a developed world, rather than traditional ones. It is promising that many efforts and undertakings are being carried out all over the world. Onecan find loads of blockchain ventures in hundreds of technology fields on blockchain-related websites [10][13]. In the literature, there are still few blockchain attempts.

For instance, a blockchain science information system is suggested to decrease the expense of accessing scientific information and making it free and universal. A blockchain credit global higher education network is proposed for an internationally trusted, transparent university education payment and ranking framework that will provide learners and institutions of higher education and other future stakeholders with a globally united perspective [10][14]. A blockchain digital infrastructure has been built to create protected digital identities that help minimize identity fraud and promote public safety, allowing people to conduct high-value and everyday online transactions [10][15].

1.9.5 Blockchains for Public Services

There is no awareness of current credit structures due to different brokerage systems, in appropriation, centralized and stagnant appraisal models, and inadequate funding. The autonomous blockchain technology is known to be the next version of the credit system because it is exchange based and suits all parties participating in trading. It is planned to be an interconnected, traceable, customized, and dynamic blockchain ecosystem. In addition to reliable information in such a blockchain scheme, the aim is to allow the participants and the transactions credibility. It promotes credible market promises with lifecycle, multimedia monitoring, and credit brokerage dependence.

1.9.6 Underdeveloped Blockchain Techniques

The groundbreaking decentralized project, Bitcoin cryptocurrency, has many detractors around, while much of the deviated cryptocurrency projects except Bitcoin have collapsed. A significant number of blockchain implementations have also been terminated, and in another implementation case, no blockchain project has been found to succeed. Yet, the magical innovations of blockchain are so enticing that people never give up. Many investigations have been carried out to develop their key strategies or to identify viable and successful worldwide use scenarios.

There are many common and exciting blockchain strategies, like blockchain creditworthiness, performance, safety/privacy, supervision, and integration online. The underdeveloped approaches are aimed at solving key issues that obstruct the adoption of blockchain systems and their growth. Blockchain networks are creditable by the devoted credit processes, but blockchains are a creditworthy framework to store and run records. It is commercially driven to please all the participants in the exchange.

The credit framework offers an open, fair, and credible platform to implement a decentralized creditworthiness environment, and all blockchain processes are processed by a series of intelligent contracts. The creditworthiness method is designed to enhance the integration, traceability, dynamics, and customization of the credit system. In order to test the viability and efficacy of a suggested independent credit system, numerous pilot programs have been created. As public consumer and creditworthiness query systems, four loan worthiness clouds have been created. Four forms of blockchain networks have been identified which include public blockchains, private blockchains, consortium blockchains, and hybrid blockchains. It is difficult to attain public blockchains while private blockchains don't really display their technological ability. Most of the initiatives currently in development use a consortia or hybrid blockchains that take some central mechanisms and some decentralized mechanisms [10].

For the time being, Bitcoin's characteristics remain paramount in blockchains. As seen in Figure 1.12, Libra, DCEP, and Bitcoin have their numerous views. There is a need for a range of developments in blockchain strategies, which are the online protection of blockchain, and the efficiency of PoW public

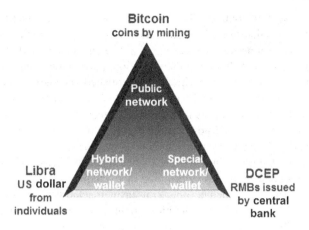

FIGURE 1.12   Features of Bitcoin, Libra, and DCEP.

blockchains has been considered quite low [10][16]. A variety of basic technologies for critical blockchain problems are given as follows:

1. Distributions of computers with central public blockchains such as the theorem limit, ACID, and Paxos/Raft.
2. Stable multiparty computing advanced techniques for decentralized networks, including a consensus system, Byzantine concerns, and algorithms.
3. Blockchain data mechanism has been developed to fulfill particular business functions through triggers for blockchain ventures, and a number of business levels for blockchain-related implementations with the technology on the market technology. Advanced strategies include shared storage data attribute-based encryption and zero knowledge–based attributes.

The blockchain architecture develops to investigate integrated blockchain networks with MSR, identify producer-based block data structure, replace blockchain PoW with corporate rewards, and establish blockchain network consensus structures and gates to co-locate blockchain and Internet facilities to promote efficient and complicated trading processes. Smart contracts for stable authentication and immersive models should be built for unmanned sector. Further data management methods for combining data both in and out of the blockchain systems have been developed to overcome data shortage and inadequacy through auto-regulated blockchain data.

1.9.7 Blockchain Applying Strategies

A viable and effective blockchain technology platform has many important issues to solve. A traditional blockchain ecosystem has four layers for the computing framework, including the blockchain, intelligent transactions, services, and interfaces.

Critical problems for an ecosystem include developing a network model, the ecosystem architecture, member and approval practices, polling and nodes, benefits, intelligent contracts, and consumers. In addition, algorithms for data collection and analysis are expected to solve crucial problems in blockchain applications. For most existing ventures, the blockchain network architecture remains an obstacle. The blockchain methods have evolved quickly, and there have been no well-accepted technological standards. Many Bitcoin ventures have not been accepted because of their inefficiency and performance costs.

Some take blockchain as an infrastructure in distributed databases. More projects are built for hybrid networks or variety network models that are self-designed. A traditional blockchain environment consists of a decentralized blockchain, participants' knowledge systems with blockchain programming interfaces, and a series of intelligent operating contracts. The blockchain offers, among other things, a transparent and self-regulating computer system that stores both data and transactions. Information systems for participants are designed for blockchain consumers and enable business data on blockchains to be accessed or uploaded.

Depending on the Bitcoin blockchain and their position, participants must be identified. The nodes of the polling system and organizational priorities are established. The admission policy and the necessary details are referred to as network model and in case of blockchain consortia. To render blockchain to prevail and design an effective consensus mechanism, a fair and efficient reward mechanism should be created. Intelligent contracts are well known as the biggest blockchain technologies with the equality, transparency, approval and legitimacy of a blockchain ecosystem [12].

The blockchains can work without human interference through a series of intelligent contracts. The intelligent contracts are designed for the predetermined blockchain numerals.

Callbacks from the blockchain scheme, other consensus mechanisms, or information structures of the parties may be invoked. In general, both the blockchain processes and implementation rules can be coded as smart contracts. There seem to be three types of cryptocurrency applications that communicate through programming interfaces with the Bitcoin community. In the stakeholders' data systems, the first class of customers is developed; both management accounting systems and integrated systems are one of them. The second category of customers is intelligent contracts or the blockchain operating system, like the decentralized clients. The third form of consumer is the blockchain public utilities, which provide the participants and future participants with a public interface.

Techniques for gathering data are important to help companies rooted on blockchain. It is assumed that the information are self-regulated and privately owned by the blockchain users, which poses some of the common problems in data processing. For lost data, characteristics, and redundant data, you need to build excellently compensation mechanisms. During the same period, it will be important to build weighting and cross-checking algorithms to leverage interconnected data on engagement from within and outside of Bitcoin and blockchain, which can be built as smart contracted knowledge collection systems.

1.9.8 Application Development Environments for Blockchain

For particular purposes or scenarios like supply chain funding, financial clearance and company regulation, and tracking hundreds of cryptocurrency, development environments have also been established. Improved infrastructure, consensus processes and design patterns have been developed to achieve higher efficiency and better suit special scenarios in the generic production environment of blockchain applications.

For example, with their specific consensus mechanisms, frameworks, and architecture, a permitted cryptocurrency called Beihangchain was already created. The blockchain uses the blockchain account and a blockchain exchange tool to cover a range of applications [10][17]. Hyperchain is indeed a blockchain application that offers blockchain network applications at a market level. The software provides organizations with the possibility for implementation, extension, and maintenance of their blockchain network on established data centers [10][18].

1.10 BLOCKCHAIN USER AUTHENTICATION AND PERMISSION

Utilizing public key encryption is to secure the permission of blockchain customer. Within its simplest form, blockchain technology-based properties are inherent; for example, the possession of an object is determined by hidden key data [19]. Dedicated wallet providers may be used to incorporate authenticating two-factor or other authentication protocols near the centralized electronic money networks.

A Bitcoin-like scripting language renders custodial bags. Special hardware wallets can boost the security capabilities of the public-key cryptography (PKC) for signing transactions.

- Overall, blockchain offers security decentralization, removing single failure points inherent in central e-money books.
- Blockchain users can use hierarchies of deterministic wallets and a payment to contract protocols to preserve user anonymity that allows the development of publicly unlinkable on-demand audit addresses. Using range evidence, transaction amounts might be masked. And in the case of even more complicated payment systems, for example for intelligent contracts, secret sharing proofs and stable multipartisan formulas may be used to operate contracts without exposing data to any computer.
- As a full-fledged event ordering infrastructure, blockchain could be used for distributed public key infrastructure that connects the identity of individuals and organizations to their public key. Public infrastructure may be structured in the form of blockchain or a particular network protocol. The legitimate value conversion and asset issuance will be allowed by PKI.

1.10.1 Blockchain Authentication

Blockchain security applies to schemes that test users for the resources of blockchain and other virtual money underlying technologies. Blockchain uses PKC to encrypt wallets or locations where value and function are safely stored. The ledger uses PKC [19]. There are therefore interesting parallels between blockchain authentication and technology protecting. As the key feature, identity and access management (IAM) for both the blockchain would be a cryptocurrency wallet; its user experience (UX) and user interface (UI) designs are nevertheless very weak without even a modern verification component, including true password-free protection. It is worth mentioning that encryption developers and blockchain designers also have an enthusiasm with both markets, which allows blockchain programmers an essential aspect of security and innovation.

1.10.2 Blockchain-Based Authentication of Devices and People

Using blockchain technology for providing secure identification and authentication of individuals and devices with publicly available encryption. The Internet of things is a system of devices, actuators, software and connective devices for the connection, interaction and exchange of data across gadgets, cars, and homes. Every element of our daily life is affected by IoT systems, from aircraft, vehicles, and drones to hospital devices, robotics, security cameras, and smartphones.

Primechain-API blends blockchain technology power and public key encryption to allow:

1. Smartphones, other computers, and consumers are securely authenticated and marked.
2. Internet correspondence is secure and encrypted.
3. Login schemes without password.
4. Preventing counterfeit emails.
5. DNS tracks authentication and spoofing prevention.
6. Electronic signatures.

Authentication centered on blockchain has certain special characteristics:

1. On the computer, keys to sign and decrypt will remain.
2. Authentication and encryption keys are stored on the blockchain.
3. Safe from sensitive cyberattacks like phishing, intermediary, play attacks.

Figure 1.13 indicates the following steps:

Step 1—Recovery of the verifier's public RSA key.
Step 2—Encrypt the requester's blockchain address.
Step 3—The blockchain address is submitted to the verifier.
Step 4—Decoding the encoded address.
Step 5—Return of the requester's public RSA key.

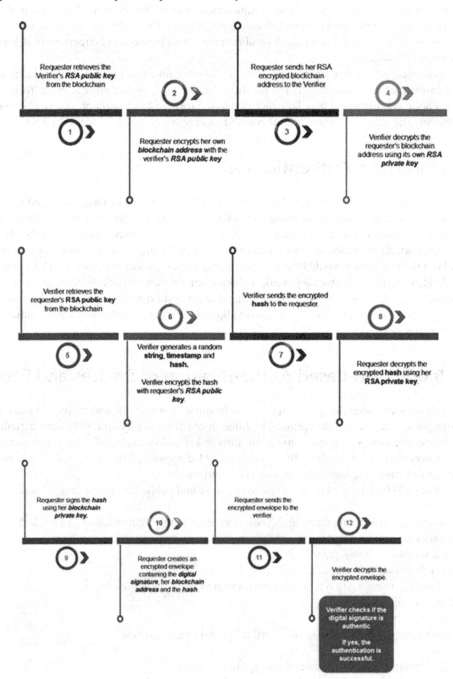

FIGURE 1.13   Flow of blockchain-based authentication.

Step 6—Build a random timeline and a hash.

Step 7—Give the key to the claimant.

Step 8—Hash decoding.

Step 09—The requester signs the hash.

Step 10—Build the enclosure.

Step 11—The envelope would be submitted to the verifier.

Step 12—The verifier decodes the encrypted envelope.

Step 13—Digital signature monitoring.

1.11 COMPUTER AND HARDWARE ENCRYPTION IMPLEMENTATIONS OF BLOCKCHAIN TECHNOLOGY

The advent of the Internet led to the rise of e-commerce that contributed to financial transfers between various organizations [20][21]. A single agency is responsible for protected correspondence and stable financial transfers between the two organizations. In the event of a loss or theft, this core body is liable still and may be challenged. Any structured processes can also be prone to lead to a device collapse at such a catastrophic rate at one point of failure. A central agency also poses problems of faith, privacy, and protection.

In comparison, unlike a P2P technology, a pause introduced either by central entity is implemented to answer all these questions, mostly during the transaction [20][21]. The blockchain technology uses a decentralized directory where all networking members retain the synchronized full or partial directory. All transactions between various organizations are saved in the distributed directory and the directory is synchronized across each node of the network after each successful transaction. That eliminates the need for a main agency, and thus removes several other problems.

Figure 1.14 shows the potential implementations of blockchain technology. The IoT is the foundation for many diverse fields of intelligent applications, including intelligent cities, intelligent wellbeing, and

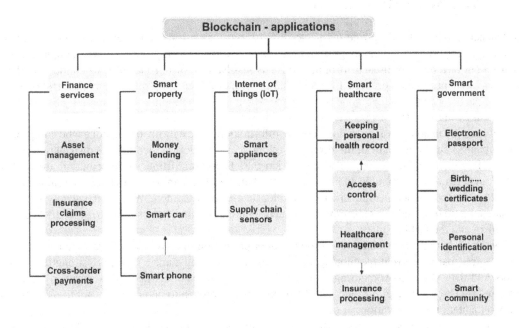

FIGURE 1.14 Blockchain technology potential implementations.

intelligent transportation. Essentially, "instrumentation," "interconnections," and "intelligence," referred to the three 'I's of a smart city, are due to the IoT.

The Internet of All is a philosophy that integrates IoT into its infrastructure and environment; the other three elements of an IoE system are individuals, data, and procedures. One of the main components of IoE is data collection. In the IOE ecosystem, the data processing takes place in a number of areas, and the volume of data gathered is expanded every day in the IoE system. The devices used in these applications were reduced power consuming devices that do not provide the architecture with high calculating power.

The inclusion of an "edge layer" in these cases aims to reduce the processing burden across the whole computer network. In certain instances, an edge data center may be used for near–real-time computing. Edge computing helps improve the applications in which computer processing has to be discharged, but there are no large volumes of data transmission through the network. The machines in the IoE network have no high processing power and are typically devoted to the processing of data.

However, it is still not ideal to move all the data into a cloud in such a case, due to network bandwidth restrictions. Protection and confidentiality were two other aspects that must be of primary significance in the design process of a system environment. Studies over the years create different methods to solve these challenges, such that computing demands are moved to the network's edge. Integrating edge data centers allows cracking the resource constraints and low performance. Those other technologies are part of many mission-critical implementations including military, medical, and manufacturing IoT scenarios.

These vital mission applications often require optimum reliability, protection, and privacy. Different ideas were suggested in the IoT architectures for the privacy and security aspects. It suggested the use of cryptographic algorithms to improve IoT stability, but if a cryptographic mechanism is to be seen as an IoT protection instrument, a central agent is necessary. To eliminate the need of a central authority from IoT architectures, blockchain technologies can be used. The blockchain is used to organize and execute data by means of a transparent public ledger. A duplicate of the database is available to each node connecting to the network. This helps to ensure coherence and protection. A blockchain is secure, tamper-proof, and is a list of numerous transactions between network participants.

1.11.1 Blockchain Technology Can Transform the Security Industry

The blockchain has not only a role in crypto devices, but may use these to develop security strategies, according to experts. Computer bugs cannot actually cause security problems, for example a privacy infringement or a network breach. If human error is involved or an intruder tries to manipulate data or processes in the production process, the blockchain may fix problems by splitting any doubtful operation. When all parties know what everyone is doing and when, they can monitor and potentially fix lax protection, mistakes, and inside risks before there is real harm.

Obviously, you do not want a recipient of the information to be willing, or someone who compromises a participant to alter it all data in the directory of applications such as identities or distribution network tracking. Intelligent contracts may also be carried out. These small lines of information are held in a blockchain network on each node and implement the behavior that can be carried out. The same outcome must be obtained if machines attached to the blockchain are executed. When participants know who has planned activities and the reasoning associated with them, this inspires more trust in the "deal" and mechanism and the right result.

The blockchain itself presents very little threat or protection in conventional cybersecurity solutions, but offers transparency, event monitoring, cryptographic technology, and a chance to strengthen security sensors and data sharing—something that is missing in some business network security solutions and deployments. The wholesale introduction of IoT devices has proven to be necessary not to move through the implementation of innovations at the earliest level.

At a period of vital system trust, though, one can also see the blockchain embedded into systems that manage confidential financial information transactions or monitor the IoT and mobile phones. The software will also deliver secure infrastructure to manufacturers, to help maintain ownership over enterprise networks, which do what they're doing to fix weaknesses in safety protocols.

1.12 CONCLUSION

Blockchain is a public ledger in one form. Distributed ledgers use freelance machines in many electronic ledgers to register exchanges and synchronize transactions. Overall, the blockchain infrastructure offers shared authentication and removes individual failure points found in centralized systems. Blockchain's main goal is to create a credible ecosystem in some kind of a non-trustable network system among independent participants. Because of its clustered blocks, consensus-based ledgers, peer-to-peer nodes, anonymous accounts for auto-regulated information protection, and configurable intelligent agreements, a decentralized system is safe.

The need to assess a blockchain venture is critical to sustainability, performance, and potential benefits. Various common and promising blockchain strategies—such as creditworthiness, performance, productivity, protection, privacy, oversight, and Internet-based integration—have been underdeveloped. The blockchain has been one of the most significant innovations that can serve diverse applications.

New consensus mechanisms, as well as a novel blockchain design, are introduced in this article as a response to a certain problems, such as interoperability, processing time, and stability. Applications have addressed the convergence of the strength of blockchain technologies: secure public key authentication cryptography, and recognition of individuals and computers. DLT/blockchain is an innovative and important emerging arena in technical advancement, which we have discussed in this chapter with various applications. DLT/blockchain operations have been rising in various industries over the last few years, having potential impacts on industry, the government, and community.

We assessed the existing DLT/blockchain ecosystem and thoroughly explored the problems important to DLT/blockchain creation using a mixed methodology approach that involves a concise analysis of the findings and interactions with such a variety of stakeholders. Our research shows that the DLT/blockchain prospects are vast; however, multiple obstacles must be addressed. While it is an environment of radical transition and complexity, measures should be taken to further evaluate the present realities, causes of change, and sectors affected. In this respect, the review in this article states that standards will contribute in fostering technology; for example, in allowing the creation and implementation in DLT/blockchain, as well as its market to be developed as a space.

However, the times for designing and implementing standards are critical, as is usually the case for modern innovations. A too-late standards strategy for a technology may risk losing opportunities to optimize the advantages of technology. The review that we have carried out attempts to offer a rounded view of the scientific basis can be used for potential analysis and decision making on the position of DLT/blockchain standards.

REFERENCES

[1] Roeck, Dominik, Henrik Sternberg, and Erik Hofmann. "Distributed ledger technology in supply chains: A transaction cost perspective." *International Journal of Production Research* 58, no. 7 (2020): 2124–2141.
[2] Hawlitschek, Florian, Benedikt Notheisen, and Timm Teubner. "The limits of trust-free systems: A literature review on blockchain technology and trust in the sharing economy." *Electronic Commerce Research and Applications* 29 (2018): 50–63.
[3] Underwood, Sarah. "Blockchain beyond bitcoin." *Communications of the ACM* 59, no. 11 (2016): 15–17.
[4] Natarajan, Harish, Solvej Krause, and Helen Gradstein. *Distributed Ledger Technology and Blockchain*. World Bank, 2017.

[5] Deshpande, Advait, Katherine Stewart, Louise Lepetit, and Salil Gunashekar. "Distributed ledger technologies/blockchain: Challenges, opportunities and the prospects for standards." *Overview Report the British Standards Institution (BSI)* 40 (2017): 40.

[6] Attiya, Hagit, and Jennifer Welch. *Distributed Computing: Fundamentals, Simulations, and Advanced Topics.* Vol. 19. John Wiley & Sons, 2004.

[7] Xiao, Yang, Ning Zhang, Jin Li, Wenjing Lou, and Y. Thomas Hou. "Distributed consensus protocols and algorithms." *Blockchain for Distributed Systems Security* 25 (2019).

[8] Xiao, Yang, Ning Zhang, Wenjing Lou, and Y. Thomas Hou. "A survey of distributed consensus protocols for blockchain networks." *IEEE Communications Surveys & Tutorials* 22, no. 2 (2020): 1432–1465.

[9] Liu, Xing, Bahar Farahani, and Farshad Firouzi. "Distributed ledger technology." In *Intelligent Internet of Things*, pp. 393–431. Springer, 2020.

[10] Li, Yinsheng. "Emerging blockchain-based applications and techniques." *Service Oriented Computing and Applications* (2019): 279–285.

[11] Engelhardt, Mark A. "Hitching healthcare to the chain: An introduction to blockchain technology in the healthcare sector." *Technology Innovation Management Review* 7, no. 10 (2017).

[12] Deng, Miaolei, and Pan Feng. "A food traceability system based on blockchain and radio frequency identification technologies." *Journal of Computer and Communications* 8, no. 9 (2020): 17–27.

[13] Vujičić, Dejan, Dijana Jagodić, and Siniša Ranđić. "Blockchain technology, bitcoin, and Ethereum: A brief overview." In *2018 17th International Symposium Infoteh-Jahorina (Infoteh)*, pp. 1–6. IEEE, 2018.

[14] Turkanović, Muhamed, Marko Hölbl, Kristjan Košič, Marjan Heričko, and Aida Kamišalić. "EduCTX: A blockchain-based higher education credit platform." *IEEE Access* 6 (2018): 5112–5127.

[15] Wolfond, Greg. "A blockchain ecosystem for digital identity: Improving service delivery in Canada's public and private sectors." *Technology Innovation Management Review* 7, no. 10 (2017).

[16] Illing, Sean. "Why bitcoin is bullshit, explained by an expert." *Vox* 17 (2018).

[17] Yli-Huumo, Jesse, Deokyoon Ko, Sujin Choi, Sooyong Park, and Kari Smolander. "Where is current research on blockchain technology?—A systematic review." *PloS One* 11, no. 10 (2016): e0163477.

[18] Nguyen, Dinh, Ming Ding, Pubudu N. Pathirana, and Aruna Seneviratne. *Blockchain and AI-based Solutions to Combat Coronavirus (COVID-19)-Like Epidemics: A Survey.* (2020).

[19] Tahir, Muhammad, Muhammad Sardaraz, Shakoor Muhammad, and Muhammad Saud Khan. "A lightweight authentication and authorization framework for blockchain-enabled IoT network in health-informatics." *Sustainability* 12, no. 17 (2020): 6960.

[20] Puthal, Deepak, Nisha Malik, Saraju P. Mohanty, Elias Kougianos, and Gautam Das. "Everything you wanted to know about the blockchain: Its promise, components, processes, and problems." *IEEE Consumer Electronics Magazine* 7, no. 4 (2018): 6–14.

[21] Puthal, Deepak, Nisha Malik, Saraju P. Mohanty, Elias Kougianos, and Chi Yang. "The blockchain as a decentralized security framework [future directions]." *IEEE Consumer Electronics Magazine* 7, no. 2 (2018): 18–21.

Blockchain for Information Systems Applications

2

Divya Stephen, Blesmi Rose Joseph, Neeraja James, and Aswathy S.U.

Contents

2.1 INTRODUCTION

A blockchain is a digital record of transactions which is used for recording transactions with crypto-currencies like Bitcoin. The potential of blockchain technology is increasing rapidly as the technology becomes more secure and immutable. The blockchain comprises distributed blocks, every one of which can record and store all transactions. The members can share records and question information nodes in a decentralized structure. The blockchain technology does not have any central authority. In other words, there is no intermediate party required for transferring and storing the assets from one to another using peer-to-peer (P2P) communication. All the participants in the network can view and verify the accessed and transferred information via ledger. Blockchain relies on container data structure. Blockchain has three main parts: block, chain, and network [1].

2.2 STATE OF THE ART OF BLOCKCHAIN TECHNOLOGY AND CYBERSECURITY FOR INFORMATION SYSTEMS

A blockchain is a record of transactions of digital data. The blockchain is a structure in which individual data stored in blocks are connected to a single list, called blockchain. Blockchains are used for recording exchanges like digital forms of money—for example, Ethereum—and have numerous different applications. Numerous PCs approve every exchange added to a blockchain on the Internet. These frameworks are designed to follow specific types of blockchain deals, structure, and distributed organization. They work jointly to make sure each transaction is checked before it is connected to the blockchain. This decentralized computer network gives a single system that cannot add invalid blocks to the chain. When a new block is created, it is added to the blockchain, it will be linked to the previous block using a cryptographic hash generated from the contents of the preceding block. This will confirm that the chain never fragmented and that each block is permanently recorded.

2.2.1 History of Blockchain

1. 1991: Stuart Haber and W. Scott Stornetta described a cryptographically secured chain of blocks.
2. 1998: Nick Szabo, a computer scientist, works on a decentralized digital currency known as "bit gold."

3. 2000: Stefan Konst published the theory of cryptographic secured chains and ideas for their implementation.
4. 2008: The developer working under the pseudonym Satoshi Nakamoto releases a white paper establishing the model for a blockchain.
5. 2009: By using Bitcoin, Nakamoto introduces the first blockchain as the public ledger for transactions.
6. 2014: Blockchain technology is sorted out from currency and its future for other financial interorganizational transactions is explored. Blockchain 2.0 is introduced, referring to requests beyond currency. The Ethereum blockchain introduces computer programs into the blocks, representing financial instruments like bonds. These are called smart contracts.

2.2.1.1 The Second Generation

Some other blockchains incorporate those that run the few hundred "altcoins"—other comparable currencies which stick out with various principles—just as genuinely various applications. For example:

- Ethereum: It is the second largest blockchain execution after Bitcoin. The cash flow by Ethereum is the ether, yet additionally considers the capacity and activity of PC code, taking into account keen agreements.
- Ripple: A constant gross settlement framework, cash trade and settlement organization, in view of a public record.

2.2.1.2 Characteristics of Blockchain

- Decentralization: The blockchain comprises distributed blocks, each of which can record and store all transactions. In fact, data is consequently shared and disseminated between hubs with no outsider intercession. In this decentralized framework, all members and hubs are dynamic to join the exercises and exchanges.
- Detrusting: Since blockchain innovation is executed in a decentralized framework, information moves between hubs in the organization and does not need common trust between members.
- Transparency: Through the blockchain, all members share records and question information in hubs in a decentralized structure. The blockchain innovation guarantees that frameworks record and move information and data. Every member can query the records in the blockchain to make the data in the disseminated framework straightforward and reliable.
- Traceable and unforgettable: The blockchain utilizes timestamps to distinguish and to record every transaction, in this way upgrading the time measurement of the information. This permits the hub to maintain control of exchanges and to make the information detectable.
- Anonymity: The blockchain encodes information utilizing lopsided encryption methods. This unbalanced encryption has two uses in blockchains: information encryption and advanced marks. Information encryption in the blockchain guarantees the security of transfer information and diminishes the danger of losing or misrepresenting exchange information. Exchange information is communicated over the organization and is carefully endorsed to show the personality of the signatory and whether the exchange has been distinguished.
- Credibility: The information trade of the blockchain is totally subject to restraint. It depends on every hub to frame an incredible figure to guard against outside assaults without human mediation. Members can finish the exchange in a detrusting climate under states of complete obscurity. Through the blockchain, all members share records and question information in hubs in a decentralized structure. The blockchain innovation guarantees that frameworks record and move information and data. Every member can question the records in the blockchain to make the data in the appropriated framework straightforward and steady.

2.2.1.3 Cybersecurity for Information Systems

The cybersecurity monitoring technology is based on experience, observation, vulnerabilities, classification of attacks, and countermeasures. Today, the two key parts of the innovation are the methods of detection and the types of tools available. There are numerous terms utilized for depicting techniques of location—all the procedures we have seen described fall into either of two classes:

1. Statistical deviation detection: Here, the cybersecurity monitoring (CSMn) instrument searches for deviations from factual measures. A standard of qualities is characterized for subjects and items; for example, clients, gatherings, workstations, workers, documents, and organization connectors. One can utilize chronicled information or basic checking, or anticipate that qualities should set up the pattern. As activities being checked occur, the CSMn instrument refreshes a rundown of factual factors for each subject or object of revenue. For example, the engine may count the amount of records read by a particular customer over a given period. This method treats any inadmissible deviation from foreseen characteristics as an irregularity. For example, when the quantity of records read by a particular customer over a given period outperforms the ordinary motivation for that period, the CSMn instrument articulates a possible inconsistency. Experts use various terms for and explanations of this sort of ID. Some are:
   - Anomaly recognition: Distinguishing deviation from an ordinary example of utilization, similarly as with an insider's utilization of a venture organization.
   - Statistical abnormality: Location depends on the assumption that clients and organizations show unsurprising examples of conduct from which they do not digress altogether throughout brief time frames; a deviation from the typical demonstrates a potential assault.
   - Rule-based recognition: identification dependent on a library of factual portrayals of worthy practices.
2. Pattern matching detection: In this methodology, the CSMn apparatus analyzes action to put away examples that model assaults or inadmissible states referred to as assaults or kinds of assaults, just as appropriate designs or framework security arrangements are demonstrated as examples of information. Examples can be made out of single occasions, arrangements of occasions, limits of occasions, or articulations utilizing AND, OR, and NOT operators. This technique treats any action or expression that coordinates an example as an expected issue. Practitioners use varied terms for and explanations of this sort of detection. Some are:
   - Misuse detection: Attempted exploitation misuse of a particular weakness.
   - Signature detection: Identifying explicit qualities of a transmission or of the message being received.
   - Rule-based detection: Location dependent on a library of realized attack designs, unapproved movement, or inadmissible framework boundary is calculated [2].

2.3 BLOCKCHAIN TECHNOLOGIES AND METHODOLOGIES FOR INFORMATION SYSTEMS

2.3.1 Types of Blockchain Technologies

Blockchain is the basic form of the digital cryptocurrency, such as Bitcoin. It has a character of decentralization, anonymity, suitableness, and unchangeability for digital cash dealings method. There are four varieties of blockchain [3][4]:

- Public blockchain: This is an open source, decentralized blockchain. There are no limitations for users. Anybody can access it; they can read, write, and audit the blockchain without any restrictions. Clients who take part in the organization have no limitations. They all have control over the organization. Anyone can make changes in the blockchain; they can add data into it. Public blockchain structures are good for securing user confidentiality. It is publicly available to all; decisions are made by a few consensus algorithms like proof of work, proof of stake, etc. Public blockchain stage keeps a motivating force component predefined in the convention through some gaming hypothesis; that is, the members in the organization are financially compensated for keeping up the most amazing aspect practices and genuineness in the framework.
- Private blockchain: This is the earliest starting point somewhat allowing for client personality for deciding their particular assignments in the organizations and their controlling access; for example, reading, writing, and auditing of explicit data in the blockchain. The private blockchain has the personality that it is more unique than public blockchain, so the decisions are very secure. Private blockchain is utilized by associations or ventures that require versatility, information insurance security, and administrative principles for stated consistency. Thus, particular members who are pre-characterized with explicit measures in the organization approach the blocks of data for inside confirming and approving the exchanges [3].
- Consortium/federated blockchain: This is a half-decentralized blockchain, which is in between the public and private blockchains. It has the properties of both blockchains. Unlike a private blockchain, the organization of a consortium blockchain is worked by a gathering of elements. Rather than a public blockchain, a consortium blockchain does not permit anyone to enter the organization; rather, it requires the consent of the organization administrators to grant someone admittance. This kind of blockchain is frequently referred to as "semi-private" blockchain, since the authority of the organization is given ahead of time to a specifically predefined node dependent on a few consensus algorithms.
- Hybrid blockchain: This is the combination of private and public blockchains. It solidifies the central focus characteristics of each blockchain independently; that is, it hinders the security focal points of private blockchain and straightforwardness favorable circumstances of a public blockchain according to requirements. The secured Internet limit offered rise to the combination thought of the blockchain, enabling the hybrid blockchain to have different chain associations of blockchains. The hybrid blockchain is controlled by a group of individuals; each transaction made is kept private and can be verified whenever needed. They are not open to all; some restrictions are there for entering the participants into the hybrid blockchain. This upholds the immutability of the transactions [3][4].

2.3.2 Methodologies for Information Systems

Blockchain advancement works by building up a platform which is secure and clear for the money-related trades of virtual characteristics, for instance. The hash of each block guards data in the blockchain. It is fundamentally in light of the fact that regardless of size of the data or archive, the numerical hash work gives a hash code of a similar length for each block. Thus, attempting to change a block of data would create a totally new hash value. An association which is accessible to all and all while keeps up customers' anonymity in actuality brings up trust issues with respect to the individuals. Along these lines, to assemble trust, members should experience a couple of understanding counts.

The computerized digital money Bitcoin utilizes the first-ever blockchain innovation. It is a computerized store of significant worth that empowers shared exchanges over the web without the intercession of an outsider. The blockchain network is a decentralized design that contains dispersed hubs (PCs) that survey and approve the validity of any new trades that are attempted. This joint game plan is carried out through a couple of arrangement models by the route toward mining. The route toward mining displays that each center endeavoring to add another trade has encountered and tended to the complex computational conundrum through wide work and has the privilege to get an honor as a compromise for their organization. For the approval of an exchange, the organization should affirm the accompanying states; the sufficient Bitcoin will be held in the sender account that it plans to move. The amount planned to send has not previously been sent to some other beneficiary. When an exchange is approved and is settled upon by all the hubs, it then gets added to the high-level record and is guaranteed using cryptography which uses the public key and that is available to wide scope of different center points and a private key, that should remain Confidential/Private.

To keep up the exchanges utilizing advanced cash in the blockchain network, we need to be aware of the automated wallet which is used to store, send, and receive processed cash. This public location is utilized at whatever point an exchange happens—that is, the Bitcoin money is relegated to the public location of the particular wallet; in any case, to demonstrate that the responsibility for public location there be a private key related with the wallet that fills in as the client's advanced mark that is utilized to affirm the handling of any exchange. The customer's public key is the abbreviated rendition of his private key made through complex and progressed numerical calculations [5].

2.3.3 Block Structure

A block contains several parts:

- Main data: Here, the blocks will contain exchange of information. The data depends upon the use factor of blockchain, which is the important administrations which the blockchain executed. This exchange information will be stored for financial institutions like banks, etc.
- Timestamp: These additionally exist in the blocks themselves. When a specific block is created, the timestamp includes the date and time.
- Hash: Each block has a hash which is a unique identifier created by using a cryptographic hash calculation (e.g.: SHA-256). The new block is added to the chain by connecting it to the previous block by using the hash. The hash of the current block and hash of the past block are connected together. Hashes make the block constant. By utilizing the Merkle tree, these hashes were created and are put away in the header of the block.

2.3.3.1 Block Properties

In a blockchain, each block includes three sections: hash of the previous block, current data, and hash of current block. The information may be anything that can be exchanged: records, clinical records, protection records, etc. There are mainly two types of blockchain: the first is private blockchain and the second is public blockchain. Then there is one more type, a mix of both private and public blockchain called hybrid blockchain. Each block is associated with past blocks utilizing the hash value. When we are making a change in the value of a single piece of information in a block, it will bring about an adjustment in the hash value of that block.

2.3.3.2 Hash Function

When a hash works, it will take data and return a fixed-length yield (e.g., SHA-1). The yield must be different for various data/messages and the equivalent for similar information. In a hash, its work has some internal states. On the basis of the message it receives, it makes changes for those internal states. It is very difficult to figure out the input message from the hash output when the stages and mixes are taking place and the interior states will change. This implies that the output cannot be known or it cannot be guessed anymore. When we make a change in the input marginally, it will change the output of the hash wildly. There is no standard on how these progressions happen and give off an impression of being irregular; by the way, it is only irregular.

2.3.3.3 Consensus Algorithm

The major consensus algorithm is proof of work. When we are searching for a solution, it needs a large computational force and consumption of energy [6]. In proof of work, when we are adding a new block to the chain, blockchain calculations check if the newly introduced block is valid or invalid. We know in DLT networks, trust is built on the framework, not on any users. PoW checks if each block's hash value is in a fixed range. If it is in range, then the block is received; otherwise, it will be rejected. In the blockchain, the miners compete with each other in the PoW idea to mine blocks, which intends to discover a block's hash value in a predetermined range.

PoW is a relay between the miners in the blockchain network to discover the answer to a mathematical puzzle. In this competition, whoever gets the answer will be the winner; as a part of this, they get rewards for mining that block. To add a malicious block in a PoW network, one needs to have at least 51% computational power over the whole network. Otherwise, one trying to add maliciously would be unsuccessful [6].

2.4 RECENT DEVELOPMENTS AND EMERGING TRENDS USING BLOCKCHAIN FOR SECURING INFORMATION SYSTEMS

2.4.1 Supply Chain Management

Blockchain builds a trust layer for supply chain management. The process involves being transparent at the point at which order is placed, manufacturer/producer of the product, followed by the transportation and supply to the end user. Difficulties in blockchain are record keeping and following of items. Provenance exchanges are the point at which countless products are dealt with by the PCs; it is hard to monitor all the records. It results in straightforward need and cost issues. With the utilization of blockchain, item data are acquired through installed sensors and labels, so the items from the creation stage to end stage can be checked and used to identify any false exercises. Blockchain decreases the expense of moving things in the store network.

Elimination of third party middlemen and intermediaries in the supply chain avoids the risk of fraud and duplicated product. It gives a solitary view and wellspring of reality with respect to the lifecycle of the buy request. Payments are made between client and provider as digital forms of money, with shadow ledgers capturing buyer, seller, and carrier data to the blockchain and a web-based user interface providing enhanced visibility. Risk of misplacement turns into an uncommon factor. It has the ability of interfacing record and information foci, keeping up the information trustworthiness.

2.4.2 Healthcare

In order to enhance the quality level of patient health management, the rules and regulations are a tedious and lengthy procedural process. So the plausibility isn't accomplished. The issue is to overcome any issues between specialist co-ops and payers. Outsider reliance exacerbates things. For instance, critical patient information is required urgently. The scattered information in various departments and systems has to be connected in order to fetch the details immediately. This will not give us the smooth working of the task, dealing with and the trade of data. It gets repetitive—for example, missing or abusing of information, which is a significant danger for persistent consideration and medical care association. Blockchain is one of the main advancements that impact the world with its high-market procedures. When the data is added to the circulated record, adjustment is impossible. The high upgraded security is the strength. On the off chance that any progressions are made, the entire ensuing blocks are additionally to be modified. It provides a safe and secure digital relationship. When the blockchain is used for medical services, the member will be answerable for their own reports dealing with them, and the client will have all entrance rights to control the information. Along these lines, understanding consideration quality has been ad-libbed by less support cost and different levels of verifications are dropped. Predominantly, it permits the creation and appropriation of a single information base of wellbeing data and simple availability to all the elements in the framework. Higher security and straightforwardness is permitted, and exceptional consideration and concern is applied to patients by the specialist for their treatment. Permissioned blockchain allows information to be divided between the members, and it is for utilization inside the association. So, exchange is performed safely. Once a transaction is made through consensus, it will be the permanent record and it is added to the new block of existing one. Without blockchain, the information stored is centralized and is difficult to fetch. Here patient details are isolated. Once it is decentralized, smooth flow of information takes place with the scarce datasets. In the studies, a group of participants enrolled themselves and monetized data in the form of tokens. With the emerging datasets, the implementation of new technologies such as machine learning and artificial intelligence would be possible to enable discovery of the threat and risk factors.

2.4.3 Smart Contracts

Brilliant agreements are a sort of an understanding or agreement that actualize oneself executing modified PC code. It has three center components: a pace of repeat to test conditions, a gathering of conditions, and an activity that gets enacted by those conditions. The shrewd agreements become unchanging, self-executing portions of program meetings on a straightforward and auditable public record. Once programmed, smart contracts are not taken control of by central authority. It causes us to trade offers, property, and cash by dodging the administration of outsiders. By the utilization of smart agreements, we pay as spot coins into the record, and the concerned offers or property are traded. The working of keen agreements incorporates a discretionary agreement between the members that are written as code into public record, which additionally incorporates expiry date, strike cost, and so forth. Protection of an individual entertainer is kept up by controllers and receipt of exchange is held as virtual agreement and installment as cryptographic forms of money. Ethereum was intended to help savvy contracts.

2.4.4 B-Voting

To limit the defects and along these lines of improving the precision of legitimate votes surveyed and to check whether the qualified applicants are the electors and consequently license them to login and cast a ballot from any workstation, the reconciliation of blockchain in democratic framework is presented. The circulated records are utilized to give the democratic tokens to a survey station, which thus issue tokens to electors independently and in this manner track casting a ballot in sidechain toward the end the sidechain is joined together to frame primary democratic blockchain executed under Ethereum. Toward the finish of casting a ballot multimark is applied by surveying stations to the new vote from the citizens and shrewd agreements will be moved to voting form or competitor. To keep up mystery survey stations have capacity to keep the votes of the blockchain and the votes are approved utilizing the savvy contract for example multisignature component which implies both surveying station and citizen need to sign before the arrival of blockchain. By isolating the cryptographic hashes we can assemble an open, evident and unknown democratic framework.

2.4.5 Insurance

By the use of blockchain, insurance fraud can be eliminated and efficiencies of claiming can be improved for the operation costs of insurers who need to minimize fraud; this very well may be prepared utilizing keen agreements. The participants who wish to claim the insurance could access the distributed ledger to learn the policy details. The datasets added to the disseminated record are the verification of protection, guarantee of structure, and proof to help claims. Blockchain technology can influence the following processes: minimizing paperwork and frameworks so claims can be verified and handled quickly, reducing fraud, and improving quality of data and efficiency of the insurance value chain. Dispersed record utilizes cryptostrategies to forestall expansion, alteration, and release of information.

2.4.6 Smart Land Registry

Land data is put on the decentralized public record—those records that deal with property rights. It empowers the protected and quick moment of land property, when the specific conditions are met from the purchaser and vendor points of view. Blockchain-based land vaults dispose of the registration gap, and naturally update the record all the while. The users would be allowed to access the information about the property, and it also provides the automatic assurance about the property ownership. Blockchain-based land libraries diminish the dangers associated with cheats, middle charges, and flawed circumstances. Initially, the buyer and seller should register to the permissioned blockchain network with their identity, which is connected with their mobile devices for instant updating. The buyer generates a request and forwards it to the seller and asks in return for details of the land. The seller takes the buyer's request and passes it to the land. Then the land (blockchain) responds to the seller with the buyer's request, the land's public key, other details of the land (ownership, area, location, etc.), the current owner's public key, and the transaction details of the prior ownership transaction. This information is enough for the buyer to know about the land and the seller. Once the buyer is satisfied, the transaction will be initialized and ownership will be transferred.

2.4.7 B-Music

Serious issues in the music business contain proprietorship rights, royalties distribution, and straightforwardness. The advanced music industry essentially centers around proprietorship rights for cash or resource creations. Blockchain technology creates a decentralized database of music rights, and the distributed ledger gives transparent communication of artist royalties. Contingent on the predefined contract, the clients are paid with computerized money. Digital copies of artists' music can be sold and paid from the customers directly without publishers, which will improve the relationship between musicians and their fans. Specialists accomplish more autonomy to showcase their own music. Blockchain innovation gives unlimited authority and admittance to their substance. For instance, Ujo Music is an Ethereum upheld music programming services company or the cutting-edge financial scene of music.

2.4.8 Digital Identity

Individuals are known by their character; it drives business and social communications. Character is an assortment of traits like age, name, financial history, address history, and social history. Numerous identity thefts have been ongoing because of absence of validity, approval, and checks. There is no visibility over the identity attributes. Character information is ordinarily decentralized in identification, driving permits, citizen cards, Aadhaar cards, and banking passbooks. Single identity is replicating for multiple purposes. Instead of maintaining multiple copies of a single document, place blockchain technology to decentralize the identities accessed through one password called single sign on (SSO). Every individual ought to have full control and responsibility for personal data. Individuals can handle the use of their own character profiles for business and social communications; this ensures the distributed trust model, defines multiple different vendors, and can access identity profiles for different purposes. Users can give the two solutions: namely consent for identity usage and control of identity attributes and identity profiles.

An automated and real-time verification of identity through smart contracts can verify identity without revealing the identity data, so no one can tamper with the identity information of individuals and auditable record of information access. Hyperledger Indy provides the platform of sharing the user's identity, and working principles are defined with trust anchors; it verifies the distributed identifier. Indy calls the pairwise relationship for sharing and verifying the user's identity. Plenum is one of the examples of distributed ledger platforms for verifying digital identity [7].

2.5 THEORY OF BLOCKCHAIN FOR INFORMATION SYSTEMS

Most of the trust issues in an information system are unpredictable when there is no confirmation or surveying is not done properly. When we need to manage very sensitive information—for instance, financial transactions—with these digital formats, it should be confirmed for proper understanding. In 2008, Satoshi Nakamoto introduced a big change in the digital world [8] with Bitcoin, a virtual cryptocurrency that maintains its value without any support from any centralized authority or financial entity. Blockchain has three main pillars: decentralization, transparency, and immutability. The proper structure of a blockchain is a growing list of records which are known as blocks, and they are linked with the previous and following blocks by using a cryptographic hash. The blockchain system grants the exchange to be confirmed by a group of people in the network. It is a secure, distributed, immutable, clear, and auditable record. The blockchain gives permission to all the traders to transfer data, adding new blocks to the network. Blockchain is the basic form of digital cryptocurrency such as Bitcoin. it has a character of decentralization, anonymity, suitableness, and unchangeability for digital cash dealings methods. There are four varieties of blockchain: private, public, hybrid, and consortium. The blockchain gives the information in the form of the block, whereby each block takes a large number of Bitcoin trades executed at a fixed time.

According to the capacities they give, different sorts of hubs can be fundamental for the association. The capacity work is answerable for keeping a duplicate of the chain in the node.

Wallet administrations give security keys that permit clients to arrange exchanges to work with their Bitcoins. At last, the mining limit is liable for making new blocks by settling the verification of work. The center points that play out the affirmation of work are known as diggers, and they get as of late delivered Bitcoins, and costs, as a prize. PoW is the key to empower trustless arrangements in blockchain networks. The PoW contains a computationally intensive work that is basically for the generation of blocks. The work is very complex to settle and simultaneously effectively obvious once finished. At the point when a miner has finished the confirmation of work, the newly entering block in the association and other blocks in the association check its authenticity preceding, adding it to the chain.

Since the generation of blocks is done at the same time in the association, it is very expensive for a cyberattack to make a change in a block and degenerate the blockchain. The assailant in the block generation measure—and thus, the acknowledged piece of blocks—will invalidate the one made by the aggressor. As a result of a large computational limit expected to change the blockchain, the debasement of its blocks is, all things considered, immense. This implies that whether or not the individuals are absolutely genuine in the use of Bitcoin, an arrangement is continually reached in the association as long as by far most of the association is outlined by reasonable individuals. Blockchain has similarly given a development that the idea of a smart contract can arise. Generally speaking, a smart contract refers to the PC shows or tasks that grant consent to be subsequently executed and actualized, considering a bunch of predefined conditions. In smart contracts, conditions and limits can be characterized past the exchanging of digital currencies—for instance, the approval of assets to a particular extent of trades with non-financial components—which makes it an ideal fragment to develop blockchain advancement to various zones.

Ethereum is one of the explorer blockchains to consolidate sharp arrangements. Today, splendid arrangements have been related with most existing blockchain executions; for example, Hyperledger got ready for associations that licenses parts to be passed on by the necessities of clients with the assistance of huge organizations [9].

2.6 BLOCKCHAIN-BASED SECURITY OF FINANCIAL INFORMATION SYSTEMS

Blockchain plays a vital role in the financial sector due to its high efficiency and security. Blockchain is an advanced technology which supports financial services in a decentralized manner. As the financial system undergoes more technical changes in coming years, blockchain technology stands as a pillar to the various substantial disruptions, but the rate of risk factors, potential threats, and challenges are also a major issue in this system, like the data leakage which can happen during the transactions through the network. The major issue is the lack of security with the authentication part, which is not incorporated. Financial institutions are trying to develop systems which decrease the number of users involved in transactions. There are various proposed systems which provide security to the financial information systems which make use of the different technologies and applications. Blockchain also has the facility to record the transactions between two different parties, and once a transaction has been recorded, it cannot be modified or altered. The authentication problem can be solved by using the hashing technique, which empowers the security in the blockchain. There are many blockchain-based applications in the financial systems, and numerous patents are also being developed for the use of blockchain in trading and transaction settlements. As the blockchain uses cryptographic tools for empowering the security system, the central financial systems are also taking the effort in improving monetary policies and transaction capabilities; moreover, the Bank of America, JP Morgan Chase, and Goldman Sachs use blockchain technology significantly for their operational activities. The financial sector has put tremendous amounts into the execution of blockchain; it is reported that $1.6 billion has been speculated in the previous three years, and 80% of banks have launched ventures that contribute to innovation in blockchain [10]. From this, we can conclude that blockchain technology has a prominent role in the financial information systems and thus provides a high-security layer to the financial sector.

2.7 BLOCKCHAIN-BASED SECURITY OF HEALTH INFORMATION SYSTEMS

The healthcare sector is improving day by day with the latest technologies and reforming its structure with technological transitions. In almost everything from health records to drug supplies, a drastic change has occurred, but when all these improvements take place effectively, there is one thing that still plays a crucial role: security. Information regarding patients is very useful to hackers as they get detailed identity information, which makes securing electronic health records (EHRs) and related personal details a high priority in the healthcare sector. Therefore, blockchain plays a vital role in protecting as well as in enhancing the healthcare sector more significantly. Features like decentralized storage, cryptographic tools, and smart contracts provide an outline for organizations to secure data by maintaining accuracy and preventing unauthorized access to or alteration of the patient details.

Blockchain in medical services generated a potential scope in the healthcare business for various stakeholders by providing secure and efficient data storing and sharing.

2.7.1 Potential of Blockchain Healthcare Systems

Blockchain can facilitate electronic health records interoperability, which would provide access to clinical records, current medicines, and previous examinations of patients. It is stated that maximum interoperability can save $77.8 billion every year in the US medical system. Blockchain will verify the transactions between drug manufacturers, suppliers, distributors, and the consumers, as well as a safe supply of medicines, which could minimize the counterfeit drugs market (annual losses of $200 billion). By making patient outcomes public, blockchain can support new drug production. Rule-based protocols could be generated using blockchain in situations in which transactions are executed when the criteria are met; for example, a health insurance patient has the policy information linked to their profile that is triggered when they seek medical services, ensuring that providers are paid appropriately [11].

Companies like MedChain and MedRec are presently working on permissioned blockchain systems to deliver the features of blockchain into healthcare organizations and the patients they serve. By moving health records and related patient information to a decentralized storage, where they are broken down into small blocks and distributed across the blockchain, these companies look forward to delivering an efficient method for healthcare organizations to secure patient information.

2.8 BLOCKCHAIN-BASED SECURITY SOLUTIONS FOR SMART CITIES INFORMATION SYSTEMS

A smart city is a network consisting mainly of ICT (information and communication technologies) for design and improvement of social development processes to resolve urbanization's growing challenges [123]. Smart city technology can contribute to improving the urban standard of living. Nevertheless, with multiple connected devices and robust communication networks, this "smart" urban environment opens up a whole new set of security challenges that cannot be solved by current traditional security solutions. Smart city merges ICT and other IoT network-connected devices to improve the quality of urban operations and facilities, thus connecting people [13][14]. The technology helps to monitor the city and its residents to live better lives.

2.8.1 Security Challenges in Smart Cities

Even though there are multiple examples of using this so-called smart technology, we also face many challenges regarding security issues. Digital security is the biggest challenge faced when smart city technology is introduced. Confidential information is uploaded to the cloud, and it is also linked with digital devices, which share the data between multiple users. Therefore, securing this data from unauthorized use is important. A few studies are the Open Web Application Protection Project, which points out the common security challenges, computer emergency response teams offering a visual representation of security breaches, and G-Cloud providing a set of specifications for the cloud computer service provider [15][16]. There are various categories of threats that come under the smart cities like security threats on availability, integrity, confidentiality, authenticity, and accountability.

2.8.2 Role of Blockchain

Blockchain focuses on improving faith in an untrustworthy environment that keeps a record of the transactions, exports, and commitments, and has become a potential guide to security-related issues.

The major reason for using blockchain technology is because it can resist various security-related issues; it also gives some of the unique functions which include advanced reliability, the higher capability of fault tolerance, green operation, and scalability. Moreover, an attacker must be brilliant enough in hashing techniques to breach the targeted network. Therefore, incorporating the technology of blockchain with smart city devices can communicate and transfer information more securely and efficiently in the distributed environment. Blockchain has systematic methods for each problem that arises in the smart cities, but in practice, implementation of this technology would be based on government rules and interests.

2.9 BLOCKCHAIN FOR INTERNET OF THINGS (IOT) INFORMATION SYSTEMS

2.9.1 IoT and Blockchain

The Internet of Things (IoT) is an extensive network of daily entities, called "things," and individuals. IoT allows any "thing" to communicate and interact, thus transforming the material world into a tremendous data system. Numerous applications are constantly becoming an integral part of the IoT, such as cloud computing and machine learning, to data development and information mapping. The rapid evolution of IoT is also triggering the commercial success of information and communication technology (ICT). Protection is one of the major concerns of IoT. The unique nature of IoT, on the other hand, promotes the development of creative end-user applications; however, lack of security measures can lead to severe problems. Protection has another factor connected with it: the issue of privacy. Blockchain is a distributed ledger which is more advantageous than traditional databases due to security and immutability. Blockchain technology has evolved dramatically in recent years and is seen as a potential option for the major security-related issues.

2.9.2 Blockchain in IoT

The missing link in the IoT to address scalability, safety, and security issues is blockchain technology. Blockchain technology can be used to monitor billions of smart devices, allow transaction processing and device-to-device management, and enable substantial savings for producers in the IoT industry. This decentralized approach would remove discrete potential failures, enabling a more efficient device environment in which to run. Blockchains can make user data more private due to the cryptographic algorithms used. The blockchain's decentralized, autonomous, and cryptographic capabilities make it a perfect tool to become a vital part of IoT solutions. The blockchain can keep an enormous volume of the existence of the devices inside the IoT system. This function allows smart devices to function autonomously without the use of centralized authority. As a consequence, without it, the blockchain provides a door to a variety of IoT applications that seem to be difficult to perform. IoT applications can allow transparent and secure messaging across devices in an IoT network by utilizing the blockchain. In this model, the blockchain will manage information flows between devices which are equivalent to transactions in a Bitcoin network.

Devices can utilize smart contracts and then develop an agreement between parties to allow data transfers. There are many tremendous possibilities in the integration of blockchain and IoT. Blockchain's function in the IoT is to provide a system via IoT nodes to process protected data records. Blockchain is a safe technology that can be used publicly. This kind of technology is required by the IoT to facilitate safe connectivity between IoT nodes in a heterogeneous network. Blockchain transactions can be tracked and analyzed by someone who is authenticated within the IoT to communicate. Thus, blockchain for the IoT can help to enhance the security of communication.

2.10 APPLICATIONS OF BLOCKCHAIN TECHNOLOGIES IN DIGITAL FORENSICS FOR INFORMATION SYSTEMS

Blockchain, a decentralized organization presently utilized by Bitcoin and also other cryptocurrency organizations, furnishes a safe information base with assistance of hashing information and putting it away in blocks. We had proposed this to execute blockchain innovation for the chain of custody (CoC) that will help in following the individuals who access the information and help with guaranteeing the believability of the information given during the time of accommodation in court [17].

Step 1: The proof, from the scene of wrongdoing or the spot of examination, is gathered as DNA analysis, audio, video, text, pictures, or even framework logs, including hours of the proof gathered to get a course of events.

Step 2: The gathered information is transferred to the information base which assists with putting away the case subtleties. A URL is created by the information transferred. The produced URL is removed and utilized in blockchain for hashing.

Step 3: The extricated URL is considered to be as a string and is put through a hash calculation for hashing. A timestamp is likewise hashed alongside the URL for greater trustworthiness. The hashed esteem is put away in the square itself.

Step 4: The square is made alongside a timestamp. The timestamp assists with finding when the proof was transferred to the blockchain. In case of alteration, it will definitely swap, which prompts in breaking the chain. On the off chance that the chain is not broken, it guarantees the square is in the appropriate state.

Step 5: Proof of work (PoW) is a strategy to guarantee if the proof has been altered, as the association of the squares would have been gone after a specific point. This should be possible by repeating the current squares to cross-reference with the current information.

Hence, blockchain assists with executing the CoC in a legitimate manner. After the production of the square, it contains the timestamp, hashed esteem, and the past hash esteem, which assists with following the square. This likewise makes for an easy-to-use approach in accessing, so anybody can see the subtleties. It fulfills all the prerequisites of CoC; for example, it gives respectability and legitimacy by giving client identification for each client for utilizing the information base, and the square goes through mining to guarantee it is secure and sealed. Blockchain diminishes strife and expands conviction through the appropriated blockchain, making it difficult to adjust each square. Blockchain is the best answer for CoC for computerized criminology.

2.11 SCALABILITY AND EFFICIENCY OF BLOCKCHAIN-BASED INFORMATION SYSTEMS

At the point when the quantity of clients of blockchain frameworks increases broadly, the adaptability and effectiveness problem of significant public-chain platforms (for example, Ethereum and Bitcoin) have emerged and enormously influenced the improvement of blockchain. Scalability in blockchain networks is the capacity of that stage to help expand the quantity of hubs in the organization [18].

2.11.1 Factors Influencing Performance of Blockchain

1. Mechanism in consensus: The procedure or instrument by which an exchange is spread, approved, and settled in the blockchain network is called the agreement convention or calculation. Furthermore, this agreement instrument is additionally liable for accomplishing fine harmony between the blockchain network's level of decentralization, adaptability, and security. Thus, the decision of agreement instrument is straightforwardly identified with the blockchain network performance.

2. Node infrastructure: Blockchain hubs involve a runtime motor and an information base that is facilitated on premises or in the cloud. Without committed foundation assets (for example, a computer processor, memory, hard plate), the hub execution is well on the way to being hampered. In this way, it is basic that foundation measuring and satisfactory IOPS (input/output activities per Second) distribution is provisioned.

3. Number of nodes: As the quantity of nodes increases, the more it takes for an exchange to be spread and for agreement to be accomplished—the more it corrupts the general exhibition. Procedures to decrease the correspondence overhead and permit hubs to depend on approval history of a pioneer node—and additionally, other companion nodes—are being notified to reduce this issue.

4. Complexity in smart contracts: The greater part of the benchmarking studies or claims depend on tests led in the controlled lab climate for the easiest of exchanges. As the unpredictability of brilliant agreements increments regarding the approval rationale and the quantity of reading and writing from/to the record builds, the preparing inactivity likewise expands, consequently affecting the general presentation.

5. Size of transaction payload: As the exchange and its payload should be transferred over the organization to every hub, greater payloads set aside more effort for replication across hubs. So perhaps the best practice is to store enormous payloads and archives in an off-chain stockpiling, and record their references in blockchain.

6. Local storage node: Commonly, blockchain networks uphold key-esteem pair datastores to keep up the exchange and condition of the record. There is a lot of read-compose that happens, and the productivity of the hidden information base is a vital factor in impacting the exhibition of the whole organization [19].

2.11.2 Improving the Scalability of Blockchain

In view of the adaptability issue, Bitcoin encountered difficult work and was split into the two blockchain branches, Bitcoin and Bitcoin Cash. Bitcoin Cash and Bitcoin have expanded their square size to 8 MB, which has is much larger than the size of its past version (only 1 MB in size). From that point onward, Bitcoin Cash updated further, to grow the square size up to 32 MB. The normal square time frame Bitcoin Cash is as yet kept up at the first ten minutes. In principle, the exchange throughput will be extraordinarily increased. There is likewise another type of blockchain stages, named Blockchain 3.0, that depends on the standards of DLT (disseminated record innovation). These stages help settle the issues of execution and versatility by utilizing information structures.

2.12 BLOCKCHAIN-BASED OPEN SOURCE TOOLS FOR INFORMATION SYSTEMS

When blockchain innovation became public, it fundamentally focused on the monetary area. Specifically, the Bitcoin white paper delineated a framework that would empower clients to move money from point

A to point B without depending on conventional channels. Its applications are widely used in web-based business, e-administration, and Internet casting of ballots, energy, gaming, and different areas [20].

2.12.1 Some of the Best Blockchain Open Source Projects

1. Enterprise Ethereum: Notwithstanding being the stage that advocated savvy contracts, Ethereum is vital to enterprises. Basically, this stage is an execution of the Ethereum codebase. With this organization, associations can make decentralized applications (DApps). The DApps can be tried and conveyed inside the biological system with no personal time. Because of the inalienable attributes of blockchain innovation, the DApps made here cannot be blue-penciled, meddled with by outsiders, or utilized for deceitful undertakings.

2. Corda: Corda is another well-known blockchain stage, particularly since it puts severe accentuation on the protection of the data concerning exchanges among peers. Corda is business arranged. It is underlined by the capacity for engineers to make blockchain networks which are interoperable yet with the severe protection strategy. Organizations utilizing arrangements based on Corda can execute straightforwardly.

   The vital highlights of Corda incorporate keen agreements which can be written in JVM dialects such as Java. Additionally, the stage is worked around a stream system whereby arrangements and interchanges between clients can be overseen easily.

3. Quorum Majority was created by JP Morgan. The stage is a fork of Ethereum, and it expects to furnish the financial area with the full advantages of blockchain. Prominently, the onboarding of JP Morgan onto the blockchain biological system is a significant advance toward the standard appropriation of the innovation. The essential goal of the organization is to give a permissioned blockchain network dependent on the Ethereum codebase, which empowers private exchanges.

4. OpenChain: Rather than chains of squares, OpenChain engineering joins exchanges together straightforwardly the second clients submit them. This is very progressive, regardless of whether the entire blockchain biological system is simply starting to acquire worldwide attention. This can be followed as: OpenChain is all the more halfway oversaw contrasted with conventional blockchain networks. This is on the grounds that the approval of exchanges is finished by a solitary position. Besides, every hub inside the OpenChain biological system has its own record and high command over to access it. This conflicts with the customary design of a blockchain network where there is a solitary record that is shared across all the hubs.

5. MultiChain: Another fascinating blockchain open source project is MultiChain. It is an endeavor blockchain. As per the authority site, any association utilizing MultiChain can cut its improvement time by 80 percent. At the center, its thought is to give the instruments and strategies to make blockchain application arrangement quicker.

2.13 FORENSICS READINESS OF BLOCKCHAIN TECHNOLOGIES

Advanced forensics is an unmistakable and unavoidable piece of an incident response plan covering electronic information and a set up ability region in the digital protection industry. The objective is to reject or help speculation identified with a lawbreaker or common case. The principle motivation behind digital forensics is mainly to perform specialized examinations inside the limits of the overall set of laws in light of crimes that include electronic gadgets. The blockchain is framed with a fundamental rundown of records, namely blocks, and these are connected utilizing cryptographic calculations. The strong association and progression of squares forestall the adjustment of existing information blocks and with any composed substance will, in this manner, be undeniable and forever open. This has set off a great deal of revenue from different enterprises—for example, banking and energy—while different propositions were introduced to help administration models. Consortiums have been set up, and examination in private labs is opened to explore capable models that would assist with cutting the center man (as practical) and mechanize measures for organizations' backend frameworks. Moreover, the disseminated idea of the innovation eliminates any single-purpose of-disappointment and provides the way to consider/taking an interest parties who are responsible for their records on the grounds, i.e., each recorded exchange will be accessed by completely associated hubs and only few colossal measures of processing force can supersede their information.

Conceivable in principle, i.e., non-reasonable assaulting the organization, becomes more diligently when the more self-inspired gadgets become a part of a circulated framework. The requirement for provenance goes beyond the monetary and production network advertises, likewise an extremely basic necessity for scientific examinations. These starting point and development of case-related information (for example held onto things) is used as/for human mistake/ blunder, robbery and forging [21][22]. During a legal examination, all the elaborate specialists might want to store their discoveries in a changeless manner with the goal that they cannot be adjusted and be brought to a courtroom. Essentially, blockchains give straightforwardness and auditability as a necessity for a chain of care of the related proof. In such a manner, in the previous few years, a few scientists have examined these chances and have proposed blockchain-based answers for legal sciences.

2.13.1 Blockchain-Based Forensics

- Mobile forensics: Versatile criminology incorporates the investigation of advanced and actual proof given by cell phones and comparable devices (for example, those having comparable design bodies and basic working frameworks, such as tablets or other handheld gadgets). All things considered, the distinguished blockchain–put together criminological exploration predominantly centers with respect to applications and malware identification. All the more solidly, creators propose the utilization of consortium blockchains and center around malware recognition and measurable examination dependent on every application included [17][21]. Hence, more work needs to be provided in this field, with regard to holistic systems definition and hardware inclusion, as well as its implementation.
- Cloud forensics: Another basic part of cloud crime scene investigation may allude to logs of the executives. Specifically, secure safeguarding and examination of the different logs are fundamental components of cloud crime scene investigation. Be that as it may, because of the inborn vulnerabilities of the cloud climate, a few troubles exist concerning the assortment of real logs from a cloud climate while safeguarding honesty and secrecy. Blockchain innovation might be utilized as a logging-as-an-administration apparatus for safely putting away and preparing logs while adapting to issues of the multipartner conspiracy and trustworthiness and privacy of logs.
- Multimedia forensics: Media forensics utilizes different logical methods for analyzing a sight and sound record (sound, video, or potentially picture) concerning its: (i) honesty (build up the linkage between an interactive media yield and its source recognizable proof), and (ii) genuineness (check for the veracity of the sight and sound yield). For instance, a blockchain-based methodology is mainly proposed for classifying CCTV video proof. The creators give a practical execution of a blockchain-based framework that oversees a high volume of CCTV proof. The creators present E-Witness, a framework that utilizes blockchain innovation for defending the uprightness and spatiotransient attributes of computerized proof caught by cell phones. To confirm the trustworthiness and temporal-spatio cases of the proof, the proposed framework utilizes hashes of pictures/recordings alongside certificates of location which are stored in the blockchain.

2.13.2 Challenges in Blockchain Digital Forensics

- Management of data volume in the chain of custody efficiently: The principle worries of digital forensics are the content of information, since proof may incorporate a huge number of mixed media documents or log records per case. In such a manner, the fact that information stockpiling of crude archives must be accommodated in all cases ought to be founded on off-chain innovations (for example, Storj, IPFS). For this situation, just hashes ought to be utilized in the blockchain (for example, or on the other hand, meta-hashes if information is handled as squares, to ease survey) [22] [23].
- Parse forensic sound approaches in blockchain systems: Sound measurable and standard streams must be given, in any event, when utilizing blockchain as a stage to give undeniable nature and chain of care sealed certifications. In this way, legitimate normalized streams and brilliant agreements that map the satisfactory capacities must be given to empower last court approval, just as affirmation by forensic digital labs and law authorization organizations.
- Timeline of events and chronology: Standard and sound measurable streams must be given, in any event, when utilizing blockchain as a stage to give undeniable nature and chain of care sealed certifications. In this way, legitimate normalized streams and brilliant agreements that map the satisfactory capacities must be given to empower last court approval just as affirmation by forensic digital labs and law authorization organizations.

2.14 CONCLUSION

Blockchain is a distributed ledger which is more advantageous than traditional databases due to the security and immutability. In today's world, the interaction between blockchain and IT systems has played a crucial role. The chapter is divided into different parts that cover the various aspects of the blockchain–information systems relationship. At present, there is an increasing expectation that blockchain technology will have a massive influence on many industries, including security, healthcare systems, the financial industry, the forensic sector, and many more. Many researchers take efforts to improve the efficiency and interoperability of blockchain tools. We make use of many functionalities for digital health record projects. The computer protocol that digitally facilitates, verifies, or enforces the negotiation or performance is known as a smart contract. These have a broad spectrum of applications, like financial services, prediction markets, and the IoT. The blockchain implemented in the technology of Bitcoin is spreading to many other areas. When the use of blockchain increased, issues like the scalability of major public-chain platforms came to the fore, which affects the development of blockchain. To keep a record that enables developers to develop a decentralized application that provides solutions, we make use of an open source tool, which is a public transparent way; the demand for open source software is growing as businesses gradually adopt the technology. Blockchain is going to be a more well-known technology and will become something that will be more strong than it is now.

REFERENCES

[1] Hewa, T., M. Ylianttila, M. Liyanage. "Survey on blockchain based smart contracts: Applications, opportunities and challenges." *Journal of Network and Computer Applications* (2020). https://doi.org/10.1016/j.jnca.2020.102857.
[2] LaPadula, Leonard J. *State of the Art in CyberSecurity Monitoring*. Center for Integrated Intelligence Systems, 2000.

[3] CoinSutra—Bitcoin Community. "Different types of blockchains in the market and why we need them." 2017. https://coinsutra.com/different-types-blockchains.

[4] Voshmgir, Shermin. *Blockchains Distributed Ledger Technologies*. BlockchainHub, 2019.

[5] Haque, A. K. M. Bahalul, and Mahbubur Rahman. *Blockchain Technology: Methodology Application and Security Issues*. North South University, 2020.

[6] Reyna, Ana, Cristian Mart´ın, Jaime Chen, Enrique Soler, and Manuel D´ıaz. "Proof-of-stake consensus mechanisms for future blockchain networks: Fundamentals, applications and opportunities." *IEEE Access* 7 (2019).

[7] Saranya, A., and R. Mythili. "A survey on blockchain based smart applications." *Journal of Network and Computer Applications* 177 (2021).

[8] Nakamoto, S. "Bitcoin: A peer-to-peer electronic cash system." 2008. https://bitcoin.org/bitcoin.pdf.

[9] Nguyen, C. T., D. T. Hoang, D. N. Nguyen, D. Niyato, H. T. Nguyen, and E. Dutkiewicz. "On blockchain and its integration with IoT. Challenges and opportunities." *Future Generation Computer Systems* 88 (2018).

[10] McWaters, J. "The future of financial infrastructure." In *World Economic Forum*. Deloitte Consulting LLP, 2016.

[11] R. Hanna, D. Auquier, Toumi, "PHP115—Could Healthcoin be a revolution in healthcare? *Value in Health*, 20, no. 9 (2017): A672.

[12] Chan, Karin. "What is a 'smart city'?" *Expatriate Lifestyle*. Retrieved 23 January 2018.

[13] Trindade, E. P., M. P. F. Hinnig, E. Moreira da Costa, J. S. Marques, R. C. Bastos, and T. Yigitcanlar. "Sustainable development of smart cities: A systematic review of the literature." *Journal of Open Innovation: Technology, Market, and Complexity* 3 (2017): 11.

[14] Peris-Ortiz, Marta, Dag R. Bennett, and Diana P´erez-Bustamante Y´abar. "Sustainable smart cities: Creating spaces for technological." *Social and Business Development. Springer* (2016). ISBN 9783319408958.

[15] Bhatt, Devanshu. "Cyber security risks for modern web applications: Case study paper for developers and security testers." *International Journal of Scientific & Technology Research* 7, no. 5 (2018).

[16] Claycomb, W. R., and A. Nicoll. "Insider threats to cloud computing: Directions for new research challenges." *36th Annual Computer Software and Applications Conference* (2012): 387–394.

[17] Harihara Gopalan Dr., S., S. Akila Suba, C. Ashmithashree, A. Gayathri, and V. Jebin Andrews. "Digital forensics using blockchain." *International Journal of Recent Technology and Engineering (IJRTE)*, 8, no. 2S11 (2019). ISSN: 2277-3878.

[18] Zhou, Qiheng, Huawei Huang, Zibin Zheng, and Jing Bian. "Solutions to scalability of blockchain: A survey." *IEEE Access* 4 (2016).

[19] www.wipro.com/blogs/hitarshi-buch/improving-performance-and-scalability-of-blockchain-networks/.

[20] https://101blockchains.com/blockchain-open-source/.

[21] Dasaklis, Thomas K., Fran Casino, and Constantinos Patsakis. *SoK: Blockchain Solutions for Forensics*. University of Piraeus, 2020.

[22] al-Khateeb, Haider M., Gregory Epiphaniou, and Herbert Daly. "Blockchain for modern digital forensics: The chain-of-custody as a distributed ledger." *Blockchain and Clinical Trial* (2019): 149–168.

[23] Mr. Nelson, S., Mr. S. Karuppusamy, Mr. K. Ponvasanth, and Mr. R. Ezhumalai. "Blockchain based digital forensics investigation framework in the internet of things and social systems." *IEEE Transactions on Computational Social Systems* (2019): 104–108.

A Dynamic Trust Model for Blockchain-Based Supply Chain Management Networks

3

Shivam Narula, Annapurna Jonnalgadda, and Aswani Kumar Cherukuri

Contents

3.1 INTRODUCTION

A blockchain architecture lacks central authority, so control of single unit cannot be implemented in this structure. All the actions that happen involve one or another single node which is part of the network. The main objective of this work is to implement a dynamic trust model for a blockchain network for each node connected. The actions that are performed by the nodes while in the network would be monitored and based on negative and positive points being given to nodes. These points will constitute in calculating the rank or the reputation factor of a node in the network. These factors have given some weight which is accounted to build up the trust value and trust rank, which is visible to all the nodes and can decide which

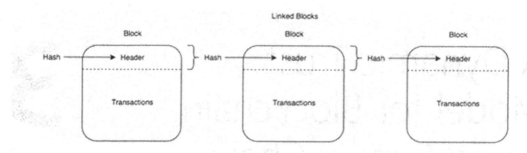

FIGURE 3.1 Block structure in blockchain.

node is more trustable and which is not. The lower ranking in the network means a malicious node and higher rank would mean the genuine node. After ranking, we can find the node which may or may not misbehave in the future and try to prevent those nodes to cause serious security threats like Sybil attacks and Byzantine fault tolerance. These passive attacks are hard to discover and harder to prevent. Hence, this dynamic trust model will incorporate methods by which blockchain could be more secure and resilient. To get the application-based advantage of the following dynamic trust model, a supply chain model application would be used to record the peer-to-peer transactions for recording in the blockchain and further processing for trust ranking of the nodes. This application would generalize the use of all blockchain applications.

Since the introduction of blockchain, everyone talks about the properties it offers—and they are actually quite unique. The introduction of blockchain was not made only to build application of Bitcoin, but to support the decentralized architecture and its work in the transaction processing. Therefore, blockchain also involves threats like any other new technology. Now, to remove those threats, as well as using blockchain widely, is the motivation for this project. Two of the threats which could be solved by devising a dynamic trust model are Sybil attacks and Byzantine fault tolerance. These passive attacks have disrupting impact on the whole network and are proven to be lethal for destroying architecture and applications running over it. The literature has wide discussion on security of blockchain, security, and trust of blockchain and its applications in different environments (Zyskind and Nathan, 2015; Li et al., 2020; Shala et al., 2020; Kouicem et al., 2020).

Today's supply chains have high standards for their requirements and even when the software works just fine, maybe it is not recent enough or it was not specified and built to satisfy these requirements. For instance, concurrent payment and transaction verifiability might be a huge issue nowadays in the supply chain finance, but maybe it was not rated as a high importance problem 12 years ago. Therefore, the software from 12 years ago complied with different requirements than the ones from today and was not built to handle that specific problem well. Requirements evolve, and so should the technology, in order to support them.

The characteristics of blockchain architecture and dynamic trust models seem to be a good solution for many of the identified problems in supply chains to be reduced or neutralized (Pournader, 2020). Figure 3.1 shows the general architecture of a blockchain with few blocks. More details of the blockchain can be found in the literature (Berdik et al., 2021; Namasudra et al., 2020). These architectures are the perfect means to achieve traceability of a supply chain transaction, and so, they are useful to achieve provenance, as well. At the same time, they are a secure, incorruptible, and immutable way to store information, with a fast synchronization time, being perpetually available to anyone who has permission, anywhere within the network. It would also be the way to close the analog gaps, turning the chain fully digital, and leading to the possibility of a global overview.

3.2 BACKGROUND

A dynamic trust model has been implemented and maintained for mobile ad hoc networks (MANETs) by Liu et al. (2004). The main aim of this chapter is to prevent ad hoc networks from malicious nodes and provide secure routing paths for communication and sending data packets. The need for a dynamic trust model is to enhance message routing and reducing existing threats by evaluation of nodes for choosing the best route path for developing a collaborative ad hoc model. They found an approach where there is no need for time-synchronization and authentication systems, as well as maintaining route and behavior, and integration of current routing protocols which are used in mobile ad hoc networks. This model can be applied to any general application and is not specific.

In a different work, Boukerche et al. (2009) considered the previous history record of nodes to take account of dynamic and adaptive trust evaluation. Their work focused primarily on the adaptive condition for wireless and mobile infrastructure. They aimed to find an effective approach by looking at the previous record as evidence to predict future behavior of the current node which involves mathematical computations. This at last is useful to prevent improper behavior, as well as to install new security measures to ensure reliability of the environment.

The Bayesian trust model has been introduced by Melaye and Demazeau (2005) that has taken the dynamics of trust calculation and evaluation to a whole new level. The belief of statistical models and symbolic approaches are used as complementary. Formation of low-level and high-level layers guides to focus on two different aspects. The basic trust dynamics are taken into account by a low-level layer which integrates with the actor by calculating the weight of components involved in it. Basically, the negative and positive experiences play a major role in making the system learn how to build up a dynamic model, whereas the high-level layer takes a symbolic approach into account which involves trust components manipulation. The dynamic form discussed here is believed to have dependent on social norms, as well. These social norms will make the connection between both the layers.

Wu et al. (2014) focused on a dynamic model for Wireless Sensor Networks (WSNs) to resist selfish node behaviors. Their model uses fuzzy sets and gray theory to calculate and rank the reputation factor for neighboring nodes based on their relationship with them. The dynamic nature of the model is evaluated into time slices, which are used to recover those selfish nodes. These time slices are eventually used to predict the time that network has performed negatively and positively, and based on that, giving positive and negative values for itself and the neighboring nodes.

The self-monitoring and dynamic model for trust is very important when someone is looking to move their architecture to the distributed architecture (Jiang et al., 2014). Efficient Distributed Trust Model is such a method, which solves the problem by efficiently exchanging data and information and also involving only the trusted nodes to prevent leaks in information. After the simulation has been achieved, this method can be inferred to the attack-resistant trust model, but at the same time requires some prior assumptions for absolute results. The challenge of selecting a true assumption value is still not known, and requires deep analysis for working which will be out in following research. This chapter describes an approach for how to monitor and synchronize the trust level for detection of malicious node in WSNs and also preventing the most common and threatening attack of Byzantine fault.

Work by Zhuo et al. (2006) gives the proper and quoted relationship between time and trust value using the ant colony algorithm. The base theory and argument for this is to provide a real-time trust calculation and updating model using ant colony. After this implementation, they have aimed to achieve a relationship between trust, time, and inter-operation events. There are certain assumptions which are used to simulate the results that all the inter-operations are successful, and the complexity of this algorithm for updating trust is $O(n^2)$.

3.3 PROPOSED METHOD

After thorough research, the goal of this work is to devise a dynamic trust model for a blockchain network which would prevent the passive attack like Sybil, etc., on the network and generalize this model so that it can be used for any decentralized application. This would prevent the transaction and its record stored over the blockchain. One such application used here is the supply chain. We define trust model as reliable, timeliness model for storing transactions on a blockchain in a secure way and later preventing malicious attacks from hackers. This integrity is maintained by knowing which node is used to authenticate the corresponding transaction and which is responsible for writing that over a block. Some assumptions while making this base structure are that nodes are already present to be part of the network, which is synchronized based on their physical and logical IP (internet protocol) address. Each node has a script which is running continuously in sync, as well as dynamically updating the trust ranking for each node.

Based on these stated assumptions and specifications, we design the trust model as follows. Initially, a layout or the base structure of blockchain is developed using NodeJs, which has all the basic functionalities that a blockchain should possess. These include consensus algorithm, mining algorithm, and hash functions. When the node initially joins, it needs to copy the first block, which is the Genesis block, and later on all application programming interface (API)-endpoints are automated for successful launch of nodes. After launching of desired number of nodes for the first time, initial trust values would be assigned based on the past activity (if nothing found, then 0 would be assigned by default). These scripts work in synchronization and regular updating phases of 100 seconds, which ensures eradication of any mismatch between the trust ranking. A period of 100 seconds is taken by default, to bypass or give ample overhead for all the desired steps to happen in a single iteration. When a node does not agree with the majority decisions of authenticating, mining, or validating a new transaction and block, respectively, then it is treated as if it wants to deceive the network and there would be reduction in the trust value, which would ultimately lower the reputation factor. If it goes below a certain point, then the node is permanently banned from the network and would not be able to become a part of it again. On the other hand, if a node behaves positively in the network and is not involved in any malicious activity, it will be rewarded with incentives. These will be added to the trust value of the node, and will eventually increase the node's rank in the network.

For adding dynamic nature to the model, there is time-based incentive. A node which stays longer in the network will be given more points than a node which often comes online in the network for short periods. The reason for this consideration is because they somehow by staying online make a 51% attack difficult to execute. For example, if there are seven nodes, then to gain control over the network, the attacker needs to change the data stores on four nodes. If the number of nodes increases to 11, it takes six nodes being attacked to take control of the network. Hence, time-based incentive will be provided which contributes to the trust value of nodes which are connected.

One example of an application that could be implemented over this trust model for blockchain networks is supply chain management (Korpela et al., 2017; Kouhizadeh et al., 2021; Rao et al, 2021). Literature has already addressed blockchain-based models for supply chain environment (Chang and Chen, 2020; Kamble et al., 2021; Moosavi et al., 2021; Pournader et al., 2020). The peer-to-peer transfer of goods would be stored, which first authenticates the correct address and then adds the transaction in the block in the blockchain. The node which gets a request for transaction processing, first for authenticating and then later for mining the blocks, if they have high trust value, the decision would be accepted by other nodes. However, if the trust rank is lower, then approval of at least majority of nodes would be needed for future progression. Figure 3.2 shows the high-level diagram and the flow of the project like how transactions have been made between peer-to-peer and then being stored over the blockchain, and the trust values which are operated on each node in a synchronized way involving these discussed factors and contribute to trust ranking.

3.4 PROPOSED ALGORITHM

As we have discussed until now, there are some positive and negative values which are going to decide the ranking of the nodes in the network. Now, if we talk in context of the blockchain architecture and functionalities which govern seamless transaction processing of applications, some of the methods which could be used to find the trust values are as follows:

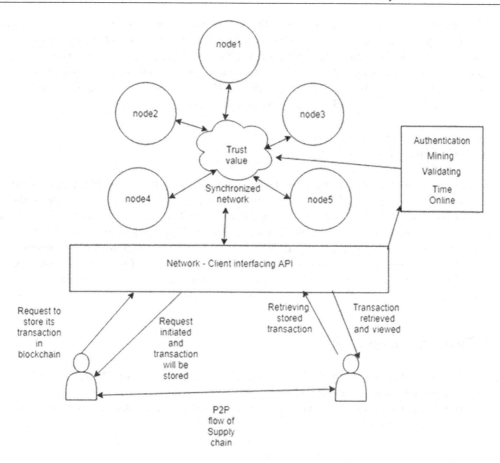

FIGURE 3.2 High-level design of dynamic trust model for supply chain.

3.4.1 Authentication

Authentication of transactions prior to storing over the permanent blockchain is very important because if we are storing the illegitimate data which cannot be over-ridden later, this would soon bring into question the integrity and safety of the blockchain. The node that is going to authenticate would be provided the incentives.

Trust_node ← trust_node + 1 (for positive)
Trust_node ← trust_node − 2 (for negative)

It is self-explanatory that if the authentication results are positive, the node will gain 1 point (+1), and if the authentication results are negative, it will lose 2 points (−2) per transaction. To be considered correct, you need to agree with majority of the nodes, i.e. with N + 1/2 (if N is odd) and N/2 + 1 (if N is even).

3.4.2 Miner

Miner is defined as the block which is going to mine the block—or in simpler terms, we can say, adding new blocks to existing blockchain. The mining function is as complex as it seems, as mining awards are provided by the network after validation of new block. So, every node will come under race conditions and try to solve the cryptographic puzzle; whoever solves that puzzle first will get the reward, as well as increase in trust rank if validation is successful. The factors of selection of mining nodes in this case are dependent on the previous records, as well as connectivity in the network, so the node which has low latency tends to have higher connectivity in the network. The choice depends on these factors solely and after the mining is done, the trust value will be updated as follows.

Trust_node ← trust_node + 8 (for positive)
Trust_node ← trust_node − 16 (for negative)

If, after the validation, the block is found to be legitimate, it is added in the blockchain, trust value increases and mining rewards would be provided to that node. However, deduction is done if the block is found out to be selfish and disrupting. If a node has created a block just now, there is a wait time for that node. The wait time is of increase in N/3 length of blockchain; until then, that node would not been able to participate in the mining process again. There could be a DOS attack node there which can stop the service of other nodes and try to mine maximum blocks possible, i.e. if node A has mined the block of #32 and there are presently 11 connected nodes in the network. Then A has to wait until the length of blockchain reaches #35; only then can A participate in the maximum process.

3.4.3 Time-Connected

This is most important factor which is the base of implementing the time-trust relationship and providing the dynamic nature of trust model for blockchain.
For every 100 seconds of nodes given to the network, +1 value will be added in the trust value, which then reflects in the ranks of nodes.

Trust_node ← trust_node + 1 (for every 100s)

These mentioned methods and helper functions have been implemented in a script which will run infinitely and continuously update trust ranks for each node connected in the network. If a certain node is disconnected, the checkpoint will be stored in that node and every node indicating the last rank of the connected node. When it joins again, consensus would synchronize the new length of chain and start calculating trust ranks from that point.
Following is a flowchart of the working algorithm, where the flow of each value, variable, and function explained in detail. It follows a methodology of continuous integration (CI) and monitoring of node by a never-ending infinite loop which would be running on each node and with synchronization.

3.4.4 Algorithm

Step 1: Initialize trust value for each node and no_of_operations value
Step 2: while True
Step 3: if no_of_operations < 10
Step 4: node ← Select a node from connected_nodes //based on latency
Step 5: trust_node ← trust_node + (no. of txns) * (txn validation credit) //txn validation credit = +1
Step 6: node ← Select a node from connected_nodes //based on latency
Step 7: trust_node ← trust_node + (no of blocks mined) * (mining credit) //mining credit = +8
Step 8: trust_node ← trust_node + (time-based incentives = +1) //for every 100s presence in network
Step 9: no_of_operations++
Step 10: node ← Select a node from connected_nodes //based on latency

Step 11: if trust_node == max_trust in network
Step 12: trust_node ← trust_node + (no. of txns) * (txn validation credit) //txn validation credit = +1
Step 13: node ← Select a node from connected_nodes //based on latency
Step 14: if trust_node == max_trust in network
Step 15: trust_node ← trust_node + (no of blocks mined) * (mining credit) //mining credit = +8
Step 16: trust_node ← trust_node + (time-based incentives = +1) //for every 100s presence in network
Step 17: no_of_operations++
Step 18: else
Step 19: trust_node ← trust_node + (no of blocks mined) * (mining credit) //mining credit = +8
Step 20: for all trust_node > current
Step 21: Verify block mined
Step 22: if block verified
Step 23: trust_node ← trust_node + (time-based incentives = +1) //for every 100s presence in network
Step 24: else {trust_node ← trust_node -16} //reduction in trust value
Step 25 trust_node ← trust_node + (time-based incentives = +1) //for every 100s presence in network
Step 26: no_of_operations++
Step 27: else
Step 28: trust_node ← trust_node + (no. of txns) * (txn validation credit) //txn validation credit = +1
Step 29: for all trust_node > current
Step 30: verify transactions
Step 31: if Verified
Step 32: trust_node ← trust_node + (time-based incentives = +1) //for every 100s presence in network
Step 33: else {trust_value ← trust_value -2} //reduction in trust value
Step 34: no_of_operations++

3.4.5 Trust Ranking Calculation

Figure 3.3 provides a detailed flowchart of the algorithm discussed previously. The procedure of building trust as follows:

> After the synchronization of the nodes, the algorithm starts the script, which in each iteration gives out a trust value for each node. Those values received would be fed into the trust rank function with a predefined range. A mapping would take place between trust value and its correspondence rank, and then the visible rank would be displayed. The values for each role and final value of each node is hidden and they cannot be viewed for security purposes; otherwise, the most weight factor would be chosen by nodes, and this greediness would exploit the network flow and compromise everything. It is as similar as calculating Elo ranking in multiplayer online gaming. Table 3.1 provides trust ranks.

3.5 RESULTS AND DISCUSSION

Figure 3.4 depicts the schematic diagram of the experimental setup that was used in this project to continue to obtain trust values after each iteration. One complete cycle represents a single iteration. The first step is to synchronize the nodes in the network to avoid getting mismatch details and sharing data. Then, a continuous loop will follow; keep an eye on the action of each node. Each action will result in a positive or negative outcome, depending on the decision made by the majority. If it comes out to be positive, the

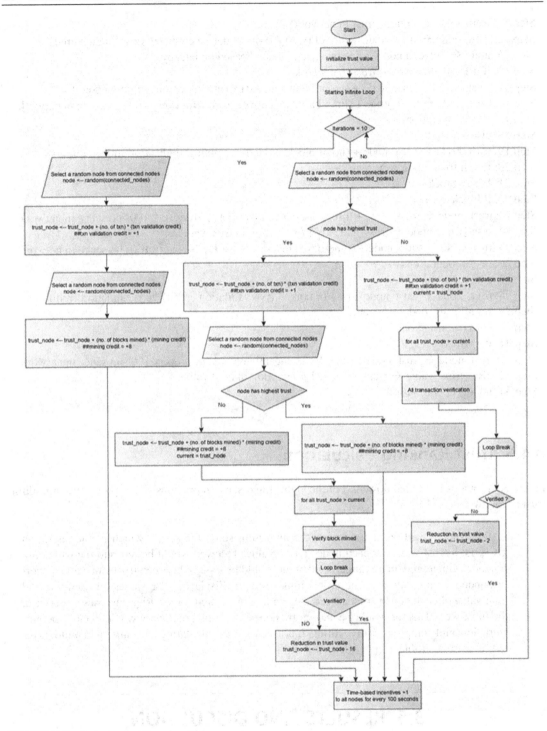

FIGURE 3.3 Flowchart of the algorithm.

points will be added in the trust value; otherwise, points are deducted. A node could be not able to see how many points are being added or deducted, or the value of trust; these are hidden to avoid selfishness nature by them. However, they can always see rankings of connected nodes and make self-intuitions of how much they can trust them.

TABLE 3.1   Trust Ranks with Their Trust Value Ranges and Descriptions

TRUST VALUE RANGE	TRUST RANK	DESCRIPTION
$T < -10$	Banned from network	Malicious node
$-10 \leq T < 0$	N/A	Could be threat to network
$0 \leq T \leq 10$	Silver 1	
$11 \leq T \leq 18$	Silver 2	Low level of trust
$19 \leq T \leq 32$	Silver 3	
$33 \leq T \leq 40$	Silver 4	
$41 \leq T \leq 52$	Silver 5	Average level of trust
$53 \leq T \leq 60$	Silver 6	
$61 \leq T \leq 75$	Silver 7	
$76 \leq T \leq 82$	Silver 8	Intermediate level of trust
$83 \leq T \leq 99$	Silver 9	
$100 \leq T \leq 120$	Silver 10	
$121 \leq T \leq 180$	Gold 1	
$181 \leq T \leq 300$	Gold 2	High level of trust
$301 \leq T$	Gold 3	

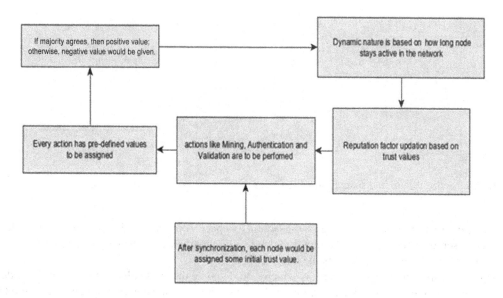

FIGURE 3.4   Schematic diagram of the experimental setup.

3.5.1 Implementation

Step 1: Launch nodes to get connect to the blockchain network. Transaction processing, storing, and trust rank would be calculated for these launch nodes. Assumption: Right now, due to limited RAM, only five nodes are launched to be the part of network. Figure 3.5 shows the initialization of the network.

Step 2: After the successful launch of five nodes, we need to synchronize the data that is going to be stored over each node. Each node should have same blockchain stored; otherwise, there is no credibility of the transaction. A consensus algorithm is used for further syncing the data of connected nodes. Figure 3.6 shows these steps.

```
C:\Users\snaru\Desktop\Final year Project\blockchain>npm run node_1

> blockchain@1.0.0 node_1 C:\Users\snaru\Desktop\Final year Project\blockchain
> nodemon --watch developer -e js developer/networkNode.js 3001 http://192.168.43.117:3001

[nodemon] 1.18.10
[nodemon] to restart at any time, enter `rs`
[nodemon] watching: C:\Users\snaru\Desktop\Final year Project\blockchain\developer/**/*
[nodemon] starting `node developer/networkNode.js 3001 http://192.168.43.117:3001`
Listening to port number 3001...
```

FIGURE 3.5 Starting node for blockchain network.

```
def registerAll():
    for i in range(len(nodes)):
        body = {'newNodeUrl': nodes[i] }
        myurl = "http://192.168.43.117:3005/register-and-broadcast-node"
        req = urllib.request.Request(myurl)
        req.add_header('Content-Type', 'application/json; charset=utf-8')
        jsondata = json.dumps(body)
        jsondataasbytes = jsondata.encode('utf-8')   # needs to be bytes
        req.add_header('Content-Length', len(jsondataasbytes))

        #print (jsondataasbytes)
        response = urllib.request.urlopen(req, jsondataasbytes)
        if response.getcode() == 200:
            print ("Nodes registered to the network successfully")
        else:
            print ("Cannnot connect to network")

registerAll()
```

FIGURE 3.6 Script that would synchronize the nodes in the network.

Step 3: In order for a user to make any transaction to a peer, A python GUI application is provided. The user just needs to enter the required details and the transaction would be stored over to the blockchain. Figure 3.7 indicates the interface.

Step 4: A script would run continuously which would update the trust values and rank of the nodes involved in the network. This script is solely responsible in implementing dynamic trust model for the blockchain network. This script involves all the methods required to get the trust value, and it offers a method for new nodes to join the network and then synchronize first with the blockchain and then update trust values based on the actions of the nodes. Figure 3.8 shows the code for trust building.

3.5.2 Analysis

Several vulnerabilities and threats with blockchain network are discussed in the introduction section. The dynamic trust model is presented in this chapter which successfully prevent network from Sybil attacks and Byzantine fault tolerances. Each node needs to maintain an ample amount of network connection and have to give computation power to stay in the network and to gain good and respected trust in the network, until they try to forge intentions and perform negative actions in the network (Sybil attack). The

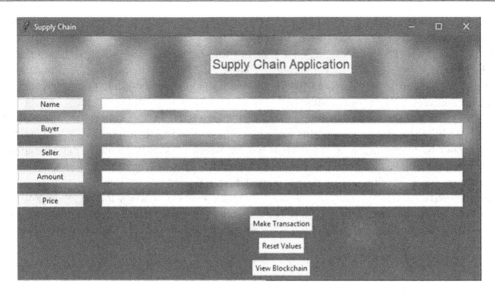

FIGURE 3.7   Python GUI to make transaction between peer-to-peer.

```
def trustRanking(trust_value):   #trust ranking based on points in network

    for node in trust_value:

        if trust_value[node] < -10:
            banned(node, trust_value[node])

        elif -10<= trust_value[node] <0:
            value = "NA"
            trust_ranking[node]=value

        elif 0<= trust_value[node] <=10:
            value = "Silver 1"
            trust_ranking[node]=value
            #node + "has Silver 1 ranking"
        elif 11 < trust_value[node] <=18:
            value = "Silver 2"
            trust_ranking[node]=value
        elif 19 < trust_value[node] <=32:
            value = "Silver 3"
            trust_ranking[node]=value
        elif 33 < trust_value[node] <=40:
            value = "Silver 4"
            trust_ranking[node]=value
        elif 41 < trust_value[node] <=52:
            value = "Silver 5"
            trust_ranking[node]=value
        elif 53 < trust_value[node]  <=60:
            value = "Silver 6"
            trust_ranking[node]=value
        elif 61 <trust_value[node]  <=75:
            value = "Silver 7"
            trust_ranking[node]=value
        elif 76 < trust_value[node]  <=82:
```

FIGURE 3.8   Code snippet for trust building algorithm.

node has to give more as they get even after successful attack execution, so the profit margin is not that great to do that. There is a connection between each node, and the decision which is made by majority will be taken into account. The node which is not agreeing with the decision or providing false information would be given negative values; hence, making Byzantine fault tolerant architecture. Additionally, in the structure of blockchain, a simple proof-of-work algorithm is implemented in the mining process, which adds another prevention layer for the same.

Figure 3.9 shows the storing of transactions of the supply chain application over the blockchain, which is done by one peer to another. This also shows the node which is responsible to authenticate the transaction and hashes of previous and current blocks, which ultimately creates a cryptographic link between blocks in blockchain, and also the nonce value, which is a solution of this block. Figure 3.10 shows a sample block which is storing transactions and other related information.

To summarize the things and results, we can say that users need to know the cryptographic address of the peer to which they are willing to make the transaction, and they also need to mention which commodity is being sold and at what price. After the transaction has been done, it would go to authentication

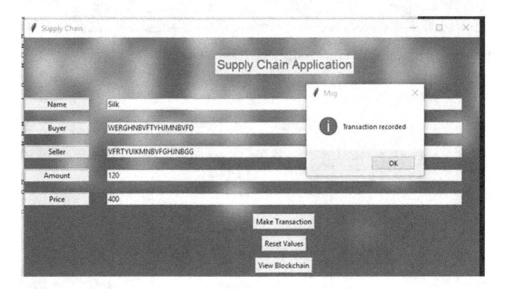

FIGURE 3.9 User is making a transaction which is storing on the blockchain.

```
"index": 2,
"timestamp": 1554671551955,
"transactions": [
    {
        "node": "http://192.168.43.117:3002",
        "name": "Silk",
        "buyer": "WERGHNBVFTYHJMNBVFD",
        "seller": "VFRTYUIKMNBVFGHJNBGG",
        "amount": "120",
        "price": "400",
        "transactionId": "30e8d170597911e9b7099bb384a29e08"
    }
],
"nonce": 210096,
"hash": "0000f6c70baa8caf59a41fc394595025d6a155aa7505a3acd15fcb7871887a11",
"previousBlockHash": "6b86b273ff34fce19d6b804eff5a3f5747ada4eaa22f1d49c01e52ddb7875b4b"
```

FIGURE 3.10 Sample block which is storing transactions and other related information.

mechanism by the nodes connected in the network. It is assumed that all the transactions are correct only if the address mentioned is in a certain format. After the transaction has been authenticated by one of the nodes and is being verified by a majority of nodes present in the network can we say the transaction is ready to be mined over the blockchain.

Figure 3.11 and Figure 3.12 show the simulation of trust values after ten and 50 iterations, respectively, for the network of five nodes. The first ten iterations, as specified, do not have any restrictions on

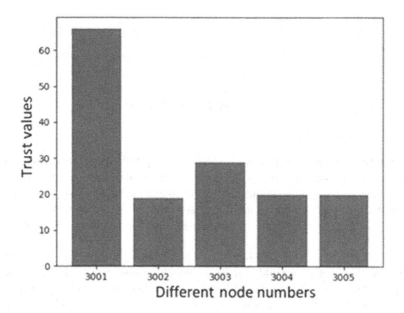

FIGURE 3.11   Trust values of nodes after ten iterations in network.

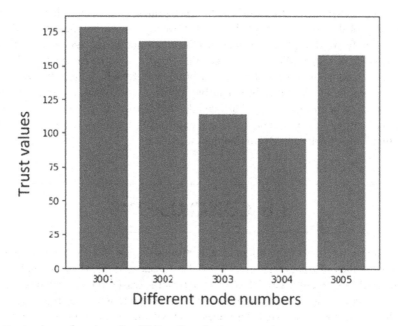

FIGURE 3.12   Trust values of nodes after 50 iterations in the network.

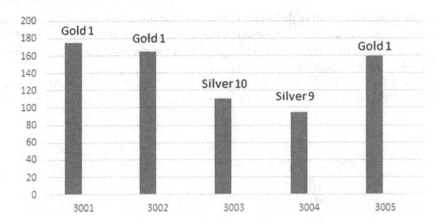

FIGURE 3.13   Reputation factor associated with each node of given trust values.

which nodes are to be selected for transaction and which are to be selected for mining. Hence, we have node 3001 become outlier with maximum trust. But as the algorithm runs, we can see there is not much increase in the 3001-node trust value and infrastructure somewhat becomes normalized. After 50 iterations, we can say the least trusted node is 3004 node and any activity which is done by this node would require a majority-based agreement to process further. That is how the above argument of attack prevention works.

Now, if we need to find the ranking of nodes after 50 iterations, the ranking are as follows.

The objective of this work is to build a dynamic model for a blockchain network which would continuously monitor and update the trust value of nodes, and also the model could be applied to any generic blockchain application. Three factors are taken into account for preparing a dynamic model which was implemented before only for the WSNs. In WSNs, they are used to find the best route to transfer messages. A similar model was implemented there, without implementing dynamic trust and giving time-based incentives for the nodes that are connected. This work aimed to find the correct way to implement and apply the model to all decentralized networks. The trust values which are gathered also depend on the relative average rank of the network. If it is below that average, suspicion may rise and only a majority decision will be taken forward. Figure 3.13 indicates the reputation factor associated with each node.

In this work, we have prepared a basic blockchain structure with major functionalities like hashing techniques, consensus algorithm, proof of work algorithm, etc., by which decentralized nodes are being created. After the Genesis block, any subsequent blocks are used to store the transactions. To monitor actions of each node, a synchronized script has been deployed which is then able to calculate the reputation factor based on trust values. This reputation factor has been used to prevent the nodes internally from passive attacks like Sybil attacks and Byzantine fault tolerance.

3.6 CONCLUSIONS

Blockchains provide an excellent decentralized mechanism to deploy and run scalable applications. There is no master to govern the information processing, so the transactions and their internal workings are visible to all. In this work, we discussed and developed a dynamic trust model for a blockchain network that could be used for seamless transaction storing over the blockchain, as well as reducing security threats. The approach discussed does not reveal the nodes' internal information and does not try to alter the information stored by the blockchain. The concepts here cannot be governed by a central authority and should only be applied for decentralized network. These are generic concepts and could be applicable to any decentralized application.

REFERENCES

Berdik, D., S. Otoum, N. Schmidt, D. Porter, and Y. Jararweh. "A survey on blockchain for information systems management and security." *Information Processing & Management* 58, no. 1 (2021): 102397.

Boukerche, A., Y. Ren, and R. W. N. Pazzi. "An adaptive computational trust model for mobile ad hoc networks." *Proceedings of the 2009 International Conference on Wireless Communications and Mobile Computing: Connecting the World Wirelessly*, pp. 191–195, June 2009.

Chang, S. E., and Y. Chen. "When blockchain meets supply chain: A systematic literature review on current development and potential applications." *IEEE Access* 8 (2020): 62478–62494.

Jiang, J., G. Han, F. Wang, L. Shu, and M. Guizani. "An efficient distributed trust model for wireless sensor networks." *IEEE Transactions on Parallel and Distributed Systems* 26, no. 5 (2014): 1228–1237.

Kamble, S. S., A. Gunasekaran, V. Kumar, A. Belhadi, and C. Foropon. "A machine learning based approach for predicting blockchain adoption in supply Chain." *Technological Forecasting and Social Change* 163 (2021): 120465.

Korpela, K., J. Hallikas, and T. Dahlberg. "Digital supply chain transformation toward blockchain integration." *Proceedings of the 50th Hawaii International Conference on System Sciences*, January 2017.

Kouhizadeh, M., S. Saberi, and J. Sarkis. "Blockchain technology and the sustainable supply chain: Theoretically exploring adoption barriers." *International Journal of Production Economics* 231 (2021): 107831.

Kouicem, D. E., Y. Imine, A. Bouabdallah, and H. Lakhlef. "A decentralized blockchain-based trust management protocol for the internet of things." *IEEE Transactions on Dependable and Secure Computing*, 2020.

Li, X., P. Jiang, T. Chen, X. Luo, and Q. Wen. "A survey on the security of blockchain systems." *Future Generation Computer Systems* 107 (2020): 841–853.

Liu, Z., A. W. Joy, and R. A. Thompson. "A dynamic trust model for mobile ad hoc networks." In *Proceedings 10th IEEE International Workshop on Future Trends of Distributed Computing Systems. FTDCS 2004*, pp. 80–85. IEEE, May 2004.

Melaye, D., and Y. Demazeau. "Bayesian dynamic trust model." In *International Central and Eastern European Conference on Multi-Agent Systems*, pp. 480–489. Springer, September 2005.

Moosavi, J., L. M. Naeni, A. M. Fathollahi-Fard, and U. Fiore. "Blockchain in supply chain management: A review, bibliometric, and network analysis." *Environmental Science and Pollution Research* (2021): 1–15.

Namasudra, S., G. C. Deka, P. Johri, M. Hosseinpour, and A. H. Gandomi. "The revolution of blockchain: State-of-the-art and research challenges." *Archives of Computational Methods in Engineering* (2020): 1–19.

Pournader, M., Y. Shi, S. Seuring, and S. L. Koh. "Blockchain applications in supply chains, transport and logistics: A systematic review of the literature." *International Journal of Production Research* 58, no. 7 (2020): 2063–2081.

Rao, S., A. Gulley, M. Russell, and J. Patton. "On the quest for supply chain transparency through blockchain: Lessons learned from two serialized data projects." *Journal of Business Logistics* 42, no 1 (2021): 88–100.

Shala, B., U. Trick, A. Lehmann, B. Ghita, and S. Shiaeles. "Blockchain and trust for secure, end-user-based and decentralized IoT service provision." *IEEE Access* 8 (2020): 119961–119979.

Wu, G., Z. Du, Y. Hu, T. Jung, U. Fiore, and K. Yim. "A dynamic trust model exploiting the time slice in WSNs." *Soft Computing* 18, no. 9 (2014): 1829–1840.

Zhuo, T., L. Zhengding, and L. Kai. "Time-based dynamic trust model using ant colony algorithm." *Wuhan University Journal of Natural Sciences* 11, no. 6 (2006): 1462–1466.

Zyskind, G., and O. Nathan. "Decentralizing privacy: Using blockchain to protect personal data." *2015 IEEE Security and Privacy Workshops*, pp. 180–184, May 2015.

TRACK 2

Blockchain for Information Systems

New Methods for Day-to-Day Problems

Blockchain and IoT Technologies to Improve the Agricultural Food Supply Chain

Saranya P, Maheswari R, and Tanmay Kulkarni

Contents

4.1 INTRODUCTION

India is a developing country; more and more people are getting educated, and the Indian economy has increased vigorously. It is inferred that a large part of the Indian economy comes from the agriculture industry, but the main aspect of the agriculture industry is the farmer who gets the lowest pay. There are many reasons behind that, such as more participants in the supply chain, lack of information about the product origin and quality, food adulteration, etc. Apart from farming, the consuming habit of India's well-educated consumers has changed. They pay more attention to food safety and the quality of the food. However, every year, many people survive with health issues, primarily because of food safety accidents. These types of food safety accidents will affect human health, as well as harm the economic system of the country. As our nation is an agriculture-dominated country, these types of losses are a big mess for the development of the country. To avoid these types of messes and to help to improve the economic system, it is the need of the hour to track the agriculture supply chain from farmers to consumers. But it is not an easy task, because there are many intermediaries between farmers and consumers. For that, it needs a traceability system to track and trace the supply chain. For developing such a type of system, we can take help from the emerging technologies like blockchain and IoT. Blockchain provides a decentralized trustful data storage of transactions between two stockholders, whereby unchangeable and encrypted copies of information are stored in each node in the network chain. It is transparent and can record transactions between two parties permanently, efficiently, and in a verifiable way. These are the features of blockchain that make it the most trustable distributed data storage system. IoT is a network in which all the IoT devices are attached with the Internet through network devices and are able to swap data. IoT allows things to be controlled from a distance without any physical connection across a network. IoT minimizes human effort, as well as making it easy to access physical equipment. IoT also has independent control factors by which any equipment can handle its responsibilities without any human physical interaction. Using these two technologies, we can build a new agriculture food supply chain system.

4.2 RELATED WORK

In this section, we will focus on the related literature work found in papers related to blockchain and IoT applications for supply chain. The blockchain application is mostly used in the financial industry like banking, insurance, finance, etc. Now food safety has become a global issue, and hence, blockchain is gaining popularity in the food industry like supply chain traceability. IoT applications provide automation and reduce the work of humans, and most probably, IoT is used in the automation industry, vehicle automation, and home automation. With food safety as a global issue, we found some solutions for food safety using IoT devices and technology. M.M. Aung and Chang (2014) proposed smart contracts with blockchain technology for the food supply chain. T. Bosona and Gebresenbet (2013) mainly focus on food traceability issues. The barriers in developing and implementing food traceability systems (FTS), benefits, traceability technologies, improvements, and performances of FTSs have been identified and discussed here. J. Hobbs (2006) explores the economic functions of traceability, examining the extent to which traceability can bolster liability incentives for firms to practice due diligence. D. Mao et al. (2018) discussed the challenges to enhance the decentralized storage-based inspection system in the milk dairy product industry. F. Tian (2017) developed a blockchain system to increase the transparency and automated process in the agriculture industry. F. Tian (2016) introduced the blockchain with IoT sensors like radio frequency identification (RFID) for trusted traceability—using RFID, they get authentic data and stored in the blockchain for security and traceability. D. Li et al. (2006) proposed a system which introduced dynamic planning and wireless identification technology like RFID and barcodes, and also used blockchain for data security and traceability. J. Trienekens and Zuurbier (2008) discussed quality and safety standards of the food and food supply chain, and also discussed challenges which have to be faced while supplying supply and delivery of the food. R. Akkerman et al. (2010) discussed food standards and how to maintain them, while the food supply also has some quality standards which have to be followed—and how to follow these standards. There are some food products which have low sustainability and this is a challenge in the supply chain; they introduce IoT devices to maintain quality, safety and sustainability. K. Sari, (2010) discussed wireless devices for transparent and traceable food supply chains like RFID and barcodes, and also try to explore food quality and sustainability using RFIDs. D. Folinas et al. (2006) discussed traceability and data management. They introduce a system to manage the data about food and traceability devices like RFIDs. C. Shanahan et al. (2009) discussed templates for food traceability from farms to customers. Also about traceability and chain monitoring using IoT devices, E. Abad et al. (2009) discussed RFID tags for food supply chain traceability and transparency. V. Mattoli et al. (2010) provide a flexible tag data logger for food logistics. Sensors and actuators, defined in H. Massias et al. (1999), show the design of a secure timestamping service with minimal trust requirements. S. Haber and Stornetta (1991) proposed using timestamps on digital documents, which is used as a digital signature. R.C. Merkle (1980) discussed a public protocol cryptosystem, how this cryptosystem will work, and what protocols are used for public keys.

4.3 PROPOSED SYSTEM

This proposed system has used blockchain and RFID together to trace and track the food products. RFIDs are the virtual identity of the product to take physical parameters in action. We proposed to utilize blockchain and RFIDs with load cell sensors to trace the supply chain, along with weight alteration detection. Our solution eliminates the third trusted party and enhances the identification of weight alteration of food containers in the supply chain.

4.3.1 Blockchain

A blockchain is a constantly growing decentralized database store that protects data against tampering and revision of data lists of records in the blockchain called blocks that are linked together using cryptographic hash values. Hash function is a method that can be used to set the discretionary size of data into a rigid size. The values returned by the hash function are called hash value. Hash function uses the SHA 256-bit algorithm to encrypt the data. Each block contains the hash value of the previous block, a timestamp, and transaction data. Blockchain is resistant to modifications. It is a transparent, distributed digital register that can record transactions between two stockholders of the supply chain permanently, and in a verifiable way (S. Nakamoto, 2008). As we defined previously, there some characteristics of blockchain are: anonymous, distributed, reliable database, and also robust because it does not follow a single point of failure. If a single block of the blockchain fails, its effect is not seen in other blocks (R.C. Merkle, 1980). In the supply chain, as shown in Figure 4.1, if one stockholder initiates a transaction, a new block will be created. The new block could be verified by hundreds of computer nodes called miners who are distributed around the world (S. Haber and Stornetta, 1991). The verified block is added to the network, creating a unique record and unique history of transaction, as well. Modifying a single record requires making changes in hundreds of block entries which is practically impossible. Blockchain transactions are free and verification of new blocks will provide rewards to miners (H. Massias et al., 1999).

FIGURE 4.1 Stock holder supply chain.

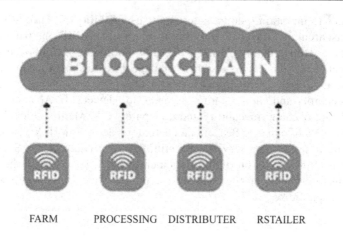

FARM   PROCESSING   DISTRIBUTER   RSTAILER

FIGURE 4.2   RFID vs. blockchain.

4.3.2 RFID

RFID leads to a system that utilizes wavelengths to automatically detect matters by using radio frequency identification. There is a reader which is used to read the RFID tags attached to the different things. In general, RFID systems are made up of an RFID label and a scanner. The reader throws electromagnetic rays that are absorbed by the labels. The consumed rays can be used to provide energy to the microchip, and the reader retrieves a signal that contains the specific tag number. Each tag has its unique identification number with other information that are stored with that unique identity number. RFID has more advantages as compared to the barcode such as mass capacity for information, antipollution, and recyclability. Probably most RFIDs are used in the supply chain systems, storage facilities like warehouses, etc. In the supply chain, when food is delivered from one stockholder to another stockholder, RFIDs get into action at that time. At the source of the delivery process, RFID tags are attached to the food containers, and at the destination, these tags are read by the reader with attached unique identity number and information, as illustrated in Figure 4.2.

4.3.3 Load Cell Sensor

The load cell is a type of cell that translates the influence of a power such as voltage, compression, pressure, or torque into electrical impulses which can be measured, regarded, and standardized. Load cell sensors are mostly found in industries. Load cell sensors are highly accurate, versatile, and cost-effective.

4.4 METHODOLOGY

Blockchain and IoT technologies in a combined form are utilized only for the virtual identity code. Virtual identity codes can be RFIDs, barcodes and quick response (QR) codes. In supply chain, every container of food has its own virtual identity known as a unique number and information. If any change or alteration is done with the virtual identity, then we can identify the weight alteration with the help of RFID, but any change occurred in physical parameters could not be addressed by virtual identity codes.

To deal with this problem in our proposed system, we introduce the load cell sensor which detects the weight of the product, as illustrated in Figure 4.3. To identify the alteration of physical parameters of

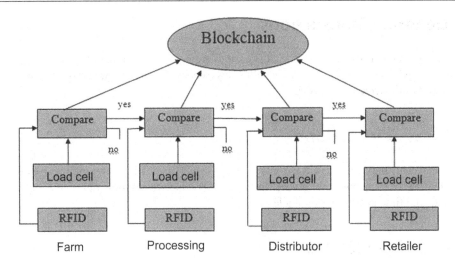

FIGURE 4.3   Load cell vs. blockchain.

the entity, we utilize this sensor along with RFID (virtual identities). The output of a load cell sensor is compared with predefined weight in RFID reader. The product will be forwarded in supply chain only if both weights are same; otherwise, it will be rejected. The output of comparison will also be added in the blockchain. It helps to detect who did the alteration, where the alteration was done, and when alteration was done.

4.5 RESULTS

4.5.1 Wallet Generator

"Wallet Generator" is basically a public and private key generator which is used to create a transaction in blockchain, as shown in Figure 4.4.

FIGURE 4.4   Wallet generator.

4.5.2 Generate Transactions

"Generate Transaction" is the window which is used to create a transaction and store it in the blockchain. It contains the sender's private key, sender's public key, receiver's public key, and description of the product and amount as depicted in Figure 4.5.

4.5.3 View Transactions

Figure 4.6 represents the "View Transactions" window, which basically shows the history of transactions of each node with the recipient's and sender's public key, product description and timestamp, which shows the exact date and time of transaction made.

4.5.4 Configure Nodes

Using the "Add Blockchain nodes" window, we can configure nodes with the new blocks in each node, as shown in Figure 4.7, which shows the transaction of each node using a "Mine" button.

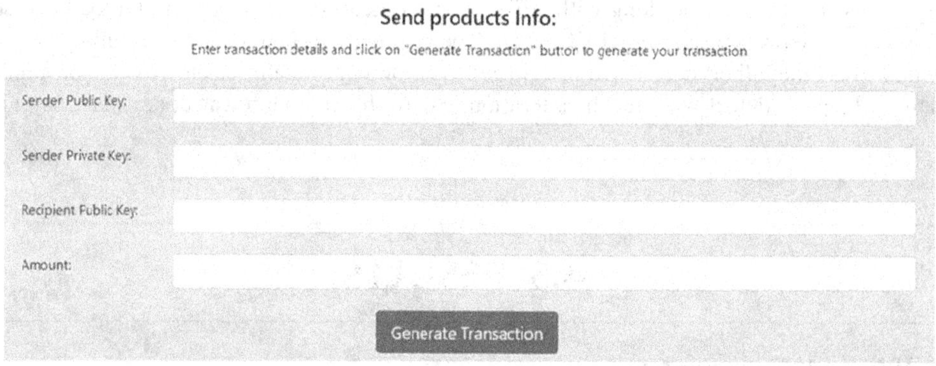

Send products Info:

Enter transaction details and click on "Generate Transaction" button to generate your transaction

Sender Public Key:

Sender Private Key:

Recipient Public Key:

Amount:

Generate Transaction

FIGURE 4.5   Generate transactions.

View Transactions

Enter a blockchain node URL and click on "View Transactions" button to check all transactions

Node URL: http://127.0.0.1:5001

View Transactions

Show 10 ▾ entries   Search:

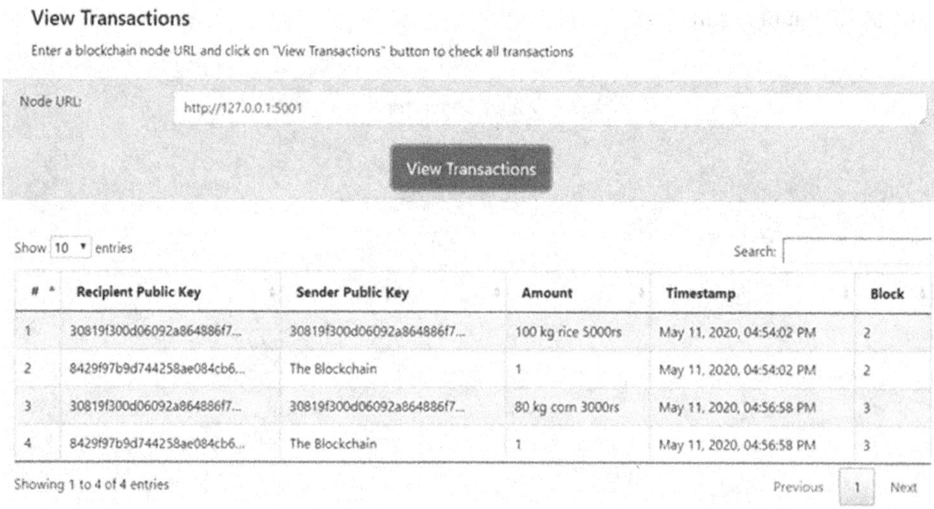

# ▲	Recipient Public Key	Sender Public Key	Amount	Timestamp	Block
1	30819f300d06092a864886f7...	30819f300d06092a864886f7...	100 kg rice 5000rs	May 11, 2020, 04:54:02 PM	2
2	8429f97b9d744258ae084cb6...	The Blockchain	1	May 11, 2020, 04:54:02 PM	2
3	30819f300d06092a864886f7...	30819f300d06092a864886f7...	80 kg corn 3000rs	May 11, 2020, 04:56:58 PM	3
4	8429f97b9d744258ae084cb6...	The Blockchain	1	May 11, 2020, 04:56:58 PM	3

Showing 1 to 4 of 4 entries   Previous   1   Next

FIGURE 4.6   View transactions.

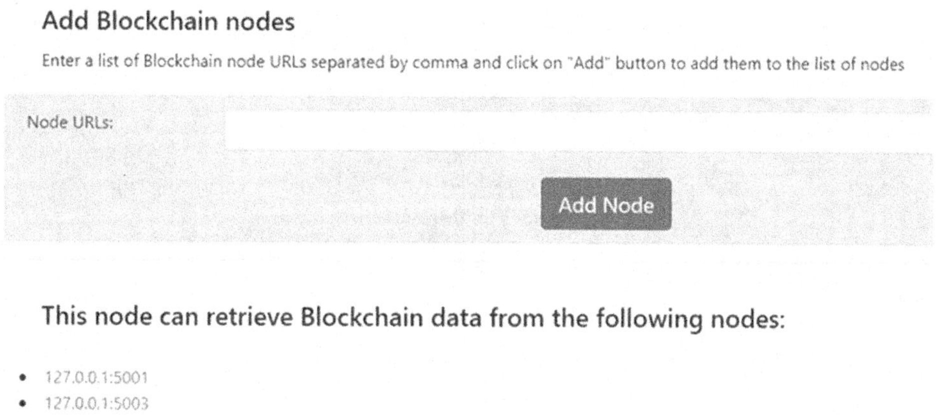

Add Blockchain nodes

Enter a list of Blockchain node URLs separated by comma and click on "Add" button to add them to the list of nodes

Node URLs:

Add Node

This node can retrieve Blockchain data from the following nodes:

- 127.0.0.1:5001
- 127.0.0.1:5003

FIGURE 4.7   Add blockchain nodes.

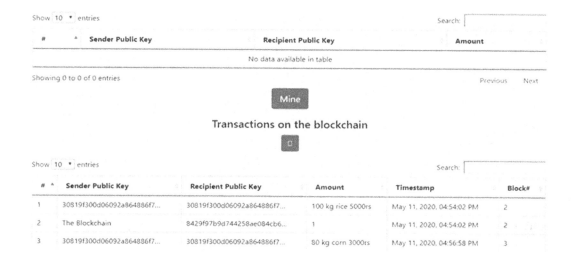

FIGURE 4.8   Node I: Public keys.

4.5.5 Transactions of Each Node

4.5.5.1 Node I

Figure 4.8 shows the transaction which is made in Node I with both public keys, description, and timestamp.

4.5.5.2 Node II

Figure 4.9 represents the transaction which is made in Node II with both public keys, description, and timestamp.

4.5.5.3 Node III

Figure 4.10 depicts the transaction which is made in Node III with both public keys, description, and timestamp.

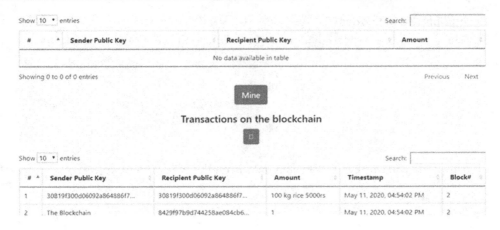

FIGURE 4.9   Node II: Public keys.

FIGURE 4.10   Node III: public keys.

4.6 CONCLUSION

In this chapter, the agriculture food supply chain traceability system is established with the help of RFID, load cell sensors, and blockchain technology. This system provides the transparency, traceability, and integrity of the food in the supply chain. It also gathers data from all the stockholders in the supply chain and stores them for future reference. The proposed system concentrated mostly on the physical parameter of the agricultural food like food containers. The current weight of the food containers is compared with the predefined weight in RFIDs, which helps to detect the weight alteration of the food containers in the agriculture food supply chain.

REFERENCES

Abad, E., et al. "RFID tag for traceability and chain monitoring of food: Demonstration in an intercontinental fresh fish logistic chain." *Journal of Food Engineering* 93, no. 4 (2009).

Akkerman, R., P. Farahani, and M. Grunow. "Quality, safety and sustainability in food distribution: A review of quantitative operations management approaches and challenges." *OR Spectrum* 32 (2010): 863–904.

Aung, M. M., and Y. S. Chang. "Traceability in a food supply chain: Safety and quality perspectives." *Food Control* 39 (May 2014): 172–184.

Bosona, T., and G. Gebresenbet, "Food traceability as an integral part of logistics management in food and agricultural supply chain." *Food Control* 33, no. 1 (2013): 32–48.

Folinas, D., I. Manikas, and B. Manos. "Traceability data management for food chains." *British Food Journal* 108, no. 8 (2006): 622–633.

Haber, S., and W. S. Stornetta. "How to time-stamp a digital document." *Journal of Cryptology* 3, no. 2 (1991): 99–111.

Hobbs, J. "Liability and traceability in agri-food supply chains." In *Quantifying the Agri-Food Supply Chain*, pp. 87–102. Springer, 2006.

Li, D., D. Kehoe, and P. Drake. "Dynamic planning with a wireless identification technology in agricultural food supply chains." *International Journal of Advanced Manufacturing Technology* 30 (2006).

Mao, D., Z. Hao, F. Wang, and H. Li. "Novel automatic food trading system using consortium blockchain." *The Arabian Journal for Science and Engineering* 44, no. 4 (April 2018): 3439–3455.

Massias, H., X. S. Avila, and J.-J. Quisquater. "Design of a secure timestamping service with minimal trust requirements." *20th Symposium on Information Theory in the Benelux*, 1999 May.

Mattoli, V., B. Mazzolai, A. Mondini, S. Zampolli, and P. Dario. "Flexible tag data logger for food logistics." *Sensors and Actuators A: Physical* 162, no. 2 (2010): 316–323.

Merkle, R. C. "Protocols for public key cryptosystems." In *Proceedings 1980 Symposium on Security and Privacy*, pp. 122–133. IEEE Computer Society, 1980 April.

Nakamoto, S. "Bitcoin: A peer-to-peer electronic cash system." (2008): 1–9.

Sari, K. "Exploring the impacts of radio frequency identification (RFID) technology on supply chain performance." *European Journal of Operational Research* 207 (2010): 174–183.

Shanahan, C., B. Kernan, G. Ayalew, K. McDonnell, F. Butler, and S. Ward. "A template for beef traceability from farm to slaughter using global standards: An Irish perspective." *Computer and IoT in Agriculture* 66, no. 1 (2009).

Tian, F. "A food supply chain traceability and identifying system for food safety refers on HACCP, blockchain & IoT." *Proceedings International Conference on Service Systems and Service Management* (ICSSSM), June, 2017.

Tian, F. "An agriculture-food supply chain traceability & identifying system for China based on RFID & blockchain technology." *Proceedings 13th International Conference on Service Systems and Service Management* (ICSSSM), June, 2016.

Trienekens, J., and Zuurbier. "Quality and safety standards in the food industry, developments and challengers." *The International Journal of Production Economics* 113 (2008): 107–122.

A Novel Hybrid Chaotic Map–Based Proactive RSA Cryptosystem in Blockchain

5

S. Selvi and M. Vimala Devi

Contents

5.1 INTRODUCTION

Blockchain, the booming technology in the world of digital cryptocurrency [1], has a dynamic adaptable structure of records, called blocks. Each block is a container of cryptographic hash of the previous linked blocks, the timestamp of the transactions, and the data transmitted through the communication channel. Each block has a nonce value which is generated at random when the block is generated. This leads to the emergence of blockchain in various fields such as grid environment, proof of evidence, etc. The consensus among the miners is achieved through digital signatures, which identify honest parties and knock out the misbehaving/untrusted miners. An RSA-based digital signature [2] scheme would enable a robust, efficient, and auditable key generation environment in blockchain.

The proposed variant of the RSA algorithm aims to reduce the overall computational time, in spite of the complexity in numerical calculation. The variant RSA comprises a generalization of key generation process, encrypted data, and its corresponding decrypted one. The encryption holds the private key of the sender and the public key of the receiver, and decryption uses vice versa. When compared to the existing

RSAs, the proposed one has a parallel implementation and hence obtains a faster encryption/decryption scenario. Also, a mixture of hybrid chaotic maps still adds an additional advantage, so that it could be well equipped for the low computability gadgets.

A variant of chaotic maps [3] are heavily being used from the earlier secured communication technologies, which creates a more secured encryption. The suggested scheme aims to provoke a minimal number of operations, thereby demanding a robust defense against several known attacks. RSA, during its first stage of encryption, would be resistant to differential and cryptographic attacks Gauss map, logistic map, and tent map (GLT maps) are the chaotic maps used to generate a pseudo-random number in the RSA algorithm. The fundamental RSA algorithm invoked a second stage of encryption using the combined GLT maps to design a secure framework against cryptographic attacks. GLT maps generate a higher degree of randomization and an unpredictable chaotic sequence, which makes the process of cryptanalysis more difficult.

The properties of confusion and diffusion are achieved by generating entropical condition, and hence it is framed as a suitable component to be applied in cryptography. The combination of chaotic maps and cryptographic keys proves to be impossible for an attacker in predicting the original plain text from the cipher text. Earlier works due to its insufficiency and inadequacy of chaotic sequences suffers from cryptanalytic attacks and slower computation.

Following are the sections organized for discussion: Section 5.2 comes up with the related works; Section 5.3 describes the working model of the proposed RSA algorithm in blockchain, and illustrates the experimental results; and finally, Section 5.4 deals with conclusions and future work.

5.2 RELATED WORKS

A survey on various papers has been made for the proposed concept and detailed as follows. Two stages of encryption were put forward by Roayat et al. [4]. Encryption at the end of first level was enhanced by XORing with a pseudo-random sequence number during the second stage. Meanwhile sine, ten, and Hénon maps—with their control parameters—were used to resist against brute force attacks, chosen plain text attacks, etc., thereby achieving integrity, authentication and non-repudiation.

Various chaotic maps combined with RSA encryption were implemented by Nedal et al. [5] focusing on limited capability communicating nodes. The variant RSA concentrated on improvising the complexity of integer factorization and discrete logarithmic axioms. An encrypt assistant multiprime RSA (EAMRSA) was developed by Saveetha et al. [6], whereby the private key was computed using the extended Euclidian algorithm. Also, the authors aimed to speed up the encryption/decryption to a speed up factor of 7.06 by moderating the exponential modulus for the private exponents.

A solid and a consistent blockchain-based private PDP [7] scheme is developed by merging blockchain and RSA. The anonymity of the clients was also being recognized by the security constraints. However, the security of the private key had to be improved further. The auditability and verification adequacies [8] were being concentrated and minimized by focusing on a threshold-based RSA key generation merged with digital signatures, but proactive-based RSA had to be looked into for further performance optimization.

Srinivas et al. [9] introduced a chaotic cryptosystem by including a pseudo-random number generator into the Lanczos algorithm. The randomness was achieved by accomplishing the shuffling pixels within the image and thereby achieving a high resistance to various known attacks. The preference for RSA and elliptic curve cryptosystems on embedded systems was done to verify how far the sensitive documents will remain secure, along with their prolonged memory and power consumption. A hybrid concept of cryptography and a video-based steganography was invoked by Nouf A. Al-Juaid [10] to overcome the tradeoff between capacity and security constraints on fixed sensitive video information. A modified RSA suitable for both signing and encryption was explored by Ravi Shankar Dhakar [11], but only known mathematical attacks and brute force attacks provoked by the algorithm.

In [12], to defend over the most common attacks, RSA has enhanced its algorithm by providing an effective solution by eliminating the occurrences of redundant messages if any in some value of n. The k-nearest values had been used for the values of either p, q, or both. Both p and q values are related to the distance calculation, which also would be changed periodically to avoid threats.

In Amare Anagaw Ayele et al. [13], multiple key pairs were assigned as public keys instead of a single value e in the RSA security process. This modified RSA was concentrated to lessen the vulnerability to brute force attack with greater communication overhead. Two sets of public keys were communicated among the parties, so as to minimize the possibility of an attacker getting hold of the cryptanalysis. Sangita et al. [14] aimed to enhance the security measures and speed up the encryption/decryption process by introducing the calculation of three prime random numbers for n value and further replacing n with the value of x. The simulation was done using MATLAB and found that their proposed work exploited the difficulties for an intruder, thereby achieving confidentiality of the message.

5.3 PROPOSED WORK

5.3.1 Modified RSA Algorithm

To secure communication of data, a variant RSA cryptosystem based on "n" prime is being proposed. This is a novel technique to maximize the security for data over the network, involving encryption, decryption, and key generation [15]. The variant RSA provides the following three phases: prime key generation, encryption, and decryption. In this technique, we used the RSA cryptosystem algorithm with hybrid chaotic maps (Gauss map, logistic map, and tent map). The public key was only used for encrypting the messages, and it can be seen to all. It is not secret key. The private key is used for decrypting the messages. Private key is also called the secret key.

Prime number used is the only component used to explore security over the networks. In this technique, we used "n" prime number with some enhancement which could not be easily breakable; "n" prime numbers are not easily decomposed. This technique would surely provide more efficiency and reliability over the networks.

RSA is a well-known asymmetric key block cipher in which the encrypted text and decrypted text should be integers and should be between 0 and n−1 for some n. Encryption and decryption could be evaluated based on the following form, for any plaintext block M and cipher text block C:

$$C = M^{b/a} \bmod n \tag{1}$$

$$M = C^d \bmod n = (M^{b/a})^d \bmod n = M^{b/ad} \bmod n. \tag{2}$$

Both sender and receiver must know the values of n, b, and a; only the receiver would be aware of the value of d. This is an asymmetric key encryption algorithm with a public key of KU = {b,n}, {a} and a private key of KR = {d,n}. For this algorithm to be more effective for public key encryption, the following requirements must be met:

1. It is possible to find values of b, a, d, n such that $M^{b/ad} = M \bmod n$ for all M < n.
2. It is relatively easy to calculate $M^{b/a}$ and C^d for all values of M < n.
3. b is a multiple of a and e (which is the public key in the normal RSA algorithm)

Steps

- Initialize by choosing two prime numbers, p and q, and evaluating their product n, which is the modulus exponent for encryption and decryption.

- Next, we need to measure φ(n), referred to as the Euler totient of n, which is the positive integer less than n and relatively co-prime to n.
- Select an integer e that is relatively prime to φ(n) (i.e., the greatest common divisor of e and φ[n] is 1).
- Choose any two numbers a and b such that b equalizes the multiplication of a and e(b = a × e).
- Having these numbers, two public keys {b,n},{a} could be equated.
- Finally, calculate d as the multiplicative inverse of e (which is public key in normal RSA), modulo φ(n). But to compute, the receiver has to choose any positive natural number and multiply it by a, then add b, divide the result by a and finally subtract the chosen value then the receiver has e. then calculate d as usual.

The variables d and e should have the following characteristics:

1. Suppose that user A has published its public key and that user B wishes to send the message M to A.
2. Then B calculates $C = M^{b/a}(\text{mod } n)$ and transmits C.
3. On receipt of this cipher text, user A decrypts by calculating $M = C^d(\text{mod } n)$.

5.3.2 Chaotic Maps

Our new secure cryptosystem depends upon two number theory concepts: Integer Factorization and Chaotic Maps Discrete Logarithm (CMDL). This requires minimal number of operations, and it would not increase the overhead during the encryption/decryption process. Designing a chaotic map setting is usually difficult, but generally creates secure and efficient protocols. That is because chaotic map–based protocols have low computational costs when compared with other modular exponential computing–based protocols or protocols that are based on scalar multiplication on elliptic curves.

It merges Gauss map, logistic map, and tent map (GLT maps) and so it has secret control parameters which increase the key space, and hence provides a good randomness and achieves a strong resistance against chosen plaintext attacks and brute force attacks. The most common mathematical hard problems used in public key enabling (PKE) are integer factorization and discrete logarithm [16]. Actually, cryptographers have found that they can achieve computational efficiency in performance and higher security with very low key size compared to other algorithms. There is no sub exponential algorithm for solving the discrete logarithm problem.

The scheme is time-efficient for two reasons: first, it has a smaller number of EC point multiplications; which is the most time consuming operation; compared to many recent EC based image encryption schemes and second, it uses elliptic curve (EC) group of pixels point multiplication instead of single-pixel EC point multiplication. This matter achieves computational time saving. Chaotic maps are highly sensitive to initial values and control parameters. Any slight change in the initial conditions causes a remarkable deviation. This sensitivity strongly limits their prediction ability [17]. Encryption schemes based on chaos use initial conditions as a cryptographic key. The chaotic maps include one-dimensional and high-dimensional chaotic maps. The one-dimensional map commonly has one variable and few parameters.

Gauss Map

The Gauss map (also known as Gaussian map), is a nonlinear iterated map of the reals into a real interval given by the Gaussian function:

$$x_{n+1} = \text{exponential}(-\alpha x_n^2) + \beta \qquad (3)$$

where α and β are real parameters.

Gauss maps are best suitable to solve discrete logarithmic problems.

Logistic Map

The logistic map is a polynomial mapping (equivalently, recurrence relation) of degree 2, often cited as an archetypal example of how complex, chaotic behavior can arise from very simple nonlinear dynamical equations:

$$x_{n+1} = rx_n(1-x_n) \qquad (4)$$

Tent Map

the tent map with parameter μ is the real-valued function fμ defined by:

$$f\mu = \mu \min\{x, 1-x\} \qquad (5)$$

5.3.3 Working Principle of the Proposed Work

A system based on chaotic theory is usually defined on real numbers. In fact, any encryption algorithm, which utilizes chaotic maps, upon its implementation on a computer (e.g., finite-state machine), turns into a transformation onto itself from a finite set.

Figure 5.1 portrays the workflow of the proposed work where the RSA encryption, invoking the public and private key generation, makes use of a Hybrid GLT chaotic map sequence. The sender converts the

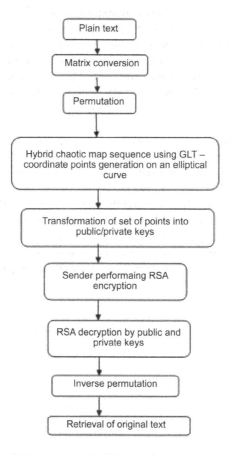

FIGURE 5.1   Working principle of RSA with hybrid GLT chaotic maps.

plain text into a row x column matrix format. The matrix undergoes the 64-bit permutation process, from which the coordinate points are chosen for an elliptic curve. The elliptic curve is chosen for the proposed work, since it has the significance of providing a higher security even for a smaller key length [18] [19] sequence. From the points, private keys are identified and public keys are being generated. The formatted text then undergoes an encryption process using the proposed RSA algorithm. At the receiver end, decryption followed by inverse permutation is performed to retrieve the original text.

5.3.4 Elliptic Curve—Coordinate Points Generation

1. Elliptic curve cryptography is involved in this work for the key generation process using the hybrid GLT sequence.
2. The proposed hybrid chaotic GLT is used to induce a pseudo-random sequence (PRS) of a variable length.
3. Perform XOR operation pseudo-random sequence generated by Gaussian map, logistic map, and tent map.
4. Restructure the resultant mapping sequence into coordinate points for the generation of an elliptic curve.

5.3.5 Blockchain with the Proposed RSA

Blockchain technology is nothing but a network of nodes dealing with a database. The nodes are entry points for new data, as well as the validation and propagation of new data that have been submitted to the blockchain. Blockchain technology offers new tools for authentication and authorization in the digital world that preclude the need for many centralized administrators. As a result, it enables the creation of new digital relationships by incorporating with the various cryptographic techniques [20] [21] [22] and also it explores its significance with IOT devices [23]. The blockchain revolution is poised to create the backbone of a layer of the Internet for transactions and interactions of value, often called the "Internet of Value."

The blocks in the blockchain consist of a hash with some information of its previous block. Hash plays an important role and turns out be a unique mathematical code which is different for different blocks. Changes in any part of information would surely reflect in the hash value. All the blocks are connected with hash keys, making the blockchain secure.

Blockchain uses the Merkle tree function and the Merkel root field that presents the hash value of the current block. When transactions are taking place in the network, their respective nodes will validate these transactions. Blockchain uses public and private keys in order to ensure security.

Authentication is achieved using these keys; authorization arises. It allows the participants to perform mathematical verifications of the network and reach a consensus on any particular value. The sender uses

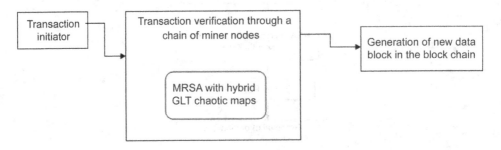

FIGURE 5.2 Transaction verification layout with hybrid chaotic maps in blockchain.

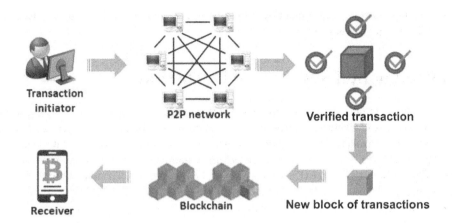

FIGURE 5.3 Block chain transactions process.

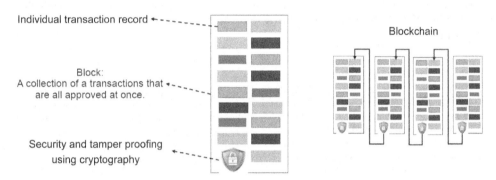

FIGURE 5.4 Block chain as records.

the private key and announces the transaction over the network. The block consists of timestamp, a digital signature, and the public key of the receiver to perform a transaction.

Once the information is broadcasted, the validation of the process starts. The nodes that are present in the network try to solve the puzzle related to the transaction in order to process it. Nodes spend computational power in order to solve the puzzle. Once the puzzle is solved, the nodes will receive a reward in the form of Bitcoins. This kind of work is known as proof of work problems.

Once the nodes in the consensus agree to a solution, the timestamp is added to the existing block. The block can contain anything from money to data. If a new block is added to the chain, the existing nodes are updated in the network. The new data will be broadcasted in the network, and all the nodes are updated.

Nelson et al. [24] have provoked that conventional RSA showed its lower performance in terms of computation cost and memory consumption over Elliptic Curve Cryptosystems. Considering these backlogs over RSA, a blockchain-based modified RSA scheme with hybrid chaotic maps is introduced. This would prove to be efficient, depending on the communication and computation costs. In other words, the computation cost and communication cost must be as low as the practical efficiency requirements.

The most currently trendable blockchains induce the RSA algorithm for the creation of blockchain and encryption of blockchain cryptocurrencies. Following is the scenario of how RSA is being applied to cryptos:

- The cryptocurrency transaction uses a public address and a private key for its generation.
- The public address utilizes the received cryptocurrencies and consults the available balance on the blockchain.

- The private key, on the other hand, will be used in correlation to this public key to access and spend the cryptocurrency.

5.3.6 Experimental Results and Discussion

The proposed work has been simulated in MATLAB. Plain text underwent the RSA encryption and decryption process in a blockchain environment. The security level has been determined and measured with respect to the time taken for the generation of public/private keys and computational time by the algorithm. The performance of the proposed MRSA (modified RSA) using chaotic maps has been compared with the RSA algorithm and MRSA algorithms. The experiment is conducted with the plain text of various sizes such as 128 bits, 256 bits, 512 bits, 1,024 bits, 2,048 bits, and 4,096 bits. From Table 5.1 and Figure 5.5, it is found that the proposed algorithm is about 1.33 times faster than the RSA algorithm and 1.11 times faster than the MRSA algorithm.

To work out the computational time, the message m is divided into equal chunks and encryption/decryption is performed. From Table 5.2 and Figure 5.6, it is projected that the computational time of the proposed algorithm is about 1.53 times faster than the RSA algorithm and 1.27 times faster than the MRSA algorithm.

TABLE 5.1   Key Generation Time: RSA vs. MRSA vs. MRSA Using Chaotic Maps

MESSAGE M IN BITS	KEY GENERATION TIME IN RSA (IN SEC.)	KEY GENERATION TIME IN MRSA (IN SEC.)	KEY GENERATION TIME IN MRSA USING CHAOTIC MAPS (IN SEC.)
128	0.0025	0.0013	0.0009
256	0.0032	0.0023	0.0016
512	0.0042	0.0036	0.003
1,024	0.0059	0.0052	0.0049
2,048	0.0096	0.0089	0.0082
4,096	0.0115	0.0096	0.0094

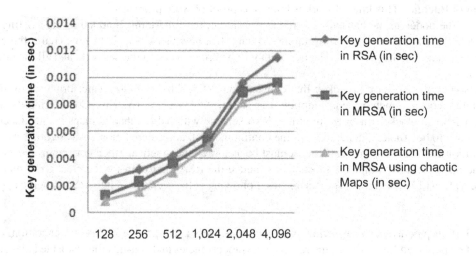

FIGURE 5.5   Key generation time: RSA vs. MRSA vs. MRSA using chaotic maps.

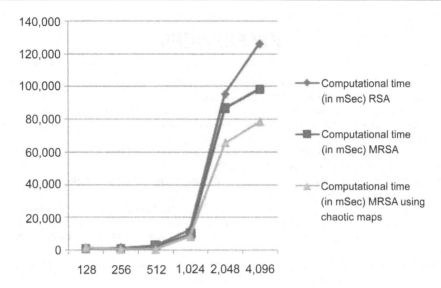

FIGURE 5.6 Computational time: RSA vs. MRSA vs. MRSA using chaotic maps.

TABLE 5.2 Computational Time: RSA vs. MRSA

MESSAGE M IN BITS	CHUNK SIZE IN BITS	COMPUTATIONAL TIME (IN MSEC.)		
		RSA	MRSA	MRSA USING CHAOTIC MAPS
128	64	1,452	896	1,986
256	128	1,568	969	840
512	128	3,256	2,812	698
1,024	256	12,568	10,058	8,650
2,048	512	95,625	87,079	65,892
4,096	512	126,585	98,567	78,633

5.4 CONCLUSION

This chapter proposed an enhanced security framework for blockchain. Authentication is achieved by employing the RSA algorithm with hybrid chaotic (GLT) mapping for the key generation process. The chaotic map sequence is mainly adopted for adding complexity to the factorization and solves discrete logarithm problems. The experiment was simulated using MATLAB. The results favored 1.33 times and 1.11 times faster than the existing RSA and MRSA algorithms, respectively, with regard to key generation. With regard to computational time taken by the proposed algorithm, it is determined that it is 1.53 times and 1.27 times faster than the existing ones. Increasing the complexity by introducing chaotic maps and multiple public keys in encryption/decryption, it has been proven that the proposed algorithm performs better than the earlier works. In the future, it could be implemented over blockchain-based real-time scenarios in order to enjoy the security advancements and reap its benefits.

REFERENCES

[1] Zheng, Z., S. Xie, H. Dai, X. Chen, and H. Wang. "An overview of blockchain technology: Architecture, consensus, and future trends." *2017 IEEE 6th International Congress on Big Data*, June 2017.

[2] Jansma, N., and B. Arrendondo. *Performance Comparison of Elliptic Curve and RSA Digital Signatures.* 2004. http://fog.misty.com/perry/ccs/ec/KF/Performance_Comparison_of_Elliptic_Curve_and_RSA_Digital_Signatures.pdf

[3] Wang, X., X. Wang, J. Zhao, and Z. Zhang. "Chaotic encryption algorithm based on alternant of stream cipher and block cipher." *Nonlinear Dynamics* 63 (2011): 587–597.

[4] Abdelfatah, Roayat Ismail. "Secure image transmission using chaotic-enhanced elliptic curve cryptography." *IEEE Access* 8 (January 2020): 3875–3890.

[5] Tahat, Nedal, Ashraf A. Tahat, Maysam Abu-Dalu, Ramzi B. Albadarneh, Alaa E. Abdallah, and Obaida M. Al-Hazaimeh. "A new RSA public key encryption scheme with chaotic maps." *International Journal of Electrical and Computer Engineering (IJECE)* 10, no. 2 (2020, April): 1430–1437. ISSN: 2088–8708. https://doi.org/10.11591/ijece.

[6] Saveetha, P., and S. Arumugam. "Study on improvement in RSA algorithm and its implementation." *International Journal of Computer & Communication Technology* 3, no. 6, 7, 8 (2012). ISSN (PRINT): 0975–7449.

[7] Wang, Huaqun, Qihua Wang, and Debiao He. "Study on improvement in RSA algorithm and its blockchain-based private provable data possession." *IEEE Transactions on Dependable and Secure Computing* (2019). ISSN: 1545–5971. https://doi.org/10.1109/TDSC.2019.2949809.

[8] Farley, Naomi, Robert Fitzpatrick, and Duncan Jones. *BADGER—Blockchain Auditable Distributed (RSA) key GEneRation.* Thales UK Limited, 2019.

[9] Koppu, Srinivas, and V. Madhu Viswanatham. "A fast enhanced secure image Chaotic cryptosystem based on hybrid chaotic magic transform." *Journal of Hindawi Modelling and Simulation in Engineering* (2017). Article ID 7470204, 12. https://doi.org/10.1155/2017/747020.

[10] Al-Juaid, Nouf A., Adnan A. Gutub, and Esam A. Khan. "Enhancing PC data security via combining RSA cryptography and video based steganography." *Journal of Information Security and Cybercrimes Research (JISCR)* 1, no. 1 (June 2018).

[11] Dhakar, Ravi Shankar, Amit Kumar Gupt, and Prashant Sharma. "Modified RSA encryption algorithm (MREA)." In *Second International Conference on Advanced Computing & Communication Technologies*, pp. 426–429. IEEE Computer Society, 2012.

[12] Dr. Hussain, Abdulameer K. "A modified RSA algorithm for security enhancement and redundant messages elimination using K-Nearest neighbor algorithm." *International Journal of Innovative Science, Engineering & Technology* 2, no. 1 (January 2015): 159–163. ISSN (Print): 2320–9798. ISSN 2348–7968.

[13] Ayele1, Amare Anagaw, and Dr. Vuda Sreenivasarao. "A modified RSA encryption technique based on multiple public keys." *International Journal of Innovative Research in Computer and Communication Engineering* 1, no. 4 (June 2013): 859–864.

[14] Jaju, Sangita A., and Santosh S. Chowhan. "A modified RSA algorithm to enhance security for digital signature." *IEEE Explore, International Conference and Workshop on Computing and Communication* (2015). https://doi.org/10.1109/IEMCON.2015.7344493.

[15] Kumar, A., S. S. Tyagi, M. Rana, N. Aggarwal, and P. Bhadana. "A comparative study of public key cryptosystem based on ECC and RSA." *International Journal on Computer Science and Engineering* 3, no. 5 (May 2011): 1904–1909.

[16] ElGamal, T. "A public-key cryptosystem and a signature scheme based on discrete logarithms advances in Cryptology." *Proceedings of CRYPTO* 84 (1985): 10–18.

[17] Han, M., R. Zhang, T. Qiu, M. Xu, and W. Ren. "Multivariate, chaotic time series prediction based on improved grey relational analysis." In *Senior Member.* IEEE, 2017.

[18] Lenstra, Arjen K. *Key Lengths: Contribution to the Handbook of Information Security.* Citibank, N. A., and Technische Universiteit Eindhoven. 1 North Gate Road, Mendham, NJ 07945–3104, U.S.A.

[19] Savari, M., M. Montazerolzohour, and Y. E. Thiam. *Comparison of ECC and RSA Algorithm in Multipurpose Smart Card Application.* IEEE, 2012.

[20] Suma, V. "Security and privacy mechanism using block chain." *Journal of Ubiquitous Computing and Communication Technologies* 1, no. 1 (2019): 45–54. https://doi.org/10.36548/jucct.2019.1.004.

[21] Chandel, Sonali, Wenxuan Cao, Zijing Sun, Jiayi Yang, and Tian-YiNi. "A multi-dimensional adversary analysis of RSA and ECC in blockchain encryption." *Future of Information and Communication Conference* 70: 988–1003.

[22] Ting-ting, G., and L. Tao. *The Implementation of RSA Public-Key Algorithm and RSA Signature Algorithm.* Department of Computer Science, Sichuan University, 1999.

[23] Huh, Seyoung, Sangrae Cho, and Soohyung Kim. "Managing IoT devices using blockchain platform." *International Conference on Advanced Communications Technology* (2017): 464–467.

[24] Saho, Nelson Josias Gb'etoho, and Eugene C. Ezin. *Securing Document by Digital Signature Through RSA and Elliptic Curve Cryptosystems.* Auckland University of Technology, IEEE Xplore, June 2020.

Institutional Technologies for Blockchain

Implications and Policies

Shyam Mohan J.S., S. Ramamoorthy, Narasimha
Krishna Amruth Vemuganti, Vankadara Naga
Venkata Kuladeep, and Raghuram Nadipalli

Contents

6.1 INTRODUCTION

Blockchain technology (introduced during 2008) has an outline that contains transactional data records of the public in various data servers; it is known as a chain and is a peer-to-peer connection. Blockchain is a conditional database pre-existing on different user systems at the same time. It is continuously growing as new assets of recordings, i.e. blocks, are added to it. Every block contains a timestamp and a chain link to the preceding block, so they form a chain. Blockchain is a kind of spreadsheet that contains information about transactions. Every transaction is going to generate a hash (string of numbers and letters). All the transactions are entered in the order of their occurrence. Any change in the order of transactions will create a new hash. A blockchain is effective as it is spread over a huge range of computers [1]. It is that dissemination of administration that makes blockchain an "institutional innovation," unmistakable from modern advancements. Modern innovations are commonly observed through a Schumpeterian focal point, affecting mechanical efficiency by reception into firms. On the other hand, institutional advances should be seen through the perspective of exchange costs and monetary association. The financial impact of the reception of blockchain innovation is portrayed by bringing down check costs and systems administration costs, which are both types of exchange costs. The essential impact of institutional advances—for example, blockchain—is on exchange expenses of financial coordination and administration between systems of financial operators instead of the profitability effect of development on a financial specialist [2]. For business purposes, blockchain holds transactional occupancy, the ability to create secure and real-time communication networks with the parties. This network plays a vital role in networking analysis [3], as shown in Figure 6.1 [4].

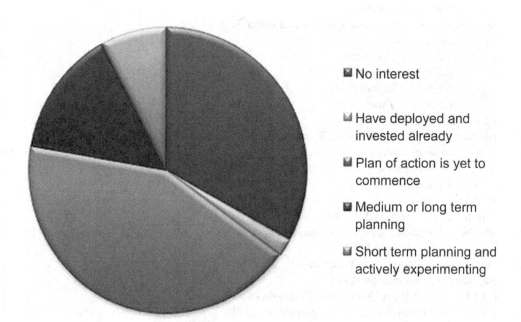

FIGURE 6.1   Blockchain plans, as indicated by Gartner Distinguished Analyst Avivah Litan.

If institutional advancement is best portrayed as another kind of development with another sort of transformative financial procedure, at that point it additionally has suggestions for development strategy. A "cryptoaccommodating" open arrangement is a versatile approach structure to encourage the selection of blockchain strategy by the changed interests occupied with creative practices. While setting up blockchain at the institutional level, utmost care should be taken using the cryptoaccommodating approach. Further, proper government orders, rules, and steps to be carried out as the costs or expenses are borne by the government at an institutional level across the country. Open approaches that serve to encourage blockchain speculation, reception, and utilization empower the rise of pioneering revelations over foundations by various entertainers, increasing existing open development hypotheses and provide better advancement and results [5][6].

6.2 SECURE INSTITUTIONAL FRAMEWORK

The secure institutional framework model introduces secure infrastructure management on the digital space and public services. The model enhances the service quality through the secure blocks, which provide the complicated framework toward the security attacks. The blockchain is a cryptographic secure and distributed ledger; it essentially is a record of transactions similar to the traditional ledger. Blockchain will not come under the classification of Bitcoin. Computerized currency forms are made sure about with cryptography and join them with their role as currency; these are mined but not printed—but they are considered as a bar of digital gold or silver. The endeavor explores the potential benefits of tech like Corda and Quora, the combination of both public as well as private key features that makes a solid advanced character reference dependent on ownership. Blockchain is likewise alluded to as distributed ledger technology (DLT) [7]; it completes the information of any digital data unalterable by using cryptographic hashing and decentralization. One can put this together in a simple way of knowing the blockchain technology function is Google Docs. When one shares a doc, it won't be copied or transferred; rather, it is distributed, which creates a decentralized distribution chain giving access at a similar instance to the pupil to whom the document is shared. There is no waiting process, while all the changes in the document are being recorded in real-time, making changes completely transparent. Blockchain is more confounded than a Google Doc, yet the similarity is adept since it outlines three basic thoughts of the innovation [8], as shown in Figure 6.2.

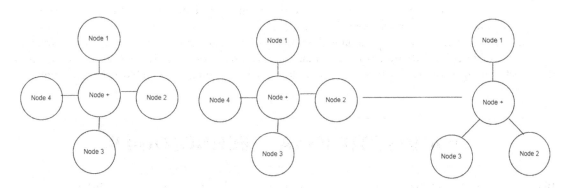

FIGURE 6.2A The blockchain core (top left: centralized network; top middle and right: decentralized network.

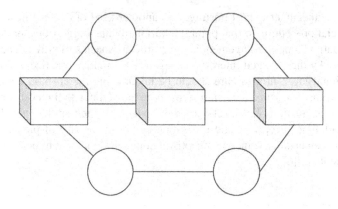

FIGURE 6.2B   A distributed ledger.

TABLE 6.1   A Short Description of DLT

THE NEW NETWORKS	
Distributed ledgers can be public or private, and they may vary in size, shape and structure	Users may or may not be anonymous
Public blockchains	Each user has a copy of the ledger and participates in confirming transactions independently
Require computer processing power to perform transactions (Mining)	At times, permission is required for users to have a copy of the ledger and confirming transactions

6.3 BLOCKCHAIN GOVERNANCE TOWARD PUBLIC SERVICES

The application of the blockchain mechanism and distributed ledgers provides better governance across the global marketing and public services. The model lowers the cost of these services by eliminating complete transaction charges associate with any public services. The utilization of institutional-level technologies opens a number of entrepreneurship models and services to the nation. The global economy and the local marketing space may get improved with this framework. Figure 6.2 and Figure 6.3 show the blockchain core and typical applications of blockchain.

These enterprises require innovation and desperate high grades of efficiency. Example: a survey [9] which was conducted in 2018 by a group says that 600 executives from 15 territories groups are involved; that is, 84% of organizations say that they have at least some collaboration with blockchain technology.

6.4 INSTITUTIONAL TECHNOLOGIES

Blockchain, when implemented at an institutional level, will reduce costs across different systems. Researchers are willing to explain the reason for particular blockchain developments which are contended to produce an incentive by upgrading prior procedures, to use blockchain innovation to build its

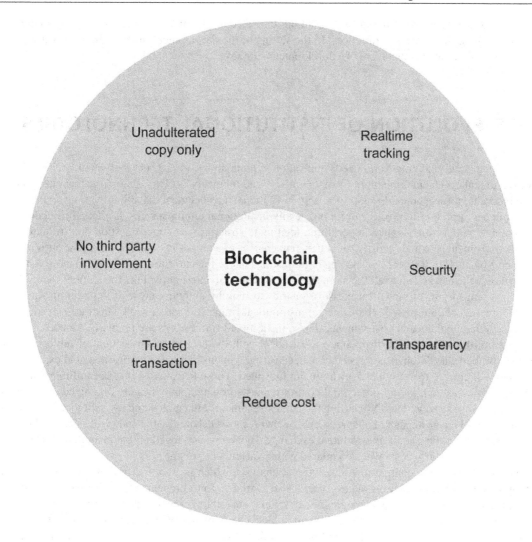

Unadulterated
copy only

Realtime
tracking

No third party
involvement

**Blockchain
technology**

Security

Trusted
transaction

Transparency

Reduce cost

FIGURE 6.3 Applications of blockchain.

value in overseeing abilities, and by empowering various types of exchanges; for example, the block-chain for quality applications. More recent research indicates the highlights potentially problematic that involve blockchain, including supporting completely new sorts of plans of action, empowering new types of administration, and producing new types of eco-friendly applications. Such investigations recommend that blockchain may make esteem by improving existing business forms, as well as by drastically chang-ing how business functions. The term "blockchain" was a popular keyword used in searching the Scopus database. These innovations require various types of organization, restricting and strengthening the limits of satisfactory conduct in the public arena. The difference of institutional cryptofinancial aspects is that the blockchain presents a sixth institutional innovation since it is separated by the idea of its development and operational blockchain conventions (for example, Bitcoin, Ethereum, and Monero) by constraining a scope of connections on web stages they can be considered as a sanctioned and incorporated by an accord calculation into a record held by a system [10]. On the off chance that institutional advancement is best portrayed as another kind of development with another sort of transformative monetary procedure, at that point, this likewise has suggestions for development strategy. A "cryptoaccommodating" open approach is a versatile arrangement structure to encourage the selection of blockchain strategy by the changed interests occupied with creative practices. In the setting of the development of institutional advances, the cryptoaccommodating arrangement is a development strategy.

6.5 EVOLUTION OF INSTITUTIONAL TECHNOLOGIES

The developing and changing world needs innovation of foundations—a way not to supplant organizations, however, to make a greater amount of them, tentatively and innovatively. This is the thing that one can find in the blockchain. Blockchain development is an institutional advancement that allows various foundations to work in one spot. It is completely fit for unfriendly institutional circumstances. It offers the opportunity to make new organizations—new algorithmic legitimate structures, contract question goal frameworks, shared government help and security, and open item courses of action—in contention with the current plan of establishments [11]. Rather than shaping organizations inside the current institutions, business visionaries can utilize the blockchain to all the more adequately work fair and square of the foundations themselves. Blockchain engages institutional business visionaries to look by chipping away at the administration or "defensive level" of enterprise [12], distinctive institutional frameworks assigned by institutional advancements including markets and governments. These institutional frameworks are regularly connected to the custom-built, the ability of the firm supervisor to deal with the exchanges on account of taking care of expenses of the value. Exchange costs emerge because agreements can never be finished, and express that the world will emerge for activities which are not indicated. These firms assist that streamlining on these exchange costs together, giving orders and control requests in which activities are organized all together instead of arranged and variated by settling the fiat. Governments are empowered by institutional administration to control the arrangement of agreement law that resolves debates by fiat and gives open products by modest requirement instead of an exorbitant exchange. By comparing together, the institutional technologies of blockchain reduce costs when compared with a variety of systems.

The tools undertake comparative institutional analysis, which is from the framework developed for institutional innovation structures of governance also available. Entrepreneurs also can create new things; they can also use institutional technologies and develop them for applying new governance structures. Few tests were conducted and proved to be successful in blockchain institutional governance. Blockchain technology, then, protects property rights, and hence, makes it productive-tier entrepreneurship. Figure 6.4 shows the typical blockchain concept.

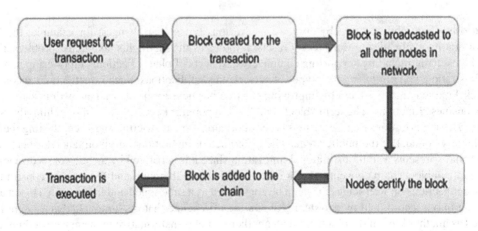

FIGURE 6.4   Blockchain concept.

Blockchain technology at institutional governance is viewed as a rare phenomenon. It is used in almost all sectors. Between 1750 and 1960, the most available forms of technical progress were developments in industrial sectors, getting higher output from lesser inputs. The 20th century witnessed many innovations in financial trade [13].

There are many innovations in technology in connection with blockchain technology. Policymakers of institutions make effective decisions based on dynamic modeling, which leads to a revolution in industrial technologies.

Blockchain reduces the enterprise costs by lowering the overhead expenses. Blockchain-put-together organizations contend concerning different edges with the prior foundations and can empower the covering of variable establishments inside a physical space [14].

6.6 GENERAL VIEW OF BLOCKCHAIN

Blockchain is a creative innovation that will arrive at its maximum capacity in 5–10 years, comprising of innovative design with the aspects of decentralization and distributed ledger technology [15]. Blockchain uses consensus mechanism. Transactions are done using cryptocurrencies without knowing the details of other parties.

Exchange records are put away in the square. Squares are then connected to the chain by utilizing hash esteems, along these lines making a blockchain and giving the most extreme uprightness of information. Each new square is connected to the past one [16]. Blockchain records all the financial transactions as it has immutable ledger to record the same. Figure 6.5 shows the blockchain-based institutional framework.

Each block in a blockchain has a timestamp that is linked with each other using cryptographic rules, therefore enabling the trusted users to work on a distributed peer-to-peer (P2P) network, whereas

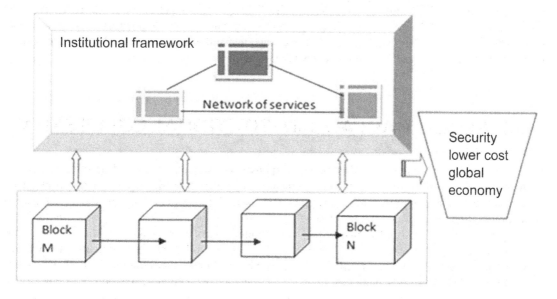

FIGURE 6.5   Blockchain-based institutional framework.

transactions from non-trusting members happen via mining the blocks. Nodes can communicate, cooperate, and collaborate with each other without knowing the details of other nodes [17].

6.7 INSTITUTIONAL FRAMEWORK AND DISTRIBUTED LEDGER TECHNOLOGY

The most recent innovative advancement in the modern division has prompted a change in perspective in producing productivity and operational cost decreases. As a rule, decrease in cost makes to ensure that data security, etc., is not compromised. Most of the institutional frameworks and technologies have technical pitfalls in terms of security by configuration approach, making frameworks exceptionally vulnerable to cyberattacks. Considering these issues, a few of the authors have proposed a building structure for the industrial Internet of Things that provided security against cyberattacks. A secure multiparty computation (SMPC) built on the top of distributed ledger technology (DLT) provides security in the institutional framework. Distributed ledger technology, also famously known as blockchain innovation, has its foundations in a paper composed of an obscure gathering of individuals under the pen name Nakamoto. Bitcoin acts a digital currency that can be traded between clients over the Internet utilizing a shared system. The trading of this advanced money, or some other computerized resource, is accomplished by giving an exchange marked by the client starting the exchange. Moreover, these exchanges are stuffed into squares utilizing a Merkle tree structure, while squares are fastened together by remembering for everyone the hash of the past square. These decentralized exchanges can be confirmed by the hubs, which are associated from one another in a shared system and hand-off new data. Every hub keeps up a duplicate of the appropriated record spoken to by the requested grouping of obstructs that make up the "world state" at a particular point in time. At the end of the day, the "world state" can be seen as a state machine. A distributed ledger must be changed by giving exchanges to one of the companions who will communicate it to the blockchain organizer. Every hub, or a subset of validator hubs, will perform essential approval of this pending exchange, for instance by checking the marks and the configuration. After approval, each pending exchange will be placed in the nearby exchange pool, from where exchanges will be brought to assemble a potential next square. As hubs will have distinctive next square competitors, they run an accord component to conclude who is permitted to propose the following square, along these lines guaranteeing an away form of exchanges. At the point when another square is communicated into the blockchain arrangement, every hub plays out another approval of every exchange inside that specific square by likewise utilizing the state machine data to guarantee consistency [18].

6.8 BLOCKCHAIN AND INSTITUTIONAL COMPLEXITY

Crypto-currencies reduce the overall institutional expenses by providing secure and effective transactions using blockchain technology without the involvement of any third party. Multifaceted nature is an unconquerable obstacle for current institutionalism that is pre-sorted out, as undertaken by the private players. Institutional structures are determined by quality, dynamic frameworks, etc. They were finally superseded by establishments created around cutting-edge frameworks of correspondence. Many of the authors have opposed the trade theories that were made during 1980s and mid-1990s, i.e., before the Internet came into existence. These theories are insufficient while inspecting Internet period foundations. Likewise, the failure of these hypotheses has quite recently been escalated on account of the passionate trouble of reality they depict. Blockchain reduces the human errors or mistakes done during financial transactions [19].

6.8.1 Blockchain Properties

The main properties of blockchain technology:

1. Decentralization.
2. Immutability.
3. Transparency.

6.8.1.1 Decentralization

It is the main part of blockchain. Data is stored inside the blockchain cannot be utilized by anyone but can be shared with other parties [20].

6.8.1.2 Immutability

Immutable means non-tamperable, i.e. remaining unchanged. Any data that individuals put inside the blockchain cannot be tampered with since the applications are decentralized in nature.

6.8.1.3 Transparency

All the transactions in a blockchain are transparent. Transparency has never pre-existed before in the financial system era that includes the responsibility of a decentralized organization. One of the cutting-edge innovations is that institutional financial matters (transactions) are limited by blockchain. Institutional framework using blockchain technology has various aspects like transparency in execution of transactions. It is viewed as homogenous framework with algorithms based on agreements like codification and decentralization [21].

6.9 BLOCKCHAIN USE CASES

Blockchain is used in many industries. Estimates by 2027 suggest that over 10% of the overall GDP will be adopted and taken care by blockchain technology. Table 6.2 shows Industry 4.0 and its use cases. The general market for Industry 4.0 is expected to grow in the coming years.

TABLE 6.2 Blockchain Use Cases

USE CASES	DESCRIPTION
Cryptocurrency	Digital mode of exchange for transactions
Smart contracts	Blockchain-based application
Crowd funding	Direct mode of exchange for capital to investments
Energy markets	Used in solar energy trading with automated payment systems and automated charging stations for electric cars
Smart assets	IPR and other digital transfers

6.10 BLOCKCHAIN APPLICATIONS TOWARD SECURITY AND GOVERNANCE

Blockchain is decentralized in nature, and cryptographic calculation makes it insusceptible to assault. In reality, as everyone knows that digital security has become a key issue for individual, corporate, and national security, blockchain is a possibly progressive innovation. Information stored in a blockchain is based upon the type of blockchain (example: Bitcoin).

6.10.1 Financial Services

Latest reports suggest that the benefit of the board business could reduce expenses by $2.7 billion consistently by moving to blockchain technology. Blockchain plays a vital role in financial sectors like security in transactions, customer screening, information storing, and various other features. Researches across the world are trying various methods and ways for applying blockchain technology for financial services, healthcare, etc. [22].

6.10.2 Smart Contracts

Blockchain and smart contract are used for making digital contracts and keeping the identities of the parties safe and secure. Smart contracts are self-executing, and there is no need for third-party involvement.

6.10.3 Digital IDs

Blockchain provides digital identification for the users, and the identities of the users or the participating parties do not know the other identities. Third-party vendors use digital ID for know-your-customer (KYC) initiatives.

6.10.4 Internet of Things (IoT) and Blockchain

Over 20.4 billion IoT-associated gadgets would be dynamic before the finish of 2020, with certain appraisals indicating the IoT market will reach $3 trillion every year by 2026. Around 90% of the data on the planet today has been made in the past two years alone. Such advancement pace will increase due to:

1. The advancement of the Internet of Things (IoT).
2. The populace build-out.

IoT and Blockchain combinely provides effective use-cases in various applications and sectors in real time. For instance, the appropriated far-off sensor frameworks, which despite their drawbacks are one of the pillars of the mechanical and human turn of events, show that blockchain configuration may improve IoT by constraining its needs and extending its latent limits.

6.10.5 Inter-Planetary File System

Blockchain stores enormous amounts of data of any type or format. For speed of access, the Inter-Planetary File System (IPFS) is utilized. IPFS is an imaginative shared conveyed information arrangement of equivalence that connects all the systems to a single data framework. IPFS is a combination of BitTorrent and Gita, for instance, distributed hash tables (DHT), block exchange system, and version control framework.

6.11 THE NEED FOR BLOCKCHAIN INSTITUTIONAL FRAMEWORK

As mentioned in previous sections, blockchain can be used across industries. It changes the priorities, the flow of transactions, income, and profits, and also ensures growth by benefiting both the company's employees and endusers.

To answer the question of how exactly can anyone use the blockchain in their business:

1. One can store data inside the blockchain that cannot be modified or changed.
2. Most companies have started using blockchain's transparency for supply chain.
3. Many companies have integrated the blockchain with artificial intelligence to expand their business by attracting more customers.

6.11.1 Utility Token Model

The total income of working satisfaction that is received by the consumption of good working goods or services is called utility. The utility token model is shown in Figure 6.6. The token utility has three important properties:

1. Role.
2. Features.
3. Purpose.

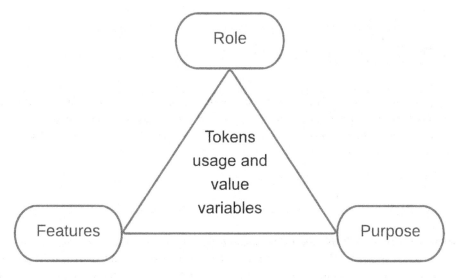

FIGURE 6.6 Tokens usage and variables.

6.12 WORKFLOW OF INSTITUTIONAL FRAMEWORKS

According to the neo-Schumpeterian model, major diagnostic origin means that the unit of variety, determination, and replication is a complex mechanical origination of information. In the first place, the system envelops the five sorts of advancement: authoritative, showcase, info, item, and procedure development. Second, the structure utilizes Schumpeterian meanings of radical and gradual advancement. It is in this feeling the structure is "neo-Schumpeterian." This information is commonly comprehended to allude to the innovative capacities of firms, along these lines shaping a modern populace. Blockchain innovation encourages the enterprising gracefully of monetary foundations as another class of administration development at the financial edge of checking and system costs. Institutional innovations (I), shaping an institutional populace, $\in I$, there exists a populace of different in situational frameworks I.

This entrepreneurial procedure makes an institutional difference. Operators pick institutional frameworks for making appropriations of specific institutional technologies [23]. A strategy to formal agreement hypothesis is situated toward the characterization of ideal agreements, where the characterization of the institutional framework in which they exist are considered. The two operators I and j of capacity $p_{ij}(x_t)$ that speak to the installments to be produced using I to J restrictive upon the acknowledgment of a specific condition of the world x_t (counting activities are taken by j) at time. According to the authors, $I \in I$ is a contribution to a creative work that changes that framework into exchanges costs $c_T(I)$ related to the all-out common expenses of composing, observing, arranging, executing, and upholding an agreement $p_{ij}(x_t)$. For effortlessness, accept exchange costs $c_T(I)$ are steady overall agreements struck inside a framework I. The institutional advances that help frameworks are chosen dependent on the degree to which they moderate exchange costs. The development of institutional innovations utilizes Fisher's essential hypothesis of determination, which expresses that the difference in mean wellness qualities is equivalent to the variety of that trademark over the populace. Hence, for the development of institutional technologies, the pace of progress of average or mean exchanges costs $V_{\in I} c_T(I)$ for institutional frameworks is equivalent to the negative of the fluctuation of those exchanges costs $V_{I \in I}[c_T(I)]$.

$$-\frac{\partial}{\partial t} E_{I \in I} c_T(I) = V_{I \in I}[c_T(I)]$$

As transaction costs decline, wellness improves where variance $V[\cdot]$ is characterized by

$$V_{I \in I}[c_T(I)] = \sum_{I \in I} \frac{|P(I)|}{|P(I)|}[c_T(I) - E_{I \in I} c_T(I)]^2$$

Where, $|P(I)|$ represents the size of the stage for which the framework I give institutional administration, known as the cardinality of the set P(I) of agreements struck which are dependent upon the arrangement of institutional administration governance. The cardinality of the set $P(I) = \bigcup_{I \in I} P(I)$ of all agreements overall frameworks $I \in I$. Thus:

$$E_{I \in I} c_T(I) = \sum_{I \in I} \frac{|P(I)|}{|P(I)|} c_T(I)$$

i.e., the mean transaction cost is mentioned frequently.

The evolution of institutional innovations relies upon the adjustment in the size of the populace with a specific trademark. The components of this set are dictated by the contracting choices of specialists i and j. As these operators or agents choose to differentially contract in one framework over another, they apply developmental determination pressures on the arrangement of institutional technologies. To strike an agreement, agents i and j should obviously at the same time agree upon the type of agreement $p_{ij}(x_t)$ to exist between them. Be that as it may, in the event that has a decent variety in institutional frameworks inside which that agreement might be struck, at that point, the decision of the institutional framework and the contract relationship will be non-trivial [23].

Hence, they occur simultaneously, $p_{ij}(x_t)$ and the institutional arrangement of administration I and the relationship will turn into a tuple $a_{k=i,j} = \{p_{ij}(x_t)I\}$. If and only if the decision of agreement and the institutional framework to which it will be subject can be composed between specialists i and j, that agreement will be struck and remembered for the set of agreements which are dependent upon the institutional arrangement of administration to which i and j have chosen to be subject. Consequently, the equation is

$$p_{ij}(x_t) \in P(I) \Leftrightarrow a_i^* = a_j^* \ \& \ I \in a_i^*, a_j^*$$

The set of contracts that are dependent on the arrangement of institutional administration I at some random point is given as

$$P(I) = \left\{ p_{ij}(x_t) : a_i^* = a_j^* \ \& \ I \in a_i^*, a_j^* \right\}$$

Change in the cardinality rate is given as

$$\frac{\partial |P(I)|}{\partial t} = \frac{\partial}{\partial t} \left| \left\{ p_{ij}(x_t) : a_i^* = a_j^* \ \& \ I \in a_i^*, a_j^* \right\} \right|$$

If this difference is positive in the Institutional system (I), it will be chosen as the innovation in institutional framework. If the difference is negative, the institutional system is rejected, which is illustrated by the Fischer condition.

6.13 BLOCKCHAIN AS INNOVATION POLICY

6.13.1 Role of Blockchain Smart Contracts in the Power Sector

Blockchain brings more advantages in the power sector. Effective implementation of blockchain in the power sector brings rapid changes in transactions related to electricity bills, as it uses the concept of decentralization and executes all the transactions with a high degree of transparency. Consumers can buy or sell their electricity without any third party, as all the transactions are safe and secure. Use of smart meters gives a clear picture of generated data into the blockchain technology as the power is produced, and how to reduce carbon emissions by compensating the green certificates that can be determined and earned instantly. All the transactions happen via smart contracts. On the other hand, it offers several efficient, effective, and compatible solutions to help that transform the power sector, and may ultimately enable truly transitive energy systems [24].

6.13.2 Key Factors to Enable Deployment

Transactions in the digital era along with blockchain technology can be safe and secure. Number of transactions per second (TPS) when deployed by blockchain technology reduces the transaction time. Early conventions which incorporate Bitcoin and Ethereum both bragged about throughputs of about 10TPS and

30TPS, respectively; VisaNet, the concentrated preparing administration for the global Visa arrangement can deal with more than 65,000TPS.

Basic selection in the force segment and others will require a great many TPS, especially as the quantity of web-associated gadgets will in general increase. There exists, nonetheless, a compromise: the more decentralized a system becomes, the harder it is to keep up a higher rate of TPS. In the event that decentralization isn't a significant thought for a specific use case, blockchain is—in all probability—not the fitting device to start exchanges. The upsides and downsides of decentralization and speed are—to a great extent—talked about in different for today. A promising method for handling scaling is the utilization of equal sidechains. This methodology purposefully designates some computational reactions to subordinate chains, which report and notice their outcomes to different squares. This system along these lines accomplishes agreement by equal preparing calculations, contrasted with troubling a solitary chain. This design can likewise address information power guidelines that expect information to be put away inside explicit topographical limits. Certain information can be put away off the blockchain or solidified permitting augmentations in handling times. Most likely, blockchain innovation is as yet creating, and execution and adaptability will keep on improving, with time. There is large gap for blockchain developers in the world, and hence, costs are higher for implementation.

6.13.3 Blockchain and Cryptofriendliness

Changing the expenses of attestation and checking of information constancy, and enabling decentralized frameworks of trading monetary worth, blockchain is consistently conceptualized as an institutional framework class with specified terms and conditions. Policymakers and decision makers do not consider the critical obligations when adopting blockchain to institutional frameworks, unless there are major variations during implementation. Making an accommodative situation for the uncommon arrangement of institutional advances portrayed over a generalizable technique in blockchain known as "cryptokind demeanor" ought to be valued as an improvement method. The scale and level of blockchain-related exercises have pulled in the possibility of policymakers' late years, changing over into the degree of appraisal grouping, administrative and authoritative reactions. It is feasible to watch a design for seeing levels of strategy convenience toward dissipated record improvement. This miracle has been suggested in progressing composing as "cryptoneighborliness," with a more crypto-obliging condition illustrative of techniques for methodology improvement that empower an expansive apportionment and use by various on-screen characters (individuals and social events fusing both private and open fragments) inside the appropriate politico-jurisdictional settings. The advancement of open arrangements concerning blockchain seems aroused by a longing to oblige this innovation inside the boundaries of existing financial and administrative practices and understandings. Efforts of policy to fit blockchain innovation inside the occupant strategy device might be considered as endeavors to limit the expenses of auxiliary institutional modification conceivably presented by this innovation, or—drawing upon bits of knowledge from the open decision or Chicago School administrative speculations—to keep up capacities with regards to monetary lease age through intermediated records.

It is feasible to expand the premise of the crypto-obliging open technique as one of the improvement frameworks that can reshape the entire scenario of trade relations that help in supply chain avoiding the intermediation of any third-party players. It benefits the users or firms, as they are paid directly.

A valuation for blockchain-related methodology as another arm of progression technique prompts thought of the integrative thought of system territories, emphatically concerning the treatment of monetary movement happening using scattered records. For instance, concerning burden assortment, fiscal rule, contention methodology, and strategy, the executives—the widely inclusive methodology structure of the cryptopleasantness model—gives the reason to policymakers to recognize interdependencies of technique settings, and examine discontinuities in the system, from the position of contextualizing attempts to improve the coordinative and authoritative constraints of blockchain as an institutional innovation [25].

6.13.4 Dimensions of Policy Accommodation toward Blockchain

Countenancing the chance of heterogeneous strategy reactions toward the blockchain, it is conceivable to observe differing degrees of strategy. The expression "cryptofriendliness" is planned to embody the degree of strategy convenience toward disseminated record innovation. A more cryptoaccommodating condition reflects styles of strategy advancement that successfully treats blockchain as a positive open door for cryptofinancial improvement. On the other hand, cryptoantagonism is probably going to relate with arrangements that seriously oblige open doors for commitment and learning with blockchain, from strategy convenience (cryptofriendly) to strategy concealment (cryptounfriendly). The bolts in the figure mirror the idea that political locales may move along an understood blockchain strategy commitment range. Relating to these two polar places of cryptobenevolence and cryptodisagreeableness are varying approach packs. Purviews toward the cryptoaccommodating finish of the blockchain strategy range are bound to proactively explain the duty treatment of blockchain tokens and resources, and to not burden those instruments correction ally. Measures endeavoring administrative assurance as for cryptomonetary exercises, without sabotaging the development and advancement of blockchain use and appropriation, are additionally steady with cryptoinvitingness. Different highlights of a cryptoaccommodating strategy condition incorporate the help of utilization cases, the induction of "sandboxing" or other administrative preliminaries of blockchain, just as political proclamations and authority reports featuring the expected advantages of blockchain. There are a few likenesses between strategy cryptoinvitingness and the more nonexclusive position that a sound financial approach improves the capacity of private segment business visionaries aware of new open doors for emergent economic coordination. This proposes that cryptoaccommodating arrangements are bound to be rule-arranged and non-biased in character, empowering all entertainers to adjust, perceive openings, and improve their learning abilities because of blockchain. In another sense, cryptoamicability could give the underpinnings of the standardization of record development, even notwithstanding the dissemination of blocks and failures coming about because of blockchain reception [27].

6.13.5 Matching the Ways of Policy Engagement with Blockchain

By and large, there is a connection between physical or virtual advances, which change crude materials or mental information into new setups for characterized uses or purposes, and social advancements which are the foundations, mores, and practices which request human participation. An open approach, comprehended as a type of social innovation, could animate or impede the reception and speed of innovative change inside the economy. By doling out the status of legitimacy toward the utilization of innovation, and telling non-state entertainers to watch any lawful norms, therefore, set up, open strategies can, without a doubt, shape open mentalities and regard toward certain physical or virtual innovative setups. Policy entrepreneurship impacts mechanical change and development through the sanctioning of strategy change; however, by affecting view of open interest. Is the engendering of dispersed record advancements predictable with the advancement of the prosperity of the individuals from the network? No doubt the response to such an inquiry changes, depending upon whether policymakers are seeking after, fundamentally, a cryptofriendliness or cryptounfriendliness arrangement toward blockchain.

Policymakers, paying little heed to their blockchain perspectives, have been conveying to possible clients and individuals from the overall population the same about the expected dangers encompassing the utilization of blockchain. Not exclusively are blockchain exchanges defenseless to extortion; what's more, robbery, as has appeared comparable to brought-together symbolic trades, yet a few blockchain-empowered exercises might be identified with unlawful activity, for example, tax evasion. A key contrast between strategy correspondence in cryptofriendly and cryptounfriendly edges is that, in the first, the possible advantages of blockchain are bound to be compared against the articulation of dangers, while in the last, the benefits are—to a great extent—left implicit. To the degree that singular convictions about the attractive quality of mechanical change are in any event incompletely encircled by the perspectives of others, it follows that strategy talks may influence the rate and speed of blockchain appropriation.

6.14 CONCLUSION

The proposed research model highlighted the application of blockchain-based institutional technology in various governance and public services. The quality of the services improved due to the enormous amount of support extended by blockchain and its associated components. The various aspects of institutional technology and its application environments are discussed in this chapter. The proposed blockchain-based framework not only improves the quality; it is also strength the process of global marketing services. Records state that institutional advancements have been in the space of history specialists; however, not just in the developing economy. This is because institutional manifestations have been—for the most part—differentiable and pitiful occasions punctuated by many years of steadiness. The significance of blockchain innovation brings up significant issues to this specific institutional framework. Blockchains provide a new method of security by decentralization. Developers have created blockchain financial models for institutional frameworks by using the latest technologies. Institutional advances show a troublesome portrayal issue. The proposed model catches the procedure of blockchain development, accentuating the coordination issues and system externalities portrayed around the selection of the institutional technology.

REFERENCES

[1] Gaikwad, Akshay S. "Overview of blockchain." *International Journal for Research in Applied Science & Engineering Technology* 8, no. VI (2020): 2268–2272. ISSN: 2321-9653.

[2] Davidson, S., P. de Filippi, and J. Potts. " Blockchains and the economic institutions of capitalism." *Journal of Institutional Economics* 14, no. 4 (2018): 639–658.

[3] Catalini, C., and J. S. Gans. " Some simple economics of the blockchain." *Communications of the ACM* 63, no. 7 (2020): 80–90.

[4] Computer World.www.computerworld.com/article/3191077/what-is-blockchain-the-complete- guide.html.

[5] Berg, C., S. Davidson, and J. Potts. "Towards crypto-friendly public policy." *Markets, Communications Networks, and Algorithmic Reality* 1 (2019): 215–232. https://doi.org/10.1142/9781786346391_0011.

[6] Novak, M. "Crypto-friendliness: Understanding blockchain public policy." *Journal of Entrepreneurship and Public Policy* 1 (2018): 1–26. http://dx.doi.org/10.2139/ssrn.3215629.

[7] Cheng, S., et al. "Research on application model of blockchain technology in the distributed electricity market." *IOP Conference Series: Earth and Environmental Science* 93 (2017): 012065.

[8] Subramanian, N., et al. *Blockchain and Supply Chain Logistics*. 1st Edition. Palgrave Pivot, 2020. https://doi.org/10.1007/978-3-030-47531-4.

[9] PWC-Global. www.pwc.com/blockchainsurvey.

[10] Allen, Darcy W. E., et al. "Blockchain and the evolution of institutional technologies: Implications for innovation policy." *Research Policy* 49 (2019).

[11] Bylund, P. L. "The firm vs. the market: Demonizing the transaction cost theories of Coase and Williamson." *Strategic Management Review* (2019): 1–50.

[12] Aldrich, H. "Heroes, villains, and fools: Institutional entrepreneurship, NOT institutional entrepreneurs." *Entrepreneurship Research Journal* 1, no. 2 (2011): 2. https://doi.org/10.2202/2157-5665.1024.

[13] Parker, G. G., et al. *Platform Revolution: How Networked Markets Are Transforming the Economy and How to Make Them Work for you*. WW Norton & Company, 2016.

[14] MacDonald, T., D. Allen, J. and Potts. "Blockchains and the boundaries of self-organized economies: predictions for the future of banking." In *Banking Beyond Banks and Money: A Guide to Banking Services in the Twenty First Century* (2016). SSRN. http://dx.doi.org/10.2139/ssrn.2749514.

[15] Tasca, P. "Token-Based Business Models." In Lynn, T., Mooney, J., Rosati, P., and Cummins, M. (eds.). *Disrupting Finance. Palgrave Studies in Digital Business & Enabling Technologies.* Palgrave Pivot, 2019. https://doi.org/10.1007/978-3-030-02330-0_9.

[16] Jovovic, I., S. Husnjak, I. Forenbacher, and S. Maček. "Innovative Application of 5G and Blockchain Technology in Industry 4.0." *Industrial Networks and Intelligent Systems* 6 (2019): 1–6. https://doi.org/10.4108/eai.28-3-2019.157122.

[17] Ismail, L., H. Hameed, M. Alshamsi, M. Alhammadi, and N. Aldhanhani. "Towards a blockchain deployment at UAE university: Performance evaluation and blockchain taxonomy." In *ICBCT 2019: Proceedings of the 2019 International Conference on Blockchain Technology,* 2019. https://doi.org/10.1145/3320154.3320156.

[18] Lupascu, C., A. Lupascu, and I. Bica. "DLT based authentication framework for industrial IoT devices." *Sensors* 20, no. 9 (2020): 2621. https://doi.org/10.3390/s20092621.

[19] Frolov, D. "Blockchain and institutional complexity: an extended institutional approach." *Journal of Institutional Economics* 17 (2020): 1–16. https://doi.org/10.1017/S1744137420000272.

[20] Atlam, H., A. Alenezi, M. Alassafi, and G. Wills. "Blockchain with Internet of things: benefits, challenges and future directions." *International Journal of Intelligent Systems and Applications* (2018). https://doi.org/10.10.5815/ijisa.2018.06.05.

[21] Frolov, D. "Blockchain and institutional complexity: An extended institutional approach." *Journal of Institutional Economics* 17, no. 1 (2021): 21–36. https://doi.org/10.1017/S1744137420000272

[22] Casino, F., T. K. Dasaklis, and C. Patsakis. "A systematic literature review of blockchain-based applications: Current status, classification and open issues." *Telematics and Informatics* 36 (2019): 55–81. ISSN 0736-5853. https://doi.org/10.1016/j.tele.2018.11.006.

[23] Chowdhury, E. K. "Transformation of business model through blockchain technology." *The Cost and Management* 47, no. 05 (2019). ISSN1817-5090.

[24] Windrum, P., and M. García-Goñi. "A neo-Schumpeterian model of health services innovation." *Research Policy* 37, no. 4 (2008): 649–672. ISSN 0048-7333. https://doi.org/10.1016/j.respol.2007.12.011.

[25] Kaal, W. A., and C. Calcaterra. "Crypto Transaction Dispute Resolution." *Business Lawyer,* 2018, U of St. Thomas (Minnesota) Legal Studies Research Paper No. 17-12 (June 26, (2017). http://dx.doi.org/10.2139/ssrn.2992962.

[26] IRENA. "Innovation landscape brief: Blockchain", In *International Renewable Energy Agency,* IRENA, 2019. ISBN 978-92-9260-117-1

[27] Andoni, M., V. Robu, D. Flynn, S. Abram, D. Geach, D. Jenkins, P. McCallum, and A. Peacock. "Blockchain technology in the energy sector: A systematic review of challenges and opportunities." *Renewable and Sustainable Energy Reviews* 100 (2019): 143–174. ISSN 1364-0321. https://doi.org/10.1016/j.rser.2018.10.014.

[28] Schot, J., and W. Edward Steinmueller. "Three frames for innovation policy: R&D, systems of innovation and transformative change." *Research Policy* 47, no. 9 (2018): 1554–1567. ISSN 0048-7333. https://doi.org/10.1016/j.respol.2018.08.011.

Two-Fold Security Model Using 2D-Vector Key Bunch and Privacy Preservation of the EHRs in the Distributed Network Involving Blockchain

7

Shirisha Kakarla, Geeta Kakarla, and D. Narsinga Rao

Contents

7.1 INTRODUCTION

In recent decades, a tremendous surge is observed in the production of electronic equipment and gadgets, especially in the developed and developing countries, catering to the needs of specific domains. With the developments in the networking infrastructure and the computing taking place ubiquitously, the flow and sharing of the electronic information has made every organization, office, and agency almost paperless [1]. The primary, secondary, and tertiary sectors are adopting the technological evolution, with primary sectors involving the agriculture, aqua-culture, and mining activities; the secondary sector referring to product manufacturing establishments which use raw produce; and the tertiary sector including financial institutions, the retail industry, education institutions, healthcare organizations, hospitality and recreation centers, media and communications, IT (information technology) and ITES (IT-enabled services), and supply of civic amenities. With the establishments, sized bigger or smaller in terms of personnel, investments made, and/or space, the data remains the asset and is considered to be sensitive. Although the technological advancement of the paperless recording of the details has its own pros, it faces few inherent challenges. It needs to be safeguarded against theft, misappropriations, or eventualities by internal or external handlers.

In the case of the healthcare industry, one of the services providing sectors, the information stored in the electronic health records (EHRs) is often critical, detailing the diagnosis, treatment, and history of the illness and other private and sensitive health factors of the patients. In the course of seeking treatment, patients may visit multiple hospitals and diagnostic centers. At each, the patient's subjected details are registered. Consent from the patients is obtained to liberate the anonymized information to the concerned stakeholders for the greater good, thus abiding by the legislative laws of restoring the patient's private and sensitive data. The patient's attributes can be classified into three types, namely, explicit identifiers (EIs), quasi-identifiers (QIs) and sensitive identifiers (SIs). The EIs are the patient's name and other unique credentials by which a patient may be directly identified. QIs relate to the attributes which can be combined together to re-identify an entity uniquely in the dataset. A few examples of QIs are race, ethnicity, occupation, hospital name, dates of hospital visit, admission, discharge, and languages spoken. Financial details and the medical condition are among the few examples of the SIs. The risks involved with the loss of the health data is inevitable and remains vulnerable to hacking, malicious tampering, and natural disasters.

Privacy of the sensitive personal data stored in the EHRs and shared across the public channels must indeed be protected from misuse and illicit gains [2]. In recent times, hacking into data stores that manage the personalized medical records of the patients in the healthcare organization, and stealing the large amount of the private healthcare information for financial gains or propelling bigger attacks like ransomware, have become one of the widely induced data breaching practices used by attackers [3]. From the reports of the healthcare data breaches, each with more than 500 records, it is found that the daily average of breaches has increased to 1.76 from an earlier level of one. Those breaches [4][5] have resulted in the theft of personal data, loss, exposure, or impermissible disclosure for financial gains. With the healthcare data being more susceptible, the loads of the EHRs are breached at the behest of the gullible personnel or the accidental leakage of the credentials leading to compromise of the private information. The ever-increasing usage of the smart devices and Internet connectivity round the clock, and remote operation of the applications and data, have additionally led to oblivious dissipation, along with the ease-of-use provisions [6].

The techniques are discussed in this chapter to safeguard the privacy of the sensitive fields of the healthcare dataset. For privacy preservation of the considered EHRs, the k-anonymity technique is used to anonymize the individuals. In this, the quasi-identifiers (QIs) are handled with suppression and generalization technique. By doing so, the utility of the data is maintained for potential study by the stakeholders with no revelation of the private identifiers of the patient. The sanitized data of the EHR dataset of the medical center is blockchained before sharing.

In this chapter, the model developed is contributing to the two-fold security of the EHRs in the distributed environment. First, the cryptic procedures are implemented to secure the confidential information of the EHRs using the 2D-vector key bunch. The procedures designed are computationally low cost and robust. Second, the privacy of the quasi-identifiers is preserved in the records. The resulting EHRs are then stored in the blockchain using the DApp. In Section 7.2, a literature review is presented for the existing privacy-preserving and security mechanisms. In Section 7.3, healthcare information systems and blockchain technology are briefed. The proposed framework is presented in detail in the Section 7.4, with installation and performance details in Section 7.5. Security analysis in relevance to the popular attacks is in Section 7.6, and conclusions with future scope are made in Section 7.7.

7.2 EXISTING PRIVACY-PRESERVING AND SECURITY MECHANISMS

In this section, the available and researched privacy-preserving mechanisms used for the sensitive data are detailed. The sharing of datasets containing some sensitive fields like personal data of the data owner—such as financial status, residential details, health history, his/her identifiable information—over public Internet channels must essentially seal the susceptible data and thwart its misuse. The procedures widely used [7] for preserving the privacy of the sensitive information of the entities are:

- k-anonymity.
- l-diversity.
- t-closeness.
- Randomization.

7.2.1 k-Anonymity

A version of dataset is said to observe the k-anonymity property [8][9] in case a tuple is indistinguishable from at least $(k-1)$ similar tuples existing in the same dataset. The *k-anonymization* technique mainly handles the quasi-identifiers (QI) of the dataset. The equation governing *k-anonymity* property within a given arbitrary dataset T where $\forall t \in T, \exists (t_{i_1}, t_{i_2}, \dots t_{i_{k-1}}) \in T$ such that $t[C] = t_{i_1}[C] \cup t_{i_2}[C] \cup \dots \cup t_{i_{k-1}}[C], \forall C \in QI$. The application of *k-anonymization* can be performed in either of two techniques, namely suppression and generalization. In suppression technique, certain values of the attributes are replaced by a special character. All or some values of the attribute are affected accordingly to conceal the identity of an individual. In the latter, individual values of the attributes are replaced with a broader category, such as range or bin representation, to get the anonymized table T^*, with $T_1 \cup T_2 \cup \cdots \cup T_n = T^*$ for communicating with the other stakeholders.

7.2.2 l-Diversity

Unlike k-anonymity, the *l-diversity* technique [10] handles sensitive attributes of the dataset, namely disease and financial status. The dataset obtained after *k-anonymization* would contain the same values under each of the QIs in $\forall T_i | 1 \leq i \leq n$. However, to introduce more privacy, the l-diversity technique ensure to re-distribute the tuples in T^*, in such a way that in each T_1^*, the order under each sensitive attribute would be at least $(l-1)$ distinct values. The governing equation followed by each $T_1^* | 1 \leq i \leq n$ to be diverse is given by the following:

$$-\sum_{s \in S} p\left(T_1^*, s\right) \log\left(p\left(T_1^*, s\right)\right) \geq \log(l)$$

where $p\left(T_1^*, s\right) = \dfrac{n\left(T_1^*, s\right)}{\sum\limits_{s' \in S} n\left(T_1^*, s'\right)}$ indicates the ratio of the records in the T_1^*, with sensitive attribute.

7.2.3 t-Closeness

T-closeness [11] is the procedures adopted to ensure the threshold difference between the contents of the T^* with that of the $T_1^* | 1 \leq i \leq n$ to obtain $T_{t-close}^*$. Thus, an equivalence class has t-closeness if the distance between the distribution of a sensitive attribute in this class and the distribution of the attribute in the whole table is no more than a threshold t.

A table is said to have t-closeness if all equivalence classes have t-closeness.

7.2.4 Randomization

One of the well-known techniques to preserve the privacy of an individual is to introduce a certain amount of the noise in the dataset. The nature, position, and type of the noise to be introduced in the raw data are discretionary to the beholder of the data. The original aggregate can be reconstructed by removing the noise introduced from the inferences drawn.

7.3 HEALTHCARE INFORMATION SYSTEMS AND SECURITY MODELS ADOPTED WORLDWIDE

The healthcare ecosystem involves the central entity as patient registered with the healthcare unit and the various stakeholders providing services directly and indirectly in the treatment and operational feasibility of the ecosystem. The distributed ledger system provides storage and access feasibility for the classified information of the healthcare system through blockchain. The types of the blockchain and features are described with the application scenario in this section.

7.3.1 Stakeholders and Threats in the Healthcare Environment

Very often, the details of the patients registered with a hospital or a medical-care unit are needed to be shared among the stakeholders of the healthcare environment, like healthcare professionals, clinical staff and care takers. Exchange of EHRs effectively speeds up the diagnostic process, enhances the patient care and cooperation, and improves the practice efficiency as the patients' health information remain accessible all the time. The other participatory stakeholders [12] in this ecosystem, as shown in Figure 7.1, are the insurance firms, governmental bodies, and research organizations. The available data utilized in the direction of research offer potential possibilities for the betterment of humanity like inventing new drugs or antidotes, designing sophisticated medical equipment, amending strategic policies/schemes for the poor, or building enhanced medical infrastructure for providing seamless services to the society at affordable prices. However, the entrusted parties with whom the EHRs are shared, at times, delegate the tasks to the third party, thereby raising a serious concern of mishandling of the private and sensitive data of the patients registered with the hospital for personal or financial gain.

The conventional model of storing the EHRs on the centralized database servers remains vulnerable to attacks and misuse, either deliberate or accidental. With the Internet spread widely, the EHRs are accessible, thereby defying the geographic boundaries of the data staged or origin. However, storing the data at a single location would raise serious concerns during data access in terms of the network congestion leading to delayed response times, low throughput, and at times, server failure. The management of sensitive data would further demand the security framework to be placed on the data storage units, as well as on the transmission. Regular risk assessments are needed for identifying any potential threats and essentially designing mitigation techniques. The security procedures, in order to restore privacy and confidentiality, may involve cryptic procedures and access control policies. Although the cryptographic procedures provide much solace in maintaining the secrecy of the data during transmission over public networks, the privacy of the same remains at stake at the receiver end. As a matter of fact, the procedures to preserve the data confidentiality are universally the same, whereas the privacy laws and the related procedures adopted are geographically varied.

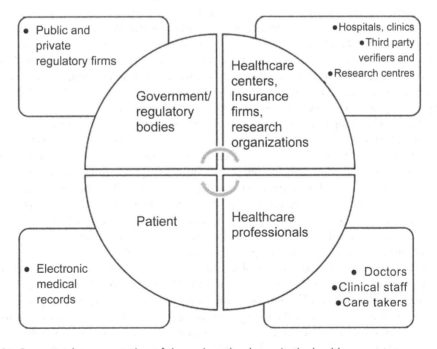

FIGURE 7.1   Conceptual representation of the major role-players in the healthcare system.

7.3.2 Distributed Ledger System through Blockchain and its Classification

Blockchain technology [13] is revolutionary of the disruptive technologies with its promising features to address a multitude of questions in trustless scenarios. It can be plainly described as a technology to decentralize data storage so that it cannot be owned, controlled, or manipulated by a central actor, and so that it can be shared in trustworthy manner. The blockchain acts as distributed ledger for recording the provenance of the digital entity, regarded as a digital asset. The changes imperative to be carried out in the committed data must have the consensus of all the blockchained nodes. This would entrust all the players in the blockchain network to vote in the consensus exercise.

According to Orkutt [14], "The whole point of using a blockchain is to let people—in particular, people who don't trust one another—share valuable data in a secure, tamperproof way." Particularly, blockchain potentially cuts down the risks and squashes out the fraud of non-repudiated records in the data storage by bringing in absolute transparency and scalability.

In each block of the blockchain network, the records are stored pertaining to the transactions between two parties, in a verifiable and immutable manner. Blockchain is considered to be open source, by virtue of the open source nature of the blockchain protocols and its code development. The other important feature offered by the blockchain is that it acts as a "distributed ledger," which refers to the fact that the blocks of data on which transactions are recorded are shared to several participants in the network, with no single node/entity either fully owning or controlling it. Whenever the entities enter into the blockchain, they are agreed upon the immutability condition of the transaction recorded into the distributed ledger. The cryptographic primitives and the algorithmic rules used for developing blockchain models allow the transactional data be verifiable and helps ensure the permanency of the records. The different types of blockchain available for development are private, public, consortium, and hybrid blockchain, with diagrammatic models presented in Figure 7.2.

> *Private blockchain:* The private blockchain is custom-built among the entrusted stakeholders with permissions to access and append. The participating entities are provided with the access rights by the network administrators, and unlike peer-to-peer decentralized database systems, the validators ensure the appending/updating of the nodes on the blockchain by running the consensus protocols. The private blockchain network is also widely termed as distributed ledger. As the number of participants is smaller, the characteristic features of the private blockchain are faster transactions, higher scalability, and better consensus due to the usage of different consensus algorithm such as Byzantine fault tolerance (BFT). Ripple (XRP) and Hyperledger are popular platforms for developing private blockchain networks.
>
> *Public blockchain:* An open blockchain network with absolutely no access restrictions is termed as public blockchain. Usually, public blockchains support ad hoc compute clusters. Anybody on the Internet can access its content, append their transactions, and be a validator. Usually, the miners lease the processing power of their mining equipment to execute proof of stake (PoS) or proof of work (PoW) algorithms, and are rewarded with economic incentives in the form of the cryptocurrencies remotely from digital wallets. Comparative to the private blockchain networks, the order of magnitude of a public blockchain is lesser. The well-known platform for developing public blockchain is Ethereum, and the popular public cryptocurrency is Bitcoin, involving proof of stake and proof of work, respectively.
>
> *Consortium blockchain:* Unlike private blockchain in which a single organization governs the data/blocks of the blockchain, the consortium blockchain is a blockchain technology which is managed and controlled by multiple organizations. Being a permissioned platform, a pre-designated set of nodes, out of the total participating nodes, validate every block on the blockchain by exercising the consensus process. In a way, every other organization of the preselected set on the platform will keep a check on the validity of the blocks and the new appends. The

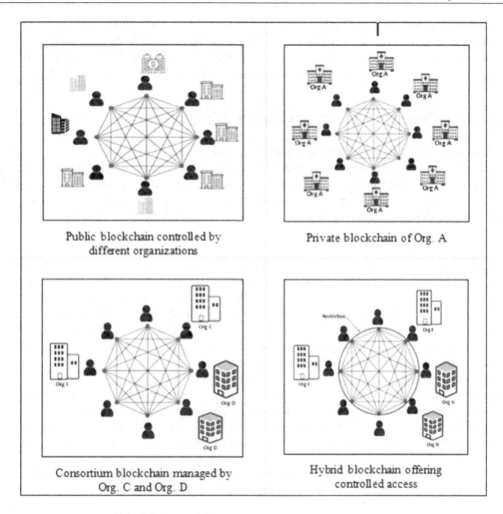

FIGURE 7.2   Four types of blockchain models.

whole concept of consortium blockchain is developed to help enterprises work on the issues and collaborate with each other. Quorum, Hyperledger and Corda provide platforms to develop consortium blockchains.

Hybrid blockchain: A hybrid blockchain is best defined as the combination of good features of the private and public blockchains, thereby offering centralized and decentralized properties. The hybrid blockchain [15] is entirely customizable and exact workings of the chain can vary based on which aspects of centralization and decentralization are used. The participating entities can decide who can validate the data in the blockchain or which transactions are to be made public. Ideally, a hybrid blockchain tends to offer controlled access and freedom at the same time. A distinguishable feature of the hybrid blockchain is that it is not open to everyone, but still offers the fundamental qualities of security, transparency, and integrity.

Sidechain: Designated as a secondary blockchain with parallel ledger to the primary blockchain and practicing the independent operations, the sidechains are an alternate means of record keeping, alternate consensus algorithm, and validations. The digital assets, i.e. entries of the blocks in the main chain, can be linked to and from the sidechain. The two-way channel between the sidechain and the primary chain enables the exchange of digital information with a pre-agreed order from the primary chain to the sidechain. The reverse happens when moving back from a sidechain to the main chain.

A variety of sectors, including healthcare [16], are favoring blockchain technology for its features of better transparency and efficiency. For general healthcare management, medical supplies inventory, clinical trial outcomes, regulation compliance, supervising drugs, and recording diagnostic and pathological results, the usage of the ledger can revolutionize the secure sharing of confidential private data.

7.3.3 EHRs Security through Public Blockchain

With the possibility of using blockchain technology, the storage and management of healthcare data has raised interest among developers and academics [17]. Although the usage of the blockchain is widely used for the financial sector and banking institutions, in our work, our focus remains on creating a blockchain for storing the EHRs of the patients, with their follow-up records with all diagnostic test reports, and implementing the same practically which can be effectively used for sharing among the stakeholders with no scope for discontent.

The confidentiality of the sensitive fields identified in the EHRs are kept up by introducing cryptic procedures using key bunch matrix block cipher technique. The privacy-preserving technique of k-anonymization is used for the QIs to maintain the anonymity of the patients' identifiable data stored in the EHRs. The modified EHRs are thus chained into the distributed ledger, which can be shared among the authorized data seekers. The immutable feature of the ledger which also maintain transparently the history of all the patients enrolled with a healthcare network (like doctors' details, patient modifying permissions, uploading reports and consultations, and sharing data for research) will provide the privacy to the identifiable details, as desired.

Rather than depending upon the centralized control for the healthcare data management as in traditional set up, blockchain technology will guarantee fair access to the different actors of the network with privacy of patients' sensitive data. A transaction, in the healthcare environment, can be viewed as a patient's information exchanged among the connected peers. A state of the blockchain network can be represented as the set of transactions that are created and added as the block to the existing network.

The key benefits of applying the blockchain technology in healthcare are the following: verifiable and immutable transactions; tamper resistance, transparency, and integrity of distributed sensitive medical data. This is mainly achieved by employing consensus protocol and cryptographic primitives such as hashing and digital signatures [18].

7.3.4 Blockchain Development Platform Using Ethereum

In its simplest form, each block of a blockchain can be viewed as a data structure with the following fields in general: block header, transaction counter, and transaction(s). The block header additionally stores three types of metadata. First is the hash of the parent block, also termed as previous hash. Second, data pertaining to the mining procedure of a new block are difficulty, timestamp, and nonce. The difficulty and nonce are the input parameters for mining the new block to be added to the blockchain, and the timestamp is the time at which block is added. Third, the hash value generated from the SHA-256 cryptographic algorithm, summarizing all the transactions in the block. The transaction counter is the unique sequence identifier of the block, whereas the transaction is the actual data record stored. The hash of the current block is the previous hash of the next block. The diagrammatic representation of the blocks in the blockchain are shown in Figure 7.3.

For inclusion, the agreed-upon consensus algorithm is executed by the miners to validate the new transaction for its authenticity, and the miners are rewarded with cryptocurrencies.

Ethereum [19] is a distributed and open source blockchain development platform, formally introduced in 2015, to create a trustless smart contract model. The four core technological building blocks of Ethereum are peer-to-peer networking, Turing-complete virtual machine, cryptographic tokens

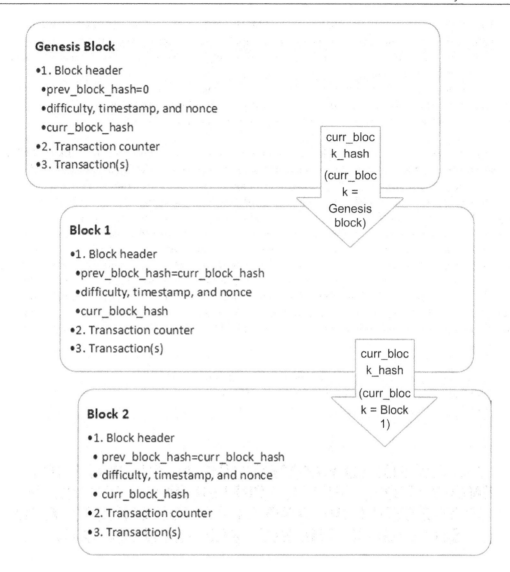

FIGURE 7.3 Structural representation of a blockchain.

and addresses, and consensus algorithms. The peer-to-peer networking approach on the Ethereum platform makes the model developed as distributed. A customized blockchain can be developed using the Solidity programming language, thereby implementing the smart contracts. Ether, as its own cryptocurrency, is used for sharing between accounts connected on Ethereum blockchain. Information exchange happens among the entities with the transaction entry into the blocks of the Ethereum blockchain.

A transaction is a record of the details of give-and-take among the two entities having the following formal properties:

- From: Sender address (20 bytes).
- To: Recipient address (20 bytes).
- Value: The fund amount transferred from sender to recipient.
- Data (optional): Contains the message that is being sent to the recipient.

- Gas: For every transaction entered into the blockchain, the sender needs to pay some fees—called gas—to the miner who expends his computational power to generate hash value of the new transaction and club it with the existing transactions. Every transaction contains the gas limit and gas price in it.
- Gas limit: The maximum amount of gas that can be paid for this transaction.
- Gas price: The amount of gas the sender is willing to pay for this transaction.
- Timestamp: The date and time of the transaction entered into the blockchain.

In order to perform any task on the blockchain, a program called *smart contract* is implemented which is executed when the users send the transactions. In Ethereum blockchain development, Solidity language is used for writing the smart contracts. These can be compiled using Turing-complete virtual machine, or Ethereum Virtual Machine (EVM), bytecode, executed and deployed on the Ethereum blockchain. Once deployed, the transaction become resistant to any kind of tampering or non-repudiation.

Inter-Planetary File System (IPFS) protocol is used in the peer-to-peer network for data storage. It generates an identifier comprising of cryptographic tokens and addresses that protects the data from alteration. In negotiation, to make changes to the data stored on IPFS, the identifier has to be changed using consensus algorithm. It is unique and is used for identification of stored data file on the IPFS. This secure storage strategy of IPFS protocol makes it a favorable choice for storing critical and sensitive data. The cryptographic hash that is generated could be stored on the decentralized application to reduce the exhaustive computational operations over the blockchain. The following properties offered by the IPFS protocols are:

- Files stored on IPFS are assigned a unique cryptographic hash.
- Duplicate files are not allowed to exist on the IPFS network.
- A node on the network stores content and index information of the node.

7.4 PROPOSED FRAMEWORK INVOLVING EHRS ENCRYPTION, PRIVACY-PRESERVING TECHNIQUE FOR THE SENSITIVE AND QUASI-IDENTIFIERS, AND STORAGE IN THE BLOCKCHAIN NETWORK

In this section, the mathematical models and cryptographic procedures developed are presented for enciphering the confidential fields of the patient dataset. First, the name of the person and unique ID, like Aadhar number, are individually encrypted, as these are the explicit identifiers which can directly identify a particular person. For preserving the privacy of the quasi-identifiers, k-anonymization technique is elaborated further. To embed the resultants of the patients' information in the blockchain, the pseudo-codes developed are discussed.

7.4.1 Handling Confidentiality of the Sensitive Fields of EHRs Involving Key Bunch Matrix Block Cipher

Presently, the objective to render confidentiality to the sensitive and personal attributes in the patients' records is done by developing a key-based substitution block cipher technique [20] involving a key bunch encryption matrix [21]. The procedure must be computationally cost economic, as well as strong, to thwart the majority of cryptographic attacks. The key-based substitution, presented here, strengthens the cipher in a significant manner.

Consider a sensitive feature value of a patient record, say Pt_k, as S, which can be represented in the matrix form of decimal numbers lying in [0–255], corresponding to the EBCDIC code of the characters:

$$S = \left[s_{ij} \right], i = 1...n, j = 1...n, \tag{7.4.1}$$

Let the encryption key bunch matrix Key_Enc be represented as

$$Key\_Enc = \left[e_{ij} \right], i = 1...n, j = 1...n, \tag{7.4.2}$$

in which each e_{ij} is an odd number lying in [1–255]. The corresponding decryption key bunch matrix, with the governing principle of $(\times) \, mod \, 256 = 1$, can be expressed as

$$Key\_Dec = \left[d_{ij} \right], i = 1...n, j = 1...n, \tag{7.4.3}$$

wherein each d_{ij} is an odd number lying in [1–255]. It may be noted that each d_{ij} can be computed uniquely for the e_{ij} by the governing principle. The basic equations used in the cryptic procedures are expressed as shown following:

$$C = [c_{ij}] = [e_{ij} \times s_{ij}] \, mod \, 256, i = 1...n, j = 1...n \tag{7.4.4}$$

and

$$S = [s_{ij}] = [d_{ij} \times c_{ij}] \, mod \, 256, i = 1...n, j = 1...n. \tag{7.4.5}$$

With the number of iterations considered as r, taken here as 16, the procedures used in the encryption and the decryption are expressed in the pseudo-codes given hereunder. The insights into the key-dependant substitution process are provided illustratively further. The function $Rev\_Substitute()$ of the decryption procedure is the reversed process of the function $Substitute()$. The function $Mult()$ computes the corresponding elements of the Key_Dec matrix of the given Key_Enc.

ENCRYPTION PSEUDO-CODE	DECRYPTION PSEUDO-CODE
1. Read S,Key_Enc,K,n,r	1. Read C,Key_Enc,K,n,r
2. For k = 1 … r do	2. Key_Dec = Mult(Key_Enc)
begin	3. For k = 1 … r do
3. For i = 1 … n do	begin
begin	4. C = Rev_Substitute(C)
4. For j=1 … n do	5. For i = 1 … n do
begin	begin
5. s_{ij} = (e_{ij} × s_{ij}) mod 256	6. For j = 1 … n do
end	begin
end	7. c_{ij} = (d_{ij} × c_{ij}) mod 256
6. S = [s_{ij}]	end
7. S = Substitute(S)	end
end	8. C = [c_{ij}]
8. C = S	end
9. Write(C)	9. S = C
	10. Write (S)

The key-based $Subsitute()$, termed as Key_Sub, function developed is typically described using an example. An arbitrary key K in the range of [1–255] follows, with the form as:

$$K = \begin{bmatrix} 209 & 113 & 200 & 217 \\ 127 & 184 & 55 & 131 \\ 59 & 216 & 237 & 218 \\ 191 & 26 & 235 & 139 \end{bmatrix} \tag{7.4.6}$$

The elements of this example K is presented in the vector form, say K_Vector taken in row-wise, as shown in Table 7.1.

TABLE 7.1 K_Vector Table: Elements of K in One-Dimensional Array

1	2	3	4	5	6	7	8	9	10	11	12	13	14	15	16
209	113	200	217	127	184	55	131	59	216	237	218	191	26	235	139

The order of the magnitude of elements in the $K\_Vector\_Ordered$ is shown in the second row of Table 7.2:

TABLE 7.2 K_Vector_Ordered Table: Relation between Serial Numbers and Numbers in Ascending Order

1	2	3	4	5	6	7	8	9	10	11	12	13	14	15	16
209	113	200	217	127	184	55	131	59	216	237	218	191	26	235	139
11	4	10	13	5	8	2	6	3	12	16	14	9	1	15	7

The pairs from $K\_Vector\_Ordered$ are considered for generating the substitution matrix, which is further used in the cryptic procedures. Let the numbers given in the first and third rows are represented by $x_1, x_2, x_3, ..., x_{14}, x_{15}, x_{16}$. The enlisted elements in the pairs: $(x_1, x_{11}), (x_2, x_4), (x_3, x_{10}), (x_6, x_8), (x_{12}, x_{14}), (x_{13}, x_9)$ are swapped mutually. It may be noted here that x_4 and x_{13} are not swapped, as x_4 has already undergone the swapping. Similarly, the other pairs which do not swap are $(x_7, x_2), (x_8, x_6), (x_9, x_3), (x_{10}, x_{12}), (x_{11}, x_{16}), (x_{14}, x_1) and (x_{16}, x_7)$. In case of columns, too, the previously mentioned pairs are used for mutual swaps. Let the EBCDIC integers ranging between [0–255] be represented as a squared matrix of size 16 and represented in the form:

$$EBCDIC(i, j) = \left[16(i-1) + (j-1) \right], i = 1...16, j = 1...16. \tag{7.4.7}$$

Using the previously mentioned pairs of mutual swaps, first the rows of *EBCDIC* are interchanged, and then the columns resulting into the matrix as shown following:

$$SB = \begin{bmatrix} 170 & 163 & 169 & 161 & 164 & 167 & 166 & 165 & 172 & 162 & 160 & 173 & 168 & 171 & 174 & 175 \\ 58 & 51 & 57 & 49 & 52 & 55 & 54 & 53 & 60 & 50 & 48 & 61 & 56 & 59 & 62 & 63 \\ 42 & 35 & 41 & 33 & 36 & 39 & 38 & 37 & 44 & 34 & 32 & 45 & 40 & 43 & 46 & 47 \\ 26 & 19 & 25 & 17 & 20 & 23 & 22 & 21 & 28 & 18 & 16 & 29 & 24 & 27 & 30 & 31 \\ 74 & 67 & 73 & 65 & 68 & 71 & 70 & 69 & 76 & 66 & 64 & 77 & 72 & 75 & 78 & 79 \\ 122 & 115 & 121 & 113 & 116 & 119 & 118 & 117 & 124 & 114 & 112 & 125 & 120 & 123 & 126 & 127 \\ 106 & 99 & 105 & 97 & 100 & 103 & 102 & 101 & 108 & 98 & 96 & 109 & 104 & 107 & 110 & 111 \\ 90 & 83 & 89 & 81 & 84 & 87 & 86 & 85 & 92 & 82 & 80 & 93 & 88 & 91 & 94 & 95 \\ 202 & 195 & 201 & 193 & 196 & 199 & 198 & 197 & 204 & 194 & 192 & 205 & 200 & 203 & 206 & 207 \\ 42 & 35 & 41 & 33 & 36 & 39 & 38 & 37 & 44 & 34 & 32 & 45 & 40 & 43 & 46 & 47 \\ 10 & 3 & 9 & 1 & 4 & 7 & 6 & 5 & 12 & 2 & 0 & 13 & 8 & 11 & 14 & 15 \\ 218 & 211 & 217 & 209 & 212 & 215 & 214 & 213 & 220 & 210 & 208 & 221 & 216 & 219 & 222 & 223 \\ 138 & 131 & 137 & 129 & 132 & 135 & 134 & 133 & 140 & 130 & 128 & 141 & 136 & 139 & 142 & 143 \\ 186 & 179 & 185 & 177 & 180 & 183 & 182 & 181 & 188 & 178 & 176 & 189 & 184 & 187 & 190 & 191 \\ 234 & 227 & 233 & 225 & 228 & 231 & 230 & 229 & 236 & 226 & 224 & 237 & 232 & 235 & 238 & 239 \\ 250 & 243 & 249 & 241 & 244 & 247 & 246 & 245 & 252 & 242 & 240 & 253 & 248 & 251 & 254 & 255 \end{bmatrix} \tag{7.4.8}$$

The resulting matrix, generated in Equation 7.4.8, is used in the substitution process in each iteration of the enciphering process. Let, the characters of a sensitive field in any record be represented as $S = [s_{ij}], i = 1\ldots4, j = 1\ldots4$, in its EBCDIC form. After an arbitrary round of enciphering with the encryption key bunch matrix, the S is converted to $S' = [s'_{ij}], i = 1\ldots4, j = 1\ldots4$. The substitution takes place in the following manner:

For each value of S' in SB matrix, the row and column are identified which are used as indices to find the corresponding value, in the EBCDIC table, say e_B. The integer s'_{ij} is substituted with e_B. Likewise, all the values are filled in the S' to get a S'_B matrix. However, if the size of the square matrix is less than 16, the process of swapping is restricted according to the least value of either rows or columns. Suppose the matrix is of size 4, as represented in Equation 7.4.9,

$$S' = \begin{bmatrix} 21 & 109 & 56 & 89 \\ 12 & 39 & 221 & 200 \\ 167 & 23 & 78 & 93 \\ 45 & 210 & 173 & 238 \end{bmatrix}$$

(7.4.9)

and applying the previously mentioned procedure on Equation 7.4.9, the resultant 2-dimensional vector obtained is represented as

$$S_B' = \begin{bmatrix} 55 & 107 & 28 & 114 \\ 168 & 37 & 187 & 140 \\ 5 & 53 & 78 & 123 \\ 43 & 185 & 11 & 238 \end{bmatrix}$$

(7.4.10)

This completes the process of the substitution, denoted by the function $Substitute()$ and its reverse by $Rev\_Substitute()$. The function $Mult()$ is used to find the Key_Dec for the given Key_Enc.

7.4.2 Privacy Preservation of the Encrypted Dataset Using k-Anonymization

In this regard, it is of utmost importance to sanitize the valuable information resulting from the quasi-identifier before making it public, so that de-identification is not possible. The privacy preservation algorithm k-anonymization is designed to anonymize the quasi-identifiers, and will lead to k-indistinguishable records, thwarting any attempt to distinguish them. Quasi-identifiers (QI) are the

TABLE 7.3 Patients' EHRs before Anonymization under the QIs

PATIENT_ID	AGE	GENDER	POSTAL CODE	PLACE OF BIRTH	DISEASE
P101	49	M	560011	Adilabad	Liver cirrhosis
P102	48	M	560005	Warangal	Nerve Disorder
P103	58	M	560014	Karimnagar	Cancer
P104	35	M	520004	Karimnagar	Liver cirrhosis
P105	35	F	520012	Ailoni	Skin allergy
P106	39	F	530007	Sircilla	Cancer
P107	55	M	111011	Delhi	Nerve Disorder
P108	65	F	110003	Delhi East	Cardiac problem
P109	62	M	110028	Gopalganj	Cardiac problem

TABLE 7.4   Patients' EHRs after k-Anonymization

PATIENT_ID	AGE	POSTAL CODE	PLACE OF BIRTH	DISEASE
P101	>45	560***	Telangana	Liver cirrhosis
P102	>45	560***	Telangana	Nerve Disorder
P103	>45	560***	Telangana	Cancer
P104	3*	5200**	Telangana	Liver cirrhosis
P105	3*	5200**	Telangana	Skin allergy
P106	3*	5300**	Telangana	Cancer
P107	>50	11****	Delhi	Nerve Disorder
P108	>50	11****	Delhi	Cardiac problem
P109	>50	11****	Bihar	Cardiac problem

attributes which can be combined together in order to re-identify particular individuals in the table. In addition to the examples of QIs mentioned in Section 7.1, few more are age; gender; six-digit postal code; date of birth; place of birth; names of parents, siblings, and children; work status; company name, etc. These QIs can be handled with generalization and suppression techniques. As per the k-anonymity principle, each record must be indistinguishable from at least $k - 1$ records with respect to certain identifying attributes.

K-anonymization is applied with k value as 3 to Table 7.3, thus ensuring that at least three indistinguishable records emerge during any attempt to decipher the anonymized EHR data. In this illustration, k-anonymity is applied on the two quasi-identifiers: age and postal code. The other quasi-identifier, place of birth, is suppressed with the higher concept hierarchy, as shown in Table 7.4.

7.4.3 Blockchain-Based Distribution of the Privacy Preserved and Cryptic Dataset Records

To present the insights into the process involved in storing the EHR of a patient, with encrypted sensitive fields and generalized quasi-fields, in the form of a transaction into the blockchain network, the architecture of the proposed blockchain-based distribution of the privacy preserved and cryptic dataset records is presented in Figure 7.4. Each interaction between the entity and the blockchain network is auditable and encapsulates transparency and security.

Decentralized applications (DApps) developed using the blockchain-enabled information system enable medical care-teams and patients to interact and share the much-valued digitized information thus, empowering the patient with no intermediary costs. At the behest of the patient, telemedicine can also be practiced in a trustworthy environment provided by the blockchain network, maintaining EHRs on the nodes of the external entities.

To be operational in the blockchain network, patients must enroll themselves to the network, upon which the public account on the blockchain, roles, and pre-designated access privileges are assigned. The private key corresponding to the public account is provided as the secret key to the individual account holders. The role of the new entity may be classifying into patient, doctor, diagnostic center where the patient's clinical tests take place, insurance agency, and local or national government body in terms of health ministry. The set of access privileges would encompass adding the EHRs; updating, retrieving, and archiving into the library; and purging when patient EHRs are no more required. Few of the access privileges can only be accomplished after entity validations, which are further mentioned in the pseudo-codes.

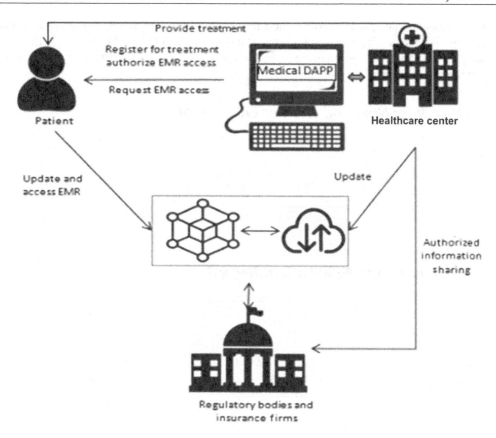

FIGURE 7.4 Blockchain-based distribution of the records among stakeholders.

In the blockchain network, each EHR is maintained as a transaction on the blockchain. Upon receiving the new transaction, the following steps are observed:

- In order to add the new transaction to the nodes of the blockchain, the miner—or the mining algorithm—computes the hash of the block containing the new transaction, using the SHA-256 cryptographic algorithm with the agreed upon difficulty level. The hash value is embedded in the newly created block, along with other parameters and broadcasted to all the nodes of the peer-to-peer network of the blockchain.
- The other nodes verify the new addition is unaltered by any means. Upon successful verification, the block is added in their own copy of the blockchain.
- The whole process of addition is completed by all nodes of the blockchain after a consensus algorithm is executed. Here, the consensus algorithm is developed using the principle of 51% whereby the more than half of the nodes validate successfully the new entrant-block contents.
- With the addition of the new block into each node of the blockchain network, the transaction entry is committed.

In view of these steps, a smart contract is developed which allows the records to be inserted and shared securely among the stakeholders for better and unhampered consultation and medical-care. The procedures can be designed to help patients control, organize, retrieve, and donate their sensitive data with the research organizations. The pseudo-code of the smart contract for new transaction addition, updating, retrieval, archiving, and purging by the appropriate stakeholders, are presented in the rest of this section. Additionally, a procedure is developed to enroll and assign the new stakeholder entrant to the appropriate user-type with the access privileges.

7.4.3.1 Procedure: New Stakeholder Enrollment

```
procedure new_entrant_enrol (new account, user_type,
  access_previleges)
begin
create new_account and map with user_type,
assign access_previleges
return succcess
end
```

7.4.3.2 Procedure: Add New Patient Record

```
procedure add_new_transaction (patient_id,
  transaction_attributes)
begin
find patient_id from the blockchain
if (patient_id exists and transaction_sender == doctor) then
append transaction_attributes to the patient_id block
return succcess
else
call new_entrant_enrol (new_account, patient_type,
  access_previleges),
add transaction_attributes to the patient_id block
return succcess
end
```

7.4.3.3 Procedure: Update Patient Record

```
procedure update_patient_record (initiator, patient_id,
  new_attributes)
begin
if (initiator.matches(doctor, diagnostic_center, same_patient))
  then
find block(s) with block.patient_id == patient_id
if (block(s)) exists then
update block with new_attributes
return success
else
abort procedure
return fail
else
abort procedure
return fail
end
```

The diagnostic_center is the lab facility where the patient undergoes diagnostic tests

7.4.3.4 Procedure: Retrieve Patient Record

```
procedure retrieve_patient_record (initiator, patient_id)
begin
if (initiator.matches(doctor, diagnostic_center, same_patient))
  then
find block(s) with block.patient_id == patient_id
if (matched.block(s) found) then
retrieve data from matched.block(s)
return data to initiator
else
return patient_not_found_error
end
```

7.4.3.5 Procedure: Archive Patient Data

```
procedure archive_patient_data (initiator, patient_id)
begin
if (initiator.matches(doctor, same_patient)) then
find block(s) with block.patient_id == patient_id
if (matched.block(s) found) then
retrieve data from matched.block(s)
archive data to archive_library_blockchain
return success
else
return patient_not_found_error
end
```

7.4.3.6 Procedure: Purge Patient Record

```
procedure purge_patient_details (initiator, patient_id)
begin
if (initiator.matches(doctor, same_patient)) then
find block(s) with block.patient_id == patient_id
if (matched.blocks(s) found) then
retrieve data from matched.block(s)
return data to patient_id
delete matched.block(s) in the blockchain
return success
else
return patient_not_found_error
end
```

7.5 INSTALLATION SETUP AND PERFORMANCE EVALUATION

For implementing the proposed model, the computer system with the following configuration is used: Intel Core i5 processor 8250U CPU @ 1.60 GHz 1.80 GHz, with 8.00 GB RAM and Windows 10 Pro as 64-bit OS.

TABLE 7.5   Expended Time for the Smart Contract Procedures

SMART CONTRACT PROCEDURES	COMPUTATIONAL TIME ELAPSED (IN MINUTES)
New stakeholder enrollment: new_entrant_enrol	0.52
Add new patient record: add_new_transaction	1.48
Update patient record: update_patient_record	1.07
Retrieve patient record: retrieve_patient_record	1.04
Archive patient data: archive_patient_data	2.28
Purge patient record: purge_patient_details	1.09

The cryptic procedures and the privacy-preserving techniques are implemented using the Java SE 13 release. The decentralized application is developed using the Ethereum platform, and the Solidity programming language is used for defining the procedures, as described in the preceding section, of the smart contract.

For maintaining the confidentiality of the patient record, considered as the digital record containing structured data of 12 KB, through encryption is 0.014 seconds. The privacy-preserving method adopted to seal the anonymity of the quasi-attributes of the patient would add another 0.01 seconds.

The mining time computed for generating a new block as per the given difficulty level is found to be 42 seconds. On an average, the time lapsed for computing the hash value is 28 seconds. Overall, approximately, the time for adding a new block with the patient record is observed to be 1.48 minutes. The computational times for executing the smart contract's other procedures are presented in Table 7.5.

The size of the new block obtained on mining and after appending the cryptographic hash of the previous block, nonce, a timestamp, current block hash value to the transaction data enhances to additional payload ranging between 64 bytes and 196 bytes in the testing phase. The values presented here are the real values obtained while working with the mentioned configuration for the Ethereum blockchain network.

Any interaction with the network, as mentioned in the pseudo-codes in the preceding section, including the mining for adding the new block and validating the nodes of the network, by the entity would incur certain *Transaction_fee* and is rewarded to the miner who mines that block. In general, the more data payload for processing, the greater the transaction fee which is computed as the product of gas consumed and the gas price, as follows:

$$Transaction\_fee = gas\_consumed \times gas\_price$$

In Ethereum, the *Transaction_fee* refers to the amount of cost necessary to perform a transaction on the network. The *gas_price* is denoted in Gwei, a denomination of ETH, such that each Gwei is equal to $10^{-9} ETH$. The *gas_consumed* is the maximum amount of gas one is willing to spend on a transaction. The gas consumption takes place during the computations, involved in the operation of the blockchain and the recommended value for *gas_consumed* is 21000 and *gas_price* is 21 Gwei. Thus:

$$Transaction\_fee = 21000 \times 21 Gwei = 0.000441 ETH.$$

Although use of private cryptocurrencies is geographically conditional, the other parameter for the varied *Transaction_fee* is the longer waiting times and faster execution. The latter would cost more *Transaction_fee*.

7.6 SECURITY ANALYSIS

To test the strength of the cryptic procedures developed, a security analysis is performed. In this chapter, a study is made to assess the impact of popular attacks, which is presented in the following subsection.

7.6.1 Cryptanalysis

The different attacks which are widely used by adversaries for breaking into enciphered information are:

1. Ciphertext only (brute force) attack.
2. Known plaintext attack.
3. Chosen ciphertext attack.
4. Chosen plaintext attack.

In general, every cipher is designed to withstand the first two attacks [22]. The latter two attacks are examined intuitively to check whether the cipher can be broken with these attacks. In the ciphertext only attack, the key size chosen, of the Key _ Enc in the present cipher, is $n \times n$. With this, the key space size is

$$2^{n^2} = \left(2^{10}\right)^{0.7n^2} \approx 10^{2.1n^2} \tag{7.6.1}$$

On assuming that the time taken to check one key out of the previously mentioned key space is 10^{-7} seconds, then the total time required to check all possible permutations and combinations of the of the key space would be

$$\frac{10^{2.1n^2} \times 10^{-7}}{365 \times 24 \times 60 \times 60} = 3.12 \times 10^{2.1n^2 - 15} \, years \tag{7.6.2}$$

In the present analysis, the value for n is chosen as 4. With this, the total time evolves to be $3.12 \times 10^{18.6}$ years, which is formidably an enormous amount of time to uncover the encrypted data.

In the known plaintext attack, the adversary is assumed to be holding as many pairs of sensitive raw information and the encrypted information. In order to reveal the secret key and the substitution key used during the encryption process, the corresponding information from each pair are analyzed, as is shown following for one round of the iteration cycle:

$$s_{ij} = \left(e_{ij} \times s_{ij}\right) mod \, 256, 1 \le i, j \le n, \tag{7.6.3}$$

$$S = \left[s_{ij}\right], \tag{7.6.4}$$

$$S = Substitute\left(S\right), \tag{7.6.5}$$

$$C = S. \tag{7.6.6}$$

The data denoted by the C in Equation 7.6.6 and S in the right side of Equation 7.6.3 are known. Though known, the value of S, mentioned in the right side of Equation 7.6.5, cannot be determined with unless the Key_Sub is known for performing inverse of the Substitute(). For determining the Key_Sub, comprising of the 16 integers ranging in [0–255], the time using brute force method is $3.12 \times 10^{23.4}$ years. The preceding set of equations is for one round, and in the present cryptic procedures implemented, 16 rounds are taken to create enough confusion and diffusion. As the equations governing the cryptic process are complex and the time requirements to break the cipher is nonlinear, the possibility of the gaining the keys using the known plaintext attack is not possible. With the latter two attack models being intuitive, it can be envisaged that the cipher developed is unbreakable.

In the block ciphered cryptosystems, the *avalanche effect* plays a vital role in assessing the impact on the outcomes when a single bit is flipped in one of the inputs supplied to the encryption procedure, discussed previously. It was practically found that more than 50% of the bits flipped in the enciphered block as compared to the original ciphered block, when one bit is flipped in the *Key _ Enc*.

TABLE 7.6   Comparative Features among the Models Addressing EHRs Security

FEATURE	[22]	[23]	[24]	PROPOSED: TWO-FOLD SECURITY MODEL
Confidentiality	No	No	No	Yes
Privacy preservation	Yes	Yes	Yes	Yes
Scalability	No	Yes	Yes	Yes
Resource-poor Aptness	No	No	No	Yes
Owner-controlled access privileges	Yes	Yes	No	Yes
Decentralization	Yes	Yes	Yes	Yes
Transparent, trustworthy EHR sharing	Yes	Yes	Yes	Yes

7.6.2 Comparative Study

The comparative study is made on the desirable features of security that the healthcare ecosystem must possess to safeguard the confidentiality and privacy of the registered patients' EHRs. Defence of confidentiality, privacy preservation, scalability, low-cost computing for the resource-poor configurations, patient-controlled access privileges, decentralized access among the stakeholders, and being a transparent, trustworthy, and crash-free system are the strong properties. In the Table 7.6, the comparative features among the models which address the EHR privacy and security in the healthcare are presented.

7.7 CONCLUSIONS AND FUTURE SCOPE

In this chapter, a two-fold security model is detailed using 2D-vector key bunch and privacy preservation of the EHRs in the distributed network involving blockchain. With the confidential fields encrypted and the quasi-identifiable fields anonymized, the EHRs can be publicly shared among the stakeholders. The cryptic procedures designed and implemented utilize low resources for the computation, unlike other block ciphers exhibiting the same strength. The added advantage of the encryption and the decryption procedures involve enhancement of the key to a much larger size with minimal enhanced computing costs. With these additional properties in the encryption procedure, the user-end module can be fairly operated with low-end devices. The use of blockchain for decentralized storage with inherent features of transparency and robustness brings in trustworthy access and updating of the personal data as compared to the otherwise centralized storage. Besides, the control to modify the access privileges of the others in the environment vests with the data owner and is role-based, thus solving the information skew found in the conventional EHR maintenance system.

For the future, the model designed shall be qualified to migrate to the hybrid blockchain with the integration of online consultation and payment gateways. This would enhance the model to an end-to-end version for the healthcare ecosystem.

REFERENCES

[1] Pathan, Al-Sakib Khan. "Technological advancements and innovations are often detrimental for concerned technology companies." *International Journal of Computers and Applications* 40, no. 4 (2018): 189–191. DOI: 10.1080/1206212X.2018.1515412.

[2] Such, J. M., and N. Criado. "Multiparty privacy in social media." *Commun ACM* 61, no. 8 (2018): 74–81.

[3] By Davis, Jessica. "UPDATE: The 10 Biggest healthcare data breaches of 2020, so far." Retrieved July 8, 2020, from https://healthitsecurity.com/news/the-10-biggest-healthcare-data-breaches-of-2020-so-far.

[4] Johnson, Joseph. "Annual number of data breaches and exposed records in the United States from 2005 to 2020." Retrieved March 3, 2021, from www.statista.com/statistics/273550/ data-breaches-recorded-in-the-united-states-by-number-of-breaches-and-records-exposed/.

[5] Seh, A. H., M. Zarour, M. Alenezi, A. K. Sarkar, A. Agrawal, R. Kumar, and R. Ahmad Khan. "Healthcare data breaches: Insights and implications." *Healthcare* 8 (2020): 133. https://doi.org/10.3390/healthcare8020133.

[6] Khan, M. K. "Technological advancements and 2020."*Telecommunication Systems* 73 (2020): 1–2. https://doi.org/10.1007/s11235-019-00647-8.

[7] Ram Mohan Rao, P., S. Murali Krishna, and A. P. Siva Kumar. "Privacy preservation techniques in big data analytics: A survey." *Journal Big Data* 5 (2018): 33. https://doi.org/10.1186/s40537-018-0141-8.

[8] Sweeney, Latanya. "k-Anonymity: A model for protecting privacy." *International Journal of Uncertainty, Fuzziness and Knowledge-Based Systems* 10, no. 5 (2002): 557–570.

[9] El Emam, Khaled, Fida Kamal Dankar, Romeo Issa, Elizabeth Jonker, Daniel Amyot, Elise Cogo, Jean-Pierre Corriveau, Mark Walker, Sadrul Chowdhury, Regis Vaillancourt, Tyson Roffey, and Jim Bottomley. "A globally optimal k-Anonymity method for the De-identification of health data." *Journal of the American Medical Informatics Association* 16, no. 5 (September 2009): 670–682. https://doi.org/10.1197/jamia.M3144.

[10] Machanavajjhala, Ashwin, Daniel Kifer, Johannes Gehrke, and Muthuramakrishnan Venkitasubramaniam. "l-Diversity: Privacy beyond k-Anonymity." *ACM Transactions on Knowledge Discovery from Data* 1, no. 1 (March 2007): 3–es. DOI: 10.1145/1217299.1217302. ISSN1556-4681.S2CID679934.

[11] Li, N., T. Li, and S. Venkatasubramanian. "t-Closeness: Privacy beyond k-Anonymity and l-Diversity." *IEEE 23rd International Conference on Data Engineering, Istanbul, Turkey*, pp.106–115, 2007. DOI: 10.1109/ICDE.2007.367856, 2007.

[12] Wu, Juhua, Yu Wang, Lei Tao, and Jiamin Peng. "Stakeholders in the healthcare service ecosystem." *Procedia CIRP* 83 (2019): 375–379. ISSN 2212–8271. https://doi.org/10.1016/j. procir.2019.04.085.

[13] Casino, Fran, Thomas K. Dasaklis, and Constantinos Patsakis. "A systematic literature review of blockchain-based applications: Current status, classification and open issues." *Telematics and Informatics* 36 (2019): 55–81. ISSN 0736–5853.

[14] Orkutt, Mike. "How secure is blockchain really?" *MIT Technology Review* (2018): 1. Retrieved from https://www.technologyreview.com/2018/04/25/143246/how-secure-is-blockchain-really/

[15] Walker, Martin. "Distributed ledger technology: Hybrid approach, front-to-back designing and changing trade processing infrastructure." ISBN 978-1-78272-389-9, 2018.

[16] Castellanos, Sara. "A Cryptocurrency technology finds new use tackling coronavirus." *The Wall Street Journal.* Retrieved October 21, 2020.

[17] Ben Fekih, R., and M. Lahami. "Application of blockchain technology in healthcare: A comprehensive study." In Jmaiel, M., Mokhtari, M., Abdulrazak, B., Aloulou, H., and Kallel, S. (eds.). *The Impact of Digital Technologies on Public Health in Developed and Developing Countries. ICOST Lecture Notes in Computer Science.* Vol. 12157. Springer, 2020. https://doi.org/10.1007/978-3-030-51517-1_23, 2020.

[18] Dubovitskaya, A, Z. Xu, S. Ryu, M. Schumacher, and F. Wang. "Secure and trustable electronic medical records sharing using blockchain." *AMIA Annual Symposium Proceedings* 2018 (2017): 650–659. Published April 16, 2018.

[19] Dannen, Chris. *Introducing Ethereum and Solidity: Foundations of Cryptocurrency and Blockchain Programming for Beginners.* 1st Edition. Apress, 2017.

[20] Dr. Sastry, V. U. K., and K. Shirisha. "A novel block cipher involving a key bunch matrix and a key-based permutation and substitution." *International Journal of Advanced Computer Science and Applications (IJACSA)* 3, no. 12 (2012): 116–122.

[21] Dr. Sastry, V. U. K., and K. Shirisha. "A novel block cipher involving a key Bunch Matrix." *International Journal of Computer Applications* (0975–8887) 55, no.16 (October 2012): 1–6.

[22] Stallings, William. *Cryptography and Network Security: Principle and Practices.* 3rd Edition, Chapter 2, 29. Pearson, 2003.

TRACK 3

Blockchain in the Near Future

Possible Uses and Research Gaps

Analysis of Security and Privacy Aspects of Blockchain Technologies from Smart Era' Perspective: The Challenges and a Way Forward to Future

8

Amit Kumar Tyagi

Contents

8.1 INTRODUCTION

With the rapid rise in innovation, digital transformation, and digital revolution in both academia and industry, people are making use of smart devices a lot in many possible applications [1]. These applications are making people's daily lives easier and their lives longer. But today, many cyberattacks and exploits (on these smart devices and Internet of Things [IoT] infrastructure) have become disturbingly common on systems and networks. After providing several efficient solutions, it still is hard to even count all the victims who have fallen prey to cybercrime, data fraud, and/or theft. Such attacks and breaches have been damaging to hard-earned reputations, and affect people's lives a lot. From such attacks and concerns, we require freedom and want complete protection for a better tomorrow. Note that nothing is as secure on the web as we believe it is. For example, thousands of websites are hacked every day. Even also, hundreds of millions of profiles (e.g., Cambridge Analytica scandal) are up for grabs by hackers and in a constant state of compromise. Recently, Facebook has fined $5 billion for violation of privacy rights.

We always have dangers of oversharing data on social media and the lack of control over who gets to keep it. Today's issue of data protection for every sector and application (like medical care, online social networking, etc.) is a big challenge [2]. Blockchain security is a most reliable technique and is being used in many applications like finance, land records, etc., for better results [3], but small blockchains or those which are in the early stages of growth tend to be especially vulnerable to attacks. If threat actors get control of 51% of nodes (computers) on the system, they can ruin the integrity of the network. But, on a scale of thousands or millions of machines, blockchain hacks seem most improbable. Until now, we have not observed a single case of hacking blockchain (except inside attackers). Blockchain emerged as a novel distributed consensus scheme that allows transactions, and any other data, to be securely stored and verified without the need of any centralized authority. For some time, the notion of blockchain was tightly coupled with a now well-known proof of work hash-based mechanism of Bitcoin. Today, there are more than 100 alternate blockchains—some are simple variants of Bitcoin, whereas others significantly differ in their design as well as provide different functional and security guarantees. This shows that the research community is in search of a simple, scalable, and deployable blockchain technology. Various reports further point to an increased interest in the use of blockchain across many applications and to a significant investment in the development of blockchain by different industries. It is expected that the blockchain will induce considerable change to a large number of systems and businesses. Blockchain is a digitized, decentralized, and public ledger of all cryptocurrency transactions. Distributed database is one of the key features of blockchain [4]. It means many copies across various computer systems form a peer-to-peer network, denoting that no solitary, centralized database or server exists. Essential elements of blockchain are decentralization, consensus model(s), transparency, open source, autonomy, immutability, anonymity, identity, and access. On another side, key characteristics of blockchain are decentralization, persistence, auditability, and anonymity. Blockchain variations are Blockchain 1.0, Blockchain 2.0, Blockchain 3.0, and Blockchain 4.0 (DApps).

Blockchain has tremendous potential for avoiding many risks in possible applications. It has the potential to either make an application a success or cause it to fail. For example, in smart contract, we need to provide (stored) error-free and attack-free smart contracts in blockchain. We can provide possibility of correctness of smart contracts until a certain level in terms of accuracy using blockchain. Remember the increasing number of surveillance and security breaches leaking user privacy. We need to calculate the number of attacks or vulnerabilities, and also growth rate in research and industry with respect to IoT. We can find answers to questions like how blockchain technology is used to provide security and privacy in peer-to-peer networks with topologies such as IoT. In summary, we need to design a decentralized personal data management system that guarantees user's ownership and control over their data (all the time, providing access anytime, anywhere). In the past decade, many papers have been published with respect to the security of blockchain technology and its future trends. We find that no research discusses the various fields in blockchain can be used and how security and privacy issues can be challenging in those sectors.

Hence, this work is structured in nine following sections. Section 8.2 consists of discussion about related work with respect to security privacy aspects. Section 8.3 discusses the importance and scope of blockchain today and in the near future. Section 8.4 discusses motivation, i.e. motivation behind this work. Section 8.5 discusses a useful use case, i.e. using blockchain with the Internet of Things (IoT), explaining an architecture which overcomes general issues of the IoT. Section 8.6 discusses several issues and challenges raised in blockchain technology. Further, Section 8.7 deliberates on the classifications of security- and privacy-related issues in the smart era of the 21st century (considering blockchain in many applications). Section 8.8 discusses various solutions (available in the present) for raised security and privacy concerns toward blockchain-based applications. Section 8.9 sheds light on some of the future challenges and the vast array of opportunities provided with the growth of blockchain technology, explicated with respect to its privacy and security aspects. Finally, Section 8.10 summarizes this work in brief with some useful footprints for future researchers and readers.

8.2 RELATED WORK

The idea behind blockchain technology was started in 1991 by research scientists Stuart Haber and W. Scott Stornetta [5]. They implemented a computationally practical solution for timestamping digital documents so that they could not be backed up or tampered with. The implemented system used cryptographically secured blocks of chain to store the timestamp documents. In 1992, Merkle trees were integrated into the design to make it more effective by allowing the collection of several document certificates in one block. In 2004, the license for this technology was cancelled. In 2004, Hal Finney—a computer scientist and cryptographic activist—introduced a system called RPoW (reusable proof of work). RPoW receives a non-exchangeable hash-cash based proof of work token and it generates an RSA-signed token that could then be transferred from person to person. RPoW stores the registered tokens on trusted servers to avoid the double spending problem, and it allows the people overall the world to verify the correctness and integrity in real time. This was the first step in the history of Bitcoin (cryptocurrency).

In 2008, Satoshi Nakamoto is the inventor of Bitcoin [6]. It is a cryptocurrency and it is known as a decentralized peer-to-peer electronic cash system. It was posted by Satoshi Nakamoto in a cryptography mail list. It works based on hash-cash proof of work algorithm. Instead of using RPoW to avoid double spending problem, we can use Bitcoin, which provides a decentralized peer-to-peer protocol for verifying the correctness of all transactions. Bitcoins are "mined" by individual miners for a reward using the proof of work system and then verified by the network's decentralized nodes. Bitcoin came into existence on January 3, 2009, when Satoshi Nakamoto mined the first Bitcoin block, which had a reward of 50 Bitcoins. In the world, the first Bitcoin transaction is made on January 12, 2009. Santoshi Nakamoto is the first sender of Bitcoin, transferring 10 Bitcoins to Hal Finney (first receipt of Bitcoins). The first application of blockchain is Bitcoin. For the first time, it is possible to transfer money without any trusted third party.

In 2013, Vitalik Buterin [7], *Bitcoin Magazine* co-founder and programmer, stated that for building decentralized applications, Bitcoin needed a scripting language. This belief was not shared by everyone in the community, so Buterin started developing a new blockchain-based distributed computing platform, Ethereum (global, open source platform) which had scripting features called smart contracts. Smart contracts are used for exchanging shares, property documents, or anything of value among unknown people in conflict-free transparent manner. It avoids trusted third parties (services of an intermediary). Smart contracts are the executable logic that runs on blockchain network. Key properties of smart contracts are that it is autonomous (the creator does not have to participate after deploying a contract) and decentralized (it does not have a central server). The first application of smart contracts electronic transactions was proposed by Nick Szabo. In particular, programming languages smart contracts are written, compiled, and converted into byte code by Ethereum Virtual Machine (EVM) [8]. Developers are also able to code applications that run inside Ethereum blockchain. These types of applications are called as DApps (decentralized applications), i.e. gambling, financial exchanges. Ether is the cryptocurrency of Ethereum. It can be used to make online payments when executing smart contracts. Ether can be transferred between accounts. In blockchain, some consensus algorithms are used to provide reliable and trusted services to end users. These consensus algorithms are included here as: proof of work (PoW), proof of stake (PoS), practical Byzantine fault tolerance (PBFT), delegated proof of stake (DPoS), and scalable Byzantine consensus protocol (SCP) design.

Hence, this section discusses work related to blockchain technology, i.e. evolution of blockchain technology while considering several essential aspects of this new technology. The next section will discuss the importance and scope of blockchain technology today and in the near future.

8.3 IMPORTANCE AND SCOPE OF BLOCKCHAIN TODAY AND IN THE NEAR FUTURE

Today there are several uses of blockchain technology like in cryptocurrency, smart contract, protecting network, reducing intermediary services, etc., i.e., blockchain is being used in many applications as an emerging technology. Blockchain is popular in many useful applications because of following features:

- Disintermediation: Blockchain offers immutability in transactions and distributed ledger design which are essential criteria to remove the need for an organization trust enforcer. Tamper-proof shared data allows an area in which trust is not a concern and enables counterparties to work with the confidence that at all times they all have the same version of the events and their past cannot be modified.
- Transparency: Blockchain technology would increase the transparency among market participants considerably. Blockchain implementations facilitate the development in the ecosystem of a shared record of operation to which all market players have real-time access.
- Provenance: From the moment the asset first appears in a transaction on the blockchain, it retains a permanent record of transactions and thus asset ownership ever. This greatly decreases the risk of multiple asset types and the need for related mitigation operations. This capacity would enable the incidence of theft, fraud, and the abuse of high-value assets and intellectual property rights to be reduced. It will also support assets where worth is determined by its provenance by having a digital footprint on the blockchain.

Decentralization, accountability, and security (with building trust) are some core properties of a blockchain technology. Apart from characteristics of blockchain, for business, blockchain technology has the following benefits to users/organizations:

- Time savings: Transaction times for complex, multi-party interactions are slashed from days to minutes. Transaction settlement is faster, because it does not require verification by a central authority.
- Cost savings: Blockchain takes the edge off expenses in several ways:
  - Marginal oversight is needed because the network is self-policed by network participants, all of whom are known on the network.
  - Intermediaries are reduced because participants can exchange items of value directly.
  - Duplication of effort is eliminated because all participants have access to the shared ledger.
- Data validity and tighter security: Blockchain's security features protect against tampering, fraud, and cybercrime. Once you are in, the data is hard to tamper due to blockchain's

nature. If a network is granted permission, it enables creation of members-only network with proof that members are who they say they are and that goods or assets traded are exactly as represented.

In near future, we will see blockchain use in protecting internet or data over internet, decentralized Web, decentralized cloud, decentralized economy, or other decentralized services. Decentralized application will be in trend in future, because there is no intermediary involved to make delay or take charge/commission for doing any task or verifying records.

Hence, this section discusses several applications where blockchain is more useful than other existing concepts. Blockchain usually provides several advantages (which are listed in Section 8.4), also providing trust in the network, i.e., among many peers (in decentralized and distributed networks). Section 8.5 will discuss several possible applications in near future which will use the blockchain concept for increasing profits and security.

8.4 MOTIVATION

Note that toward the end of 2020, 20 billion physician things were expected to be able to connect to the Internet, and all of these devices can work collectively by implementing the Internet of Things. These smart (or Internet of Things) devices will store all of communicated data at cloud which can be accessed by many users anytime, anywhere. There may be a possibility of many attacks on this stored and communicated data, with the probability of revealing or breaching personal information (of users) by unauthorized users. We need to protect this data by updated techniques and in an efficient manner. Blockchain technology is currently in a winning race, i.e., in providing tighter security to stored or communicating data. Also, blockchain provides better flexibility in accessing this data. It is used for anonymity among many users and builds trusts among users. As discussed previously, this novel concept was coined in 2008–2009 by an anonymous person or group of people. We need to understand blockchain security risks in many applications, and need to provide solutions accordingly. There are many benefits of blockchain, which will change the future or security systems complexly (i.e., clear-cut and promising). The capability of powerful (strong) blockchain must be to provide assured record of data ownership in a cloud environment, determining vulnerabilities of blockchain cloud with a high detection rate [11]. In general, a blockchain is a sequence of time-stamped transactions, where each transaction includes a variable number of output addresses (each address is a 160-bit number). In a blockchain, each block contains contents of the block and a "header" which contains the data about the block. blockchain technology is composed of the following six key characteristics:

- Decentralized: Blockchain never counts on a central node/framework for logging the data, recording it, or for upgrading purposes.
- Transparent: All gathered or collected data which is stored and maintained in the blockchain is highly transparent and flexible with respect to one other, as well as for updating of data.
- Open source: Predominantly, blockchain is a system which is accessible to quite a lot of people due to which records are easily accessible and visible. Even more, people can exploit blockchain techniques to create any application of their choice.
- Autonomous: Since the nodes have their foundations based on consensus, each individual node can assure the safe transmission of data with the core idea or perspective of making the entire system trustworthy without any malicious interventions.
- Immutable: All data will be recorded and saved for good, and cannot be modified unless an individual takes charge of more than 51% of the nodes simultaneously.

- Anonymous: Blockchain methodologies solve and eradicate trust issues between nodes, such that the data transfer or transactions are highly anonymous and calls are for the individual blockchain addresses alone.

Note that decentralization, accountability, and security (with building trust) are some core properties of a blockchain technology. Apart from characteristics of blockchain for business, blockchain technology has the following benefits to users/ organizations:

- Time savings: Transaction times for complex, multiparty interactions are slashed from days to minutes. Transaction settlement is faster, because it does not require verification by a central authority.
- Cost savings: Blockchain takes the edge off expenses in several ways:
  - Marginal oversight is needed because the network is self-policed by network participants, all of whom are known on the network.
  - Intermediaries are reduced because participants can exchange items of value directly.
  - Duplication of effort is eliminated because all participants have access to the shared ledger.
- Data validity and tighter security: Blockchain's security features protect against tampering, fraud, and cybercrime. Once you are in, the data is hard to tamper due to blockchain's nature. If a network is granted permission, it enables creation of a members-only network with proof that members are who they say they are and that goods or assets traded are exactly as represented.

Note that blockchain can be used in any application to store data securely and anonymously. Then it does not mean that similar blockchain can be used or built for business. As discussed previously, blockchain technology can be established as public or private (permission to specific persons only; some are granted permission, while others are not). A permissioned network is critical for blockchain for business, especially within regulated industries. It enhances privacy, improves auditability, and increases operational efficiency. Blockchain technology builds trust through the following five attributes in business and individual applications:

- Distributed and sustainable: The ledger is commonly shared, updated, and upgraded every time a processing happens, and it is easily duplicated or replicated among the users in real time. Because it is not under the ownership of any particular establishment, the blockchain offers a framework which is immaculately independent of individual instances.
- Secured, private, and indelible: Authorizations and encryption aid to keep away data flowing into malicious hands, thus assuring and verifying the validity and identity of the participants. Privacy is easily imposed through cryptography, complemented by data partitioning methods, to ensure that participants (i.e., other people available in the network) are fail to resist pressure to selective access about a data/ visibility of data in the distributive ledger form. As per the agreement of the conditions, users will not be allowed to modify/harm the record filled with processed transactions.
- Transparent and auditable: Since the users participating in a particular process can access the same records, they are capable of validating the transaction procedures and authorizing ownership identities for the third-party intermediaries.
- Consensus-based and transactional: All the active users of the network are obliged to agree to the validity of a process, and this is moderated with consensus algorithms. Each of these networks is efficient enough to develop the situations under which a process can take place.
- Orchestrated and flexible: Since business rules and smart contracts can be easily incorporated into this framework, blockchain networks evolve to be mature enough to complement end-to-end business techniques and a plethora of other activities.

As discussed previously, technical measures such as proof of work, practical Byzantine fault tolerance, delegated proof of stake and proof of stake have been used to improve the security of blockchain. Hence, virtually anything of value can be tracked and traded on a blockchain network (due to using consensus function/ledger mechanism), reducing risk and cutting costs for all involved. Applications or domains where blockchain is being deployed include finance, retail, decentralized economy, decentralized web, decentralized infrastructure/networking, smart contract/land reforms, and future generation computing environments like the distributed cloud.

In general, blockchain builds trust through the following five attributes in business/ individual applications:

- Distributed and sustainable: The ledger is shared, updated with every transaction, and selectively replicated among participants in near real time. Because it is not owned or controlled by any single organization, the blockchain platform's continued existence is not dependent on any individual entity.
- Secure, private, and indelible: Permissions and cryptography prevent unauthorized access to the network and ensure that participants are who they claim to be. Privacy is maintained through cryptographic techniques and/or data partitioning techniques to give participants selective visibility into the ledger; both transactions and the identity of transacting parties can be masked. Post conditions are agreed to, participants cannot tamper with a record of the transaction, and errors can be reversed only with new transactions.
- Transparent and auditable: Because participants in a transaction have access to the same records, they can validate transactions and verify identities or ownership without the need for third-party intermediaries. Transactions are time-stamped and can be verified in near real time.
- Consensus-based and transactional: All relevant network participants must agree that a transaction is valid. This is achieved through the use of consensus algorithms. Each blockchain network can establish the conditions under which a transaction or asset exchange can occur.
- Orchestrated and flexible: Business rules and smart contracts (that execute based on one or more conditions) can be built into the platform. Blockchain business networks can evolve as they mature to support end-to-end business processes and a wide range of activities.

Today there are many benefits of blockchain, through which we are forced to use blockchain in many applications in this smart era. But always, we have one question "Will it be the end in field of security" or "Will the technology revolutionize the field of data security and justify the hopes of many Industries/ people"? So, the world is waiting for more and more innovative solutions with blockchain. Hence, this section discusses motivation behind this work, used of blockchain in many possible applications. The next section will discuss several possible applications with blockchain in near future.

8.5 REAL-WORLD APPLICATIONS WITH BLOCKCHAIN: USE CASES

The communication between Internet-Connected Things and network IoT architecture is giving great range for massive generation of data allowing dependable and well-founded services over the wide area network of things through centralized data management servers (CDMS). The mentioned facilities of IoT do not ensure high levels of security. Chances of security and privacy issues with the data are high risk factors due to the high sensitivity of the data involved. High provision and chances exist of revealing highly sensitive aspects of data to the outside world (outside of NPT [Network of Plentiful Things]) through false authentications and device spoofing. This leads to the various security and privacy issues in IoT, thereby giving rise to a challenge that must be fixed. To address the security and privacy issues in IoT, we eliminate centralized maintenance of NPT-produced data and thereby introduce the new distributed ledger–based technology called "a blockchain technology" (p. 1) [12].

A consensus protocol has three properties (safety, liveness, and fault tolerance) based on applicability and efficiency. There also exist three forms of blockchain available presently, including public blockchain, private blockchain, and consortium blockchain.

8.5.1 Blockchain Technology Solutions for Internet of Things Devices

Blockchain technology will give a finer solution to the issues faced by Internet of Things systems [13]. Due to the increasing scenarios of IoT systems, the chances for having an increased number of interacting things or devices in it have also increased. This increased number of devices will try to interact with each other, using the Internet as a medium. This would lead to many issues because, in IoT systems, the data that is collected is maintained in the central servers. If the devices want access to the data, they must interact using the centralized network and the data will flow will through the central server; this flow in the process is clearly depicted in Figure 8.1. The growing needs of IoT and its applications were showcasing IoT as large-scale systems with integration of advanced technologies. In such large-scale IoT systems, the centralized server will not prove to be an effective approach. Most of the IoT systems that are implemented as of now are relying on the centralized server concept. In IoT systems, the sensor devices collect the information from the focused things and allow the data transmission to the central server by means of a wired/wireless network, i.e., this data moves over Internet from one destination to another destination. From the centralized server, analytics were performed as per the user requirements and convenience. Similarly, the large-scale IoT system wishes to perform the analysis; the processing capabilities of existing Internet infrastructure may not support effectively.

For handling the huge data processed in large-scale IoT systems, there is a need for increasing the Internet infrastructure. One best way to solve this is to have decentralized or distributed networks on which peer-to-peer networking (PPN), distributed file sharing (DFS), and autonomous device coordination (ADC) functions could be capable. Blockchain can carry out these three functions, allowing the IoT systems to track the huge number of connected and networked devices. Blockchain allows the IoT

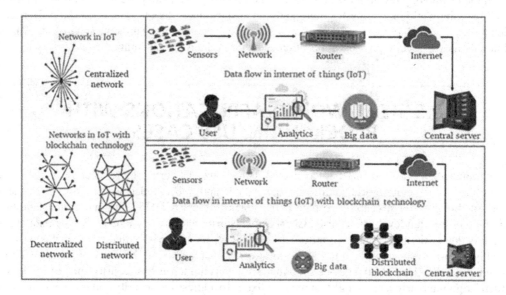

FIGURE 8.1   Internet of Things network types, data flow in Internet of Things, data flow in Internet of Things with blockchain technology.

systems to process transactions between the devices in coordination. Blockchain will enhance the privacy and reliability of IoT systems, making them robust [14]. Blockchain allows a peer-to-peer messaging in faster way with the help of distributed ledger, as shown in Figure 8.1. The data flow process in IoT with blockchain technology is different from IoT-only systems. In IoT with blockchain, the data flow is from sensors-network-router-Internet-distributed blockchain-analytics-user. Here, the distributed ledger is tamperproof, which does not allow in misinterpretation or wrong authentications in data. Blockchain complexly eliminates the single thread communication (STC) in IoT making the system more trustless. With the adoption of blockchain in IoT, the data flow will become more secure. Blockchain technology has the following advantages when applied to large-scale IoT systems:

- Tamperproof data.
- Trustless and peer-to-peer (P2P) messaging capability.
- Robust.
- Highly reliable.
- More private data.
- Records the historic actions.
- Records data of old transactions in smart devices.
- Permits self-directed functioning.
- Distributed file sharing.
- Elimination of single control authority.
- Cost reduction in developing huge Internet infrastructure.
- Built-in trust.
- Accelerates transactions.

The blockchain concept began in 2008 (by an anonymous person or group), but was used only in Bitcoin, a cryptocurrency, in 2009. The blockchain (a decentralized database which works on complex cryptographic techniques) emerged as a novel distributed consensus scheme that allows transactions, and any other data, to be securely stored and verified without the need for any centralized authority. Distributed trust—and therefore, security and privacy—are at the core of blockchain technologies, and have the potential to either make them a success or cause them to fail. Hence, some important ideas and principles in security follow:

- Defense in penetration: This is a strategy which uses numerous corrective measures to protect the data. It follows the principle that protecting data in multiple layers is more efficient as opposed to a single security layer.
- Minimum privilege: In this strategy, the access to data is reduced to the lowest level possible to reinforce an elevated level of security.
- Manage vulnerabilities: In this strategy, we check for vulnerabilities and manage them by identifying, authenticating, modifying, and patching.
- Manage risks: In this strategy, we process the risks in an environment by identifying, assessing, and controlling risks.
- Manage patches: In this strategy, we patch the words like code, application or any type error, etc.

Some applications using blockchain technology are listed in Table 8.1.

Hence, similar to IoT, the blockchain technology has wider applications, and can be used in various sectors like agriculture, business, distribution, energy, food, finance, healthcare, manufacturing, and other sectors. This section has included several possible sectors and applications using blockchain technology in the near future. In other words, which applications may use blockchain technology in near future and where it can be used; such questions are listed with proper explanations. The next section will discuss several raised issues and challenges, currently and in past years, related to blockchain technology.

TABLE 8.1 Several applications and use of blockchain technology in the Internet of Things

APPLICATIONS	USES (CATEGORY WISE)	ISSUES	CHALLENGES
Agriculture	Soil data, processing records related to agriculture data, shipping of agro- products, sales and marketing data of agro-seeds, yields etc., growth.	Secured data storage, remote monitoring, automation	Challenges related to security and privacy
Business	Import and export data, digital records By software industries, transaction processing data, and all other which has the value for finance.	Increase in transaction cost, Transaction delay, inevitable mistakes	Security, Privacy, Latency and Computational Cost
Distribution	Transport records, storage records, sales records, marketplace, digital currencies, mining chips, used goods and sales.	Data storage	Legal and compliance issues
Energy	Energy generation data, energy raw material data, resource availability, energy supplier and demand data records, tariff data maintenance, supply on demand, tracking of resources, condition maintaining of the utility.	Development cost, cost for validation and verification of data	Scalability, speed, security [4]
Food	Food packing data, food delivery and shipping data records, food online ordering and transaction data, food quality assurance data.	Lack of sufficient records, change in consumer preference	Tracability, lack of unifying requirement
Finance	Currency exchange, money deposit, money transfer, crowd funding, smart securities, smart contract, social banking, digital transaction assets, cryptocurrency.	Legal issues	Regulatory challenges, security and privacy
Healthcare	Genome data, electronic medical records, digital case reports, Digitalizing old medical data, Prescription records, information system at hospital, healthcare costs, vital signs.	Storage of massive data, lack of standardization	Security, privacy
Manufacturing	Product assurance, product guarantee information, product warranty information, manufacturing management, robotics, sensors/actuators, product production data, packaging data, product delivery transaction data, supplier and components or raw material tracking.		Technical challenges, human related challenges
Smart city	Smart service offerings, energy management data, water management data, pollution control data, digital data, enabling digital transactions, smart data maintenance, smart transaction.	Data maintenance	Lack of knowledge, lack of standards, lack of regulation
Transport and logistics	Transport records, good delivery and shipping data, logistics service identifiers, toll data maintenance, vehicle tracking, shipping container tracking.	Scalability and performance issues	Lack of experts, security, privacy and reliability
Others	Digital content, economy sharing, artwork, ownership, jewels and precious metals, space developments, government and voting, virtual nations.	Platform scalability, energy consumption for validation and verification	Cost, regulation, security

8.6 ISSUES AND CHALLENGES IN BLOCKCHAIN TECHNOLOGY FROM A 'SMART ERA' VIEW

Common security-related concerns of any organization while using blockchain are ensuring authorized parties to access correct and appropriate data. Warranting the security of data and data access in the blockchain network is fundamental. The Internet of Things (IoT) is defined as "a system of interconnected computing devices, mechanical and digital machines, objects, animals or people that are provided with unique identifiers and the ability to transfer data over a network without requiring human-to-human or human-to-computer interaction" [13]. The Internet of Things is being are being used in many applications like animal farming, healthcare, manufacturing, etc. In the near future, we have a possibility of using blockchain in IoT-based applications. Together, we face several (similar) challenges like today's in the respective applications. In the current era, there are five blockchain problems: security, privacy, legal, regulatory, and ethical issues. Also, one popular attack on blockchain network is the 51% attack, which occurs when a hacker (or group of hackers) produces more than 50% of a blockchain's computing power or tries to occupy more than 50% of a blockchain's network.

Today's blockchain is one of the most-hyped technologies. Even though privacy-enhancing technologies are deployed, they still produce metadata. Statistical analysis will reveal some information, even if the data itself is encrypted, making, for example, pattern recognition possible. Furthermore, scalability is an emerging challenge, since the consensus process is currently too expensive. If currency or any other value is traded on a blockchain-based application, a much higher transaction speed is needed. Ethereum is currently capable of 2.8 transactions per second, while Bitcoin is capable of approximately 3.2 transactions per second. It takes so long because of the complex consensus process for each transaction (currently proof of work or proof of stake) [10]. Another attack to keep in mind is the 51%-attack or "majority hash rate attack." If an organization or individual has 51% of the hash power, the attacker can reverse transactions he sent, prevent transactions from gaining confirmations, and prevent other miners from mining [15]. Blockchain technology faces a few future opportunities, as well as challenges. Although significant, the challenges can be overcome with the maturity and enhancement of the technology in the future. This will lead to a plethora of future opportunities for blockchain to be implemented and accepted. The challenges in blockchain and its applications are discussed in the rest of this section.

8.6.1 Challenges in Blockchain (in General)

A challenge can be defined as an implicit demand for proof. Some of the major challenges currently faced by blockchain technology include:

- Scalability: With ever-increasing volume of blockchain usage and the surge in the sheer number of transactions daily, the blockchain is becoming progressively colossal in size. All transactions are stored in each node to be validated. The source of the current transaction needs to be validated first before it can be validated. The restricted block size and the time interlude used to produce a new block also plays a part in not fulfilling the requirement of processing millions of transactions simultaneously in real-time scenarios. In the meantime, the size of the blocks in blockchain might create an issue of transaction delay in case of small transactions, as miners would prefer to validate transactions with bigger transactional fees. As mentioned in [16], the proposed solutions to the scalability issue of blockchains can be categorized in two categories: storage optimization and redesigning of blockchains. This database would maintain rest of the non-empty addresses. A lightweight client could also be used as an alternate to fix the scalability issue. In redesigning, the blockchain can be fragmented into a key block and a micro block, with the key block being responsible for leader elections and the micro block being responsible for transaction storage.

- Privacy leakage: The blockchain is mainly vulnerable to leakage of transactional privacy due to the fact that the details and balances of all public keys are visible to everyone in the network. The proposed solutions to achieve anonymity in blockchains can be broadly classified into the mixing and anonymous solutions. Mixing is a service that offers anonymity by transferring funds from multiple input addresses to multiple output addresses. Anonymity is a service which unlinks the payment origins for a transaction to prevent transaction graph analysis.
- Selfish mining: A block is susceptible to cheating if a small portion of hashing power is used. In selfish mining, the miners keep the mined blocks without broadcasting to the network and create a private branch which gets broadcast only after certain requirements are met. In this case, honest miners waste a lot of time and resources, while the private chain is mined by selfish miners.
- Personal identifiable information: Personal identifiable information (PII) is any information that can be used to extricate an individual's identity. In [17], authors discuss the PII with respect to communication and location privacy.
- Security: Security can be discussed in terms of confidentiality, integrity, and availability, as discussed in [18]. It is always a challenge in open networks such as public blockchains. Confidentiality is low in distributed systems that imitate information over their networks. Integrity is the métier of blockchains. Blockchain faces other challenges, like availability in blockchains is high in terms of readability due to wide replication compared to write availability. The 51% majority attack is more theoretical in a large blockchain network because of these properties.

In summary, there are no single-owner applications available (in current) but maximum applications are used or shared by a group of competitors. It means when a member uses the technology, there is chance of leaking information or a breach of information. This is the biggest challenge or issue to overcome in blockchain technology or the computing environment.

8.6.2 Challenges in Blockchain Technology–Integrated Internet of Things (IoT)

Even though blockchain technology when integrated with IoT, it may overcome the privacy and reliability (general) concerns of IoT also (automatically). However, the blockchain technology is also having some limitations making it as a challenge. These challenges include limitations with the ledger storage facility, limited developments in technology, lack of skilled workforce, lack of proper legal codes and standards, variations in processing speeds and time, computing capabilities, and scalability issues. Some critical challenges have been included in Table 8.2.

Internet of Things (IoT) security is gaining a lot of attention these days from both academia and industry. Until 2025, most of the Internet-connected devices will be connected with other smart devices for doing or performing many everyday tasks of our daily lives [12]. Existing security solutions are not necessarily suited for IoT due to high energy consumption and processing overhead. In Figure 8.1, we discussed a use case study on IoT using blockchain (with core components of architecture). In that, we provide higher authentication using blockchain technology, i.e., also having an aim of low and manageable for low resource IoT devices. Hence, this section discusses several issues and challenges in different applications using blockchain technology. The next section will discuss several serious concerns (especially security and privacy concerns) in the smart era of the 21st century.

TABLE 8.2   Challenges in Blockchain Technology Integrated with Internet of Things [13]

S. NO.	APPLICATION	NAME OF THE CHALLENGES	DESCRIPTION WITH APPLICATION—WISE
1	Agriculture	Limitation with storage facility	In IoT ecosystem, the storage capacity required for sensors and actuators is very less when compared to the ledger based Blockchain technology. In IoT, a single central server storage is facilitated, where as in Blockchain, each ledger must be stored at the node on themselves. This increase the storage size with time when compared to the traditional storage seen in IoT devices.
		Lack of skills in the field	Still the technology is new, many challenges are to be sought out to make it more convenient.
2	Manpower	Lack of workforce (Skilled)	Skilled force on this technology is very much limited, this number is extremely less when it is integrated with the concept of IoT. That means skilled work force who are knowing about the Blockchain integrated IoT concept is very less.
		Legal issues	This technology does not have any legal codes to follow. This is one of most challenging issue to be tacked.
		Variation in computing capabilities	As it a known fact that IoT systems are diverse and connected over vast network, this becomes much more complex when the Blockchain technology is integrated with it. The need for running the encryption from all the things that are connected Blockchain based IoT system is essential. In such cases, all the algorithm for running the encryption may not have similar computing capabilities.
3	Execution Time	Processing time	When these computing capabilities are varying, the time required to perform the encryption would vary leading to the variations in processing time.
		Scalability	This might lead to the centralization. If it becomes centralized the technique behind the cryptocurrency like Bitcoin would be revealed.

8.7 SECURITY AND PRIVACY ISSUES IN THE 'SMART ERA' (IN THE 21ST CENTURY)

In a blockchain, some essential elements are being used, i.e., these essential elements or components protect respective applications from any kind of attacks (internal or external). Some essential building blocks of blockchain security are decentralization (no centralized database), security by the blocks (security to a linear series of "blocks" of code), encryption, consensus mechanisms, and privacy protection. Protecting cryptographic keys is another essential ingredient to blockchain security. If everything is encrypted, we run the risk of losing it all if the key is lost. Using hardware security modules and trusted computers instead of digital wallets may well provide protection for users' digital assets.

Transactions are globally published and are not encrypted in most applications. If this data is personal data, for example medical or financial data, this leads to regulatory and legal problems, especially in Germany. One solution is to store only encrypted data in the blockchain, which leads to another problem: if the key to decrypt specific information is lost, the data may not be recovered accurately. Furthermore, if a key is stolen and published, all the data is forever decrypted in the blockchain, since the data cannot be altered. However, blockchain can also help to improve defensive cybersecurity strategies, especially in terms of identity and access. There are several problems raised in blockchain, most popular among them security and privacy, discussed as follows:

- Man-in-the-middle (MITM) attacks: One attack scheme for MITM attacks is to get the certificate authority (CA) to provide the user with forged public keys (public key substitution MITM attack). This can lead to the decryption of sensitive information. In a blockchain approach whereby users put their public keys in published blocks, the information is distributed over the participating nodes with links to previous and following blocks. This makes the public key immutable and it becomes harder for attackers to publish fake keys. Furthermore, the single point of failure, the CA, is also distributed, meaning it is harder to bring this service down. Projects that try to solve this problem include okTurtles [19].
- Data tampering: Since every transaction is signed and distributed over all blockchain nodes, it is practically impossible to manipulate data without the network knowing about it. How do we prove that Germany won the World Cup in 2014? We do not have to prove it, since it is general knowledge distributed across the people. In healthcare, the blockchain could be used to create immutable audit trails, maintain the integrity of health trials, and ensure the integrity of patient data shared across different medical environments.
- DDoS attacks: If DNS systems were based on blockchain technology, attacks like the one from the Mirai botnet would be harder to successfully complete. Such a system would provide transparency and security. The domain name system (DNS) infrastructure could not be targeted if it were a distributed system, since the data is distributed and the data entries cannot be tampered with, due to the append-only nature of the blockchain. The project "okTurtle" is also realizing a blockchain-based DNS service. For example, a DDoS attack is one in which the attacker uses several infected IoT devices to overwhelm a particular target node. Several recent attacks included in [20] have come to light which have exploited IoT devices to launch massive DDoS attacks.
- Privacy: The blockchain technology is a great example for the unrelatedness of security (at least in terms of immutability) and privacy. While it is possible to design an immutable, tamper-resistant transaction, this transaction can be seen throughout all of the nodes on the network. The most promising research on privacy (or private transactions) for blockchain technology is currently zk-SNARKs, which are implemented by zCash and Ethereum (zCash on Ethereum). The combination of both technologies makes it possible to implement anonymous payments, blind auctions, and voting systems. Since the mechanisms behind zk-SNARKS are not trivial, they cannot be described in this chapter (due to limited space).
- Linking attacks: To protect against this attack, each device's data is shared and stored by a unique key. The miner creates a unique ledger of data in the cloud storage for each device using a different public key. From the overlay point of view, the miner should use a unique key for each transaction.

Hence, this section discusses how security and privacy can be enhanced by blockchain technology in the next decade or during the 21st century. This section discusses several issues or attacks related to blockchain technology. The next section will discuss several solutions, available for security and privacy problems raised in blockchain (while using other sectors or applications).

8.8 EXISTING SOLUTIONS FOR SECURITY AND PRIVACY CONCERNS IN VARIOUS COMPUTING ENVIRONMENTS

Blockchain technology ensures adequate benefits to overcome both technological and governance hurdles and attain widespread use in the future. Note that data like personal data, or medical or financial data, leads to regulatory and legal problems in critical applications. Blockchain technology also fails to protect such data with required efficiency. Note that in blockchain, transactions (digitally signed with a public key) are documented in chronological order. Apart from blockchain method, several methods for security are trust authentication, password authentication, GSSAPI (generic security service application program interface) authentication, SSPI (security support provider interface) authentication, Kerberos authentication, Ident authentication, peer-to-peer authentication, LDAP (lightweight directory access protocol) authentication, and RADIUS (remote authentication dial-in user service) authentication—but these methods are not enough to secure available computing environments against critical attacks. On another side, privacy-preserving mechanisms are in computing environment [21, 22] like anonymity method (k-anonymity, l-diversity, t-closeness, etc.), mix zone method (pro-mix, silent mix, mobi-mix, etc.), position dummies (fake points), position sharing, path confusion, obfuscation and coordinate transformation, pseudonyms, the silent period (SP), swing and swap, certificate authentication, cryptography-based approaches, PAMs (pluggable authentication models), etc.

Apart from this concept, blockchain has provided far better secure infrastructure (or mechanisms) or secure computing environments, but still, we need to go far, i.e. identification of a threat to a network before it occurs (proactively). The entire world is watching and looking for such efficient solutions from research community and scientists. Hence, this section discusses several solutions for identified problems like security and privacy with(in) blockchain technology when it is being used in many applications in this smart era. Many problems, issues, and challenges in blockchain have been discussed here and in [14]. The next section will provide several opportunities and research directions (including identified research gaps) for future researchers and scientists. Those people can look forward to continue their work in and toward respective opportunities and directions.

8.9 OPPORTUNITIES AND RESEARCH DIRECTIONS FOR THE NEAR FUTURE WITH BLOCKCHAIN

As discussed in this chapter, the Internet during past years has observed the initiation of numerous bottom-up, significant applications that resolve problems using accommodating and distributed techniques. Many opportunities lie with respect to blockchain in many applications in the near future. For example, in the near future, blockchain distributive nature can help IoT security and also can be useful for a variety of areas, including applications for manufacturing, finance, trading, etc. Implementing blockchain in such applications can help farmers or users to grow or increase profits in their respective business. As a result, many areas such like banking, business, and government organizations are today displaying mounting interest in blockchain technology. For a little information, blockchain has received attention from this world and popularity because of acceptance of the Bitcoin currency by many countries and markets. Bitcoin technology is constantly evolving, and its deployment is susceptible to human infirmities and conflicting standards. Now, opportunities in blockchain can be stated as a chance to integrate blockchain technology in existing applications to improve efficiency and use, as well as to promote this technology in future applications. Some of the future opportunities are listed in more detail following:

- Strategic alignment and governance: Active management of connections between enterprise progressions and administrative priorities that aim to facilitate operative actions for business performance improvement can be referred to as strategic alignment. The analysis includes the evaluation of different processes and how they can be improved with the use of blockchain technology. The risks of these strategies analogous to the lock-in effects might also need to be analyzed.
- Others: First, dedicated roles that coordinate both internal and external cohorts for setting up blockchain support need to be defined. This requires both technical and jurisprudential facts.

Second, policies need to be defined for the usage and the related process of blockchain. Third, a set of guidelines needs to be defined for the usage of public, private, and consortium block-chains. Finally, smart contracts can be used to launch new models of governance epitomized by decentralized autonomous blockchain (DAO).

Blockchain-based approaches provide decentralized security and privacy, yet they involve significant energy, delay, and computational overhead that is not suitable for most resource-constrained IoT devices. We need to overcome (while introducing some efficient mechanisms) these raised (security and privacy) issues in IoT. For example, we can found several uses of blockchain technology in day-to-day (most useful) applications [23–28]. Also, several serious concerns also have been discussed [23–28] in the integration of blockchain technology with other technologies like IoT, machine learning, etc. In the near future, we need to develop a framework to integrate blockchain with IoT, which can provide great assurance for IoT data and various functionalities and desirable scalability, including authentication, decentralized payment, and so on. Hence, this section discusses serval opportunities and research directions with respect to blockchain for near future. The next section will summarize this work in brief with several interesting remarks related to the future of blockchain technology.

8.10 SUMMARY

Blockchain is a melting pot of high value, high risks, and low maturity. Several useful or related terms are discussed in this work, starting from the use of blockchain in the current century and shifting to many issues, challenges, variations and extensions, opportunities, etc., to future researchers. Throughout this chapter, we find out that security and privacy are serious in this current smart era. Even having innovative solutions, we are still in a growing phase with respect to protecting user data and privacy. This work has also discussed various applications in the near future which can use blockchain technology. In another words, this chapter helps us in finding other applications of blockchain technology (Like IoT, IoT-based cloud, or cloud-based IoT) in the near future. For such applications, we require proactive security and privacy or strong mechanisms to protect user's information (on cloud). The structure of used applications in near future can be IoT-based cloud or cloud-based IoT. Today's blockchain technology is identified as a perfect solution for addressing raised issues and challenges in IoT, but we still face similar issues and do not have perfect (and unique) solutions against serious attacks like DDoS, MITM, etc. We require programmers and security specialists to think like attackers to ensure the resiliency of blockchain ecosystems. In our future research, we will investigate the applications of our framework to other IoT domains.

REFERENCES

[1] Schwab, K. *The Fourth Industrial Revolution*. Currency, 2017.
[2] Karafiloski, E., and A. Mishev. "Blockchain solutions for big data challenges: A literature review." In *IEEE EUROCON 2017–17th International Conference on Smart Technologies*, pp. 763–768. IEEE, July 2017.
[3] Crosby, M., P. Pattanayak, S. Verma, and V. Kalyanaraman. "Blockchain technology: Beyond bitcoin." *Applied Innovation* 2, no. 6–10 (2016): 71.
[4] Mattila, J. "The blockchain phenomenon—the disruptive potential of distributed consensus architectures (No. 38)." *ETLA Working Papers*, 2016.
[5] Haber, S. A., and W. S. Stornetta Jr. Surety Tech Inc. 1998. "Digital document authentication system." U.S. Patent 5,781,629.
[6] Nakamoto, S. *Bitcoin: A Peer-to-Peer Electronic Cash System*. 2008.

[7] Buterin, V. "A next-generation smart contract and decentralized application platform." *White Paper* 3 (2014): 37.

[8] Hirai, Y. "Defining the ethereum virtual machine for interactive theorem provers." In *International Conference on Financial Cryptography and Data Security*, pp. 520–535. Springer, April 2017.

[9] Haber, S., and W. S. Stornetta. "Secure names for bit-strings." In *Proceedings of the 4th ACM Conference on Computer and Communications Security*, pp. 28–35. ACM, April 1997.

[10] Finney, H. *Rpow: Reusable Proofs of Work.* 2004. https://cryptome.org/rpow.htm.

[11] Liang, X., S. Shetty, D. Tosh, C. Kamhoua, K. Kwiat, and L. Njilla. "Provchain: A blockchain-based data provenance architecture in cloud environment with enhanced privacy and availability." In *Proceedings of the 17th IEEE/ACM International Symposium on Cluster, Cloud and Grid Computing*, pp. 468–477. IEEE Press, May 2017.

[12] Kshetri, N. "Can blockchain strengthen the internet of things?" *IT Professional* 19, no. 4 (2017): 68–72.

[13] Banafa, A. *IoT and Blockchain Convergence: Benefits and Challenges.* IEEE Internet of Things, 2017. https://www.iotforall.com/what-is-internet-of-things.

[14] Kumar, N. M., and P. K. Mallick. "Blockchain technology for security issues and challenges in IoT." *Procedia Computer Science* 132 (2018): 1815–1823.

[15] Triantafyllidis, N. P., and T. N. O. Oskar van Deventer. *Developing an Ethereum Blockchain Application.* 2016. Retrieved from https://www.slideshare.net/socialmediadna/trial-by-blockhain-developing-an-ethereum-blockchain-application.

[16] Vukolić, M. "The quest for scalable blockchain fabric: Proof-of-work vs. BFT replication." In *International Workshop on Open Problems in Network Security*, pp. 112–125. Springer, October 2015.

[17] Jain, P., M. Gyanchandani, and N. Khare. "Big data privacy: A technological perspective and review." *Journal of Big Data* 3, no. 1 (2016): 25.

[18] Halpin, H., and M. Piekarska. "Introduction to Security and Privacy on the Blockchain." In *2017 IEEE European Symposium on Security and Privacy Workshops* (EuroS&PW), pp. 1–3. IEEE, April 2017.

[19] Pretschner, A. *Public Key Tracing Framework Using Blockchain*, 2017 (Thesis).

[20] Kolias, C., G. Kambourakis, A. Stavrou, and J. Voas. "DDoS in the IoT: Mirai and other botnets." *Computer* 50, no. 7 (2017): 80–84.

[21] Sweeney, L. "k-anonymity: A model for protecting privacy." *International Journal of Uncertainty, Fuzziness and Knowledge-Based Systems* 10, no. 5 (2002): 557–570.

[22] Tyagi, A., and N. Sreenath. "A comparative study on privacy preserving techniques for location based services." *Journal of Advances in Mathematics and Computer Science* 10, no. 4 (2015): 1–25. https://doi.org/10.9734/BJMCS/2015/16995.

[23] Tyagi, A. K., S. U. Aswathy, and Abraham, Ajith. "Integrating blockchain technology and artificial intelligence: Synergies, perspectives, challenges and research directions." *Journal of Information Assurance and Security* 15, no. 5 (2020). ISSN: 1554–1010.

[24] Tyagi, A. K., S. Kumari, T. F. Fernandez, and C. Aravindan. "P3 block: Privacy preserved, trusted smart parking allotment for future vehicles of tomorrow." In Gervasi, O., et al. (eds.). *Computational Science and Its Applications—ICCSA 2020. ICCSA 2020. Lecture Notes in Computer Science.* Vol. 12254. Springer, 2020. https://doi.org/10.1007/978-3-030-58817-5_56.

[25] Tyagi, A. K., T. F. Fernandez, and S. U. Aswathy. "Blockchain and aadhaar based electronic voting system." *2020 4th International Conference on Electronics, Communication and Aerospace Technology (ICECA)*, pp. 498–504, Coimbatore, 2020. DOI: 10.1109/ICECA49313.2020.9297655.

[26] Tyagi, Amit Kumar, Meghna Manoj Nair, Sreenath Niladhuri, and Ajith Abraham. "Security, privacy research issues in various computing platforms: A survey and the road ahead." *Journal of Information Assurance & Security* 15, no. 1 (2020): 1–16.16p.

[27] Tyagi, Amit Kumar, and Meghna Manoj Nair. "Internet of everything (IoE) and internet of things (IoTs): Threat analyses." *Possible Opportunities for Future* 15, no. 4 (2020).

[28] Nair, Siddharth M., Varsha Ramesh, and Amit Kumar Tyagi. "Issues and challenges (privacy, security, and trust) in blockchain-based applications." *Book: Opportunities and Challenges for Blockchain Technology in Autonomous Vehicles* (2021): 14. DOI: 10.4018/978-1-7998-3295-9.ch012.

Applications of Blockchain Technologies in Digital Forensics and Threat Hunting

9

Shabnam Kumari, Amit Kumar Tyagi and G. Rekha

Contents

9.1 INTRODUCTION: DIGITAL FORENSICS AND THREAT HUNTING

Digital forensics and threat hunting are two essential processes in this current digital environment to track cybercrimes and avoid cybercrimes before they occur. Digital forensics (sometimes known as digital forensic science) is a part of forensic science with digitalization. It investigates the crime with an emphasis on recovery of content related to computer crimes found in digital devices [1]. In general, digital forensics is the process of exploring and interpreting data in electronic form. The main motto of the process is to find the original evidence and to perform structured investigation by digital data collection, identification, and validation to reconstruct past events. Sometimes, it also called computer forensics. The main application

159

of computer forensics is to investigate digital attacks and crimes. It is a vital part of an overall incident response strategy. In simple terms, digital forensics (or cyber forensics) is a branch of forensic science that includes the identification, recovery, investigation, validation, and presentation of facts regarding digital evidence. On another side, Digital forensics and forensic science are two different terms (domains). In [2], the accepted definition is: "Forensic science is the application of science to matters of law." One more definition of digital forensics (by the first Digital Forensic Research Workshop [DFRWS]) is:

> The use of scientifically derived and proven methods toward the preservation, collection, validation, identification, analysis, interpretation, documentation and presentation of digital evidence derived from digital sources for the purpose of facilitating or furthering the reconstruction of events found to be criminal, or helping to anticipate unauthorized actions shown to be disruptive to planned operations [3].

Forensic science requires careful examination to find some extremely important insights from the data. It needs scientific methods to be applied both in general and for specific investigations. The term "forensic" refers to how to make decision according to law. Forensic scientists obey the law and will not take over the authority and role of the court in reaching its decision. But there will be a drastic difference between scientific fact-finding and legal fact-finding in decision making. The most challenging part for forensic investigators is uncovering evidence which will be useful in court. The cultures and expectations of legal and scientific fact-finding are different, as are their impact and how each is likely to affect the lives of others. So it is required to define "science and scientific methods" and the way it operates within the forensic science domain. Next, some different types of digital forensics are discussed in detail in the following subsections.

9.1.1 Different Types of Digital Forensics

Digital forensics is a constantly evolving scientific field with many sub-disciplines (Figure 9.1). Some of these sub-disciplines of digital forensics are:

1. Computer forensics: The interaction of distinguishing proof, assortment, analysis, and reporting of proof found on systems such as workstations and personal computers, and furthermore stockpiling media for examinations and legitimate procedures [4].
2. Network forensics: Deals with discovery of network attacks and the source of attacks. Network forensics continuously monitor, capture, and analyze the network behavior in order to find the attacks such as intrusions and internal incidents, i.e. worms, virus, or malware attacks, and abnormal network traffic and security breaches [4].
3. Mobile devices forensics: The way toward recuperating electronic proof from cell phones, SIM cards, PDAs, GPS gadgets, tablets, and game consoles.

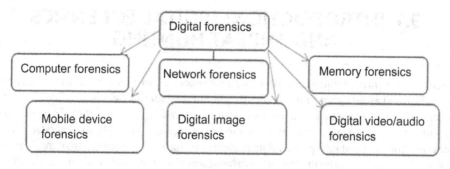

FIGURE 9.1 Digital forensics and its types.

4. Digital image forensics: The extraction and examination of carefully obtained photographic images to prove their authenticity by recuperating the metadata of the image record to discover the set of experiences in its digital history.
5. Digital video/audio forensics: The assortment, examination, and assessment of sound and video accounts. The science is the foundation of legitimacy regarding whether a chronicle is unique and whether it has been altered, either malevolently or inadvertently.
6. Memory forensics: The recuperation of proof from the RAM of a running PC, additionally called live procurement.

By and by, there are exemptions which obscure this classification in light of the fact that the grouping by the supplier is directed by staff ranges of abilities, authoritative necessities, lab space, and so on; for instance:

1. Tablets or cell phones without SIM cards could be viewed as systems.
2. Memory cards (and other removable stockpiling media) are regularly found in cell phones and tablets, so they could be considered under portable or system forensics.
3. Tablets with consoles could be viewed as systems and fit under system or portable forensics.

Today, more than 80% of all cyber-attacks penetrate from outsider rather from inside security groups [5]. Much of the time, enemies (or attackers) have been working inside the victim's' organization undetected for quite a long time or even years. For that, we need to distinguish such insider threats immediately (in an organization) in a productive way (proactively or time to time). Be that as it may, digital forensics has boundless future with advances in innovation. Likewise, with development in innovation, new advancements are prompted. Even though digital forensics started outside the standards of forensic science, it is presently completely encompassed and perceived as a part of forensic science.

9.1.2 Threat Hunting in Information Systems

In today's smart era, detecting an attack on a big network is a complex and critical task [5][6]. For example, physical computerized systems and cyber infrastructure are part of a big network called the Internet of Things (IoT), where we unable to find actual devices which face attacks or any vulnerability from outside users and networks. The primary concern is to distinguish interruptions in advancement by continually taking a look at the attacks that move beyond the security frameworks. The fundamental goal is to discover the attack ahead of time, as opposed to after the attacks have finished their targets, prompting huge harm to the association. For the incident responder, this communication is known as "threat hunting" [7]. Threat hunting uses adversary practices to proactively investigate the association and endpoints to perceive new data breaches. Such tests should be possible by an individual who is skilled. An appropriately prepared and GIAC (Global Information Assurance Certification)-certified incident responder could be the solitary guard an association has during a tradeoff; as a forensic sciences examiner, we generally know what we are up against, and we need to have the most modern information on the best way to identify and battle it. Also, a couple of hunting threats and incident response systems and techniques have progressed rapidly in recent times. Note that when we neglect to fittingly recognize compromised structures, give inadequate control of the penetration, and finally neglect to rapidly remediate the occurrence, incident response and threat hunting are used to endure/perceive such certifiable threats. The group joined with incident response and threat tracker distinguishes and notices malware in the organization. They recognize the patterns of action to create precise insights of threats that can be utilized to identify current and future interruptions. Note that the threat hunting and examining the incident, i.e., a typical misguided judgment, are pre-examination activities. And yet, the yield of automated identification frameworks, and hunting are equivalent: both produce likely applicants' examination. Through providing alerts to cybersecurity experts or administrators of a system, we can prevent or mitigate any critical attacks on such information systems.

Continuous monitoring and real-time alerting are not adequate alone to reduce hazards (or any attacks/breaches). We likewise require smoothed-out work processes to quickly issue emergency alerts, explore underlying root causes, remediate threats, and proactively hunt for new ones. Each alarm gives brief logical data about the particular action that was noticed and which gadgets were included. We need to determine the following:

- How the breach occurred.
- Identification of systems that are affected.
- Analyzing what all was stolen and give assessment of damage.
- Find an immediate remedy for the incident.
- Generating key sources of intelligence of threats.
- With method or a way by the adversary (a person who opposes attacks) can easily solve extra breaches if any.

As the present digital threats are increasing and becoming more unsafe, cybersecurity experts are turning to new methodologies—for example, threat hunting—to safeguard themselves against digital threats. Trackers who analyze threats have higher certainty, which can undoubtedly recognize that in the thing is really occurring in your organization. However, for that, we need to give threat hunters more prominent perceivability, speed, and a more extensive comprehension of all threats in the organization. Note that with more grounded security, we can proactively seek and addresses obscure issues and attacks. We need to assemble some productive calculations or components which can be utilized effectively to identify, counter, and react to genuine breach cases (in individual applications). The remaining part of this article is organized as follows. Section 9.2 discusses history of digital forensics and threat hunting process. Further, section 9.3 discusses work related to digital forensics and threat hunters. Section 9.4 discusses motivation behind doing this work. Section 9.5 discusses the importance and scope of digital forensics and threat hunting in today's era. Section 9.6 discusses popular tools, mechanisms, and methods used in digital forensics and threat hunting processes. Section 9.7 discusses several issues and challenges in digital forensics and threat hunting, then section 9.8 discusses useful points or opportunity for future researchers (including several research gaps). Finally, this work is summarized with some future remarks (which will be more helpful for our readers) in section 9.9. Note that this discusses an overview of incident handling and threat hunting tools, techniques and procedures, identification of compromised systems, detecting active and passive malware, incident handling, and incident management frameworks.

9.2 HISTORY OF DIGITAL FORENSICS AND THREAT HUNTING

The term digital forensics was called computer forensics after the late 1990s. A law enforcement officer was the first person to work as computer forensic technician for the U.S. FBI's Computer Analysis and Response Team (CART), in 1984. A year later, the UK's Metropolitan Police set up a unit under the oversight of John Austen then called the Fraud Squad. A huge change happened around the beginning of the 1990s. Specialists and specialized assistance specialists inside the UK law enforcement associations, closely with prepared experts, perceived that forensics required standard systems, conventions, and techniques. As the rules were casually referenced, an emergent requirement for formalization was required. Continuous conferences, from the outset met by the Serious Fraud Office and the Department of Inland Revenue, happened at the Police Staff College at Bramshill in 1994 and 1995, during which the cutting-edge British forensic technique was set up. In the UK in 1998, the Association of Chief Police Officers (ACPO) conveyed the essential type of its *Good Practice Guide for Digital Evidence* (Association of Chief

Police Officers, 2012). The ACPO rules detail the crucial principles material to all high level advanced forensic sciences for law use in the UK. As the investigation of forensics has built up, these standards and best practices have continuously progressed into standards and the field has gone under the purview of the Forensic Science Regulator in the UK.

Today, we need to build some mechanisms to identify and respond to some sophisticated attacks. There are a few safety efforts—for example, firewalls, intrusion detection systems (IDSs), endpoint insurance, and simulations. Likewise, we need to make some proficient and compelling systems for upgrading threat hunting and examining the occurrence—for example, a typical misinterpretation—since hunting is pre-examination tasks. In any case, recall that at the same time, the yield of automated discovery frameworks and hunting are the equivalent, i.e. the two components are utilized to distinguish and investigate threats in an organization. Similarly, attackers may attack an autonomous system or vehicle to take control of such for its benefit. We can use blockchain in autonomous applications to securely store communicated information (data in motion). Also, we need to prevent such possible attacks on autonomous vehicles through efficient threat hunting and digital forensics processes. Note that we can provide some warning to users, so we can save many users from many serious attacks and threats. Today's blockchain technology is used in many applications like autonomous applications, financial institutions to reduce fraud, smart grids, industrial control systems, etc. We need to elaborate each respective application and identify cybercrime on such applications. These cybercrimes are very critical and complex to mitigate (proactively, i.e., before they occur), and also require attention from there search community to recover.

This section discusses history about digital forensics and threat hunting process. The next section will discuss many points and works related to digital forensics and threat hunting processes.

9.3 RELATED WORK

Blockchain as an innovation has been proposed as an answer for everything from frictionless money movement to following freight on boats. Basic effect of cyber-threats/attacks, such as unpredictability, and intensity are alleviating on numerous applications like transportation, agriculture, healthcare, manufacturing, etc. [8]. There are a few digital attacks or incidents accessible in current situations on numerous applications, which are quick and expanding in number and seriousness. At the point when a digital incident (or violation) happens, the attacked venture reacts with a series of pre-decided activities. Applying forensic science to help in the recuperation and examination of material on advanced media and organizations is one of these activities. As examined in the introduction segment, forensic science is the cycle of distinguishing, protecting, investigating and introducing computerized proof in a way that is legitimately satisfactory in any lawful procedures (i.e., a courtroom). The reason for work [9] is to give an outline of advanced forensics as it applies absolutely to cybersecurity. By and large, there are many complex and basic threats accessible on the web. We need to guard end clients' frameworks and information, and recognize enemies may have been effectively scavenging through the organization undetected for quite a long time or even years. There are many concealed threats as of now existing inside an association's organizations; however, we are consistently unaware of this. Such attacks may turn out to be more destructive than different attacks, on the off chance that we do not make any move against such breaches. No safety efforts are invulnerable, regardless of how careful their security precautionary measures may be. Likewise, anticipation frameworks alone are inadequate to counter a centered enemy who realizes how to get around most security and observing instruments. Along these lines, the idea of threat hunting appears, i.e., identifying any danger over digital world proactively (before it occurs). Basically, threat trackers are incident responders and specialists effectively searching for new threats before customary intrusion detection methods (IDMs) can discover them.

In 1998, the digital examination programming device EnCase was released by Guidance Software to settle criminal cases. Today advanced digital forensic techniques have cleared a route for network safety, corporate examinations, and e-discovery in this corporate world. Equivalently, government and state experts look for used digitized verification to convict law breakers. IT bosses, and security, can use progressed advanced forensics to accumulate and safeguard proof to take apart and guard against a cyber-attack, stop an insider danger, or complete an inside assessment. A threat tracker is taking the regular indicators of compromise (IoC) instead of latently holding on to remember them (which is outdated now). By and large, customary interruption discovery doesn't perform appropriately or is unfit to discover anticipated (current) assaults by a sly enemy, i.e., it dodges just typical interruption identification guards. It takes a threat tracker to discover those (digital) attacks [10]. Threat hunting, in general, is the process of proactively seeking for and detecting digital threats, i.e., prior to presenting or unexploited organizational flaws should have been mitigated with some appropriate solutions. The interaction of threat detection is to characterize a few speculations as far as cybercriminal attacks and the conduct methods that lead to misuse in organization. At that point, threat trackers use insight to perceive gaps in their cybersecurity walls and do the vital activities to secure their frameworks. There are a few stages engaged with the act of threat hunting including planning, speculation creation, validating patterns, discovery response, and information sharing. All the more explicitly, threat trackers should be outfitted with applicable threat insight information before they can continue. Whenever this has been obtained, they can proceed onward to create speculations and pose inquiries: for example, "which regions have the most noteworthy likelihood of being focused on?" and "what strategies might attackers actually utilize?" One stage of threat hunting is containing "verification"; i.e., wherein the trackers look for an association among dangers and the produced theories. During this stage, a few speculations might be dismissed for other people. At the point when hypothesis and genuine threat matches, the last advance is to follow up on discoveries by conveying a group to determine the issues. Many crimes like physical crimes and cybercrimes are being traced nowadays. These crimes influence our society a lot; thus, we need to overcome and plan to identify and detect such crimes (cyberattacks on open network) using blockchain-based applications with proper organization, and planning and execution of methods and rules.

This section discusses evolution of digital forensics and threat hunting, and also work done for some popular cyberattacks (in the past decade, by many researchers and there search community). The next section will discuss motivation behind this work, i.e. why this topic or area is necessary to read about and the importance of having knowledge for threat detection (including some explanation of digital forensics in real-world application).

9.4 MOTIVATION

Blockchain is considered as the future of technology. Many industries (related to several applications) are using blockchain concepts in their businesses. We need to identify popular business in many popular sectors like healthcare, finance, transportation, etc. [11] that can be improved or enabled by blockchain technology. There are many attacks or vulnerabilities occurring everyday on many applications requiring mitigation; for that, similarly, we have cyber threat intelligence fields to recover those applications from any kind of attacks. For example, financial institutions use blockchain-based applications to reduce fraud. Fraud is one type of cybercrime to provide benefits of some purpose to others. We need to identify such cybercrimes and attacks using threat hunting and digital forensics processes.

In cyber physical systems, many attacks have been mitigated in the previous decade. For example, in 2010, the Stuxnet worm attack repeatedly affected Iran's nuclear facilities [12]. Also, in recent years, some attackers/hackers have entered into various services of the United States, like air traffic control mission-support systems, to make systems ineffective. Additionally, in 2010, a few attacks were related to a product apparatus called "Carshark" [13], which could cut off a car engine distantly, turn off the brakes so the car would not pause, and make instruments give incorrect error readings by checking correspondences between the electronic control units (ECUs) and supplement counterfeit parcels of information to complete attacks. Additionally, in earlier years, attackers executed a fix/worm/infection to influence or control the Siemens plant-control framework [14]. Nowadays, some hackers can also hack medical devices (implanted in human body, working based on wireless communications with Android applications).

Preventing users from any kind of breaches or cybercrimes is our main intention and motivation behind this work. As examined in section 9.1, advanced forensics is a digital forensic sciences method in the recognizable proof of cybercrimes. It's worth noting that digital forensics is an imaging procedure with a cycle. We must work with the copy rather than the original in order to provide appropriate security/countermeasures, and we must approve with a "hash." Nowadays, many data breaches are on the rise like ransomware, "WannaCry," etc.; also, many evidence systems are connected over the Internet to identify such breaches [15]. But during protection or providing security, one question arises: "how do we ensure integrity?" For that, we see that several researchers have made their best attempts at digital forensics and threat hunting, but due to having several requirements of users and complex structures of a network (or infrastructure), making it difficult to detect an attack. In basic words, we need to extricate and make urgent digital threat knowledge that can help future exploration local areas (counting clients) appropriately scope the tradeoffs and recognize future breaches in an organization. Many cybercrimes have been mitigated in several past years. For that, several researchers have tried several mechanisms and tools, but none of the algorithms/tools are sufficient to overcome such cybercrimes. This work has tried to include all possible mitigated techniques/ algorithms, etc., to detect threats or cybercrime. Digital forensics is the popular mechanism to detect cybercrime over the network. Threat hunting is also mechanism which is used to hunt threats proactively on public networks.

This section discusses motivation, i.e. our interest toward this area with a specific reason. The next section will discuss importance and scope of digital forensics and threat hunting in today's era (with respect to blockchain applications).

9.5 IMPORTANCE AND SCOPE OF DIGITAL FORENSICS AND THREAT HUNTING IN TODAY'S ERA (IN BLOCKCHAIN APPLICATIONS)

As discussed in Section 1, advanced digital forensics is an essential component of a general occurrence response strategy. Advanced forensics is the combination and evaluation of digital evidence living on electronic devices and the subsequent response to danger and attacks. Digital forensics is a part of forensic science and is perceived as such by most courts [16]. We can, by and large, separate forensics on every one of these gadgets into two fields: e-disclosure, and digital forensics and incident response (DFIR).

- E-disclosure is the legal side of forensics. From a broad perspective, the individual being analyzed is the situation, and digital forensic devices and methods are being utilized to help a case including them.
- DFIR is more the information security side of forensics. The digital framework is the situation, which means rather than our primary target being researching, the digital gadget is being explored. Instances of this are a wide range of security incidents, from information breaches to malware. In basic words, DFIR is the utilization of digital forensics for network safety use cases to analyze information breaches and malware, and the sky is the limit from there. Some experts perform both types, some on one case.

Generally, advanced forensics arrangements incorporate the accompanying capacities:

- The capacity to secure information from a wide assortment of gadgets, including customary computers and frameworks, cell phones, and so forth.

- Deep perceivability into cycles and activities that happened on gadgets and working frameworks.
- The capacity to finish a complete, forensically solid examination.
- Extensive revealing highlights.

Digital forensics is not exclusively about the cycles of obtaining, protecting, examining, and covering information concerning a incident. A forensic researcher should stay up with the most recent examinations on advanced forensic strategies. On another side, hunting threats has exhibited itself to be incredibly practical and is obtaining energy as associations look for better ways to deal with fabricating their security and destroying malware and tireless threats. As emerging and advanced persistent threats (APT) continue testing security operations centers (SOC) staff, specialists are logically utilizing hunting threat stages to uncover attacks. Since 100% disclosure is hard to achieve, and since existing wellbeing endeavors and game plans like intrusion detection systems (IDSs) and security information and event management (SIEM) are essentially deficient any more, there is an increasing need to set up security groups which will adequately "chase" for dangers zeroing in on their affiliation. Some advantages of threat hunting in the current era are:

- Proactively uncover all the security incidents.
- Improve the speed and efficiency of threat response.
- Reduce investigation time.
- Aid cybersecurity analysts in understanding the company.
- Will support to neglect threats so that we get improved IDS.
- Companies should force them to have professionals who can technically support the organization from these attacks.
- Brings security operations centers (SOCs) into the future.
- Reduces false positives and improves SOC efficiency.
- The overall cause and damage is being reduced.
- Understanding the organization's threat-discovery maturity.

This section discusses importance and scope of digital forensics and threat hunting in today's era with one example, including role of blockchain, in detail. The next section will discuss tools available for digital forensics and threat hunting processes.

9.6 TOOLS AVAILABLE FOR DIGITAL FORENSICS AND THREAT HUNTING

We can—without much of a stretch—quest for related occasions across all pertinent measurements including time span, IP or MAC address, and ports, in addition to convention explicit inquiries dependent on explicit capacity codes, convention administrations, modules, and so forth. The present threats require a more dynamic part in recognizing and reacting to refined attacks. Customary safety efforts—for example, firewalls, IDSs, endpoint assurance, and sims—are just essential for the riddle of organization security. The danger of chasing might be a manual cycle where a security examiner filters data of different information utilizing their own insight and knowledge of the organization to produce theories about likely threats; for example, yet not restricted to, horizontal development by threat entertainers. To be significantly more productive and powerful, in any case, the threat of hunting can be somewhat automatic supported, too. For this situation, the expert uses programming that utilizes ML computer language and user and object behavior analytics (UEBA) to advise the investigator regarding the possible threats. The examiner at that point inspects the possible threats, following detected dubious conduct. The process of digital forensics can be discussed in the following five basic stages:

1. Identification: The principal stage distinguishes likely wellsprings of potential proof/data (gadgets) just as key overseers and areas of information.
2. Preservation: The way toward saving important electronically stored information (ESI) by securing the incident, catching visual pictures of the scene, and reporting all significant data about the proof and how it was procured.
3. Collection: Collecting advanced data that might be potential to the examination. Assortment may include eliminating the electronic device(s) from the incident and afterward imaging, duplicating, or printing out relevant content.
4. Analysis: An inside-and-out precise pursuit of proof identifying with the incident being explored. The yields of assessment are information objects found in the gathered data; they may incorporate framework and client created records. Investigations expect to reach determinations dependent on the proof found.
5. Reporting: First, reports depend on demonstrated strategies and systems; and besides, other skillful legal analysts ought to have the option to copy and repeat similar outcomes.

Note that the initial four stages are utilized for an essential action following what we have done in adequate detail for someone else to replicate from the notes alone. Apart from that, there are some other processes which are also used in digital forensics:

- Forensics based on coercive law: The law enforcement community uses forensic software and hardware to collect, triage, investigate, and report on evidence from devices and networks [16]. Digital forensics helps investigators find evidence directly related to a criminal investigation. It also helps confirm statements, authenticate documents, create timelines, etc. As the number of digital devices and services explodes, so do the digital footprints we all leave behind. Criminological apparatuses permit agents to look at and comprehend these digital footprints as they attempt to demonstrate current realities of the case. Numerous celebrated criminal indictments incorporate the utilization of forensic sciences. Agents overall use EnCase forensic software from Guidance today, and did as such for some acclaimed indictments including the shoe aircraft bomber Richard Reid, the BTK Killer, and Scott Peterson.
- Digital forensics aid in investigations in a corporate setting: Each association will confront the need to direct digital examinations. Cases, information breaches, extortion, insider dangers, HR issues, and other network protection habits are unavoidable [18]. Prosecution concerns center more around e-discovery. DFIR groups utilize digital forensics to distinguish dubious action on their organizations, figure out who is making the issue, contain the occurrence, and find a way to protect their framework to forestall comparable future attacks. Exactly when an event is suspected, experienced security specialists will presumably have a communication work measure recently depicted to help direct them, along with the methods they expected to use to manage the issue. Routinely, this begins with a discrete arrangement of each possible source—for instance, real hard drives—followed by web program and email histories, record library logs, and even off-network endpoints. Regular corporate endpoints—for instance, PCs and workstations—are by all account not the only devices that can be relied on during criminological assessment. As mobile phones and tablets increase in step-by-step work usage, strong interest for convenient criminological capacities has gone along with it. Basically, every action taken on a device will remain on the machine as a "relic" which can be reviewed through cutting-edge forensic examination. It is fundamental to secure all data and forestall any possible adjusting to ensure that the inescapable consequence of the assessment can be viewed as reliable. At

the point when the information sources are gathered, specific inspectors will regularly use an irrefutable progressed forensic gadget. Guidance Software's EnCase Endpoint Investigator and EnCase Mobile Investigator are occasions of instruments used to take apart the proof, figuring out the mystery of the fundamental explanation behind the issue, who is to be blamed, what moves were made, and what the impact is. It is essential that security responders use top-tier progressed forensic examination advancement to correctly review the event. Since data security aces are dealing with a high volume of expected threats, profitability is also a huge attribute of a quality DFIR instrument.

- "Incident response" is a part of DFIR: Therefore, looking at the proof and assembling the enigma, incident reaction comes into the condition. The goal is to at first contain the issue, so that it does not spread to various devices, restricting the number of endpoints that are affected. The following stage is to dispense with the reason for the issue—this could incorporate malware, unapproved admittance to the organization framework, or traded-off records, among other malevolent strategies. With the threat dealt with, DFIR [19] professionals need to decide the best way ahead. This incorporates completely investigating and surveying the episode, at that point taking those learning and actualizing cycles and systems that will keep the attack from happening once more. By utilizing forensic instruments, security groups can find a way to react appropriately to a potential danger. The individuals who can gather the information, examine the circumstance utilizing progressed apparatuses and advances, and react to the occurrence rapidly, will set their associations up for free from any harm tasks while additionally diminishing future danger.

On another side, *cyberthreat intelligence* exercises empower groups of examiners to center their assets to accomplish most extreme impact, while they foresee danger distinguishing proof utilizing a threat hunting approach. It is a technique which is moving from receptive (in light of assaults) to proactive, with organizations searching for approaches to manage issues in a quicker, more efficient route, and to assemble sufficient information to forestall further issues and fabricate more grounded (yet economical) protections. There are numerous systems and approaches to secure clients against any digital attacks.

1. Attackers hide in blind spots—threat hunting identifies the unknown: Attackers are refined and plan threats to sidestep customary counteraction and recognition strategies. In numerous penetrations, the attacker has been inside the association's current circumstances for quite a long time. Threat hunting is the disclosure of malicious relics: action or location strategies not represented in passive monitoring capacities. Basically, danger chasing is the way toward distinguishing obscure dangers that generally would stow away in your organization and on your endpoints, taking sensitive information.
2. Threat hunting and detection are not one and the same: Threat hunting is regularly abused as "discovery." While danger recognition is tied in with distinguishing realized threats utilizing pointers and practices, threat hunting takes it to another level by recognizing the obscure. To do threat hunting right, we require right apparatuses, and above all, the correct information. Rich metadata gathered from network sensors, endpoints, and cloud conditions take into account cross-meeting examination, just as multifaceted and malware behavior investigation, which are basic for post-break recognition and danger chasing of the obscure.

As a rundown, digital defenders have a wide collection of instruments open to perceive, pursue, and track foe development in an association. Each attacker's movement leaves a contrasting relic, and understanding what is deserted as impressions can be fundamental among individuals. Attacks follow a foreseen pattern, and we base our agent attempts on unchanging pieces of that design. For example, sometimes an assailant should run code to accomplish its objectives. We can recognize this activity through application execution collectibles. The attack will likewise require at least one record to run code. Therefore, account examining is an incredible method for recognizing malevolent activities. Consequently, this section examines numerous apparatuses accessible for advanced criminology and threat hunting measures. The next section will talk about a few issues and difficulties brought up in digital forensics and threat hunting measures.

9.7 ISSUES AND CHALLENGES IN PROCESSES OF DIGITAL FORENSICS AND THREAT HUNTING

During a targeted attack, an affiliation needs the finest incident response groups in the field. Incident reaction and threat trackers should be furnished with the latest mechanical assemblies and memory examination techniques, and try ways to deal with recognizing, tracking, and containing enemies, and to remediate events. Incident reaction and threat hunting specialists ought to have the alternative to scale their assessments across an enormous number of structures in their endeavors. One famous attack as for digital forensics is advanced persistent threat (APT) [20]. It can be defined as "a prolonged and targeted cyberattack in which an intruder gains access to a network and remains undetected for a period of time." In general, the intention of an APT attack is to monitor network activity and steal data rather than to cause damage to the network or organization. This attack usually occurs on many networks. For detecting such serious threat, in current we use the endpoint detection and response (EDR) method. EDR abilities are progressively a necessity to follow focused attacks by an APT or a coordinated criminal organization that can quickly propagate through many frameworks. Fast response to numerous appropriated frameworks cannot be cultivated utilizing the standard "pull the hard drive" scientific assessment technique. Such sorts of approaches may alarm the attackers, and permit them to rapidly access delicate data accordingly.

Some of these critical (serious) issues are as follows: There are two types of issues available, in digital forensics, i.e. hardware and software issues. Modulating technical requirements and hardware upgrades are a key imperative. Software as a service (SaaS) and Platform as a service (PaaS) models have changed the design of configuring software and networks.

- Legal issues: Propelling security and data protection rules across geographies and creating regulatory definitions/approvals on such points may add to the multifaceted nature of get-together criminological confirmation. For instance, information open on the suspected machine (given by the association) may contain certain private, non-sensitive information which may be useful in assessments. In any case, permission to access this information may be seen as an encroachment in explicit countries. Basically, with the hour of "bring your own device" (BYOD), associations allowing staff to use singular mobile phones for having the opportunity to generate correspondence may add to the troubles of get-together verification. For instance, permission to an email from webmail through a cell phone and the download of associated files may be a wellspring of data burglary/private information robbery. In any case, explicit information on the device on which such information was downloaded and nuances on which records were downloaded may be difficult to continue in the current environment.
- Other issues: Cloud-based applications grant customers the ability to get to data from different devices. For instance, if one of a customer's two devices is subverted and the two devices make changes to the application data or organization at the same time, it very well may be difficult to recognize the wellsprings of the changes. With expanded chances of accreditation of bargain and wholesale fraud in a cloud-based climate, the difficulties in get-together of such proof stay obscure. Essentially, an email which was seen on a cell phone and along these lines erased might not have any hint of it on a system. Frequently, one may not explicitly analyze the mail worker logs to recognize proof of such correspondence.

Now coming to challenges in digital forensics and threat hunting, some challenges in digital forensics can be categorized into three parts [21]:

- Technical challenges: For instance, varying media designs, encryption, steganography, hostile to criminology, live securing and investigation. Some anti-forensic techniques (remembered for [22]) can be ordered into classifications like encryption, steganography, covert channel, data stowing away space, residual data wiping, tail obfuscation, attacking the devices, and attacking the examiners.
- Legal challenges: Protection is likewise critical to any association or attack casualty. By and large, it could be necessitated that the forensic expert shares information or compromised protection to get to reality. A privately owned business or an individual client may produce sets of private data in their everyday utilization. Along these lines, requesting that an examiner inspect their information may risk their security being uncovered; for instance, jurisdictional issues, security issues, and an absence of normalized worldwide enactment.
- Resource challenges: Depending upon the situation, the volume of information associated with the case may be enormous. All things considered, the specialist needs to experience all the gathered information to accumulate proof. It might require some investment for the examination. Since time is a restricting variable, it turns into another significant test in the field of forensics. In unstable memory forensics, since the information put away in the unpredictable memory is fleeting, client exercises are overwritten in the unpredictable memory. Consequently, agents can break down just ongoing data that is put away in the unstable memory. This decreases the criminological estimation of the information for the examination. When gathering information from the source, an agent should ensure that none of the information is changed or missed during the examination, and the information should be all secured. Information sources which are harmed can't be handily utilized in examinations. So, it is a significant issue when a specialist finds an important source that isn't usable; for instance, volumes of information and time taken to secure and break down legal media.

9.7.1 Challenges in Threat Hunting

The primary test that prevents information technology (IT) groups from completing threat hunting is time. Sadly, IT groups are regularly restricted in size, and one individual is probably going to be the IT manager, professional, and chief information security officer (CISO) all folded into one—all of which implies that we most likely do not have the opportunity we need to complete these assignments.

- Time is expected to look for threats, to assemble information, and to make legitimate theories. In addition, it's additionally required to explore pointers of attack, indicators of attack (IOAs) and indicators of compromise (IOCs), and patterns. Accordingly, time is critical.
- Threat hunters should be skilled, in addition to other things, of checking the conduct of systems, the applications running on them, and specifically, their clients.
- Threat hunting measures depend on an enormous pool of information with respect to all the conduct of the monitored segments and refreshed progressively as new occasions happen.
- In the proposed stage, new instruments should be able to examine this massive collection of data in order to generate new attack hypotheses.
- In the earlier decade, "white hat" hackers have arisen as threat trackers. Threat trackers are part proactive programmer, part measurable agent, part interruption indicator, and part incident responder (IR), with accentuation on the last aspect.

As examined in this chapter, we have never seen a quicker development in innovation than we have in the previous five years, and future advancement might be sufficiently quick to find a portion of the previously mentioned issues. We look forward excitedly to perceiving how innovation shapes the future in streamlining the way toward get-together proof. This section discusses several issues and challenges raised in digital forensics and threat hunting processes. The next section will discuss several opportunities for researchers and scientists with respect to role of digital forensics and threat hunting in blockchain applications.

9.8 OPPORTUNITIES FOR FUTURE RESEARCHERS (ESPECIALLY IN COMPUTER SCIENCE)

A real-world APT assault on big business organizations may prompt numerous difficulties and arrangements. We discover from the previous conversation that a phenomenal expansion in the absolute number of digital attacks increment a few genuine concerns, i.e. loss of time in identifying threats, deficiency of cash, and so on. We construct and execute key plans that resound with other businesses to stay away from such concerns, threats, and attacks. It makes successful data security strategy, and creates the executives and authorities abilities to all the more likely lead, rouse, and propel their groups. By consolidating threat hunting and threat insight, associations can find and manage weaknesses in their organizations to improve overall information security.

The present cybersecurity, trust and privacy (CTP) considerations are squeezing the needs of governments, organizations, and people who are getting most extreme need for authorization and improvement in practically every social order around the globe [23]. Then again, fast advances are being made in arising blockchain innovation, with comprehensively different applications that guarantee to more readily meet business and individual necessities. Currently, blockchain is a promising infrastructural innovation and can possibly be utilized in various parts of network safety, trust, and protection. Blockchain qualities—for example, decentralization, evidence, and its unchanging nature—may rotate current network safety components (or can help in getting the web, as decentralized web) for guaranteeing the genuineness, dependability, and uprightness of information. These highlights bring forth new applications which may utilize blockchain for different purposes (in the not so distant future).

- Cyberthreats are dramatically on the rise. It is not just data exfiltration, but data integrity is a growing concern, so blockchain can provide highest integrity.
- Cyberforensics is maturing, but needs to be improved.
- Hashing is improving with timestamps and blockchaining.
- Forensics workstations and systems integrity could be improved with blockchain technologies.
- Evidence control systems could be made forensics-ready for improved security and validation.

Note that readers are recommended to read or to know about several uses of blockchain technology or issues in day-to-day (most useful) applications (in integration of blockchain with other technology like IoT, machine learning, etc.) in [24–29]. Also, in [30–31], readers can find several opportunities for detecting or mitigating intrusion over the Internet and opportunities as cybersecurity professionals to handle information systems safely and securely. We have seen many possibilities or new innovations with blockchain in the near future. This section discusses several interesting opportunities for future researchers with respect to blockchain applications (and the roles of digital forensics and threat hunting). The next section will summarize this chapter in brief with several interesting facts and remarks for future researchers and readers.

9.9 CONCLUSIONS

For a perfect solution for identify threats online, digital forensics and threat hunting are the best options. While using blockchain in many applications like uses of the IoT-based blockchain in agriculture, smart homes, e-healthcare, etc., we may face several vulnerabilities or attacks. We need to shield our smart systems against such critical or serious attacks. This chapter discusses digital forensics and threat hunting process starting from the introduction, related work, importance and scope, tools available and algorithms, issues and challenges to opportunities, and research directions (including research gaps) for future researchers. We find out throughout this research work to "be proactive to be protected" against any breaches or attacks. The digital forensics cycle contains accompanying advances like search authority, chain of care, imaging/hashing capacity, validated apparatuses, analysis, repeatability, reporting, and possible master introduction. On another side, the threat hunting process is ambiguous and not complete, i.e. as a perfect answer for threat detection that is driven by an automated system, such as intrusion detection systems (IDSs) or security information and event management (SIEM) tools. Hence, there is a lot of scope in the near future with respect to digital forensics and threat hunting with blockchain applications.

REFERENCES

[1]   Garfinkel, S. L. "Digital forensics research: The next 10 years." *Digital Investigation* 7 (2010): S64–S73.
[2]   Lee, H. C. "Forensic science and the law." *Connecticut Law Review* 25 (1992): 1117.
[3]   Palmer, G. "A road map for digital forensic research." DFRWS Technical Report, DTR-T001–01 Final, Air Force Research Laboratory, Rome, New York, 2001.
[4]   Corey, V., C. Peterman, S. Shearin, M. S. Greenberg, and J. Van Bokkelen. "Network forensics analysis." *IEEE Internet Computing* 6, no. 6 (2002): 60–66.
[5]   Needles, S. A. "The data game: Learning to love the state-based approach to data breach notification law." *The North Carolina Law Review* 88 (2009): 267.
[6]   Shanmugasundaram, K., N. Memon, A. Savant, and H. Bronnimann. "ForNet: A distributed forensics network." In *International Workshop on Mathematical Methods, Models, and Architectures for Computer Network Security*, pp. 1–16. Springer, September 2003.
[7]   Homayoun, S., A. Dehghantanha, M. Ahmadzadeh, S. Hashemi, and R. Khayami. "Know abnormal, find evil: Frequent pattern mining for ransomware threat hunting and intelligence." *IEEE Transactions on Emerging Topics in Computing* (2017).
[8]   Shackelford, S. J., and S. Myers. "Block-by-block: Leveraging the power of blockchain technology to build trust and promote cyber peace." *Yale Journal of Law & Technology* 19 (2017): 334.
[9]   Daryabar, F., A. Dehghantanha, N. I. Udzir, N. F. B. M. Sani, S. Shamsuddin, and F. Norouzizadeh. "A survey about impacts of cloud computing on digital forensics." *International Journal of Cyber-Security and Digital Forensics* 2, no. 2 (2013): 77–94.
[10] Klaper, D., and E. Hovy. "A taxonomy and a knowledge portal for cybersecurity." In *Proceedings of the 15th Annual International Conference on Digital Government Research*, pp. 79–85. ACM, June 2014.
[11] Cebe, M., E. Erdin, K. Akkaya, H. Aksu, and S. Uluagac. "Block4forensic: An integrated lightweight blockchain framework for forensics applications of connected vehicles." *IEEE Communications Magazine* 56, no. 10 (2018): 50–57.
[12] Tyagi, A. K. "Cyber physical systems (cpss) â [euro]" opportunities and challenges for improving cyber security." *International Journal of Computer Applications* 137, no. 14 (2016).
[13] Koscher, K., A. Czeskis, F. Roesner, S. Patel, T. Kohno, S. Checkoway, D. McCoy, B. Kantor, D. Anderson, H. Shacham, and S. Savage. "Experimental security analysis of a modern automobile." *Proceedings of the 31st IEEE Symposium on Security and Privacy*, May 2010.
[14] Nicholson, A., S. Webber, S. Dyer, T. Patel, and H. Janicke. "SCADA security in the light of Cyber-Warfare." *Computers & Security* 31, no. 4 (2012): 418–436.

[15] Edwards, B., S. Hofmeyr, and S. Forrest. "Hype and heavy tails: A closer look at data breaches." *Journal of Cybersecurity* 2, no. 1 (2016): 3–14.

[16] Garfinkel, S. L. "Digital forensics research: The next 10 years." *Digital Investigation* 7 (2010): S64–S73.

[17] Hunt, R., and S. Zeadally. "Network forensics: An analysis of techniques, tools, and trends." *Computer* 45, no. 12 (2012): 36–43.

[18] Bhasin, M. L. "Contribution of forensic accounting to corporate governance: An exploratory study of an Asian Country." *International Business Management* 10, no. 4 (2015): 2016.

[19] Valjarevic, A., and H. S. Venter. "A comprehensive and harmonized digital forensic investigation process model." *Journal of forensic sciences* 60, no. 6 (2015): 1467–1483.

[20] Daly, M. K. "Advanced persistent threat." *Usenix* 4, no. 4 (November 2009): 2013–2016.

[21] Al Fahdi, M., N. L. Clarke, and S. M. Furnell. "Challenges to digital forensics: A survey of researchers & practitioners attitudes and opinions." In 2013 *Information Security for South Africa*, pp. 1–8. IEEE, August 2013.

[22] Garfinkel, S. "Anti-forensics: Techniques, detection and countermeasures." *2nd International Conference on i-Warfare and Security*. Vol. 20087, pp. 77–84, March 2007.

[23] Sawal, Neha, Anjali Yadav, Dr. Amit Kumar Tyagi, N. Sreenath, and G. Rekha. "Necessity of blockchain for building trust in today's applications: An useful explanation from user's perspective." May 15, 2019.

[24] Tyagi, Amit Kumar, S. U. Aswathy, and Ajith Abraham. "Integrating blockchain technology and artificial intelligence: Synergies, perspectives, challenges and research directions." *Journal of Information Assurance and Security* 15, no. 5 (2020). ISSN: 1554–1010.

[25] Tyagi, A. K., S. Kumari, T. F. Fernandez, and C. Aravindan. "P3 block: Privacy preserved, trusted smart parking allotment for future vehicles of tomorrow." In Gervasi, O., et al. (eds.). *Computational Science and Its Applications—ICCSA 2020. ICCSA 2020. Lecture Notes in Computer Science*. Vol. 12254. Springer, 2020. https://doi.org/10.1007/978-3-030-58817-5_56.

[26] Tyagi, A. K., T. F. Fernandez, and S. U. Aswathy. "Blockchain and aadhaar based electronic voting system." *2020 4th International Conference on Electronics, Communication and Aerospace Technology (ICECA)*, pp. 498–504, Coimbatore, 2020. DOI: 10.1109/ICECA49313.2020.9297655.

[27] Tyagi, Amit Kumar, Meghna Manoj Nair, Sreenath Niladhuri, and Ajith Abraham. "Security, privacy research issues in various computing platforms: A survey and the Road Ahead." *Journal of Information Assurance & Security* 15, no. 1 (2020): 1–16.16p.

[28] Tyagi, Amit Kumar, and Meghna Manoj Nair. "Internet of everything (IoE) and internet of things (IoTs): Threat analyses." *Possible Opportunities for Future* 15, no. 4 (2020).

[29] Nair, Siddharth M., Varsha Ramesh, and Amit Kumar Tyagi. "Issues and challenges (privacy, security, and trust) in blockchain-based applications." *Book: Opportunities and Challenges for Blockchain Technology in Autonomous Vehicles* (2021): 14. DOI: 10.4018/978-1-7998-3295-9.ch012.

[30] Rekha, G., S. Malik, A. K. Tyagi, and M. M. Nair. "Intrusion detection in cyber security: Role of machine learning and data mining in cyber security." *Advances in Science, Technology and Engineering Systems Journal* 5, no. 3 (2020): 72–81.

[31] Tyagi, Amit Kumar. "Article: Cyber physical systems (CPSs)—Opportunities and challenges for improving cyber security." *International Journal of Computer Applications* 137, no. 14 (March 2016): 19–27. Published by Foundation of Computer Science (FCS), NY, USA.

Healthcare Solutions for the Next Generation: A Useful Explanation from the User's Perspective

Amit Kumar Tyagi, Meenu Gupta,
Aswathy S.U., and Chetanya Ved

10

Contents

10.1 INTRODUCTION: HEALTHCARE DATA

Today, many applications have changed their way of doing business due to the COVID-19 pandemic. For example, education, entertainment, healthcare, retail, etc., have moved to new levels and changed the expectations of new customers. The entire world is currently going through a very difficult and unimaginable phase. The world economy has dropped, hundreds of people have lost jobs, and millions are suffering more than ever in poverty-prone areas. The world is not just going through a pandemic but a very severe scenario where people are forced to protect themselves and society by staying indoors, which is not possible for most people who are daily workers to support their families. The year 2020 has been injurious in terms of affecting human health, the economy, and the environment across the globe. Healthcare has always been an important sector in society. The Beirut explosion, Atlantic hurricane season, North American wildfires, Australian bushfires, flooding and landslides, COVID-19, and refugee and humanitarian crises have deteriorated world health; healthcare is needed more now than ever. Despite the monumental improvements in medical field technology over the years, it's just in the beginning phase. While now is a time of growth, it is also the time of growing pains. The medical and healthcare field faces a vital and challenging task as it has to carefully handle the health and internal functioning of a living species. In the year 2016, there were significant healthcare improvements due to enhanced access to patient information and groundbreaking technology incorporation, and the concept of virtual hospitals came into existence limited by Internet connectivity. The combined advancements created sweeping changes in the medical field.

Medical healthcare services are important as they help in diagnosing, managing, and preventing diseases, restoring and maintaining health, and reducing unnecessary disabilities and premature deaths. Virtualization can be applied in several ways for more efficient resource utilization and cost savings such as Virtual Desktop Infrastructure (VDI). From agile data centers and hybrid cloud architectures, to ultra-compact and powerful endpoints such as thin clients, VDI can help apply digital technologies to boost efficiency and transform care delivery. One thing about the healthcare industry is that regardless of the part of the world, we cannot run away from the challenges that confront the industry. This is because some of the problems that players in the industry face are global in dimension. One of the biggest problems in the healthcare industry today is an unstable federal reimbursement model (which means healthcare policies and services are better tailored for well-off people rather than universal care) amid an uncertain regulatory environment. Usually, the governments of different nations formulate policies that allow citizens who are qualified to access treatment via health insurance, and then the government pays whatever is expected of it to pay either annually or as it is spelled out in the contract. A workable solution to this would be that the government of each nation should formulate strict policies that will ensure that much more than playing their part in any agreement reached with the healthcare industry; they should ensure that they do it on time so that it will allow for smooth flow of the process and all the hitches that usually cause inefficiencies in the value chain will be eliminated.

Awkward incentives models in health plans, Medicare, and Medicaid pay providers for the services they deliver, regardless of whether the service truly benefits the patient. In most cases, most of the patients under these health insurance policies complain of the services received, but that does not stop the government or the health insurance company or health management organizations from paying the agreed amount. Healthcare services providers should be appraised regularly so as to ensure that they are delivering as expected and they should be delisted if they are providing services that are below standard. The patients should also appraise the healthcare service providers since they are at the receiving end. For example, if there is a private patient paying from their pocket on the spot while another patient is covered by health insurance or health management organization, they usually go through some bottleneck bureaucracy. This is usually noticed in countries with weak regulatory enforcement policies in the healthcare industries and other industries. Hence, one of the ways of ensuring that they are not biased in their customer service is to ensure that a regulatory body is maintained to oversee the services offered by these hospitals and medical care facilities. Another notable problem in the healthcare industry that cuts across lines is the lack of transparency in assigning hospitals to customers in any emergency case where a person needs immediate treatment and selecting the brand of drugs and medications that are to be prescribed to patients by the doctor. Sometimes, these prescriptions are based on profits and benefits rather than the effectiveness of the drug and medications covered for the patient under health insurance. Also, patients should be allowed to be among the stakeholders who select hospitals and select the brand of drugs and medications that should be used for treatments in hospitals that should be listed under their health insurance policy coverage. With that, the issue of lack of transparency can be dealt with.

Moreover, irregular disaster preparation policy is typical in the healthcare industry, especially in underdeveloped and developing countries of the world. If we do not expect disaster to happen frequently, that does not mean that we should not be prepared for them. As a matter of fact, it takes the intervention of the World Health Organization (WHO) and other stakeholders to be able to handle disasters in some countries. The government regulatory bodies in charge of the healthcare industry should make sure that they enforce regular disaster preparation policy in the health sector of their country and ensure provision is made for equipment and supplies in the warehouse that can take care of emergencies and unnecessary bottlenecks are eliminated when handling medical emergencies. This kind of problem happens in some countries where they are expected to deposit a fixed amount of fees before the treatment begins, even in case of an emergency situation. The governments of countries where this practice is still ongoing should ensure that they formulate policies that give preference to treat people or at least stabilize them when they are rushed in for treatment during medical emergencies, and ensure that hospitals abide by such laws.

A major concern, especially to low- or middle-income countries' condition, is worst where hospitalized patients can be affected with any disease during their stay in hospital as compared to high-income countries. Also, there is lacking in free quality healthcare to poor and senior citizen who cannot afford to pay for quality treatment. The truth is that, even if the government offers free treatments to senior citizens and the less privileged, the services or treatment they get is usually below the expected standard. One of the international bodies can oversee the healthcare industry, help build capacity with the host nation to ensure that free and quality healthcare is made available to everyone who cannot afford it, and ensure that nothing but the best healthcare services are provided. Finally, one of the biggest problems in the healthcare industry today is the interference of major financiers and policy makers in groundbreaking research in the healthcare industry as to why there still isn't a permanent cure for terminal diseases like cancer, HIV/AIDS, and others. The truth is that with the capacity of the human race in terms of resources and exposure, we should have come up with lasting solutions (drugs, medications, and treatment procedures) that will cure cancer, HIV/AIDS, Ebola, and other illnesses without care just like we did for malaria, tuberculosis, and the like. The reason why this has not been done yet is because of the inability of major financiers and policy makers to give their full support.

Major financiers and policy makers should be pressured by the masses to give their full support to research that will lead to the invention of drugs, medications, and treatment procedures that will help eliminate or cure diseases such as cancer, HIV/AIDS, and other terminal illnesses. Maybe one of the solutions would be to first identify the places or countries prone to disasters or lack healthcare so that primary, secondary, tertiary, and quaternary care could be provided depending on the complexity of cases or diseases to be treated and the skills and specialties of the provider. Currently, COVID-19 has taken many lives; though more than many have successfully recovered, some are still battling against it and we as citizens of this planet have a global responsibility to support and help each other in such a crisis and make healthcare a widespread priority. Hygiene, healthcare, and support should be a part of everyday life, even after the pandemic. It is together our responsibility to keep this planet and its people healthy. Healthcare is something that is everyone's right and there should be easy access to it, as it not only affects humans but the entire planet as a whole. The quality of healthcare services affects the health status of the world. Having better health is the central of human happiness and wellbeing as healthy populations live longer and are more productive. This chapter tries to include all possible solutions for improving healthcare for making society better and live longer.

Section 10.2 discusses related work. Then, Section 10.3 discusses our motivation behind writing this chapter on healthcare. Further, identity and access managements systems are discussed for healthcare systems in the 21st century. Real life–based application that can brings out a solution to healthcare in the case of safety and confidentiality are discussed in Section 10.5. Section 10.6 provides information about creating sustainable future with Internet of Things–based cloud services and touch-enabled handheld devices (in healthcare). Further, for maintaining safety and confidentiality in electronic health records (EHRs), technologies that have existed are taken in account in order to make a solution out of that are included in Section 10.7 (i.e. making healthcare medical documents secure and confidential; and the threats that occur in this area are analyzed and classified, and thereby result is produced). Then, various accurate models and algorithms for security and protection in e-medical documents in the "smart era" post–COVID-19 are discussed in Section 10.8. Section 10.9 discusses concepts of information security and privacy in electronic health records with analysis of threats (including countermeasures and solutions for the same). Similarly, various security and privacy issues in India and other countries for e-healthcare post–COVID-19 are discussed in Section 10.10. In continuation of this, a blockchain-based system for healthcare information systems (including privacy protection of patients) is presented in Section 10.11. Also, a blockchain-enabled healthcare insurance system is included in Section 10.12. As an essential section of this chapter, Section 10.13 discusses using blockchain and the importance of protecting medical data. Using blockchain services in healthcare, enhanced with data authentication and safety, is discussed in Section 10.14. Further, Section 10.15 discusses various healthcare services using networking and emerging technologies like edge computing, deep learning, etc., for the smart era. Finally, Section 10.6 concludes this chapter in brief with including several notable remarks, suggestions, and research gaps for future researchers.

10.2 RELATED WORK

There are always high stakes when it comes to technologies that can be a great solution in healthcare. There is a great future for smart health technologies, as advancement is growing day by day, so there is needed research and development of these technologies so as to boost accuracy (e.g., within telemedicine and early detection). When any system gives an advantage, then some disadvantage can also come. This statement looks toward the problem of hospital staff and their policies such as infrastructure, competencies, and assurance of data protection that is highly confidential. Nowadays, there are many health checking wearables available that are handy to use and capable to store all the data in short period of time. In the previous time, the hospital staff were using many software to store patients' data and that was time-consuming process. This new idea evolves the new path toward one's life, and intelligent systems are used to store and maintain the data.

The "smart" advances in healthcare fields are mainly due to the protection of quite essential medical records from being shared with a third party. MedChain [1], a successful session-based healthcare program, was proposed by Shen et al. using blockchain-based data sharing. In order to verify the credibility of a shared medical IoT data stream, MedChain uses a digest chain structure approach. This is required to address the performance problems of current systems such as Medrec and MedBlock. A patient-centered data management framework for healthcare in a cloud environment using blockchain [2] was introduced by Al Omar et al. With the help of technology, privacy issues are solved. Blockchain is a useful and advanced technology when comes to data integration, and it also takes accountability, integrity, and security into account. A safe blockchain platform for medical data was developed by Chen et al. [3]. Sharing can only be possible by making a well-protected cloud for a particular institution which acts as barriers to third party attacks. Cloud encryption comes to act when the data are fully encrypted, and it can only be decrypted by the members who are in the group by respective control action. In a similar study, Guo et al. [4] implemented an attribute-based signature scheme to guarantee and verify EHRs, using blockchain technology with multiple authorities. It promotes the broadcasting of group messages and could avoid attacks of conspiracy.

Kuo and Ohno-Machado [5] put forward a blockchain chain-model system whereby a private block is used for passing information within the organization this model trains using ML so that better results and information are passed without revealing, thereby improving accuracy, protection, and confidentiality of that model. A blockchain involving parallel healthcare framework (PHS), including artificial networks, computer experiments, and parallel execution (ACP) was proposed by Wang et al. [6]. The ACP concentrated primarily on representing the diagnosis, disease, and treatment process of a patient [7]. A consortium blockchain is added to PHS so as to link hospitals, patients, health governing bodies, and related communities.

10.3 MOTIVATION

Healthcare is a primary sector for society and very important, also sensitive for saving people's lives. In the past few decades, we have witnessed major developments in the healthcare sector, and improvement in consultations with doctors, equipment and laboratories, and generation of reports have been easier. This is possible only through the technology. Computer systems have solved many difficult problems of Medicare/healthcare. Using such systems in patient care today reduces much of the burden from doctors; now caring of patients and other patients simultaneously has become easier. Also, technology has helped in identifying specific patients who have similar symptoms, for example, in COVID-19 checking of high temperature through thermal screening, critical operations in hours, etc. Technology uses will also be increased in the near future, but using technology or machines in such critical or sensitive sectors raises several serious concerns like leaking of privacy of patients, society of patient data, etc. Any hacker or intruder may attack a healthcare system and steal information of patients and can use the same information for blackmailing the patients, or their own financial gain. Also, malicious hackers can take charge of a machine and remotely control the treatment of a patient. It is matter of a person's life; we cannot trust machines or smart devices or technology just like that. We need proper mechanisms to secure patient data, and we also need to preserve privacy of patients and need to build a high trust among doctors and healthcare officials. In previous decades, several attempts have made to solving these issues, which have been included here in detail. Hence, this chapter focuses more on patient data, which needs to be protected, and identities of patients, which need to be preserved against intruders or unknown or malicious users.

10.4 IDENTITY AND ACCESS MANAGEMENT SYSTEMS FOR HEALTHCARE

Enabling a right person to access the right resources at the right time for the right reason is the main task of every service provider. But, to manage digital identities and provide authentication, authorization is a challenging task in today's world. Identity and access management (IAM) is the framework of the system which provides a technological solution for managing digital identity and their access to different applications.

It is a cross-functional process to protect against unauthorized access to information [7]. In the context of IAM in healthcare, we human beings are living in a mobile civilization and are free to move between different cities and towns. Patients can visit different public or private hospitals to get treatment for different medical conditions and were referred by primary physicians [8]. At that time, a patient's medical history—required for their treatment—was not known by the physician. This exchange of information depended upon the patient's willingness and required security concerns that are another challenge for healthcare industries. Here, intrusion detection methods (IDMs) play a role in identify electronic health records accurately and remove barriers.

Figure 10.1 shows the functionality of IAM in healthcare. Identity and access management (IAM) primarily focuses on identification of user (or patient) like ID cards and authorization, where IAM focuses on a few questions like what we know, what we are, and what we have. Authentication mainly works on the question of what we are. These three terms—identity, authentication, and authorization (IAA)—are used to evaluate the accessible limits of digital resources [9]. The rest of this section is organized as follows: Section 10.4.1 will discuss the role of electronic health records of patients in IAM. It will discuss the relationship between doctors, patients, and hospital management. The decentralized system of healthcare is described in the following Section 10.4.2. Section 10.4.3 gives a framework of a smart healthcare

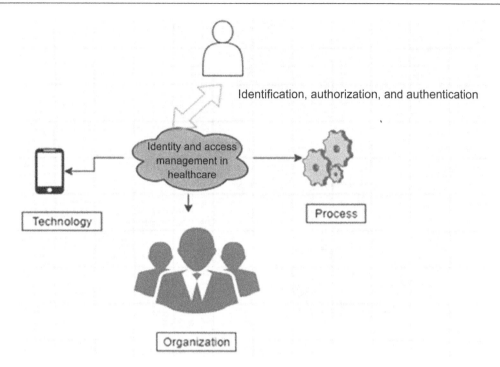

Identification, authorization, and authentication

FIGURE 10.1   Identity and access management framework.

management system using blockchain. Section 10.4.4 briefly describes the uniquely identified healthcare management card. Finally, Section 10.4.5 provides a summary of IAM in e-healthcare.

10.4.1 Electronic Health Records of Patients

Electronic health records (EHRs) consist of the records of the patient's medical history. They contain information about the patient's medications and prescriptions, and details about past treatments which help the medical practitioners in the diagnosis and treatment process. It is one of the major components of the healthcare industry which is currently required for tracking and monitoring purposes [10]. The major benefit of EHR is it gives health institutions the capability to monitor the current improvements and identification of the effectiveness of previous treatments and medications. Figure 10.2 shows maintaining patients' medical history records with blockchain.

EHR consists of the following components:

- Personal details, i.e. height, sex, weight, and BMI (body mass index).
- Treatment details.
- Medication details.
- Timestamp.
- Unique identity of report.

In EHR, each modification is considered as an addition of a block and forms a report in blockchain format. It makes the record tamper proof and secure. Security is a critical issue in maintaining these types of records, since tampering with these can be life-threatening. Blockchain plays a major role in terms of providing security and privacy of health records. Medication and treatment details are considered as an

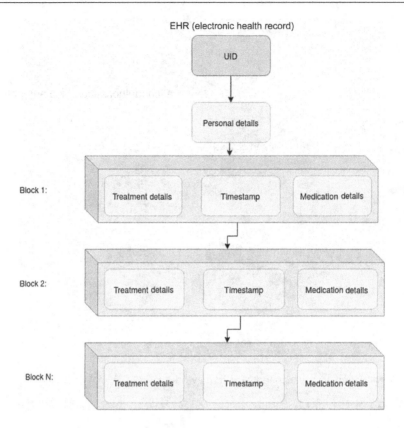

FIGURE 10.2 Blockchain-based Electronic Health Record system.

array of most important data. Restriction in user accessibility will provide extra immunity to blockchain to become a more secure and trustworthy system to its stakeholders in terms of security.

10.4.2 Decentralized System for Healthcare

The healthcare sector is the most important and necessary part of the integrated upcoming environment, where its importance and need is increasing annually. Hence, with an increase in the requirement, its infrastructure and management should be scaled up at the same pace. But scaling of any sector will invite some vulnerability with it such as trust, security, privacy, accessibility, and many other factors. To maintain its pace of scale, it needs to come up with decentralized solutions to develop a highly integrated network of such sectors. Human civilization completely depends upon this strata of centralization. The healthcare industry is vast, and to maintain its security is an utmost important responsibility. Decentralization can play a major role in this sector. It enhances trustworthiness, introduces inaccessibility, makes data secure, and many other leading factors. Decentralization is defined as integrating multiple areas together to work cooperatively, which increases its efficiency, productivity, scalability, and accessibility.

EMDR (Electronic medical diagnosis record) comes into role play as soon as EHR introduces which increases its practical application and gives a clear picture of the patient's medical problem. The basic purposes of EMDR are used to maintain records of a clinical test. EMDR is always in synchronization with EHR for the purpose of precise and effective treatment which is integrated with it. It also has a unique identity through which it gets stored in a block of the main EHR blockchain. Access for reading and writing of these reports is given to registered medical institutions and clinics only for the purpose of making this system tamperproof. Medical professionals have read access only.

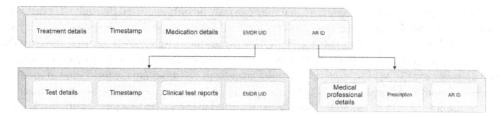

FIGURE 10.3   Integration of EHR, EMDR, and AR.

EHR is also integrated with AR (attendees record), a record which stores information about patients' medical professional details. It stores information about the prescription which is prescribed by him on the basis of diagnosed problems. AR is accessible by registered clinics and medical health institutions. Accessibility is a major concern in all these systems so that security and privacy can be maintained. Figure 10.3 shows the integration of HER, EMDR, and AR.

10.4.3 Blockchain-Based Smart Healthcare Management System

In current scenarios, mobile and wearable devices are acting like health monitoring systems which are also extracting real-time data of the body's surroundings, capturing movements such as steps, pulse rate, and calories. The patient can access everything through their mobile or portable devices [11]. In this type of management, everything is connected with the distributed ledger to store its data and every update in the ledger will be considered as a transaction. Here, the ledger is distributed among the peers (i.e., among different entities of the system) with a copy of its ledger but with different accessibility rights so that system can become tamperproof. In hospitals or medical institutions, these data have become the most important and integrated part. By tracking and monitoring the human body's movement and intakes, correct preventive measures can be suggested by doctors, practitioners, or consultants. The blockchain plays a major role in storing and forming the ledger which will help them to diagnose or be able to predict the cause of a health issue [12]. Also, it eradicates the need for tedious paperwork where the patient has to store information in the form of files and it is difficult for doctors to correctly identify earlier medical health records, that makes the task even more difficult. In some cases, people consume previously recommended and prescribed medicines which prove sometimes lethal. Here in the system, patients' EHR, EMDR, and AR can be considered as a distributed ledger. As a patient arrives at a medical consultant (or for a clinical test), then the consultant can access a patient's medical data through their UID (unique identity). The consultant has rights to only read the data of EMDR and AR, and they are allowed to read-write in EHR. This shows that blockchain-based system restricts accessibility by giving limited authorization for accessing the data, according to the organization. Earlier in hospitals, it was difficult to have information about the availability of beds, but in the present scenario, it is easy to have information about the hospital's treatment and facilities. Due to the integration of the IoT (Internet of Things), it is easy to have access to all this information. The Big Data about the health industry is generated and managed by IoT services only. This technology enables us to give real-time information and data about hospitals or clinics. The best example is during emergency times, when a GPS is integrated with the mobile application and it suggests the shortest path to reach a hospital by giving real-time traffic data feed to suggest the route.

Cloud computing is also playing a major role in developing a decentralized system for the health management industry. All the data gets stored in the cloud, which helps to eradicate the need for storage in mobile devices and it makes for an easier and secured process to access the data. All the recorded ledgers of patients and medical institutions are getting stored only in the cloud. Distributed ledgers can be stored on the cloud of individual patients' accounts so that they can only be only accessed through UID that is generated through the private key. If the record has to be accessed by the hospital staff member, then they should have patient's public key which decrypts the HER; this makes the system highly secured and trustable. In present scenario, blockchain also plays a good role in the pharmaceutical sector by decentralizing the supply chain management (SCM) system process for the purpose of fast-tracking the procedure of medical and vaccines production. SCM process needs to be transparent and trustable among the third (i.e., non-trusted) parties. The initiative has been called to avoid drug abuse and menace. This system is built for the purpose of expiry drug detection so that no pharmaceutical or chemist shop should store expire stockpiles.

10.4.4 Unique Identity Healthcare Management Card

The unique identity access management card (UIAMC) is a model that enables hospitals and other medical institution to access one's EHR. It has a unique identification number which can be authorized only by certified organizations [13]. To maintain the security and privacy of individual data, the authorized organization has limited access to it that has been given by the government. For example, pharmacist and chemist shops can only access the data of a doctor's prescriptions, and they have only information reading authorization. It will act as all-in-one document for accessing health records.

Basically, this model (as shown in Figure 10.4) works on the basis of a cryptographic key concept. The number on the card is generated by the private key of the individual which encapsulates the data in a card. The registered organization should possess the public key to decrypt the card's data. Every record has its own unique identity stored in that card which is linked with each other in hash format [14]. The hash value of successor records are stored in previous records, but they are linked together through hash values and these data can be accessed when an organization possesses authority, or a private key corresponding to the individual card.

10.4.5 Remarks

The healthcare industry plays a major role in the human ecosystem. It has a critical part in saving the lives of millions. On the other side, it faces some vulnerability in terms of security and frauds such as drug abuse, wrong treatment, and prescriptions which can prove to be life-threatening. Due to this, there is a great need to develop a secured ecosystem of the healthcare industry to stop the menace. Blockchain can play a major role in revolutionizing this industry and make it more secured and transparent, while these models and discussion can prove their caliber.

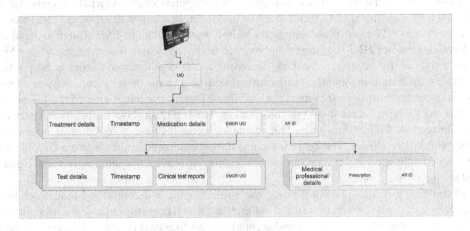

FIGURE 10.4 Model of unique identity healthcare management card.

10.5 REAL-LIFE APPLICATION-BASED ARRANGEMENT AS A SOLUTION TO HEALTHCARE IN THE CASE FOR CONFIDENTIALITY AND SECURITY

Over the years, there has been a bond between doctor and patient whereby a patient seeks advice of a doctor and a doctor accepts the patient for assistance. Due to the increasingly aging population, the healthcare industry is facing security and privacy issues. Patients hesitate to share their complete medical history due to privacy concerns that sometimes may not allow doctors to give desired solutions. The healthcare industry is facing lot of challenges when it comes to satisfaction of an individuals' health and privacy. We live in a society in which we are allowed to use public and private healthcare organizations, but there is a gap where people are less secure to share their information due to lack of trust. This section is arranged as follows: Section 10.5.1 discusses how IoT and Big Data are used for remote medical assistance. Section 10.5.2 discusses the safety and confidentiality issues faced in the field of healthcare. The solution-based blockchain application is discussed in Section 10.5.3. Finally, this section is summarized in Section 10.5.4.

10.5.1 Internet of Things and Big Data for Remote Medical Assistance

The "things" in the Internet of Things in healthcare refers to a wide range of devices such as heart monitoring implants, infusion pumps, etc., that are used in hospitals for delivery of preprogrammed fluids in patients. IoT has become a major advancement that is rapidly accepted by the scenario of modern wireless telecommunication. The mobile solutions offered by IoT are widely accepted by physicians. Measurement and monitoring methods of vital functions are improved due to combination of sensors like RFID, Bluetooth, etc. The primarily uses of IoT in healthcare are to provide remote services for cost-cutting technologies, remote monitoring, or data gathering and analysis.

Figure 10.5 shows how the components of remote patient monitoring in IoT work in a healthcare industry and the virtualization, transmission, etc., of data takes place. Recent advancements efficiently

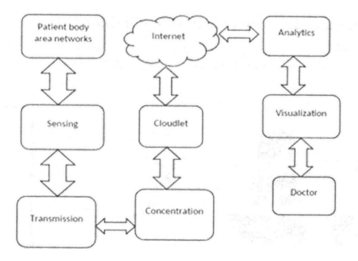

FIGURE 10.5 Components of IoT of remote patient monitoring in healthcare [15].

bring out various features in the case of wearable medical devices and many other things so as to monitor the continuous health of a patient, even in remote locations, and thanks to mobile computing that gives a great hand for researchers to reach out and bring various solutions [16]. Collecting, processing, and storage of data have become possible due to powerful computer facilities and omnipresent wearable devices.

10.5.1.1 Internet of Things and Big Data: A Patient-Centric Model

Study of patient behavior is a crucial part in diagnosis and prognosis of a disease. The only solution lies in the hand of IoT and Big Data. The Patient-Centric Healthcare Information System (PCHIS) is a system that provides ubiquitous healthcare services to patients, anytime and anywhere [17]. For reliable access to medical data, transmissions of biomedical signals, etc., are some of the emerging IoT technologies that PCHIS provides and improves. PCHIS, along with Big Data technologies, is the future of medical health industry that will allow remote monitoring, track patient records, and provide personalized medicine support and remote assistance for the patients in rural areas, as well.

10.5.1.2 Healthcare and Internet of Things Devices

For weekday treatment, a physician uses a weight scale that is enabled by Bluetooth and blood pressure cuff, along with tracking app that can track symptoms for treatment of cancer. For mild cases, cyberinfrastructure for comparative effectiveness research is used to control groups of patients. Diabetes has become a major problem these days in every generation, with physicians recommending use of insulin pens to track the blood glucose levels while taking meals or sugar. A continuous glucose monitor is also used to track the glucose level in the body.

10.5.2 Safety and Confidentiality Issues in Healthcare

As a citizen of a country, we are reliable to use public as well as private healthcare organizations to get treatment. A gap between patient and doctor relationship and lack of trust do not allow patients to share their complete medical history. Advancements in recent technologies like IoT and Big Data are trying to be best solutions for the healthcare industry, but lag behind in terms of privacy concerns. Not sharing the complete medical record may lead to incomplete treatment and guidance, and could easily affect lives or may cause deaths. Figure 10.6. shows the IoT-based challenges in healthcare organizations.

10.5.2.1 Privacy and Security Concerns in Big Data

The emerging technologies in the healthcare industry are facing security and privacy concerns because the applications are not designed to store tremendous volumes of datasets.

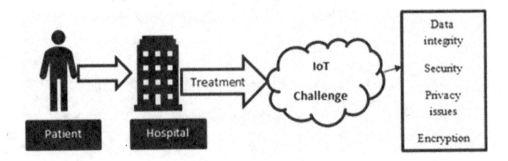

FIGURE 10.6 Internet of Things challenges in healthcare organizations.

The adoption of Big Data in healthcare increases the cause of security and privacy concern, and most of the data is stored in data centers with different security levels. Many of the data centers have Health Insurance Portability and Accountability Act (HIPAA) certification, but this certification does not provide any assurance for safety of patients' record. The emerging technologies in the healthcare industry are facing security and privacy concerns, because the applications are not designed to store tremendous volumes of datasets.

The patients' data can be lost due to centralize availability of records. The reason of breach will also be due to a regular check and management of devices used in treatment of patients for providing personalized medical healthcare facilities or monitoring remote services. Figure 10.7 shows Big Data-based challenges in healthcare organizations.

10.5.2.2 *Medical Internet of Things (MIoT): Patient Information Privacy*

The Medical Internet of Things (MIoT) or Internet of Medical Things (IoMT) is Internet-based devices which perform services that could support healthcare [18]. IoMT devices utilize many sensors and actuators to monitor the health condition of patients in real time. Patient information contains two parts: general records and sensitive data also called patient privacy. The private data should not be read out by medical organizations that could lead to misuse or may cause breaches and in extreme conditions lead to someone's health.

10.5.3 Solution-Based Blockchain Applications in the Healthcare Industry

Securing medical records and providing security is one of the most successful applications of blockchain, as shown in Figure 10.8. The working of blockchain relies on three factors: private key cryptography,

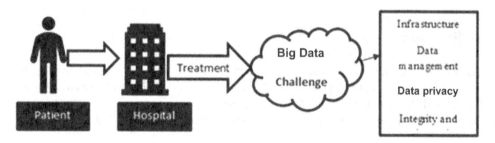

FIGURE 10.7 Big Data challenges in healthcare organizations.

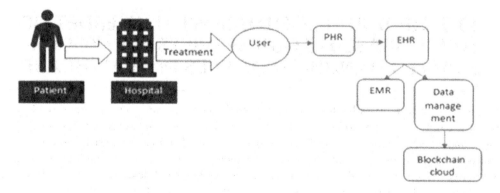

FIGURE 10.8 Role of blockchain in healthcare.

distributed ledgers, and authentication of data. Blockchain allows people to reduce the gap between patient and doctor that may allow sharing of medical records. Blockchain have several applications in healthcare such as securable healthcare setups, cryptocurrencies payment, tracing drugs, clinical trials and data breaching, managing patient data, and so on. The blockchain acts as a contract between patient and medical organizations to share the medical records on cloud storage that could not be misused by anyone or be exposed in breaches.

10.5.3.1 *Wireless Medical Sensor Networks*

Wireless Sensor Networks (WSNs) are deployed over a region when something is required to be monitored. For example, sensors are used to detect the enemy intrusion in military. WSN also plays vital role in healthcare, agriculture, environment, etc. WSNs is used to monitor the patient's health such as ECG, body temperature, blood pressure, etc. So, the work is to place sensors in an area which is unattended and then these sensors will collect sufficient data continuously from the environment and transmit those data to a base station and later those transmitted data are collected and analyzed in online or offline mode [19]. These data are sent to doctors or physicians for complete medication and treatment.

10.5.3.2 *DeStress Assistant (DeSA) iOS Application*

In the field of [20], communications and networking capabilities, sensor technologies, mobile computing, and cloud computing and network virtualization IoT brings a huge development [21, 22 and 23]. Multiple health and fitness observations are traced from that application. Some of the features include manual recording of glucose level in blood, tracing insulin, and physical activity monitoring. The App talks about the health status of the patient and ensures safety in combination. The data is stored in the cloud, allowing nobody to grant access to it for misuse.

10.5.4 Remarks

Healthcare is a big concern in today's world. To solve the challenges of privacy and security in the healthcare industry, the emerging technologies are IoT, Big Data, and blockchain. Each one has advantages over others, but IoT and Big Data lag behind blockchain in addressing privacy concerns. Blockchain removes the gap between patient and doctor to provide total privacy when it comes to sharing of medical records or data.

10.6 SUSTAINABLE FUTURE WITH INTERNET OF THINGS–BASED CLOUD SERVICES AND TOUCH-ENABLED HANDHELD DEVICES IN HEALTHCARE

In this section, the possibility of IoT has been discovered in the healthcare sector. Section 10.6.1 discusses the role of IoT in this industry, followed up by its recent application and areas of its usage. Associated challenges and problems have been also discussed in this section. Section 10.6.2 briefly describes the merits of introducing IoT in this field since it is recent technology which works with the support of Internet-enabled devices. Section 10.6.3 describes the application of handheld devices and its recent growth in terms of its use. Section 10.6.4 reveals how IoT can lead to the path of sustainable development in the healthcare industry.

10.6.1 Introduction of Internet of Things in the Healthcare Industry

Recently, the healthcare industry has gone through much technological advancement, which consists of the integration of broad range of communication technologies, wearable devices, and development of various databases for the purpose of developing smart healthcare solutions. Healthcare Providers (HPs), healthcare organizations (HOs), and practitioners are having major focus over on improvement of workflow efficiency in the industry to provide better services. To achieve such motives, HOs are ready to adopt modern solutions which are based over information communication technology (ICTs) infrastructure. In recent times, communication has played a major role in the healthcare sector, such as establishing the communication link between patients and care delivery organizations (CDOs) for the reason of receiving various medical services and facilities on time. Connectivity plays a significant role in terms of sharing recent medical histories among the stakeholders of HOs (such as doctors, hospitals, and practitioners). But it also has to face various issues with the deployment of such solutions such as integration of various stakeholders on one platform, which is one of the major challenging tasks until now. In many cases, they are not connected in an optimal way, which leads to deficiencies in the path of communication and subsequently which can cause serious problems or issues. Another challenge is to define general IoT architecture, since this industry faces a lot of variation which leads to collisions among the stakeholders. To achieve the motive of eradicating such challenges in the healthcare industry, it is required to define the proper IoT architecture which possesses the capability to deliver optimal, effective, and cost-efficient services to patients. The problem of bringing stakeholders at a single platform can be resolved by introducing the cloud-based IoT models which can synchronize with all the various data and be made it accessible to its stakeholders. A consolidated platform should be designed to provide the view of unified data and facilitates the healthcare organize to access that data according to rights provided to them by the cloud service providers (CSPs).

10.6.2 Merits of Introducing Internet of Things in the Healthcare Sector: Overview

According to [24], it is estimated that $1 trillion will be invested in the IoT sector of healthcare ICT infrastructure by 2025. The purpose of introducing IoT in this industry is to enhance the communication level and improve standard operating procedures of the healthcare sector. Since IoT is described as global network of a billion interconnected devices [25], this technology is expected to deliver efficiently various economical and non-economic benefits to this industry. This technology possesses the strong potential to provide access to the information, with efficient pathways, and also enables them to automate the task which was earlier performed by humans [26]. It has been predicted that in forthcoming years, adoption of IoT by this sector will be at massive levels due to advancements in technology and followed up by inversely proportional cost relations of enabling technological devices (such as software, hardware, or networks). Growth in the usage of IoT devices has been forecasted, and it can be observed on day-to-day basis. The IoT-based smart services and smart healthcare ecosystem involves an amalgamation of low computing capability devices to big computational devices. The IoT-based healthcare system enables efficient connectivity among its stakeholders. It offers the facility of tracking, storing, and monitoring of vital medical equipment and therapeutics, which can be proven to be profitable for the pharmaceutical sector [27].

Coalescence of the IoT with healthcare cloud enables healthcare providers to make their standard operating procedures (SOPs) smooth and seamless by increasing the efficiency of automated and monitored procedures. An IoT contribution will be accountable enhancement of work-related operations, which include service, treatment planning, and surgical operations [26]. In the current scenario, the IoT is implemented in the healthcare sector by acquisition of medical data and assistance with medical prescriptions.

Other healthcare facilities include portable healthcare monitoring systems and handheld devices which provide alerts or assist in healthy living. The purpose of bringing IoT into the healthcare sector is to provide access to health-related facilities to everyone. Diversity in technology leads to better future in this industry.

10.6.3 Application of Internet of Things–Enabled Handheld Devices in the Healthcare Industry

In the current scenario, mobile devices have been accepted as the most common handheld computing device. It has been observed that they are now part of every aspect of human life. Human interaction with such devices got recent hike due to this software's (Applications) have been develop for the purpose of providing different services to such wearable devices, for example, blood oxygen level can be detected by smart watches. These types of devices play major role in the IoT-based healthcare ecosystem, since many wireless devices are designed to broadcast data over the mobile phone. Recently, they have been used to for the purpose of determining certain body dynamics such as pulse rate, blood pressure, concentration of oxygen in blood, and breathing pattern after exercise. It provides patients with information to keep track of their medical records and history. These devices are allowed to track, store, maintain, and monitor the personal activity of humans. Further, the development is ongoing over the software of handheld devices for the purpose of streaming real-time data of patients to CDOs for the sake of real-time monitoring of patient health. Diagnosis can be done instantly by the consultant through checking the individual's day-to-day activity and other parameters. It provides facility to medical specialists to provide immediate consultation after medical tests, since reports are available on such devices immediately. These devices have to face many problems, also, such as synchronization of data over the cloud from different healthcare providers. Storage and reliable capabilities of data by such devices over long periods of time can also raise memory deficiency problems since they are stored on the local device. A long impact can be observed on the device's battery life and its interfaces of transmission.

In recent times, another technology also came into existence which is also considered as extension of mobile computing, which is known as wearable technology. These device interfaces are generally connected with mobile devices, and their interface interaction can be done through mobile software applications. These are dependent on mobile phones. Processes such as storage and transmission are carried by mobile devices and sent it to the cloud or decentralized cloud infrastructure. These devices consist of sensors which are allowed to monitor individuals' fitness parameters such as tracking sleep patterns, counting of steps while walking or distance of running, blood pressure monitoring, and breathing patterns. These devices allow patients to engage in their own fitness regimens. Early symptoms or warnings can be given to patients by such devices through measuring of all vital signs of health. They provide the facility of viewing and monitoring day-to-day activity analytics, which gives an individual an idea of their failings and weak areas to work upon. Basically, these devices are based on enabling technologies such as: system-on-chip (SOC), biosensors, low powered device-to-device (D2D) communication networks, harvesting of energy principle, bio-nanotechnology, and integrated circuits of low power, (6LoWPAN) low-power wireless personal network over IPv6 [28]. Issues faced by these technologies are inconsistency of data if sensors got damaged, privacy and security issues related to data, lack in security of transmission, breach in protocols which can ultimately lead to data leakage or theft, battery consumption, and signal interface of communication.

10.6.4 Remarks

The healthcare industry is one of the crucial and essential industries from the perspective of following vital living standards. Enabling of the IoT in such a type of sector will ultimately lead to growth in this sector by providing better healthcare services to patients. It will also raise the standards of procedure in the industry. Every technology possesses its own merits and demerits, but advancement in them will directly lead to the path of efficient workflow and maintaining the well-managed standard operating procedure for organization in every aspect. The scope and adoption of the IoT in this sector can prove to be part of future sustainable development.

10.7 SECURING HEALTHCARE/MEDICAL DOCUMENTS

In this section, we explain many methods to secure the healthcare records (or maintain confidentiality) and the cyber-threats that occur in healthcare. Also, these methods are analyzed, classified, and result is produced for future readers. This section of the chapter discusses the problems associated with maintaining electronic health records (EHR). Today's data-related technologies are facing many threats, so in this section a brief analysis have been covered up regarding healthcare data. Following up the solution related to those threats for the sake of prevention. Section 10.7.1 gives a brief overview of different types of electronic medical records. Section 10.7.2 briefly discloses the threat analysis of electronic-based records. Section 10.7.3 classifies the problems took place with EHR further. Section 10.7.4 describes the handling of privacy- and security-related issues, followed up with introduction to the healthcare cloud and its different deployed models. Section 10.7.5 describes the concept of security and privacy in the healthcare cloud. Section 10.7.6 summarizes all the points discussed in Section 10.7 and reaches conclusions regarding the solution and handling of privacy issues related to electronic records.

10.7.1 Introduction: Electronic Health Records (EHRs)

Electronic health records (EHRs) are defined as databases for storing information of medical- and health-related data of individuals which are managed by medical professionals and organizations. They are considered subsets of electronic medical records (EMRs), which are handled by care delivery organizations (CDOs). These are accessible and owned by the patients, comprising information related to the medical history of an individual. EMR is a legal entity of a patient which every health organization has to maintain. It comprises information related to patients from entry to exit, and all necessary details related to treatment given to patients. It is also owned by CDOs. It is created for the purpose of monitoring and managing of healthcare services by healthcare organizations (HOs). EMR and EHR are part of digitization which has to be brought in healthcare for the purpose of enhancing quality of services (QoS), efficiency in care of patients, and cost reduction. Health providers own the system of EMR, which manages the records of medical and treatment histories. It helps the provider to treat the patient accordingly. It depicts that blockchain technology has potential to bring a revolution in the healthcare industry in upcoming years.

10.7.2 Threat Analysis in Electronic Health Record Systems

The EHR system is considered at the secondary level of the healthcare system. Architects view it from the data layer perspective of the healthcare sector. Consideration from this perspective ignores their subsection such as networking and storage features of EHR which makes it vulnerable to attacks and data theft. Attackers have the possibility to attack from these sections and steal important personal data of patients, which makes this system insecure, and it also raises the questions of trustworthiness of its security features by healthcare providers. Possible attacks include:

- Blind Spots in encryption: Targeted attacks have been executed and planned over the encrypted data which is going through the process of being transferred from local systems to the cloud; attackers find those spots and attack over those weaknesses, it is considered one of the blind attack in IT infrastructure. It will become hard for security tools to detect such types of attacks in EHR and EMR systems.

- Ransomware and malware threats: These types of attacks have major possibility, since it can happen by taking the benefits of software vulnerabilities or by phishing emails. The potential of attack varies from data theft to data loss from host computer networks of an organization. Ransomware is different from malware; it locks out the user from the system and asks for money in exchange for regaining access. It is considered as a subset of malware attacks. This type of attack can be dangerous for CDOs or health providers (HPs) since their systems need to be up to date timely. No data loss or such attacks can be affordable in such type of ecosystem. In ransomware cases, hospitals have to pay attackers to regain access as soon as possible for the sake of safety and processing purposes of patient data, which also leads to economic loss to an organization.

10.7.3 Classification of Problems Faced by Healthcare Cloud EHR Systems

- Legal problems: Processing of data in the healthcare industry is associated with some legal complications which one has to make sure to handle initially. Here, legal refers to legislation of privacy and regulatory terms in the countries where cloud-based computation is present. Differing laws are in force in terms of policy reformation in the United States and members of the European Union. The U.S. Health Insurance Portability and Accountability Act (HIPAA) is responsible for handling matters of privacy in the healthcare sector [29].
- Technical problems: In [30], the authors have described the concept of technical problems related to privacy and security in cloud computing of the healthcare sector. Some of the key aspects of technical issues are related to data storage, processing (i.e., data centers), infrastructure management of healthcare cloud, client-side platforms, improvement in user experience, and interfaces. Certain problems related to the cloud can be resolved by cloud service providers (CSPs).

10.7.4 Handling of Privacy and Security Issues of Electronic Health Records (EHRs)

For handling privacy and security issues of EHRs, also minimizing the attack risk, combined efforts have been made in the field of data interoperability and exchange by the different nations in this sector. A turning point has been proven by cloud computing by providing various benefits such as application and services based on distributed network; it uses the collective computational resources which are formed from cluster of networks. The example of distributed computing resources and services has been cloud computing.

10.7.4.1 Introduction: Overview of the Healthcare Cloud

In the healthcare ecosystem, cloud computing plays a significant role in storing EMRs since the information retrieval process is faster in comparison to conventional management software. From a security perspective, patients' personal data is very important and a critical point of this industry; it requires certain preventive measures to protect the data from attackers, due to which organizations adopted this technology to support their complex IT infrastructure. It possesses the capability to store and share information at different locations. All of the medical-related data is stored and maintained over the private cloud, and stakeholders have the right to access the patient data according to their rights given to them by CSPs. A benefit of this technology is that anyone can access their personal data from anywhere and anytime through their credentials. There will be cost reduction for the organization in terms of maintenance of complex IT infrastructure. There are certain models of cloud which are deployed over the industry to maintain the organization's data interoperability and integrity, as discussed in the following subsection.

10.7.4.2 Classification of Different Types of Cloud Deployment Models

Figure 10.9 depicts different types of cloud models according to scalability and organization adaptability, as described in what follows.

- Private cloud: Those cloud systems which are owned or hired by single organization. Its resources are managed by that owning organization. These are generally used for multifaceted businesses. Simply, these organizations are responsible for maintaining the customer's data. Cloud service providers have comprehensive, strong policies and processes to provide the high quality of application services, network security, internal systems security, strategies for data restoration, third party authentication, and authorization features to an organization.
- Community cloud: It belongs to several organizations and its resources are utilized only by the concerned and hired organizations who are authorized. For this type of healthcare cloud, data protection is the top priority. This has certain features from the stakeholder's perspective such that no misuse of patient's data took place among the healthcare cloud ecosystem; features include physical security, encryption of data, user authentication, application security with up-to-date security standards, and replication of data with secure point-to-point network.
- Public cloud: These are open cloud-based services which individuals can have limited access to. An individual can store, access, and manage their data on their own. Microsoft Health Vault and Google Health are good examples of public healthcare cloud systems. They basically

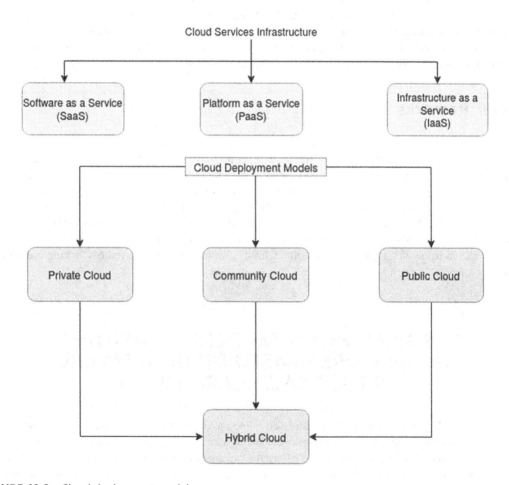

FIGURE 10.9 Cloud deployment models.

adopted a centralized architecture from patient-centric views; i.e. information stored in such ecosystem of patient will be available to CDOs, HPs, and HOs over their applications under the control of the patient.

• Hybrid clouds: It is considered as by the combination of two or more different types of cloud-deployed models such as private–community, community–public, or private–public; they possess unique entities, but they are connected by technologies they are utilizing which enable the application's portability [31][32].

10.7.5 Overview of Confidentiality and Safety in the Healthcare Cloud

In cloud computing, safety and confidentiality play major roles to protect an individual's data, which is not only protected through passwords and access enforcement. This is a multidomain-based technology; each domain acts as an individual and holds its own security and privacy policies, requirements for trust, various secured mechanisms, strategies for data backup, and certification of third party applications. Some of the issues require concrete deployed models of cloud and secured cloud services over the healthcare infrastructure. Security of the cloud includes identity-based access management, installation of firewalls, and intrusion detection software; this can be done by the internal structure of the organization at the inner surface of cloud; for external security, the CSP is primarily responsible for cloud security infrastructure. Flexibility in security over the cloud is completely dependent upon the CSP. In [33], security issues related to cloud computing are based on cloud architecture, management of identities, protection of data, and availability. It is combination of all the technology such as architecture of oriented services, virtualization, Web 3.0, and computation of utility. The author in [33] explained that the security of the cloud depends upon computation and cryptography.

10.7.6 Remarks

EHR is considered one of the crucial parts of the healthcare industry; because it holds the patient data to develop this ecosystem as user friendly, it requires integration of several stakeholders at one platform to make the process of treatment smooth and efficient. But on the other side, it is more vulnerable also from attack purposes. To safeguard it from attacks requires several levels of physical and data security. Several countermeasures should be planned by IT architectures of an organization to protect the patient data. Cloud computing is the one which comes with a solution to all the problems of EHR. Since it holds several other parts also, such as medical and personal records, it is also crucial to be protected from such types of data thefts. Cloud computing can prove to be a turning point in this industry in upcoming years.

10.8 HEALTHCARE MODELS, ALGORITHMS, FRAMEWORKS BASED ON DATA MINING IN THE HEALTHCARE SECTOR

In this section, all the problems will be addressed related to data retrieval, management, and processing. In upcoming sections of this chapter, a brief overview of data mining process related to healthcare industry will be discussed with its challenges. Different algorithms and artificial intelligence–based models will be unveiled which contribute in prediction of diseases. Section 10.8.1 introduces the importance and application of data management in healthcare industry using data mining techniques. Section 10.8.2

gives the expository view of framework which is used for data exchange and transmission in ecosystem. Section 10.8.3 addresses the challenges of data mining and Big Data. Section 10.8.4 concludes by summing up all the benefits of using these algorithms and models in this industry.

10.8.1 Overview of Data Management Process in the Healthcare Industry

There are several terms which have been used in healthcare in previous decades, like knowledge discovery in databases, data mining, machine learning, etc.

10.8.1.1 Introduction: Data Mining

Raw data gets processed through this technique by implementation of computation and extraction of certain facts.

This technique re-evaluates and processes information which was previously undiscovered and possess some potential information from voluminous unstructured data. It basically determines factual information out of the unstructured data and tries to find patterns in them to draw some conclusive outcomes. This technique is useful where there is a possibility of occurrence of error by humans; it possesses the capability to eradicate those errors and mistakes, and also it helps humans in the decision making-process. It also helps in pattern recognition, drawing relationships among different entities and developing predictive models which can be further useful for decision-making processes in treatment or diagnosis. In the modern healthcare industry, the predictive models primarily focus on the processes of decision making, reduction in subjectivity to human errors, and precise diagnostic report generation. Knowledge discovery in database (KDD) is based on scanning of data in databases to extract meaningful patterns from them. Once new patterns get discovered from this technique, this can be integrated with old ones to find meaningful information. Evaluation methods can be more refined after the extraction of new information and can improve subsequent processes to achieve new results [34]. It can be also useful for conversion of low-level data discovery to high-level data discovery [35][36]. Figure 10.10 shows steps takes place in KDD processes which are briefly described in what follows:

- Data Cleaning: This process is defined as elimination of noisy and redundant data from databases. Cleaning action takes place in case of empty values and elimination of noisy data, where the variance errors are found. Cleaning takes place by transformative and discrepancy tools.
- Integration of data: Assimilation of data from multiple sources and in heterogeneous form gets combined in the warehouse of data. It is done by using the extraction-load-transformation (ETL) process.
- Selection of data: This process takes place by the implementation of data mining algorithms for the purpose of extracting only useful data to convert it into information. It is done using neural networks, decision trees, or genetic algorithms
- Transformation of data: This can be defined as the process of converting data into useful information by mining procedures. It has two steps: mapping of data and code generation.
- Data mining: As discussed earlier, this technique is used for extracting useful patterns from analyzed data. It transforms relevant task data into patterns. It also helps in deciding the purpose of classification of information.
- Pattern analysis: This identifies strict patterns which will be used for knowledge representation and quantitatively measures the extracted pattern and scores them, Scoring is done for the purpose of drawing comparison quantitatively. It uses summarization and visualization techniques to bring that in a user-understandable format.
- Representation of knowledge: This is visualization techniques which represent the results of data mining such as generation of reports, tables, classification, and categorization rules.

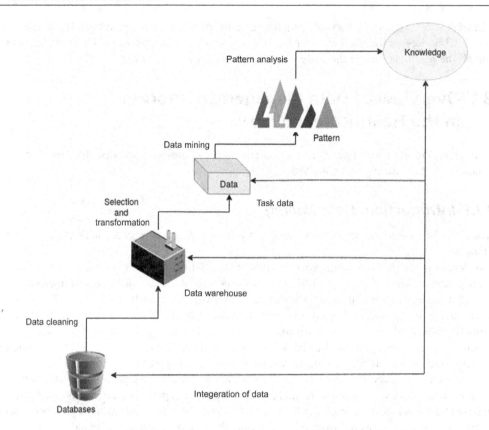

FIGURE 10.10   Processes involved in knowledge discovery in a database (KDD).

10.8.1.2 Data Mining Algorithms

Various data mining methods which are implemented in medical sector include the following:

- Artificial neural network (ANN): This technique is inspired by the working of the human brain; it is based on superior learning techniques. ANN receives large inputs through a cluster of computer networks, all having the capability to process in parallel and arranged in layers. The first layer gets the raw data as input and it gets processed by nodes which are interconnected and possess their own rules and knowledge. Then it gets passed on to the next layer of processors and nodes receive input from preceding node outputs. So at each level, the data gets more refined and it turns out to be useful information since every node as input/output possesses its own weight [37].
- Decision tree: This is graphical technique which is used to establish the relation among the different data entities of storage. It is primarily used for categorization of data. The result is in the form of a tree, and it is also used for building predictive models. Sorting of instances from bottom to root nodes leads to classification of attributes. They are faster in comparison to neural networks and are used for short-duration learning.
- Genetic algorithms: These are based on the principles of modification, natural selection, and mutation of genetics. Evolution of these algorithms leads to their optimization. From formulation purpose of hypotheses, these algorithms are used to derive the relationship among the variables and dependencies using association rule [38].

The primary advantage of using these algorithms is to simplify the process and workflow of healthcare organizations. Predictive models which are derived using these algorithms support in decision making and diagnostics processes of patient. The major aim in developing this predictive model is to give support to health providers by enhancing their procedures of treatment planning and prognosis.

10.8.2 Framework for Data Exchange and Transmission in the Healthcare Ecosystem

It is necessary for data processing to have an integrated healthcare system to continuously feed data for real time data processing and analysis. The Apache Hadoop framework is a computational model which provides this feature of distributed processing of voluminous and huge datasets of different entities in the healthcare sector. It provides the framework for distributed storage and Big Data processing. It is based on the MapReduce model of program which was originally proposed by Google for developing scalable web applications. This framework was revolutionized for the purpose of scalability to widen its reach from individual servers to clusters of server and thousands of computational devices. It provides the computational as well as storage facility with integrated healthcare system. Many healthcare companies and providers are using this framework for research and production purposes. Precise validation and evaluation of massive data are required. Hadoop plays a vital role in computation and analyzing of various and diverse types of data in this sector, which helps in various applications and reduces the cost of deliverables in the country. Hadoop is primarily dependent upon the following:

- Hadoop Distributed File System (HDFS): HDFS was developed using a file system of distributed design. It works over the commodity-based hardware. It is designed over less costly hardware due to which it also possesses high fault tolerance capability. It has a feature of parallel processing such as working upon clusters of commodities in case of any failures occurring in the hardware. It can deal with Big Datasets which are stored upon multiple machines. It provides the access of streamed information. It uses a coherency model which can be easily implemented. Hadoop provides command line interface to deal with HDFS interface. For the purpose of secured data access and authorization, it provides the file permissions and authentication features.
- Hadoop MapReduce (HMR): HMR is used for parallel processing of large datasets in clusters of Hadoop. Analysis of data in this framework primarily depends on mapping and reducing. The configuration of the job (it defines scheduling, management of files and monitoring) is map and reduces the functional analysis, and this framework contributes in providing services like scheduling, parallel processing, and distribution. In this framework, a job is segmented into two phases: map and reduce. In the map phase, input gets split for data analysis by tasks running in a cluster of Hadoop. By default, it receives data from HDFS. MarkLogic connector is used for receiving the input data from its server instance. In the reduce phase, it uses results of mapped tasks. Consolidation of data into results takes place after the reduction. MapReduce framework stores the data in HDFS, and uses MarkLogic Connector for sending the results over the HDFS.

This can be considered a possible solution for eliminating the challenges faced by Big Data organizations. Generally, these organizations face three Vs problems—i.e., volume, variety, and velocity—in data transmission over the network. In the future, it can expect to makes the process easier and less complex by migrating terabytes of data over the network without making it slow.

10.8.3 Data Mining Challenges Faced by the Healthcare Industry

Major problems faced by data mining and Big Data in the implementation phase can lead to economic and data losses. Following are the challenges that have to be faced by the data mining process in the present scenario.

- For increasing the efficiency in parallel processing to migrate the algorithm over to Hadoop platform.
- Sharing of data over the global network is still one of the major challenges. Problems related to synchronization cannot be solved.
- Increment in overheads of communication as size of datasets get increased, which has to be processed by dataset. Evolution of techniques must be there to decrease the communication overheads.
- A major challenge in the mining process is sorting of voluminous and heterogeneous raw medical data [39].
- Efficiency of the mining process depends upon the algorithm. If that is not sufficient or optimized, it will not help in the mining process effectively.
- Data visualization after the analysis is also a challenge, since complex data relations cannot be visualized on the user end.
- There can be security and privacy threats during the analysis phase which hamper the personal data of patients.

10.8.4 Remarks

According to growth and requirements of the healthcare sector, the infrastructure for maintaining the record needs to update on daily basis. Techniques such as data mining, Big Data plays key roles in updating of the complex IT infrastructure. Voluminous and heterogeneous data require management; otherwise, this can turn into a vulnerability situation for healthcare organizations. Decision-making processes are among the critical parts of the healthcare sector, but data mining techniques make this process easy and supportive for health providers. A Hadoop type of framework is a requirement for this industry, as data integration is preeminent process; otherwise, ecosystems will not be able to develop. This type of framework makes the data exchange and transmission process economically feasible and viable. Challenges can be overcome with the evolution of predictive models and algorithms.

10.9 HEALTHCARE CLOUD INFRASTRUCTURE AND SAFETY STANDARDS RELATED TO ELECTRONIC MEDICAL RECORDS (EMRS)

In this section, principles of privacy and content safety of EMRs are discussed. In the healthcare sector, the organization has the top-most priority to secure the patient personal data. Before access of data by any of the stakeholders, it is required to verify the authenticity of its identity. To maintain the trust among the participants of the healthcare cloud, it is necessary to build secured services–based infrastructure over the cloud. In Section 10.9.1, a brief overview of standards has been described which are commonly used in the healthcare sector. Section 10.9.2 describes the principles required for ensuring the security and privacy of EMR. In Section 10.9.3, classification of cloud platform services are briefly explained as to their role of maintaining security of data present on healthcare cloud infrastructure. Section 10.9.4 concludes by summing up the section.

10.9.1 Safety Standards of Electronic Medical Records (EMRs)

There are mainly two popular standards for secure data and clinical information exchange among the stakeholders. It ensures the safety of transmission of data over the ecosystem, regardless of location or medium. Standards are described in what follows:

- Health Level 7 (HL7): According to [40], this is a framework which comes into functionality when there is exchange, integration, sharing and extraction of data in electronic records of health. It sets a standard of packaging and communication of data among the stakeholders, for the purpose of integration in existing records of patients; these types of standards of information and data exchange by the other systems are necessary. HL7 supports the care delivery organizations (CDO) medical and management practices, evaluation, and provision of better healthcare facilities to patients. It is the most commonly used and recognized framework.
- ISO/TS 18308:2004: In [41], this standard came into existence for the purpose of data exchange and information among the stakeholders which are located in different countries, states, or provinces. It is developed to integrate different healthcare services and facilities at one platform for the sake of easy communication, sharing, and exchange of information among different sectors of healthcare. It is also used to integrate different healthcare models. It is commonly used in designing and development of electronic health record architecture (EHRA).

10.9.2 Principles of Security and Privacy in EMR

Four major principles are followed to ensure the safety of patients' personal data. It is also required to verify and add personal data in EMR.

1. Access to all medical related data should be secured through control of encryption, access to secured storage, and internally and externally safe transmission of data.
2. EMR is developed by taking consideration of ACID (atomicity, consistency, isolation, and durability) properties of databases, which maintain the integrity of a patient's personal data and provides less flexibility in customization of privacy by the health providers so that no tampering should take place with records.
3. Limited access rights and verification of data before entering into the cloud database and updating of EMR which is stored over the cloud database.
4. Process of sharing of EMR among the participants should be an end-to-end encrypted process by digital signatures and secured protocols which ensure the safety and privacy of data during the transmission.

These four major principles are able to manage the safety and security of patient data over the healthcare cloud. It is important in integrated systems to consolidate the system of secure medical records and ensure no tampering with personal data.

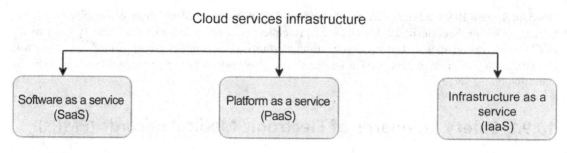

FIGURE 10.11 Categorization of cloud services.

10.9.3 Classification of Cloud Services

In healthcare, cloud services play a significant role in maintaining the security and safety standards of the system. Broadly, these services are classified into three categories [42], which are depicted in Figure 10.11.

- SaaS: Software as a service provides the facility to customers to use the provider's application running over the cloud infrastructure. It also provides the functionality of accessing the application over any device of the customer by thin interface with the client, since it runs over the web browser. The cloud service provider (CSP) manages the cloud infrastructure over which application is deployed, with the responsibility to maintain servers, storage, device accessibility, bandwidth of applications, etc. Security and privacy play a major role at such level of cloud, which is also taken care of by the CSP, and is considered as an integral part of SaaS to the consumer.
- PaaS: Platform as a service provides the feature to customers of deploying their application over the provider's cloud infrastructure by using the supported tools and programming language. The customer is not responsible for managing the cloud's environment of hosting configuration it is managed by CSP. This type of model comes with double security and privacy levels, and it is divided into two parts: lower system level (LSL) and higher system level (HSL). LSL includes the basic level of security mechanism which is provided by the cloud; it includes authorization, end-to-end encryption, and authentication. At HSL, consumers have to specify the policies of access control, requirements of authenticity, and much more.
- IaaS: Infrastructure as a service provides the capability for consumers to access processing, network, management of application, and computational resources over the cloud infrastructure. The customer has provision to run, manage, and deploy the application over the cloud. Cloud infrastructures operating system, storage, networking, and possible control over the security is not managed by the customer. The healthcare provider and organization is fully responsible for protecting security and privacy over this type of infrastructure model.

10.9.4 Remarks

With quality of service (QoS) in the medical field, ensuring data safety and confidentiality is done by CDOs. It is required to develop the safety standard exchanges and protocols which enable the data transmission among the stakeholders. The healthcare cloud provides the ability for patients to access their records from anywhere at any time. Different cloud services enable the health organizations to ensure safety and manage the access and control of their patients' records. It is required for EHR to follow the safety standards and principles to develop the integrated ecosystem of the healthcare industry.

10.10 SAFETY AND CONFIDENTIALITY ISSUES IN DIFFERENT COUNTRIES

The Internet of things is being used in many sectors and is a primary source of generating large amount of data. IoT devices are causes of leaking privacy of users/patients. There are six common implementation challenges faced with implementing the IoT in healthcare sector: the "high" investment costs; security of data at rest, data in use, and data in flight; technology infrastructure; communications infrastructure; immaturity of IoT standards; and procuring of IoT.

- Issues in India: There are many serious concerns about the healthcare industry in India, but data security/protection, privacy, and strict cybersecurity law issues are on the top of the list. Today with the development in technology, India needs to introduce strict data protection laws to protect patient privacy. Today, privacy is a global issue and needs to be protected by secure mechanisms and innovative encryption schemes. In India, privacy becomes a fundamental right, whereas in most counties, privacy is not that much of a sensitive topic for many persons. Government is tracing or stealing their citizen's information and using it to influence citizens or users. Few nations have passed strict laws for privacy and security like Germany, France, Denmark, Poland, etc. Recently in 2020, India scored 2.4 out of 5 on a global privacy index [43][44], whereas China and Russia got worse ratings than India; this means that Chinese and Russian people's privacy is more at risk. In India, when a patient uses a healthcare service using Aadhaar, the lack of data confidentiality of patients brings out a huge threat to people. In general, in India most of the applications (Android) are rooted due to design and are hosted on a Google server and Amazon Web Services (AWS) for application data, which is away from the Government of India (GoI) but rather in the hands of private companies.
- Issues in other countries: Similar issues of data protection and privacy are raised in many sectors. Another issue is in unclear specification of confidentiality policies in the case of departments or ministries using that application. These applications, such as Google and so many others, collect information which is a long list and may be quite irrelevant and unnecessary situation, but such tracing can be done by hacker who can control an app remotely and steal all data of patients or users. In recent years, we have heard many news items related to leaking of data or breaches in systems. Even big companies like Google, Facebook, etc., are also facing court cases related to breaching in user's data or violating privacy rules.

Note that during installation of any healthcare-related applications, we need to be sure about "opt in" versus "opt out" data sharing practices or privacy policies. While updating time there should be some retention rules that need to put forward for limited data collection (e.g., avoiding central server storage, deleting user data after a period). This literally shows the weak legal space in India for protecting the greatest threat to humans, which is their confidentiality. There are several challenges to the government that are been faced in the case of privacy protecting.

There are a lot of questions arising when it comes to holding sensitive data of a citizen, and when seen in depth, these data are given price tags. We need to understand differences in online privacy, data privacy, identity privacy, and its related security attitudes. In the terms of legally, technically, and politically, we need to know so many perspectives and challenges facing India and other countries.

10.11 BLOCKCHAIN-BASED HEALTH INFORMATION PRIVACY PROTECTION

Transparent yet secure information storage systems are a necessary need of the era due to the increasing number of data breaches, which could have severe consequences. Healthcare data records, including sensitive medical records, especially need to be efficiently secured. The healthcare data spans from medical information of patients, the service providers, or institutions to the entities which supply the pharmaceuticals, equipment, and drugs. The data is dynamic in nature and requires proper management, updating, and protection.

Currently, the health information exchange (HIE) system relies on three modes of information exchanges: direct, query-based and patient-centered exchanges. The direct exchange system is a A-B trustworthy transfer mechanism in which the A is an alert of the patient information. The direct transfer system stores the patient details as electronic health records (EHRs). The query-based models (lookup systems) bring detecting and ask other providers for information on a patient. A central repository plays a critical role in this exchange mechanism, where electronic medical records are aggregated from the EHR systems of multiple healthcare organizations and stored in a hub. The requesting organization could use a look-up to obtain the relevant data. Query-based mechanisms are mainly developed for interorganizational collaborations to maintain quality care treatment and related purposes. Patients are an important producer of the data and are included in the information exchange process through patient-centered exchange models. In these HIE systems, patients have access to their own healthcare information, but it is used by the care providers in reality. These HIEs are controlled and managed by the healthcare institutions for proper management of data. In such systems, the concerns and trust issues of the patients could restrict the optimal utilization of the information.

HIE is a centralized system which ensures easy collaboration between the patients, healthcare providers, and financial institutions like insurance providers. Despite the efficient collaboration between different electronic health record systems, its multiple connected networks possess a serious threat of data breach, as suggested by Vest and Gamm [66]. Some of the common possibilities for a digital data breach can be listed as follows:

- Malware and phishing attempts: With the help of links, cyber-presence is easily detected, e.g., scams from sites that look legitimate asking login information. Several viruses and other malicious nodes will compromise data and send them back to real host.
- Online medical devices: As the Internet of Medical Things (IoMT) evolves, data are exported to external sources, and this could potentially be exploited.
- General access to systems: The system where data is stored must not be accessible by third party that may be a cause of information loss or damage of data.
- Disposal of old hardware: There is still a chance to get information from carelessly throwing out hard drives, and to avoid that, one still needs to check and delete or reformat them before disposal.

10.11.1.1 Blockchain Technology

Blockchain is a decentralized technology—a digital ledger—and thus, it is also referred to as distributed ledger technology (DLT). The technology invented by Satoshi Nakamoto was first employed as a component of Bitcoin [45] (Figure 10.12). As per Crosby et al. [67], the fundamental features of blockchain technology are strong enough that it can possibly overthrow contemporary business models mainly used for information exchange purposes in healthcare systems. This technology overcomes issues of privacy. It is in the form of shared structure and used for storing history of transactions, and also it acts as chain of blocks. The Genesis block is the initial block and it contains a header, a counter for transactions, and

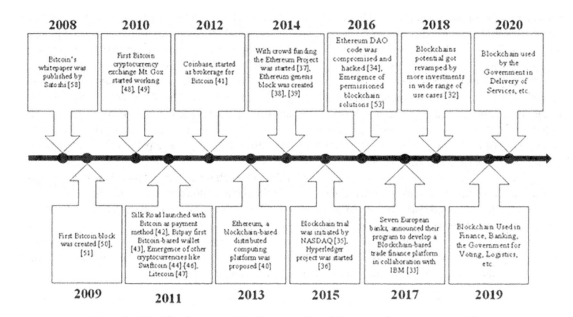

FIGURE 10.12 Evolution of blockchain year by year.

another transaction. For collecting data, it uses a decentralized manner and it works on proof of work (PoW) concept. In the form of hash function, these miners solve the puzzles. As mining takes place, new blocks are additionally added, and thereby, each of them is identified by hash which is located in header area. Hash is created using secure hash algorithm SHA-256.

Blockchain, in simple terms, is called the "chain of trust." A blockchain is a decentralized ledger of transactions across a peer-to-peer (P2P) network. A transaction ledger is just a place where something can be recorded. We say blockchains are decentralized ledgers because everyone on the network has their own synchronized copy. They can all see and confirm that a transaction has occurred and has been recorded, all at the same time. This occurs on a P2P computer network. So, instead of connecting to a central authority through a hub-and-spoke model, every participant has a computer linked to other participants. The data flow from organizations to the third parties and back can be replaced with ease using blockchain technology. Data instead travels between anonymous organizations and comes to a final assent within a short span of time, which clearly implies the combined efforts of all parties from a set of events. Data encoding assures the privacy of data, digital signatures, etc., and assures validation, data consolidation, and much more. As a result, blockchain can solve the problem of needing to trust third parties.

Note that the number of transactions and costs held in different aspects of the medical industry brings out a huge potential. It makes use of peer-to-peer computer networks rather than a centralized network. Blockchain technology employs a cryptographic hash to every block using a nonce and is unique for every block with a reference to the previous blocks. In [46][47], authors discuss how a blockchain works and how it is a foolproof technology against all odds/attacks. A blockchain is more or less permanent, since it would require improbable computational power to find the nonce to add a particular block to a chain and solve the subsequent blocks.

According to Xia et al. [68], healthcare organizations could depend upon blockchain technology in information storage and sharing on the interorganizational level. The blockchain system could ensure secure and fast information management and protection, and thus presents a solution for the data management concerns in the healthcare sector. The decentralized network and the hash on the block ensure security of the data. The information management would now become patient-centric and also interoperable. Patients could allow or deny a third-party access to their personal data, and could also acquire their data from other institutions without much complexity. The smart contract embedded in the blockchain makes the institutions capable of executing automated business interactions with minimal office operations in the sharing process. An audit trail is incorporated in the ledgers to make sure that the transactions using the blockchain are accurate; this would enable efficient financial transactions such as that of healthcare insurance.

This technology brings out a huge merit in the case of storing, information exchange, and also in managing these medical documentations. According to study done by Abdulnabi et al. [69], the more decentralized format can increase feasibility for patients when analyzing medical data (i.e., secondary) with the help of blockchain that shares at the network. There comes quantitively based work for observing the exposure of HIE with respect to this technology. It is still not clear if these patients will adopt a state of mind to accept these developments.

Hence, in summary, the primary concern regarding blockchain is the balance between transparency and confidentiality. The decentralized network and the node-to-node access of the blockchain could restrict the selective confidentiality of the information. These concerns are partially answered with the permissionless and permissioned blockchain networks. The permissionless networks are open to all and are accessible to anyone. Meanwhile, permissioned networks would make the access to the network more selective. Thus, permissioned networks would be more applicable for healthcare data management, since it could keep the confidentiality of the information to a great extent.

10.12 BLOCKCHAIN-BASED HEALTHCARE INSURANCE SYSTEMS

With the word "Insurtech," things have changed and literally focused on improving the efficiency and reduction in cost. The insurance industry stands to benefit enormously from the use of blockchain technology. While insurers can use it for help in detecting fraud, another way it will benefit is from using blockchain to help streamline the way the industry handles claims. Currently, it takes between 90 and 180 days from the time that a health claim is initiated until payment is made to a healthcare company. Not only does this mean that these organizations are owed enormous sums of money at any one time, but it also shows just how inefficient the current system is.

With the help of blockchain, insurance area becomes much more safe and transparent in today's time. Health insurance, which covers the expenses of the patient, is at risk. When comes to estimation part,

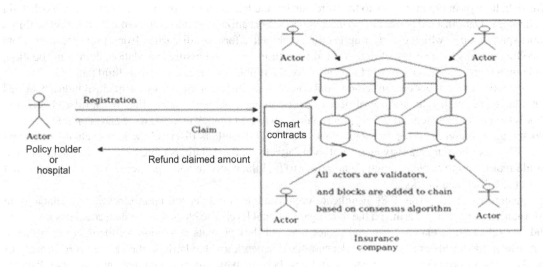

FIGURE 10.13 Blockchain-based health insurance system.

i.e., the risk and expenses of healthcare brings insurer for developing a finance structure to release claiming amount to the patient. It's a contract between the insurance provider and a policyholder, (monthly or annual) and the benefits will be to central government and private business.

In April 2018, healthcare companies like Humana, MultiPlan, Quest Diagnostics, Optum, United Healthcare, etc. announce that they will improve their system with the help of blockchain, to rectify inaccurate information of provider, or fraud people or fraud claims or avoiding multiple claims with many companies, etc. Without blockchain, it was leading to dissatisfaction, increment in costs, and lawsuits. These issues can be solved by using this blockchain technology efficiently.

10.12.1.1 Main Points for Health Insurance Providers

- Building trust among customers.
- Managing patient data.
- Unstructured/invalid documenting.

10.12.1.2 Main Points for Health Insurance Consumers

- Access to medical history of the patient as per need and ownership of medical data: This is due to changing up of plans. Patient data is carried by patients themselves and the end users have no control over access to the medical history. During an emergency, the patient's data may not be available to several other doctors, so doctors will provide services to the patient without knowing the patient's medical history.
- Processing/denying claims within a specified time period: Losing trust in customers is increased when it comes to keeping a deadline in insurance.
- Security.

Blockchain can resolve all these problems. Today's health records are typically stored within a single provider system. With blockchain, providers could either select which information to upload to a shared blockchain when a patient event occurs, or continuously upload to the blockchain.

The important features of blockchain are such as authentication, confidentiality, immutable, automated transaction, etc., which are used as distributed to the entire network, to solve several security, privacy and trust, etc., issues. Deploying blockchain on healthcare networks would help with the following points:

- Expedite and improve patient diagnoses and medical costs. Customer experience gets improved as doctors have quick access to medical documents of respective patients when that patient asks.
- Smart contracts are developed for a better transaction process, and can also improve trust factor.
- Reducing the processing costs of the insurance providers is achieved by using sharing data on networks on which data can be easily accessed by them, and thereby, loss of data or entering incorrect data is eliminated.
- Self-sovereign identity is created among all consumers and not for the centralized system.

To improve growth in market share, this technology is incorporated in this area. For example, The Office of the National Coordinator for Health Information Technology, in response to the blockchain challenge, asks how we can use this technology to make sure medical documents are well protected and are confidential in the health sector. Many possibilities with this technology like as insurance providers using smart contract, validate authentic user, etc. are widely accepted around the world by many companies. A single point can get results from multiple points, and the data that needs to be maintained is the biggest factor. A cryptographic pathway without harming person's privacy makes a better choice.

10.13 BLOCKCHAIN FOR PROTECTING MEDICAL DATA

Many authors have tried to defend many existing technologies for preserving privacy, but none of them provide reliable privacy protection mechanisms. Blockchain, a distributed ledger concept, provides a certain level of privacy protection in e-healthcare for patients. For example, authors in [46] have defined an affordable system for medical cyber-physical systems applications. Blockchain technology has gained its popularity after the proposal of the Bitcoin framework proposed by Santoshi Nakamoto [45]. Blockchain has a series of applications but is primarily known for its immutable distributed ledger technology which has the capability to encapsulate the data in a block, and arrays of blocks get arranged in a particular sequence which forms chain-like structure and hence becomes a blockchain. This has brought a paradigm to the security and privacy segment of the industry. The blockchain is known to be immutable because once the block gets added to the chain, it cannot be modified or deleted. Every piece of the chain gets added to the sequence once it is verified by the miner. Miners are the people who validate the transactions and those are authenticated nodes of the network. If any malicious user tries to mine a block or transaction, the whole chain can be invalidated. In blocks, data gets secured and encrypted by the special type of hash algorithms such as SHA-256, SHA-512, and AES [48]. Note that a few possible uses of blockchain (including serious concerns) in the near future have been discussed in [49][43][50]. Blockchain has five major components, discussed in what follows:

- Block number: Unique identity of block.
- Data: Raw pieces of information stored inside a block to transmit over the network for the purpose of maintaining trustworthiness and transparency.
- Timestamp: Generated when the block is created and added to the chain.
- Current block hash: Each block possesses its own hash value.
- Previous block hash: It can be called as a chaining component which connects the previous block to form a sequence.

In Figure 10.14, it can be observed that blockchain initiates with the Genesis block. This block does not have any type of data or information stored in it, since it consists of only the three components of block number, timestamp, and current block hash. Data in the Genesis block is initiated with null value. Blockchain plays a major role in those application areas where trust, transparency, security, and privacy are highly required for the data and where data is shared among the third-party organizations.

10.13.1 Potential Applications of Blockchain

In this section, several potential applications of blockchain will be discussed. Recently it is explored that blockchain can play a major role in fraud detection and prevention of drug abuse. It is used in the pharmaceutical sector, as well as patient-centric model. In the pharmaceutical sector, blockchain has been mainly used in supply chain management system (SCMs), since this industry is generally affected due to the involvement of all the third non-trusted parties or organizations involved. Earlier, it was impossible to detect and track which part of SCM was faulty and iterate its mistakes. But after the introduction of blockchain-based SCM, it is trackable since in this system, every moment is trackable and traceable. it is all managed by a smart contract which tracks the digital signature of each party and should be available in a distributed ledger (DL). That ledger is available to all, and every block of the transaction gets added to the ledger after validating by 50% of nodes, which makes this system more transparent and secured. Secondly, when equipment and batch of medicine get dispatch for the distribution, its batch number and the manufacturing date are coded over cartons or boxes so that it is identifiable that the medical supplies should not be outdated to avoid distribution of expired medicines to consumers, those codes get stored

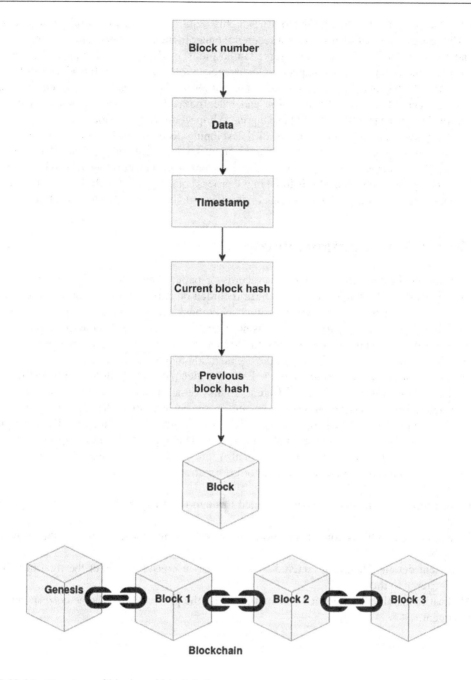

FIGURE 10.14 Structure of block and blockchain.

over the DL. So that medical regulators and bodies can have a check over the pharmaceutical production industries they are not creating any type of drug abuse.

In the upcoming time, the drug evaluation and approval process will be also based upon blockchain-based distributed ledgers, so that process should be transparent and secured among different regulatory bodies. It will turn out to be a centric process, and other government and official drug regulatory bodies can also participate in the drug and vaccine approval process. All the trials and records will be stored in the form of DL-based records such that immutability is highly required to make the whole process secure and trustable. The process can be fast-tracked in a secured manner in the case of pandemic situations.

Nowadays, most commonly it can be observed in hospitals; medical clinics are moving toward a new billing and payment system which accepts cryptocurrencies, tokens, or coins. Introduction of e-wallets will revolutionize the payment system; it will be beneficial for later stages, as well as the current scenario. It is the highly secured method of transaction and incentivized-based system which most people are inclining toward in the near future. It will have a greater impact on token economics.

Currently, developers are also focusing toward developing decentralized applications. As Web 3.0 is approaching across the globe, it is time to move applications on decentralized platforms that will enhance the process of data sharing, integrity, maintaining transparency, and building trustable relationships among different organizations. It is also helping in the process of integration of different technologies and bringing them on one platform to perform tasks in parallel and automating the process effectively.

10.13.2 Electronic Patient Records

In hospitals and medical institutions, medical records of patients have been recorded in the form of paperwork, i.e. files and discharge summaries been recorded on paper, or in current scenarios, stored in databases; hospitals have to pay hefty amounts to develop their electronic databases or to purchase software to store the information of patients, and it is not a scalable solution to handle this type of problem. Institutions have to pay directly in proportion to the storage they own. Also, these types of records can be tampered with and can be accessed by any of the organization members.

Blockchain comes up with the solution of the EHR in which patient records are stored in the form of a ledger which can have restricted access to different organizational structures, and it can be only accessed through the public keys of the patient [51]. Management of the institutions has to manage keys' corresponding records, and those keys can be also recorded in the ledger. Every record in EHR is encrypted by hash value, which makes it more secured and tamperproof. This type of system is capable of increasing security and maintaining the privacy of data. It can also function in a peer-to-peer–based network. It has the following major fields to store different types of information (Figure 10.15):

- Unique identity: This is a number generated through the encrypted private key of a patient's record.
- Personal details: This is consists of information such as name, sex, height, weight, body mass index, and vision.
- Treatment details: Detail are entered by the doctor or consultant about the treatment being administered to the patient.
- Medication details: This carries information about the prescribed medicine corresponding to treatment.

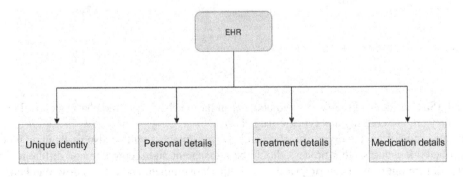

FIGURE 10.15 Electronic health records (EHRs).

These records are immutable; once the information is added to the record, it cannot be modified—and it has limited access rights, i.e. it gives restricted access to read/write information in these types of records; only specific authorized people can read or write data.

10.13.3 Benefits of Blockchain Technology

Blockchain plays a vital role in healthcare industry for security collecting information of patients' medical histories. Some of the benefits are discussed in what follows on the basis of feature analysis and distributed networks.

10.13.3.1 Features of Blockchain Technology

Features of blockchain:

- Transparency: In the healthcare sector, it is required that third parties should maintain transparency among them so that stakeholders should have surety about the treatment or diagnosis performed by institutions in the right directions.
- Scalability: Blockchain provides scalability by encapsulating all data into blocks, storing them in the ledger, and making them accessible through keys.
- Security: In the blockchain, each block is encrypted by the hash value and the block gets mined after the miner verifies it; otherwise, the whole chain can be invalid, which enhances its security feature.
- Trustworthiness: Smart contracts come into role play when the issue of trustworthiness rises. These autonomous contracts try to manage trustworthiness among different nodes of the P2P network [52].
- Privacy: Restricted access to ledgers provides privacy to data and limited access capabilities to read/write information in it.
- Sharing: Data sharing takes place via a P2P network. Distributed ledgers are meant to be sharing data among different nodes, which maintains trust ability transparency.

Popular use of blockchain, i.e., in the energy sector, has been examined in [53]. Further, we have discussed several serious concerns in blockchain technology in [54].

10.13.3.2 Distributed Network

A distributed network is defined as a network of connected individual nodes (i.e., different organizations or individuals) which has the capability to share data among each other. Transactions between any two nodes will be reflected back in all the ledgers, and every node has back up of each ledger. This system of sharing is also known as decentralization of data, whereby data storage does not depend upon a centralized system. It exemplifies the following features:

- Data sharing.
- Resiliency.
- Reliability.
- Trustworthiness.

In Figure 10.16, it can be observed all the nodes are connected together and every individual has its own copy of the ledger. The transaction between any two nodes will reflect changes in all the ledgers, which make this system more transparent and shareable.

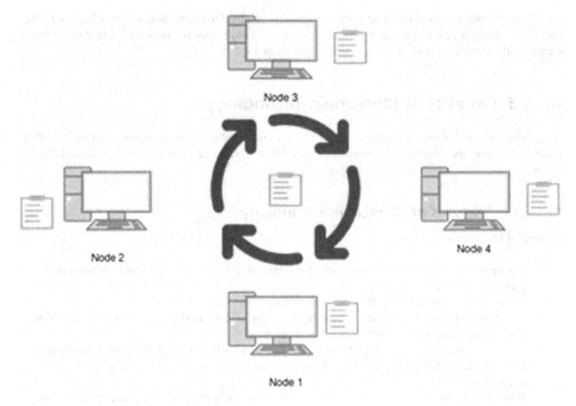

FIGURE 10.16   Peer-to-peer connected nodes sharing distributed ledger.

10.13.4 Remarks

Blockchain is that upcoming technology which integrates with another system for the purpose of providing data security, sharing data, and maintaining trustworthiness among different organizations. In the upcoming future, it will be part of the entire technology ecosystem as soon as its awareness gets increased and many organizations will rely on this for the purpose of secured data transmission and transparency. Some organizations will run autonomously due to smart contracts; it has the feature to develop a decentralized-based autonomous organization (DAO).

10.14 ENHANCED DATA AUTHENTICATION AND SAFETY IN HEALTHCARE USING BLOCKCHAIN

A lot of changes have been prompted by IT with respect to healthcare, and these affects both treatment and the data that needs to be processed carefully. When it comes to processing data, privacy issues arise and all patient data are valued, processed individually, and protected from third parties. So many attacks have taken place in several countries as they breach into the medical data that itself is kept confidential. Data breaches can cost healthcare organizations a lot, and current systems are vulnerable to numerous types of attacks. Patient data are extremely valuable to hackers looking for detailed identity information, which makes securing electronic health records (EHRs) and associated personal details a top priority in the healthcare industry. Emerging blockchain technology may offer a solution to healthcare's biggest security challenges. Features such as decentralized storage, cryptography, and smart contracts provide a framework for organizations to improve data protection while maintaining accuracy and preventing unauthorized access to or alteration of patient information. A blockchain may be set up as permissionless or permissioned. Permissionless, or public, blockchains are theoretically accessible to any user, but becoming part of a permissioned blockchain requires consent from the owner. Given the highly sensitive nature of patient data, permissioned blockchains are more appropriate for healthcare settings. Sharing of data becomes crucial as in mobile state of society. Medical service delivery can be done by leveraging the interconnectivity between networks. In 1996, the Health Insurance Portability and Accountability Act (HIPAA) was enacted by the United States to control fraud and several breaching activities of patient privacy, including five rules:

- Privacy rule: Regulation in disclosing patient medical history.
- Transactions and code sets rule: Simplifying the transaction process.
- Security rule: Controlling access of systems and securing data passage in open network.
- Unique identifiers rule: Only the national provider identifier (NPI) identifies covered entities in the standard transactions to protect the patient identity information.
- Enforcement rule: Investigation procedures and penalties for violating HIPAA rules.

Utilizing the blockchain creates an environment in which all participants, including patients, review information before it officially becomes part of a record. This provides the opportunity for healthcare providers and patients to evaluate information, thus preserving the accuracy of data throughout the blockchain. Since 40% of patient health records currently contain errors, switching to this kind of collaborative system has the potential to improve patient care and reduce the risk of life-threatening mistakes. Companies like MedChain and MedRec are currently working on permissioned blockchain platforms to bring these benefits to healthcare organizations and the patients they serve. By moving patient health information to a decentralized storage solution in which records are broken into fragments and distributed across the blockchain, these companies seek to provide a better way for healthcare organizations to protect patient information.

10.14.1 Challenges of Blockchain Implementation

While the blockchain has many potentially beneficial applications in the healthcare industry, the technology still needs time to mature before it becomes practical to pursue widespread adoption. Adherence to HIPAA regulations is a key concern when storing private patient information in a decentralized environment, and use of blockchain technology alone is not enough to ensure complete privacy. Stringent security regulations, including encryption and onsite administrative protocols, would be required of each healthcare organization retrieving, storing, or sharing patient data within a permissioned blockchain. Implementing permissioned blockchain models in existing systems requires help from IT professionals who are trained and certified in the technology and familiar with the security challenges such a framework poses in a healthcare setting. An appropriate system of checks and balances must be established at the outset to prevent data errors from becoming permanent parts of the blockchain, and provision must be made for accessing records in the event of emergencies in which patients are rendered incapable of granting access using their security keys.

10.15 HEALTHCARE SERVICES WITH EMERGING TECHNOLOGIES FOR THE 'SMART ERA'

One of the key elements of smart cities is smart healthcare. The area of smart healthcare arises from the need to enhance healthcare sector management, better use its resources, and reduce its costs while sustaining or even improving its level of quality. Smart health research can be generally divided into two major categories: the category related to patients and the category related to processes. Study in the category of processes is concerned with developing policies to guarantee certain facets of the healthcare sector. Smart city provision depends largely on the incorporation of all smart systems, including smart healthcare. The nature of the healthcare industry requires a safe and effective way to deal with the tremendous amount of data all the time. It is now possible to design and grow smart healthcare by using cloud and edge computing, as it has been established that the cloud is more reliable than traditional servers. Cloud and edge computing relies on the efficient implementation of smart healthcare services, and they deliver a stable, secure, smart healthcare platform.

Without the help of constant network structure availability, these portable IoT devices come in handy for gathering, storing, generating, and analyzing data of a patient. Patients wearing devices are quickly diagnosed on site, and the information gathering is passed as a feedback format to servers. With the help of edge computing, it can easily get the data of patent in poor connectivity areas. Securing huge amounts of data that has been produced from IoT and edge computing is a great task for providers. The data that has been fed to central servers are analyzed and processed and it may be much later when a person updates any information. Edge computing applications have the potential to solve this data problem. With the critical processing task that is been located on the edge network and with the help of that, IT gains much real-time data that is continuously processed and analyzed, and that can be extremely useful for prediction in the case of emergencies. IoT-related devices used for medical purposes can also send alerting mechanisms if the conditions are met. In the meantime, IoT with ML algorithms brings out many more solutions and also help with storing data in the cloud.

Sensor-based IoT medical devices bring out much potential. Data that has been gathered based on some patterns can be utilized for prediction cases, and smart RFID tags can be used to eliminate time-consuming processes. GPS and other tracking devices placed in fleet vehicles can track and locate them. To avoid misuse of the crucial data, edge computing comes into play in which these data are filtered locally and are not sent to central servers, thereby increasing security. COVID-19 has undoubtedly altered an already evolving healthcare landscape. As cloud computing helps in sharing data securely, edge computing goes for improved access and practical, deployable solutions. Choosing between them gives no difference because each has its own purpose. According to Vatsavai et al. [70], 91% of data is created and processed in centralized data centers. But by 2022, about 75% of all data will need analysis and action to take place at the edge. Further, there has been an explosion in healthcare data—a 900% increase in just three years. As a result, many healthcare providers have turned to edge computing to solve their challenges caused by the proliferation of devices and the latency in sending data to a cloud and back. Edge computing architecture reduces the need to use a centralized cloud and can instead exploit connectivity near the data source, improving speed and latency.

Recognition of potentially cancerous lesions in radiology images is a typical application of deep learning in healthcare. Deep learning is increasingly being applied to radiomics, or the identification of clinically important features in imaging data beyond what the human eye can perceive. In oncology-oriented image processing, both radiomics and deep learning are most commonly used.

Figure 10.17 shows edge-based smart healthcare framework. With the help of this technology, it brings out the smarter way in functions without connection to data center, so with the localized power, it will be even more useful in gathering and processing these data for delivering market. On other side, many authors have discussed various popular security and privacy concerns [54–58] toward IoT or smart

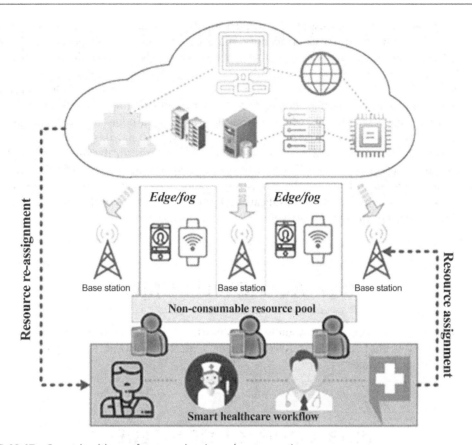

FIGURE 10.17   Smart healthcare framework using edge computing.

things and their uses in various other applications like transportation [59][60], nuclear power plants [61], healthcare, etc. Further, various possible uses of computer vision or artificial intelligence with Big Data have been discussed in [62–65]. Hence, this section discusses several healthcare services with emerging technologies like edge computing, deep learning, etc., for the smart era (21st century). The next section will conclude this work in brief, including several future remarks for scientists and researchers.

10.16 CONCLUSION

Due to recent developments in engineering and technology, we have seen major changes in the healthcare industry. As discussed in this chapter, saving people is primary goal of any human being. For example, the COVID-19 pandemic has affected billion of lives; also, through using technology, we have saved millions of other lives. We have used many smart devices or computer systems to identify COVID-19–positive people at early stages, and also many governments have launched several applications for contact tracing. Through tracing a COVID-positive person, respective authorities can trace nearby persons and provide alerts for the same, to take preventive measures against COVID-19. These solutions are only possible through artificial intelligence (or technology), but such solutions come with several negative concerns like leaking of patient privacy and breaching patient data without patient consent, etc.

In this chapter, we have discussed several (and highly cited) attempts which were proposed for solving these issues. We have discussed identity and access to management systems for healthcare, blockchain-based innovative solutions for healthcare (or protecting electronic health records), healthcare issues in India and in other countries, and the impact of emerging networking solutions like cloud computing, edge computing, etc., on healthcare. Furthermore, many other useful topics have been covered in this chapter. In this article, each section provides useful information for researchers, and also leave researchers with some research gaps which will be helpful for continuing research work in the near future. Scientists and researchers around the globe are suggested to refer this work to your colleagues and other interested readers to know more about healthcare solutions for the smart era people from a user's perspective. Note that we are still unable to find a unique solution (or standard/framework) for protecting patient data or patient's privacy, so as future work, interested researchers and scientists are invited to look over the raised issues in healthcare and provide innovative, useful, and reliable solutions to the healthcare industry (including patients).

10.17 ACKNOWLEDGMENT

This research work is funded by the Anumit Academy's Research and Innovation Network (AARIN), India. The authors would like to thank AARIN, India, a research network, for supporting the project through its financial assistance.

10.18 CONFLICT OF INTEREST

The authors have declared that they do not have any conflict with respect to publication of this chapter.

10.19 CONTRIBUTION/DISCLOSURE

All authors of this chapter have contributed equally; also, the first author was the meditation instructor of the retreat.

REFERENCES

[1] Shen, B., et al. "MedChain: Efficient healthcare data sharing via blockchain." *Applied Sciences* 9 (2019): 1207.
[2] Al Omar, A., et al. "Privacy-friendly platform for healthcare data in cloud based on blockchain environment." *Future Generation Computer Systems* 95 (2019): 511–521.
[3] Chen, Y., et al. "Blockchain-based medical records secure storage and medical service framework." *Journal of Medical Systems* 43 (2018): 5.
[4] Guo, R., et al. "Secure attribute-based signature scheme with multiple authorities for Blockchain in electronic health records systems." *IEEE Access* 776 (2018): 1–12.
[5] Kuo, T. T., et al. "ModelChain: Decentralized privacy-preserving healthcare predictive modeling framework on private blockchain networks." *arXiv* (2018), arXiv:1802.01746.

[6]   Wang, S., et al. "Blockchain-powered parallel healthcare systems based on the ACP approach." *IEEE Transactions on Computational Social Systems* 5 (2018): 942–950.

[7]   Bradford, M., J. B. Earp, and S. Grabski. "Centralized end-to-end identity and access management and ERP systems: A multi-case analysis using the Technology Organization Environment framework." *International Journal of Accounting Information Systems* 15, no. 2 (2014): 149–165.

[8]   Chen, X., D. Berry, and W. Grimson. "Identity management to support access control in e-health systems." In *4th European Conference of the International Federation for Medical and Biological Engineering*, pp. 880–886. Springer, 2009.

[9]   Xiong, J., Z. Yao, J. Ma, X. Liu, Q. Li, and J. Ma. "PRIAM: Privacy preserving identity and access management scheme in cloud." *KSII Transactions on Internet & Information Systems* 8, no. 1 (2014).

[10] Deng, M., R. Scandariato, D. De Cock, B. Preneel, and W. Joosen. "Identity in federated electronic healthcare." In *2008 1st IFIP Wireless Days*, pp. 1–5. IEEE, November 2008.

[11] Hummer, W., P. Gaubatz, M. Strembeck, U. Zdun, and S. Dustdar. "An integrated approach for identity and access management in a SOA context." *Proceedings of the 16th ACM symposium on Access control models and technologies*, pp. 21–30, June 2011.

[12] Mikula, T., and R. H. Jacobsen. "Identity and access management with blockchain in electronic healthcare records." In *2018 21st Euromicro Conference on Digital System Design (DSD)*, pp. 699–706. IEEE, August 2018.

[13] Leviss, J. "Identity and access management: The starting point for a RHIO." *Health Management Technology* 27, no. 1 (2006): 64.

[14] Gunter, C. A., D. Liebovitz, and B. Malin. "Experience-based access management: A life-cycle framework for identity and access management systems." *IEEE Security & Privacy* 9, no. 5 (2011): 48.

[15] Priyanka, A., M. Parimala, K. Sudheer, R. Kaluri, K. Lakshmanna, and M. Reddy. "BIG data based on health-care analysis using IOT devices." *MS&E* 263, no. 4 (2017): 042059.

[16] Vitabile, S., M. Marks, D. Stojanovic, S. Pllana, J. M. Molina, M. Krzyszton, . . . A. S. Ilic. "Medical data processing and analysis for remote health and activities monitoring." In *High-Performance Modelling and Simulation for Big Data Applications*, pp. 186–220. Springer, 2019.

[17] Keikhosrokiani, P., N. Mustaffa, and N. Zakaria. "Success factors in developing iHeart as a patient-centric healthcare system: A multi-group analysis." *Telematics and Informatics* 35, no. 4 (2018): 753–775.

[18] Sun, W., Z. Cai, Y. Li, F. Liu, S. Fang, and G. Wang. "Security and privacy in the medical internet of things: A review." *Security and Communication Networks* 2018 (2018).

[19] Kumar, P., and H. J. Lee. "Security issues in healthcare applications using wireless medical sensor networks: A survey." *Sensors* 12, no. 1 (2012): 55–91.

[20] Islam, S. R., D. Kwak, M. H. Kabir, M. Hossain, and K. S. Kwak. "The internet of things for health care: A comprehensive survey." *IEEE Access* 3 (2015): 678–708.

[21] Abomhara, M., and G. M. Køien. "Security and privacy in the internet of things: Current status and open issues." In *2014 International Conference on Privacy and Security in Mobile Systems (PRISMS)*, pp. 1–8. IEEE, May 2014.

[22] Štern, A., and A. Kos. "Mobile phone as a tool in the areas of health protection." *Slovenian Medical Journal* 78, no. 11 (2009).

[23] Peternel, K., M. Pogačnik, R. Tavčar, and A. Kos. "A presence-based context-aware chronic stress recognition system." *Sensors* 12, no. 11 (2012): 15888–15906.

[24] Kaaprojects. "IoT healthcare solutions and applications." *White Paper* (2019). www.kaaproject.org/healthcare/.

[25] Chordant. "The IoT breakdown eBook." *White Paper* (2017). www.chordant.io/white _ papers/101- iot-breakdown- ebook#.

[26] Zeadally, Sherali, and Oladayo Bello. "Harnessing the power of internet of things based connectivity to improve healthcare." *Internet of Things* (2019): 100074.

[27] Dharmendra, S., and G. Rakesh. "An IoT framework for healthcare monitoring systems." *The International Journal of Computer Science and Information Security* 14, no. 5 (2016): 6.

[28] Gravina, R., P. Alinia, H. Ghasemzadeh, and G. Fortino. "Multi-sensor fusion in body sensor networks: State-of-the-art and research challenges." *Information Fusion* 35 (2017): 68–80.

[29] Gavrilov, G., and V. Trajkovik. "Security and privacy issues and requirements for healthcare cloud computing." *ICT Innovations* (2012): 143–152.

[30] Löhr, H., A. R. Sadeghi, and M. Winandy. "Securing the e-health cloud." *Proceedings of the 1st ACM International Health Informatics Symposium*, pp. 220–229, November 2010.

[31] Lupşe, O. S., M. M. Vida, and L. Tivadar. "Cloud computing and interoperability in healthcare information systems." *The First International Conference on Intelligent Systems and Applications*, pp. 81–85, April 2012.

[32] Takabi, H., and J. B. Joshi. "Policy management as a service: An approach to manage policy heterogeneity in cloud computing environment." In *2012 45th Hawaii International Conference on System Sciences*, pp. 5500–5508. IEEE, January 2012.

[33] Jansen, W. A. "Cloud hooks: Security and privacy issues in cloud computing." In *2011 44th Hawaii International Conference on System Sciences*, pp. 1–10. IEEE, January 2011.

[34] Zaïane, O. R. "Principles of knowledge discovery in databases." *Department of Computing Science, University of Alberta* 20 (1999).

[35] Funatsu, K. (Ed.). *Knowledge-Oriented Applications in Data Mining*. BoD—Books on Demand, 2011.

[36] us-fsi-2018-global-blockchain-survey-report.pdf. Retrieved December 17, 2018, from https://www2.deloitte.com/content/dam/Deloitte/us/Documents/financial-services/us-fsi-2018-global-blockchain-survey-report.pdf.

[37] Gupta, S., D. Kumar, and A. Sharma. "Data mining classification techniques applied for breast cancer diagnosis and prognosis." *Indian Journal of Computer Science and Engineering (IJCSE)* 2, no. 2 (2011): 188–195.

[38] Ngan, P. S., M. L. Wong, W. Lam, K. S. Leung, and J. C. Cheng. "Medical data mining using evolutionary computation." *Artificial Intelligence in Medicine* 16, no. 1 (1999): 73–96.

[39] Cios, K. J., and G. W. Moore. "Uniqueness of medical data mining." *Artificial Intelligence in Medicine* 26, no. 1–2 (2002): 1–24.

[40] www.hl7.org/implement/standards/.

[41] www.iso.org/standard/33397.html.

[42] Zhang, Rui, and Ling Liu. "Security models and requirements for healthcare application clouds." In *2010 IEEE 3rd International Conference on cloud Computing*. IEEE, 2010.

[43] Tyagi, A. K., T. F. Fernandez, and S. U. Aswathy. "Blockchain and aadhaar based electronic voting system." *2020 4th International Conference on Electronics, Communication and Aerospace Technology (ICECA)*, pp. 498–504, Coimbatore, 2020. DOI: 10.1109/ICECA49313.2020.9297655.

[44] www.forbesindia.com.

[45] Nakamoto, S. "Bitcoin: A peer-to-peer electronic cash system." 2008. https://bitcoin.org/bitcoin.pdf.

[46] Tyagi, Amit Kumar "AARIN: Affordable, accurate, reliable and innovative mechanism to protect a medical cyber-physical system using blockchain technology." *International Journal of Intelligent Network* xx–xx (2021).

[47] Tyagi, A. K., S. Kumari, T. F. Fernandez, and C. Aravindan. "P3 block: Privacy preserved, trusted smart parking allotment for future vehicles of tomorrow." In Gervasi, O., et al. (eds.). *Computational Science and Its Applications—ICCSA 2020. ICCSA 2020. Lecture Notes in Computer Science*. Vol. 12254. Springer, 2020. https://doi.org/10.1007/978-3-030-58817-5_56.

[48] Gittins, Benjamin, Howard Landman, Sean O'Neil, and Ron Kelson. *A Presentation on VEST Hardware Performance, Chip Area Measurements, Power Consumption Estimates and Benchmarking in relation to AES, SHA-256 and SHA-512*. Synaptic Laboratories Limited, 2005.

[49] Tyagi, Amit Kumar, S. U. Aswathy, and Ajith Abraham. "Integrating blockchain technology and artificial intelligence: Synergies, perspectives, challenges and research directions." *Journal of Information Assurance and Security* 15, no. 5 (2020). ISSN: 1554–1010.

[50] Nair, Siddharth M., Varsha Ramesh, and Amit Kumar Tyagi. "Issues and challenges (privacy, security, and trust) in blockchain-based applications." *Book: Opportunities and Challenges for Blockchain Technology in Autonomous Vehicles* (2021): 14. DOI: 10.4018/978-1-7998-3295-9.ch012.

[51] Gordona, William J., and Christian Catalini. "Mini review blockchain technology for healthcare: Facilitating the transition to patient-driven interoperability." *Computational and Structural Biotechnology Journal* 16 (2018): 224–230.

[52] Wang, Yao, and Julita Vassileva. "Trust and reputation model in Peer-to-Peer Networks." *Third International Conference on Peer-to-Peer Computing* (P2P'03), 2003.

[53] Yang, Tianyu, Qinghai Guo, Xue Tai, Hongbin Sun, Boming Zhang, Wenlu Zhao, and Chenhui Lin. "Applying blockchain technology to decentralized operations in future energy internet." In 2017 *IEEE Conference on Energy Internet and Energy System Integration* (EI2) (2017): 1–5.

[54] Tyagi, Amit Kumar, Meghna Manoj Nair, Sreenath Niladhuri, and Ajith Abraham. "Security, privacy research issues in various computing platforms: A survey and the road ahead." *Journal of Information Assurance & Security* 15, no. 1 (2020): 1–16.

[55] Tyagi, A. K., and D. Goyal. "A survey of privacy leakage and security vulnerabilities in the internet of things." *2020 5th International Conference on Communication and Electronics Systems (ICCES)*, pp. 386–394, Coimbatore, India, 2020. DOI: 10.1109/ICCES48766.2020.9137886.

[56] Reddy, K. S., K. Agarwal, and A. K. Tyagi. "Beyond things: A systematic study of internet of everything." In Abraham, A., Panda, M., Pradhan, S., Garcia-Hernandez, L., and Ma, K. (eds.). *Innovations in Bio-Inspired Computing and Applications. IBICA 2019. Advances in Intelligent Systems and Computing*. Vol. 1180. Springer, 2021. https://doi.org/10.1007/978-3-030-49339-4_23.

[57] Tyagi, A. K., G. Rekha, and N. Sreenath. "Beyond the hype: Internet of things concepts, security and privacy concerns." In Satapathy, S., Raju, K., Shyamala, K., Krishna, D., and Favorskaya, M. (eds.). *Advances in Decision Sciences, Image Processing, Security and Computer Vision. ICETE 2019. Learning and Analytics in Intelligent Systems*. Vol. 3. Springer, 2020. https://doi.org/10.1007/978-3-030-24322-7_50.

[58] Shamila, M., K. Vinuthna, and Amit Tyagi. "A review on several critical issues and challenges in IoT based e-Healthcare system." (2019): 1036–1043. DOI: 10.1109/ICCS45141.2019.9065831.

[59] Tyagi, Amit Kumar, and N. Sreenath. "Preserving location privacy in location based services against Sybil attacks." *International Journal of Security and Its Applications* 9, no. 12 (December 2015): 189–210. (ISSN: 1738–9976 (Print), ISSN: 2207–9629 (Online)).

[60] Tyagi, Amit Kumar, and N. Sreenath. "A comparative study on privacy preserving techniques for location based services." *British Journal of Mathematics and Computer Science* 10, no. 4 (July 2015): 1–25. (ISSN: 2231–0851).

[61] Tyagi, Amit Kumar. "Cyber Physical Systems (CPSs)—Opportunities and challenges for improving cyber security." *International Journal of Computer Applications* 137, no. 14 (March 2016): 19–27. Published by Foundation of Computer Science (FCS), NY, USA.

[62] Tyagi, Amit Kumar, and G. Rekha. "Machine learning with Big data." *Proceedings of International Conference on Sustainable Computing in Science, Technology and Management (SUSCOM), Amity University Rajasthan, Jaipur—India*, March 20, 2019, February 26–28, 2019.

[63] Pramod, Akshara, Harsh Sankar Naicker, and Amit Kumar Tyagi. "Machine learning and deep learning: Open issues and future research directions for next Ten years." In *Book: Computational Analysis and Understanding of Deep Learning for Medical Care: Principles, Methods, and Applications.* Wiley Scrivener, 2020.

[64] Tyagi, Amit Kumar, and Poonam Chahal. "Artificial intelligence and machine learning algorithms." In *Book: Challenges and Applications for Implementing Machine Learning in Computer Vision.* IGI Global, 2020. DOI: 10.4018/978-1-7998-0182-5.ch008.

[65] Tyagi, Amit Kumar, and G. Rekha. "Challenges of applying deep learning in real-world applications." In *Book: Challenges and Applications for Implementing Machine Learning in Computer Vision*, pp. 92–118. IGI Global, 2020. DOI: 10.4018/978-1-7998-0182-5.ch004.

[66] Vest, J. R., and L. D. Gamm. "Health information exchange: persistent challenges and new strategies." *Journal of the American Medical Informatics Association* 17, no. 3 (2010): 288–294.

[67] Crosby, M., P. Pattanayak, S. Verma, and V. Kalyanaraman. "Blockchain technology: Beyond bitcoin." *Applied Innovation* 2, no. 6–10 (2016): 71.

[68] Xia, Q. I., E. B. Sifah, K. O. Asamoah, J. Gao, X. Du, and M. Guizani. "MeDShare: Trust-less medical data sharing among cloud service providers via blockchain." *IEEE Access* 5 (2017): 14757–14767.

[69] Abdulnabi, M., A. Al-Haiqi, M. L. M. Kiah, A. A. Zaidan, B. B. Zaidan, and M. Hussain. "A distributed framework for health information exchange using smartphone technologies." *Journal of Biomedical Informatics* 69 (2017): 230–250.

[70] Vatsavai, R. R., B. Ramachandra, Z. Chen, and J. Jernigan. "GeoEdge: A real-time analytics framework for geospatial applications." *Proceedings of the 8th ACM SIGSPATIAL international workshop on analytics for big geospatial data*, pp. 1–4, November 2019.

Blockchain-Based Medical Insurance Storage Systems

Ciza Thomas, Bindu V, Amrutha Ann Aby,
Anjalikrishna U.R., Anu Kesari, and Dhanya Sabu

11

Contents

11.1 INTRODUCTION

Blockchain is a distributed data storage platform where every party involved in the network records each transaction that occurs in the network. Even without third-party validation, and with participants not knowing each other in a transaction, they do exchange values, i.e., it no longer requires a central body to check trusts and transfers.

A system built on blockchain can be compared to an open book or deoxyribonucleic acid (DNA). An open book is fragmented, transparent, and irreversible such that the information is available to everyone. Likewise, blockchain systems are also inherently transparent and the responsibility of every action in the system lies in the hands of everyone associated with it. DNA is a record of genetic transactions and mutations that spread with the development of life on earth. As time goes on, our DNA grows and becomes complicated. Of course, changing DNA is not easy, as scientists estimate that it will take about a million years genetically. Similarly, in blockchain systems, a new block gets added over time, making it also complicated. Adding a new block to the blockchain is not easy, either, since every block is cryptographically interconnected with its previous block. Hence, blockchain is treated as a potential game-changing player.

The blockchain systems originated in 2008 when Satoshi Nakamoto, a pseudo-name or cluster of people, developed Bitcoin, authoring a white paper unfolding the software and its implementation. The first blockchain database was devised as part of its implementation. Further, this network has fully fledged as Bitcoin and is known to be a recognized unit of peer-to-peer digital currency. They anonymously started to transfer coins without the involvement of a third person. The potential of blockchain is so vast that it is now revolutionizing the way people do business, thereby transforming societies and making government work efficiently. Presently, the mission of the blockchain is to begin a secured ecosystem among the different independent users in a non-trustable distributed environment. As a result, many of the present-day applications are now taking the ecological architecture, operation mechanisms, and database models of this system. Prominent areas of blockchain-based application systems include the development of smart contracts, supply chain and logistics monitoring, e-commerce, social communication, etc.

The establishment of the secured ecosystem by the blockchain systems can be explained by an example. Consider the case of an ownership exchange in a business area where there will be many intermediaries or third parties involved. Usually, there will be a dedicated service meant to each party involved to guarantee efficient transfer. These services generate charges based on their policies for processing and completing the transaction. If it is a blockchain-based system, the ecosystem automatically creates public records of all transactions, and the computer checks every transaction and creates a history book of all events. The computers involved in the network are situated all around the globe. It is significant to note that they are not under any company. The third parties currently verifying the transactions—that can be auditors, accountants, legal service providers, payment processors, or other intermediaries—will be disabled by the blockchain. This is a real-time and safer process compared to the system where the third parties verify transactions.

One of the major areas that require the implementation of the blockchain is the healthcare system. Healthcare is a confidential information–concentrated domain where an enormous measure of information is produced, processed, and spread consistently. Safe, secure, and adaptable information sharing is imperative for health analysis and consolidated clinical decision making. Handling this sensitive and large volume of data is crucial and challenging. Currently, tele-medicine and e-health are two major platforms for handling clinical information. In every clinical arrangement, there are possibilities of a data breach, abuse, and exploitation of the patient's information. Subsequently, the capacity to exchange information securely, safely, and in a scalable manner is profoundly significant for supporting solid and meaningful communications.

In the medical domain, another challenge faced is the inefficient, improper, and unsystematic approach of storing medical transaction data which can lead to third-party manipulations and corruption in insurance claims. Intending to overcome these fallacies, we designed a blockchain environment to store the medical transaction data so that a decentralized tamper-resistant blockchain-based medical insurance storage system can be developed.

11.1.1 Current Scenario

When an individual is taken to a hospital for treatment, the first question posed by the hospital is whether or not the patient is covered under any insurance policy. In cashless treatment where the policyholder gets admitted and undergoes the required treatment without paying directly for the medical expenses, there are basically three steps involved:

- Intimate the third-party administrator (TPA) or the insurance company to get approval for the treatment and the claim and payment process. In the claim intimation process, the individual initially communicates to the TPA or the insurance company. In case of emergency when the policyholder gets admitted to the hospital, a family member needs to inform the hospital about health insurance.
- Then the hospital communicates to the TPA and here the intimation is done within 24 hours of hospitalization.
- TPA will send the approval letter within six to seven hours in case of emergency hospitalization.

The documents required for this include details of all medical tests conducted with their reports and bills, doctor prescriptions, health identity card, claim form, pre-authorized forms, etc. Based on these documents the TPA in case of cashless hospitalization the payment is directly made to the hospitals which may take a week normally. In general, what happens normally is that the hospital submits all the documents to the TPA and the TPA releases the payment and deposits to the hospital directly. The patients or the individuals who hold the insurance don't have access to their claims.

11.1.2 Problems

In the medical sector, basic patient information and data stay dissipated across various offices and departments. Because of this, pivotal information often is not effectively open and helpfully accessible amid urgency. Additionally, numerous medical storage systems existing today are not reliable since they are still depending on obsolete methods for keeping patient records. Today, about 40% of medical services information records are topped off with errors; hence, the existing system is inadequate for handling the exchange of information.

Handling Big Data increases the computation complexity, and data can be stolen or altered by a third party. Since any third party can access anyone's data, the trust in data security has been lost in this field. Since this sensitive data can be used for any unethical purpose, common people started losing their reliability. For the benefit of the hospital, they started claiming for the manipulated higher amounts of bills, insurance companies eventually being cheated. Misunderstanding the genuineness of true cases, insurance companies delay and deny the claims of many common people. Even as the number of patients increases, data security in medical records remains a question mark.

11.1.3 Motivation and Significance

Fraudulent activities in the medical insurance field have witnessed a steady rise in recent times. Within the limits of the present existing centralized technology, medical transactions have always been subjected to many deceitful activities either for the benefit of insurance companies or for some other intermediates in between. This includes billing even for the undone treatments, performing expensive unnecessary treatments to claim higher insurance payments, delays, and denial of genuine claims, etc. A technical solution for this existing system leads us to think of building an immutable, transparent, and decentralized platform for handling medical transaction data. Blockchain is the best platform for systematic, efficient, and secure data storage where the data can neither be manipulated nor be stolen by a third party found to be the most appropriate one. The proposed system also offers an additional advantage of two-party verification. That is, the data are entered by the patients, which are then verified by the hospital before submitting for insurance claims. In this way, deceptive activity can be limited and the system can be made secure. The advantages provided by the proposed system are three-fold.

- First, the blockchain's property of decentralization allows a client to speak with another client without the involvement of an outsider.
- Second, since the protection guarantee information given by the patients is confirmed by the hospital administrator, they can handle the case without being cheated. From the patient's viewpoint, since the information is affirmed by the hospital, the insurance agency should authorize the case along these lines, making the cases certain.
- Third, extremely significant information is evident. Specifically, the majority of information is openly verifiable. Accordingly, record nodes of blockchain can assist clients with playing out the public checks. Thus, this fundamentally decreases clients' computational intricacy.

11.1.4 Aims and Objectives

Our research work is to provide a solution to the existing problems of medical data storage using blockchain technology. With this view, we create a blockchain-based platform for the efficient storage of medical insurance data, which is the transaction data. This results in the development of a secure transparent decentralized network, providing a platform for data storage. We try to employ cryptographic techniques to data so that they can be made immutable, thereby denying false claims and participation of third-party intermediaries.

11.1.5 Literature Review

A review of literature on the subject is undertaken to understand the better prevailing aspects in the field of blockchain technology and medical insurance systems through a search of available literature from books, international journals, reputed national/international conference papers, Internet data, etc., relevant to the study. The details of some of the reviews that have been made for the work are summarized here.

Nofer et al. [1] give a detailed description of the basics of blockchain technology with its main advantages. They describe every blockchain data as stored as a chain of blocks, with a block being the smallest unit. A block has the information which is cryptographically hashed, the timestamp, the data (transaction) of the block, and the cryptographic hash of the previous block. The primary block is referred to as the Genesis block. Any change to the block information will make the block hash totally different from the previous one. This chain of blocks is put away in an organization of personal computers (PCs) with every hub having a full duplicate of the whole blockchain, making no change of information possible.

Zheng et.al. [2] present about consensus and types of the blockchain network. Mining is the process of writing data to the blockchain and a node cannot simply write this, but all nodes have to reach a consensus. Consensus calculation is used to accomplish concession to solitary information esteem among disseminated cycles or frameworks. They must be fault tolerant and should be intended to accomplish dependability in an organization including different untrustworthy hubs. It also updates the blockchain using a consensus mechanism since it also acts as a protocol for a system that is highly dynamic. The paper also describes the three classifications of the network—public, private, and consortium—based on the degree of access to data on the network. In a public blockchain, a client can turn to an individual from the blockchain network. This implies that they can store, send, and get information in the wake of downloading the necessary programming on their machine and is hence totally decentralized. Whereas in a private blockchain, consent to compose, send, and get information is constrained by one organization. Private blockchains are normally utilized inside an organization with just a couple of explicit clients permitted to get to it and complete exchanges. In a consortium blockchain, rather than permitting any client to take an interest in the check of the exchange cycle or simply permitting one single organization to have full control, a couple of chosen parties are foreordained to take part in the consensus process.

In 2008, Satoshi Nakamoto [3], the pseudonymous individual credited with creating Bitcoin, released a white paper portraying the product convention. Bitcoin is critical because it gives a mechanism to get into the blockchain—however, it's not by any means the only application that can use the stage. Bitcoin is a cryptographic wallet, decentralized digital cash without a bank that can be sent from one person to other on the peer-to-peer Bitcoin blockchain network without the prerequisite for intermediaries. Bitcoin's conditional properties are that it is irreversible, pseudonymous, fast and worldwide, secure, and permissionless.

Harry Halpin and Marta Piekarska [4] write about the security aspects related to the blockchain concerning confidentiality, integrity, and authentication. They present the analysis of problems ranging from using novel cryptographic primitives on Bitcoin to allowing use-based methods like privacy-preserving file storage. The paper also describes the basic principle of cryptography which uses advanced mathematical principles to store and transfer data in a specific form so that only those who are intended can read and process it. Three types of cryptographic techniques are also explained in general which are symmetric-key cryptography, hash functions, and public key cryptography.

Vujicic et.al. [5] present a completely decentralized version of the electronic cash system that would help to transfer payments between two parties without the involvement of financial organizations. But one of the major challenges faced by the digital currency at the time of its arrival is double spending, which happens when a person with good computation knowledge can duplicate a digital coin and thus the same currency can be spent twice illegally. This paper proposes a solution to this problem by introducing blockchain technology for transactions. Proof of work in the blockchain is carried out by a group of miners who record all the past transactions, and if again the same digital token is used for another transaction, it will detect this and prevent the fraud attempt.

Dr. Gavin Wood [6] provided the foundation for the blockchain technology Ethereum. In this paper, he substantiates the possibility of building smart contracts, new protocols like currencies, decentralized applications which can be developed on top of the Ethereum blockchain. The three major concepts discussed in this paper are accounts, transactions, and messages. Accounts are essential for each user for handling transactions. Ethereum accounts have Ethereum addresses, and their corresponding private keys. The two types of accounts are externally owned accounts that are managed by private keys and contract accounts managed by contracts code. Four fields of an Ethereum account are nonce, balance, code hash, and storage root. For externally owned accounts, nonce counts the number of transactions done, whereas for the contract accounts, it corresponds to the number of contract creations made. Balance is the total Wei (smallest unit of ether) in the account. Code hash stores the hash of the Ethereum Virtual Machine (EVM) code. Storage root is a hash of the root node of a Merkle tree. A transaction is a signed instruction sent by an external account to another account on the blockchain. It contains the recipient, sender's signature, amount of Wei to transfer, gas price, and start gas representing maximum computations required. The message is similar to the transaction except it is sent by a contract, not by an external account.

Ekblaw et al. [7] present a novel framework called MedRec which gives patients a thorough, permanent log and simple admittance to their clinical data across suppliers and treatment destinations. It facilitates verification, privacy, interoperability, responsibility, and information sharing by utilizing blockchain features. Centrally stored information has regularly demonstrated disastrous results in our advanced time of digital assaults and information spills. This framework likewise incentivizes medical stakeholders like researchers and public health authorities to partake in the network as miners. This furnishes them with admittance to total, unknown information as mining rewards as a byproduct of supporting and making sustaining and securing the network through proof of work. MedRec hence empowers the development of information financial aspects, providing large information to engage specialists while drawing in patients and suppliers in the decision to deliver metadata. It makes an available bread piece trail for clinical history. Block content refers to information possession and viewership consents shared by individuals from a private, distributed organization. It gives a solitary perspective to check for any updates to clinical history. It serves as a model that is secured by public key cryptography and empowered with critical properties of provenance and information honesty. This blockchain catalog model backs the capacity to "develop and change significantly all through its lifetime, including new members and changing authoritative connections" through stateful updates to the smart contracts.

Xia et al. [8] propose a framework called MeDShare that tends to the issue of clinical information sharing among clinical huge information overseers in a trustless condition. The framework is blockchain-based and gives information provenance, reviewing, and control for shared clinical information in cloud repositories among Big Data entities. The model utilizes smart contracts and an access control mechanism to adequately follow the conduct of the information and renounce admittance to culpable elements on the discovery of infringement of consents on the information. By executing MeDShare, cloud service providers and other data guardians will have the option for accomplishing data provenance and examination, while at the same time offering clinical information to elements, like research and medical institutions with insignificant danger to information security. A block is comprised of a solitary solicitation which ranges from when it was made until the bundle is prepared for conveyance and processing. The consensus nodes are liable for the support of the blocks and blockchain network. While checking the blocks with sideblocks, nodes alert the system breaches to the use of data. For a requester who needs admittance to sets of records from an information proprietor, the requester creates a key pair (requester private and public keys), stores the private key, and offers the public key with the information proprietor or other information proprietor the requestor might get to information from later on. The requestor makes, sign utilizing the requestor's private key, and sends a solicitation to an information proprietor. On gathering, the information proprietor affirms the solicitation by confirming the signature with the requestor's public key. The primary target of MeDShare is to give information provenance, inspecting, and making sure about clinical data.

Zyskind and Nathan [10] discuss possible future extensions that can provide efficient solutions for trusted computing problems in society. Conoscenti et al. [11] explain the possibility of using blockchain along with the peer-to-peer storage networks for IoT solutions. Van Steen., and Tanenbaum [12] explain the structure of distributed systems. Wang et al. [13] suggest a framework that combines the decentralized storage system interplanetary file system, the Ethereum blockchain, and ABE technology.

Wang et al. [14] provides a systematic study on the cryptographic primitives in blockchains by comprehensive analysis on top 30 mainstream cryptocurrencies, in terms of the usages, functionalities, and evolutions of these primitives. Henry et al. [15] provide an overview of the challenges in blockchain access privacies. Aitzhan and Svetinovic [16] explain the transaction security and privacy in one of the domains of blockchain. Hussien et al [17] review developing blockchain technology in the healthcare domain emphasizing future research directions.

Fekih and Lahami [18] provide a comprehensive study about the usage of blockchain technology in healthcare systems. Khatoon [19] describes the smart contract system using blockchain for healthcare management. Kassab et al. [20] investigates the quality requirements for blockchain-based healthcare systems.

11.2 THEORETICAL BACKGROUND

11.2.1 Smart Contracts

The idea of smart contracts was initially presented in 1994 recommending to code agreements, bonds, and authoritative reports and run them in PCs for execution, for example, on a bank centralized computer.

Before diving into the requirement for keen agreements in our framework, let us envision how a patient's visit to a hospital will work out lately without blockchain execution.

Consider a patient with influenza-like symptoms visiting for a clinical examination. The office will register the patient's details and try to recover his nearby clinical history if accessible. After the assessment, the specialist confirms that the patient requires further tests and refers the patient to another hospital to go through the proposed tests. Thus, the patient visits the clinic, registers himself, and trusts that his papers will be processed and the proposed tests will be done. The specialist gets the test results and in like manner endorses the patient a few drugs from the neighborhood medical store. Appropriately, the patient will go to the drug store, show his prescription, and buy the medicines. In this situation, we intentionally disregarded the function of the insurance accomplice. Be that as it may, we can comprehend how including another layer may entangle the preparation, the approvals, and the measure of administrative work related to a patient visit. In actuality, this situation isn't that troublesome, yet it is, as we as a whole may have encountered, a bit stressful. What blockchain innovation guarantees us is to make trustless organizations run in decentralized, straightforward, secure, quick, and also high accessible ways. The smart contract makes its functionalities even more systematic. A smart contract is essentially an executable content that dwells on top of the blockchain that will be executed if it is at the point when certain conditions are being met or in an event where it has been triggered by an outside component. Henceforth, the smart contract itself has its address in the network. To execute the smart contracts by triggering, nodes in the network issue transactions routed to those agreements legitimately. The benefit of smart contracts is that they essentially permit us to compose any rationale in code while setting the conditions and anticipated results for that rationale.

Ethereum smart contracts are agreements that depend on various scripting languages which engineers use to program their functionalities. These agreements are elevated level programming deliberations that are ordered down to Ethereum Virtual Machine (EVM) byte code and sent to the Ethereum blockchain for execution. They can be written in Solidity (a language library similar to C and JavaScript), Serpent (like Python), LLL (a low-level like language), and Mutan (Go-based). There is additionally a language in progress called Vyper (a specifically Python-determined decidable language). Smart contracts can be public, which opens up the possibility to prove usefulness.

11.2.2 DApps

Decentralized applications (DApps) are computerized applications that exist and run on a blockchain or peer-to-peer network of PCs rather than a solitary PC, and are outside the domain and control of solitary power. They have existed since the approach of peer-to-peer networks. Decentralized applications do not need to run on the head of a blockchain network. Tor, BitTorrent, Popcorn Time, and Bit Message are models for decentralized applications that run on a peer-to-peer organization, yet not on a blockchain. Decentralized applications are a bit of software product that speaks with the blockchain, which deals with the condition of all network nodes. The interface of the decentralized applications doesn't appear to be any more unique than any website or mobile application. The smart contract is the logic behind the decentralized application. The smart contracts are the vital structure of blocks of blockchains that process data from outside sensors or events and help the blockchain deal with the state of all network nodes. The frontend of a decentralized application refers to what you see, and the backend refers to the whole business rationale. This business rationale is represented by one or several smart contracts interacting with the fundamental blockchain. The frontend, as well as documents like a photograph, a video, or sound, could be facilitated on decentralized storage networks like for example, Swarm or InterPlanetary File System (IPFS). Customary Web applications use HyperText Markup Language (HTML), Cascading Style Sheets (CSS), and JavaScript or the like to deliver a website page. This page interacts with a centralized database, where all the information is put away.

11.2.2.1 Frontend–API–Database

Decentralized applications are similar to traditional web applications. The frontend utilizes precisely the same technology to render the page. It contains a "wallet" that speaks with the blockchain. The wallet manages cryptographic keys and the blockchain address. Public key is utilized for client identification and authentication. Rather than an application programming interface (API) working with an information base, a wallet software triggers exercises of the smart contract which connects with the blockchain. Ethereum DApps applications are written in one of seven diverse Turing-complete languages. Developers utilize the language to make and distribute applications that they know will run inside Ethereum. Numerous use cases have been proposed for Ethereum, including ones that are unimaginable or unfeasible. Use case recommendations have included the finance sector, IoT power sourcing, pricing, etc.

Ethereum is (as of 2017) the main blockchain stage for beginning coin offering ventures, with over half the market share. In Ethereum, all smart contracts are stored publicly on every node of blockchain. Being a blockchain implies it is secure by design and is a case of a distributed computing with high Byzantine tolerance to internal failure. The drawback is that performance issues emerge in each node is ascertaining all the smart contracts continuously, coming in and hence results in lower speeds. As of January 2016, the Ethereum convention could measure around 25 transactions every second. Ethereum's blockchain utilizes Merkle trees, for security reasons, to improve versatility and to streamline transaction hashing. Ethereum has PoW as its consensus. So according to the described derivations, we have presumed that our project implementation is basically a DaApp/smart contract on Ethereum.

11.3 PROPOSED MODEL

11.3.1 Design Environment

In our project, we have used different platforms for the implementation of each stage in the system. They are summarized here in this section.

11.3.1.1 Solidity

Solidity is an object-oriented programming language for composing smart contracts. It is utilized for executing the smart contract on different blockchain stages, most eminently Ethereum. It was created by Christian Reitwiessner, Alex Beregszaszi, Yoichi Hirai, and a few previous Ethereum center supporters for composing smart contracts on blockchain platforms like Ethereum. Solidity was at first proposed in August 2014 by Gavin Wood. The language was subsequently evolved by the Ethereum undertaking and Solidity group, driven by Christian Reitwiessner. Solidity is a statically-composed programming language intended for creating smart contracts that sudden spike in demand for the EVM Solidity is arranged to bytecode that is executable on the EVM. With Solidity, developers can compose applications that carry out self-authorizing business rationale exemplified in smart contracts, leaving a non-repudiable and definitive record of the transaction. Composing smart contracts in smart contract explicit dialects— for example, Solidity—is claimed to be simple (apparently for the individuals who have programming abilities).

11.3.1.2 Linux

Linux is a family of open source Unix-like operating systems based on the Linux kernel, an operating system kernel first released on September 17, 1991, by Linus Torvalds. Linux is typically packaged in a Linux distribution. Linux was originally developed for personal computers based on the Intel x86 architecture, but has since been ported to more platforms than any other operating system. The primary difference between Linux and many other popular contemporary operating systems is that the Linux kernel and other components are free and open source software. Linux is not the only such operating system, although it is by far the most widely used. Linux-based distributions are intended by developers for interoperability with other operating systems and established computing standards. For the project, we preferred Linux, as it is more developer-friendly with all tools needed mostly available with better handling capability than other operating systems.

11.3.1.3 Sublime Text Editor

Sublime Text is a shareware cross-platform source code editor with a Python API. It natively supports many programming languages and markup languages. The functions can be added by users with plugins, typically community-built and maintained under free software licenses. The features include quick navigation to files, symbols, or lines. A "command palette" in this editor makes use of adaptive matching for quick keyboard invocation of arbitrary commands, as well as simultaneous editing. It simultaneously makes the same interactive changes to multiple selected areas, python-based plugin API, project-specific preferences, extensive customizability via JSON settings files, including project-specific and platform-specific settings, cross-platform (Windows, macOS, and Linux) and supportive plugins for cross-platform, and also is compatible with many language grammars from TextMate.

11.3.1.4 Truffle

Truffle is a developer environment, testing system, and resource pipeline for blockchains. It permits designers to turn up a smart contract project at the snap of a catch and gives you a task structure, records, and registries that make arrangement and testing a lot simpler. To turn up a Truffle project that spreads out the design of the undertaking: *Truffle init* is used. Once coding is begun and to test the code, we need a blockchain. Presently, we can run Ganache to be this blockchain. In the deployment file (a document that Truffle gives when one makes a project), either Ganache or the main network can be used. Then to deploy the contracts with the data provided in the migration files, we use: *Truffle compile, Truffle migrate*.

11.3.1.5 Ganache

Ganache permits the formation of a private Ethereum blockchain to run tests, execute the orders, and examine the states while controlling how the chain works. It enables you to play out all activities you would on the fundamental chain without the expense. Numerous engineers utilize this to test their smart contracts during advancement. It gives advantageous instruments, for example, progressed mining controls and an inbuilt block explorer. Ganache mimics the main network and also a part of the Truffle ecosystem. Ganache can be used for the development of Ethereum. It very well may be utilized for improvement of DApp, and whenever it is created and tried on the ganache, DApp can be sent on Ethereum client like parity or geth.

11.3.1.6 MetaMask

Metamask is an Ethereum wallet in browsers and is an extension for getting to Ethereum-empowered distributed applications or DApps. The extension infuses the Ethereum web3 API into each site's JavaScript so that DApps can peruse from the blockchain. MetaMask likewise allows the client to make and deal with their own identities, so when a DApp needs to play out an exchange and keep in touch with the blockchain, the client gets a safe interface to survey the exchange, prior to endorsing or dismissing it. Since it adds usefulness to the ordinary program setting, MetaMask expects consent to peruse and keep in touch with any page.

11.3.1.7 JavaScript

JavaScript, or JS, is a programming language that adheres to the ECMA script specification. JavaScript is a high-level, multiparadigm, and is often just in-time-compiled. Along with HTML and CSS, JavaScript is one of the center advances of the World Wide Web. JavaScript empowers intelligent website pages and is a fundamental piece of web applications. By far, most sites use it for client-side page conduct, and all significant Internet browsers have a committed JavaScript engine to execute it. As a multiparadigm language, JavaScript upholds occasion-driven, useful, and basic programming styles. It has APIs for working with text, dates, standard information structures, and the Document Object Model (DOM). JavaScript engines were initially utilized uniquely in Internet browsers; however, they are currently used in servers, for the most part through Node.js. Although there are similarities between JavaScript and Java, including language name, sentence structure, and standard libraries, both are unmistakable and vary in design.

11.3.1.8 React.js

React.js is the most famous frontend framework for Web applications. It is an open source JavaScript library that is utilized for building user interfaces explicitly for single-page applications. It is utilized for taking care of the view layer for web and mobile applications. React likewise permits us to make reusable UI parts. React was first made by Jordan Walke, a programmer working for Facebook. Using React, programmers can make large web applications that can change information without reloading the page. React is widely used, as it is fast, scalable, and simple. It works just on UIs in the application. It is used alongside other JavaScript libraries or frameworks, like Angular JS in MVC.

11.3.2 System Description

As a solution to the underlying problems in the medical insurance field, we propose our solution: a blockchain-based medical insurance storage system. The system helps an insurance company to obtain the sum of patients' medical spending records. In this system, there are three parties:

1. Patient: Enters the critical medical transaction data and submits for insurance.
2. Hospital: Verifies and approves the bill.
3. Medical insurance: After getting the hospital-approved data, it can proceed to process the claim.

The working process can be explained by the following steps as shown in Figure 11.1.

- Patient logs in, uploads medical/lab test bill data creating what we call a "record" and submits it for insurance.
- The hospital admin logs in verification, and approves the records. This approval is also stored on the blockchain.
- The insurance admin can proceed to sanction the claim of the approved patients, since the admin user interface displays only the approved data.

The major outcomes/features are:

- Decentralization: No third-party involvement.
- Secure data storage: Each transaction's publicly verifiable information must be confirmed by all record nodes of the blockchain network before the transaction is recorded in the blockchain, and all related information is stored at the blockchain. Because of blockchain's property of altering resistance, information that has been incorporated by record nodes in the blockchain

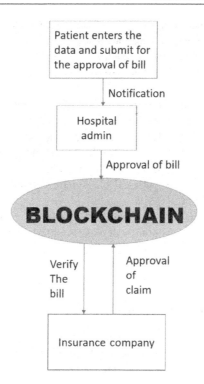

FIGURE 11.1 Working process.

can't be changed or erased by anybody. These two reasons give high validity to all clients. Therefore, when a transaction is initiated in the blockchain, all of its publicly verifiable information is solid.

• Verifiable: Key information stored at the blockchain is undeniable. In particular, anybody can check whether the verification key is legitimate. The information is recorded in the transaction's payload, and the majority of the key data is publicly verifiable. Hence, record nodes can assist different nodes with checking payloads information before the transactions are recorded in the blockchain. Thus, when a transaction has been recorded in the blockchain, the transaction's openly verifiable information is credible. Therefore, the transaction's recipient needs not to conduct the verifications performed by the record nodes. Besides, the beneficiary simply needs to perform a few verifications that can be performed only by them. Henceforth, it fundamentally decreases clients confirming computations, and users simply perform some few basic calculations instead of massive and complex ones.

11.3.3 System Implementation

11.3.3.1 Blockchain Backend

The smart contract is the backbone of our blockchain and the logic is presented in what follows.

• Create a function in the smart contract. When called in, the frontend helps to create a "record" with the function's input data.
• Create another function. When called in the frontend, JavaScript helps to sign a "record" using its ID.

- Create a migrations file to help migrate the code so that to deploy the smart contract to the personal blockchain network, any time we create a new smart contract, we are updating the state of the blockchain. Hence, whenever we permanently change it, we must migrate it from one state to another. This is very similar to a database migration in other web application development frameworks.
- Generate a new file when compiling the smart contract. This file is the smart contract ABI (abstract binary interface) file which has many responsibilities. It mainly contains the compiled bytecode version of the Solidity smart contract code that can be run on an EVM, i.e., an Ethereum node, and a JSON representation of the smart contract functions that can be exposed to external clients, like client-side JavaScript applications.
- Talk to the smart contract on the personal blockchain network inside the Truffle console by updating the project's configuration file.
- Specify the personal blockchain network by connecting to Ganache and running the newly created migration script. This will eventually deploy the smart contract to the personal blockchain network.

11.3.3.2 Frontend Web Applications

Web3.js is the main JavaScript library for interacting with the Ethereum blockchain. It is a collection of libraries that allow us to perform actions like sending Ether from one account to another, read and write data from smart contracts, create smart contracts, etc.

There should be four basic files:

- An index file: This deals with rendering the main page and linking the other three pages, i.e. patient, hospital admin, and insurance interfaces.
- A patient file: This facilitates data entry and submission by the patient.
- An admin file: This facilitates displaying of "records" created by patients and data approval by hospital admin.
- An insurance file: This facilitates viewing of hospital-approved "records."

11.4 RESULTS AND ANALYSIS

As discussed in previous sections, the project consists of two parts:

1. Blockchain part for storing the data
2. User interface (which is a web application) through which the involved parties can interact with the blockchain for entering and retrieve the data.

11.4.1 Blockchain

Ganache software is used for mimicking the behavior of the Ethereum blockchain network for securing the medical data. It provides ten free accounts, with each account having 100 ether tokens. We used the first account for deploying the smart contract into the blockchain to another address. The data entered through the web app is stored as blocks as in Figure 11.2 and Figure 11.3.

FIGURE 11.2   Blocklist.

FIGURE 11.3   Transactions list.

11.4.2 Web Applications

As discussed, the project aimed to demonstrate proof of concept through the prototype web app creation and blockchain backend. The main page created for the web app is shown in Figure 11.4. From the main web page, by clicking on the select mode dropdown menu, we can select the particular mode—parties involved—and enter the password, then click on the submit button so that it will be redirected to their respective interfaces.

11.4.3 Interface Section

We have created three prototype interfaces for the hospital, patient, and insurance company to demonstrate how data storage and retrieval through the blockchain of the network can be done through the user interface. In our case, it is a web app-making the project a DApp decentralized application. The browser, through the MetaMask extension, accesses the smart contract deployed on the Ganache.

11.4.3.1 Patient Interface

Through this interface, a patient is given provision to enter their data. Figure 11.5 indicates the interface. The patients can enter the data as per the bill issued to them by the hospital as a new record and the details include the following:

1. Patient ID, which is necessarily the bill number.
2. Name.
3. Date issued.
4. Hospital name.
5. Insurance amount.
6. Price is the amount spent by the patient.

FIGURE 11.4   Main page.

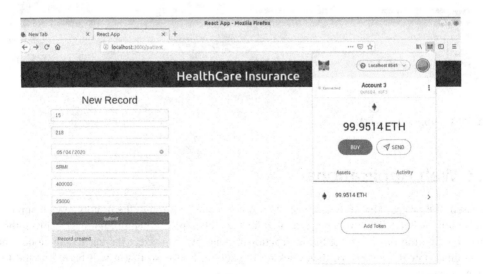

FIGURE 11.5   Patient interface.

On clicking submit, the patient gets a notification that the record is created and some ether is reduced from their MetaMask account as a transaction fee.

11.4.3.2 Hospital Admin Interface

This interface has two functionalities:

1. The medical records that are created are displayed as a table in the hospital admin interface.
2. The hospital can verify the records by cross-checking the bills they issued and can approve each with their ID, as in Figure 11.6. The approval is also stored in the blockchain as blocks.

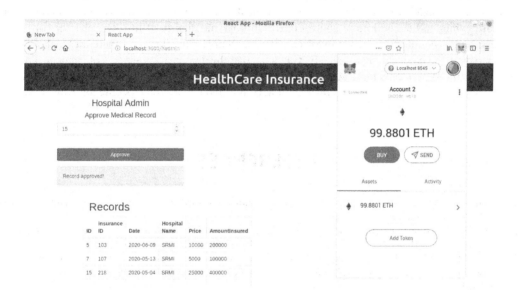

FIGURE 11.6   Hospital admin interface.

11.4.3.3 Insurance Interface

The functionality of this interface is to display the approved medical records that are approved by the hospital admin (Figure 11.7).

ID	Insurance ID	Date	Hospital Name	Price	Amountinsured
5	103	2020-06-09	SRMI	10000	200000
7	107	2020-05-13	SRMI	5000	100000
15	218	2020-05-04	SRMI	25000	400000

FIGURE 11.7   Insurance interface.

11.5 CONCLUSIONS

In this chapter, a blockchain-based medical insurance storage system is proposed. Since blockchain is used, the system obtains some special advantages like decentralization, tamper resistance, and verification of publicly verifiable data. The blockchain's property of tamper resistance gives users high credibility. Due to decentralization, users can communicate with each other without any centralized authority. The decentralized and transparent nature of blockchain is sure to prevent data from being altered or stolen, but many of the common concerns about massive data consumption still apply. This sensitive data may be sold to third parties for questionable marketing purposes and the user can still be identified indirectly through an alias or data model. But this blockchain-based health framework will involve more people in their healthcare, which in turn will more appropriately improve the quality of life. The chapter concludes by creating a prototype interface for the involved parties and deploying it on an Ethereum blockchain mimicking personalized blockchain provided by Ganache, thereby demonstrating proof of concept. The implementation of the system on a large scale will be to create a web application where any number of parties (hospital, patient, and insurance) can create their accounts and get account-specific input and output data.

REFERENCES

[1] Zhou, L., L. Wang, and Y. Sun. "Mistore: A blockchain-based medical insurance storage system." *Journal of medical systems* 42, no. 8 (2018): 149.

[2] Nofer, M., P. Gomber, O. Hinz, and D. Schiereck. "Blockchain." *Business & Information Systems Engineering* 59, no. 3 (2017): 183–187.

[3] Zheng, Z., S. Xie, H. Dai, X. Chen, and H. Wang. "An overview of blockchain technology: Architecture, consensus, and future trends." In 2017 *IEEE International Congress on Big Data (Big Data Congress)*, pp. 557–564. IEEE, June 2017.

[4] Nakamoto, S., and A. Bitcoin. *A Peer-to-Peer Electronic Cash System.* Bitcoin, 2008. https://bitcoin. org/bitcoin. pdf.

[5] Halpin, H., and M. Piekarska. "Introduction to security and privacy on the blockchain." In 2017 *IEEE European Symposium on Security and Privacy Workshops (Eu- roS&PW)*, pp. 1–3. IEEE, April 2017.

[6] Vujicic, D., D. Jagodic, and S. Ranic. "Blockchain technology, bitcoin, and Ethereum: A brief overview." In *2018 17th International Symposium Infoteh-Jahorina (Infoteh)*, pp. 1–6. IEEE, March 2018.

[7] Wood, G. "Ethereum: A secure decentralised generalised transaction ledger." *Ethereum Project Yellow Paper* 151, no. 2014 (2014): 1–32.

[8] Xia, Q. I., E. B. Sifah, K. O. Asamoah, J. Gao, X. Du, and M. Guizani. "MeDShare: Trustless medical data sharing among cloud service providers via blockchain." *IEEE Access* 5 (2017): 14757–14767.

[9] Ekblaw, A., A. Azaria, J. D. Halamka, and A. Lippman. "A case study for blockchain in healthcare: 'MedRec' prototype for electronic health records and medical research data." *Proceedings of IEEE Open & Big Data Conference.* Vol. 13, p. 13, August 2016.

[10] Zyskind, G., and O. Nathan. "Decentralizing privacy: Using blockchain to protect personal data." In *2015 IEEE Security and Privacy Workshops*, pp. 180–184. IEEE, May 2015.

[11] Conoscenti, M., A. Vetro, and J. C. De Martin. "Peer to peer for privacy and decentralization in the internet of things." In 2017 *IEEE/ACM 39th International Conference on Software Engineering Companion (ICSE-C)*, pp. 288–290. IEEE, May 2017.

[12] van Steen, M., and A. S. Tanenbaum. "A brief introduction to distributed systems." *Computing* 98, no. 10 (2016): 967–1009.

[13] Wang, S., Y. Zhang, and Y. Zhang. "A blockchain-based framework for data sharing with fine-grained access control in decentralized storage systems." *IEEE Access* 6 (2018): 38437–38450.

[14] Wang, L., X. Shen, J. Li, J. Shao, and Y. Yang. "Cryptographic primitives in blockchains." *Journal of Network and Computer Applications* 127 (2019): 43–58.

[15] Henry, R., A. Herzberg, and A. Kate. "Blockchain access privacy: Challenges and directions." *IEEE Security & Privacy* 16, no. 4 (2018): 38–45.

[16] Aitzhan, N. Z., and D. Svetinovic. "Security and privacy in decentralized energy trading through multi-signatures, blockchain and anonymous messaging streams." *IEEE Transactions on Dependable and Secure Computing* 15, no. 5 (2016): 840–852.

[17] Hussien, H. M., S. M. Yasin, S. N. I. Udzir, A. A. Zaidan, and B. B. Zaidan. "A systematic review for enabling of develop a blockchain technology in healthcare application: Taxonomy, substantially analysis, motivations, challenges, recommendations and future direction." *Journal of Medical Systems* 43, no. 10 (2019): 1–35.

[18] Fekih, R. B., and M. Lahami. "Application of blockchain technology in healthcare: A comprehensive study." In *International Conference on Smart Homes and Health Telematics*, pp. 268–276. Springer, June 2020.

[19] Khatoon, A. "A blockchain-based smart contract system for healthcare management." *Electronics* 9, no. 1 (2020): 94.

[20] Kassab, M., J. DeFranco, T. Malas, G. Destefanis, and V. V. G. Neto. "Investigating quality requirements for blockchain-based healthcare systems." In *2019 IEEE/ACM 2nd International Workshop on Emerging Trends in Software Engineering for Blockchain (WETSEB)*, pp. 52–55. IEEE, May 2019.

Hybrid Multilevel Fusion

12

Integrating Score and Decision Levels of Fusion for Multimodal Biometric Systems

Aarohi Vora, Chirag Paunwala, and Mita Paunwala

Contents

12.1 INTRODUCTION

The rising era of evolution in technologies poses high security threats to the privacy of individuals. The amount of threat posed to the access of unauthorized data is a major concern while designing any security system. Biometric systems so far have proved reliable in maintaining security and integrating privacy of the individual [1]. Despite the benefits of biometric systems, certain major issues arises due to sensitivity of biometric data to outliers and privacy invasion caused by information leakage [2]. Multibiometric system refers to integrating data from multiple biometric sources, hence enhancing system accuracy, performance, proficiency, and robustness [2][3]. The major concern in the designing of a multimodal system is choosing the level of fusion for different modalities. Besides this, the performance evaluation of biometric frameworks is fundamental in high security applications [2][3]. Integration of multibiometric data is basically achieved at primarily three different levels: feature level, score level and decision level [2][3]. Feature-level fusion integrates templates from different modalities using concatenation. However, feature vectors from different modalities are not always compatible with each other. Hence, direct augmentation of feature sets degrades the performance of fused system [2][3]. Matching scores are generated in a biometric system by comparing the user template with all templates within the database. These scores are the representation of genuineness of the users [2][3]. Thus, score-level fusion consolidates the scores from different modalities using state of art algorithms such as linear weighted sum rule (LWSR), min rule, T-norms, support vector machines, etc., which are then used to identify the authenticity of users. The scores contain abundant amounts of discriminative information about the users. In decision-level fusion, decisions of individual modalities are fused using AND rule, OR rule, etc. Among all these levels, score-level fusion has widely been accepted because of its affluence to fusion and sovereignty to choose any feature extraction and matching algorithms [2][3]. Score fusion is the most widely researched and adapted method for integration which offers the optimal tradeoff between information content and integration intricacy.

Decision fusion is less contemplated on the basis that decisions have less information content than the matching scores [2][3]. However, commercial firms provide access to the system directly on the basis of recognition output [2][3]. As a quantitative proximity measure, scores are comprised of the richest yet simplest representation of the genuineness of the user [4][5]. The major merit of score fusion is that it can easily be computed and compared, even though the features of different modalities are not compatible with each other [6–8]. As a rule, score fusion accomplishes optimal execution. A demerit of score fusion is that it is liable to substantial flexibilities [6–8]. This results into different decision boundaries by different normalization techniques, as well as over fitting of data in case of too small score sets. The decision-level fusion comprises of vague and rigid form of information yet it is the most common form of data obtained in real-time commercial applications [6–8]. As decision-level fusion is performed on Receiver Operating Characteristics (ROC) of individual modalities, it aids in optimizing false acceptance rate (FAR) in presence of outliers. A major drawback of decision fusion is the constrained probability of decision limits restricted due to the thresholding operation [6–8].

Hence, the proposed multilevel framework is designed whereby the limitations of score, as well as decision fusion, will be eliminated if a blend of both fusion mechanisms is employed. As the proposed fusion framework is oriented on performance errors minimization it helps in achieving an even more reliable and robust multibiometric system. The proposed hybrid multilevel multimodal scheme incorporates the similarity scores from different matchers corresponding to each protected modality. The individual scores obtained from different matchers for each modality are combined using the T-norm score fusion method. Further, decision-level fusion techniques AND rule and OR rule are applied to the induced scores to output the final decision. The proposed system develops an algorithm which assigns certain probabilities to the fused scores of each modality based upon the error rates GAR and EER of individual score fused modalities. Also, the proposed method is robust enough to the variability of scores and outliers satisfying the requirement of secure authentication.

12.2 LITERATURE REVIEW

The research on multimodal systems boosted up in the late 1990s. The authors in [3] combined face, fingerprint, and hand geometry at feature, score and decision level of fusion. They used sum rule, decision tree and linear discriminant classifiers for combining the scores of face, fingerprint, and hand geometry modalities. They showed that score-level fusion using sum rule gives a better recognition performance as compared to other levels. A theoretical framework for fusing scores using techniques like sum rule, product rule, max rule, min rule, median rule, and majority voting was proposed by the authors in [9]. The scores of different modalities are fused by using user specific weights by the authors in [10]. The scores of iris and fingerprint modalities are fused via SVM by authors in [11]. They also proved that normalization of scores plays a very effective role on recognition performance of the system. The author in [12] utilized techniques such as sum rule, product, exponential sum, tan-hyperbolic sum using particle swarm optimization in order to develop an adaptive score-level fusion model. The score-level fusion is implemented using T-norms by the authors in [13] and the fusion is compared with all approaches of score-level fusion in the literature and it is shown that the T-norms outperform all these approaches. In decision-level fusion literature, AND or OR decision rules are widely accepted techniques of fusion. It is proved by the authors in [6] that when decisions of individual modalities are fused using AND or OR rules, there is a risk of degradation of overall performance when the performance of individual modalities are distinct in nature. Hence, they devised another approach for the decision-level fusion using majority voting rule whereby the decision output which is in majority from different modalities is considered as the final decision. Another variant of majority voting was developed by the authors in [14] known as weighted majority voting. In this technique, weights are assigned to all modalities on the basis of their recognition performance. The weighted majority voting approach aids in improving performance of the multibiometric system at decision level. The authors in [15] and [16] devised their multibiometric systems using the Bayesian approach and Dempster–Shafer (DS) Theory, respectively. The authors in [17] optimized the match score thresholds and performed fusion using "and" or "or" rule. This technique improved the performance of fused system over the component modalities in the Neyman–Pearson sense. It also proved that the OR rule fusion does not deteriorate the recognition performance, even in the presence of outliers. A hybrid multilevel system fusing palm prints and hand dorsal veins at feature and score levels is developed by the authors in [4]. A hybrid fusion using feature-level and score-level fusion for finger veins and finger knuckle biometrics is discussed by the authors in [5]. This paper had the complexity of using nearest-neighborhood ratio method and weighted sum rule for fused matching score. The authors in [8] developed a multilevel score and feature fusion of face and finger veins. The hybrid framework involving score and decision level was developed by authors in [6] and [7]. In this paper, the ambiguity associated with the local biometric decisions are modeled by fuzzifying (the process of converting a crisp input value to a fuzzy value that is performed by the use of the information in the knowledge base) the error rates. The multimodal dataset used for the experimentation is NIST BSSR-1 which comprises scores of fingerprint and face modalities of 517 individuals [18]. The scores for face modality are obtained from two different matchers, C and G. The fingerprint scores are obtained from left index and right index fingers of an individual [18].

12.3 PROPOSED HYBRID MULTILEVEL MULTIBIOMETRIC SYSTEM

The proposed system is designed by integrating score-level and decision-level fusion in order to increase performance of the system, as well as minimize the FAR of the system. So before discussing the hybrid multilevel system, first discussion is carried about score-level and decision-level fusion individually. In this chapter, two modalities—face and fingerprint—are being fused. Face scores obtained from two different matching algorithms, and right index and left index of fingerprints are used for fusion. Hence, the proposed system is in fact a multialgorithmic and multi-instance multilevel multibiometric system. The block diagram of a multibiometric system developed by integrating the scores of individual modalities is shown in Figure 12.1.

As shown in Figure 12.1, scores from four different modalities are fused at score level using rule-based fusion technique. There are several state-of-the-art algorithms through which scores can be fused: namely, sum rule, LWSR, product rule, min rule, max rule and T-norm. It has been proven in various literatures that for modalities with statistically independent data fused using LWSR outperforms the performance of all other methods. But it is not always the case to have independent modalities, and hence, it is required to use T-norm fusion [13]. T-norms deal with the real challenge of uncertainty and imperfection encompassing the different scores from different modalities [13]. T-norms do not require the assumption

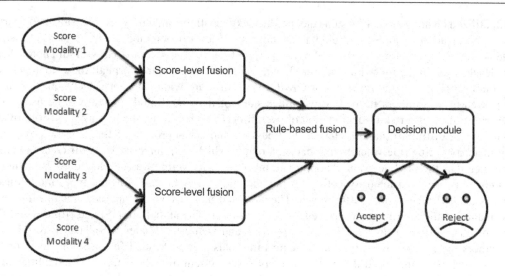

FIGURE 12.1   Score level multibiometric system.

of evidential independence of the modalities to be fused [13]. As T-norms are associative, fusion of N number of modalities can be done regardless of the order [13]. The raw scores that are obtained from the matchers are normalized into a common domain using min/max normalization technique. Thereafter, the normalized scores are fused using T-norm. Modality 1 consists of the score of face from G matcher, Modality 2 consists of the score of face from C matcher, Modality 3 consists score of right index finger, and Modality 4 consists score of left index finger. Scores normalized from M1 and M2 of face are integrated using T-norm using Equation (12.1).

$$S' = T(S_1, S_2) = \log_p(1 + ((p^{S_1} - 1)(P^{S_2} - 1))/(p-1)) \tag{12.1}$$

Where S' = fused score of face modality = multi-algorithmic fused face score
S1 = normalized score of face from G matcher
S2 = normalized score of face from C matcher
    Similarly, scores from modalities M3 and M4 of fingerprint are integrated using Equation (12.2).

$$S'' = T(S_3, S_4) = \log_p(1 + ((p^{S_3} - 1)(P^{S_4} - 1))/(p-1)) \tag{12.2}$$

Where S'' = fused score of fingerprint modality = multi-instance fused fingerprint score
S3 = normalized score of right index fingerprint
S4 = normalized score of left index fingerprint

    Thereafter, the T-norm fused scores of face and fingerprint are fused using T-norm again to get the final fused score of the system using Equation (12.3). Once the fused score is obtained, the decision module operates on these scores by varying the threshold points and hence finding out the performance metrics viz. FAR, FRR, EER and GAR of the system.

$$S = T(S', S'') = \log_p(1 + ((p^{S'} - 1)(P^{S''} - 1))/(p-1)) \tag{12.3}$$

Where S = final fused score of face and fingerprint

The block diagram of decision-level framework is shown in Figure 12.2. At this level of fusion, the decisions of individual modalities are obtained initially. After that, the modalities are used either AND rule or OR rule. Finally, the performance parameters are computed in order to find out the recognition performance of the system.

The proposed system consists of the multilevel multibiometric framework consisting of score-level and decision-level fusions of face and fingerprint scores. The block diagram of proposed hybrid system is as shown in Figure 12.3. As shown in Figure 12.3, scores from Modality 1 and 2 are first fused at score level using T-norm. Similarly scores from Modality 3 and 4 are fused using T-norm. Both the score level fused scores are used to compute the ROC of both score level fused systems. After computing the EER and GAR of both score fused modalities, the weights are computed on the basis of the error rates of the

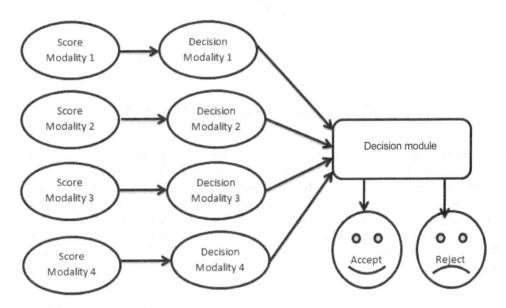

FIGURE 12.2   Decision-level multibiometric framework.

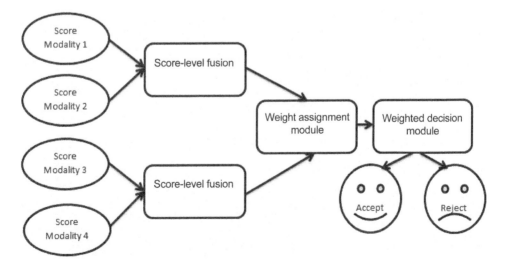

FIGURE 12.3   Proposed hybrid multilevel multibiometric framework.

individual fused system. The biometric fused modality with smaller error rate will be assigned higher weight in order to have high influence on the outcome of the final fused system.

In order to compute weights to be assigned to these modalities, find out the equal error rate (EER) of each face and fingerprint T-norm fused system. Thus, an optimum threshold point is obtained for individual T-norm fused systems. Thereafter, calculate the value of GAR and FAR of both the systems at their individual threshold points. The system which has higher EER value will be a weaker system as compared to other system. Thus, compute the weight for weaker system using Equation (12.4). Then the weight of the stronger system is given as Equation (12.5). Thereafter, these weighted scores are fused in a decision fusion module using AND rule and OR rule, as well as weighted majority voting rule.

$$w_w = \frac{(FAR_w + GAR_w)}{FAR_w * GAR_w} \tag{12.4}$$

$$w_s = 1 - w_w \tag{12.5}$$

12.4 EXPERIMENT RESULTS

The multimodal database BSSR1 used for the fusion of fingerprint and face is obtained from NIST. This dataset consist of 517 individuals' scores of face from matcher C, face from matcher G, left index fingerprint, and right index fingerprint. In this chapter, experiment is carried out on 102 user datasets from 517 individuals. The experimentation is carried out in three major phases: (i) fusion of scores at score level using T-norm, (ii) fusion of scores at decision level using AND rule and OR rule, and (iii) proposed fusion of scores at score-level fusion first and then at decision level using AND rule, OR rule, and weighted majority voting rule. The recognition performance curve of all the experiments are as shown in Figure 12.4.

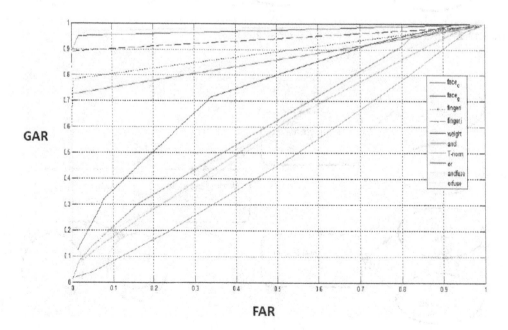

FIGURE 12.4 Performance recognition curves.

The recognition performance curve is the curve of FAR vs. GAR of face scores from C and G matches, right index finger and left index finger scores, T-norm score-level fusion, AND decision fusion, OR decision fusion, multilevel fusion using T-norm and AND, multilevel fusion using T-norm and OR, and multilevel fusion using T-norm and weighted majority voting rule. The weights obtained using (4) and (5) results in weight for face fused T-norm as 0.04, while the weight for fingerprint fused T-norm comes out to be 0.96. The performance comparison of all these systems is shown in Table 12.1.

Unimodal systems of face from C matcher achieves GAR of 1.96% at FAR of 0.04, face from G matcher achieves GAR of 7.84% at FAR of 0.004, left index finger achieves GAR of 78.43% at FAR of 0.003 and right index finger achieves GAR of 89.22% at FAR of 0.001. The score level fused system using T-norms achieves GAR of 12.75% at FAR of 0.01, whereas decision-level fusion using AND rule achieves GAR of 6.8% at FAR of 0.012, and using OR rule achieves GAR of 72.55% at FAR of 0.01. The multilevel multibiometric framework incorporating score fusion using T-norm and decision fusion using AND rule achieves GAR of 6.83% at FAR of 0.013, while score fusion blended with decision fusion using OR rule achieves GAR of 91.02% at FAR of 0.01. The proposed multimodal multilevel framework developed using T-norm at score level and weighted majority voting rule at decision-level fusion achieves a GAR of 92.16% at FAR of 0.0001. Thus, the proposed system not only increases the GAR of the system as compared to other deployments of the systems in [4–8], but also it tends to minimize the FAR of the system. Thus, the false acceptance of the system decreases, and hence, the security of the proposed system is higher as compared to other systems.

TABLE 12.1   Performance Comparison of All Systems

SR. NO.	METHOD	SYSTEM	FAR	GAR
1	Face G	Unimodal system	0.015	7.84%
2	Face C	Unimodal system	0.0047	1.96%
3	Left index finger	Unimodal system	0.0035	78.43%
4	Right index finger	Unimodal system	0.001	89.22%
5	T-norm fusion	Score level multibiometric system	0.013	12.75%
6	AND fusion	Decision-level multibiometric system	0.012	6.8%
7	OR fusion	Decision-level multibiometric system	0.01	72.55%
8	T-norm + AND	Multilevel multibiometric system (score + decision)	0.01388	6.83%
9	T-norm + OR	Multilevel multibiometric system (score + decision)	0.01	91.02%
10	T-norm + weighted majority (proposed)	Multilevel multibiometric system (score + decision)	0.0001	92.16%
11	FFV + sum rule [4]	Multilevel multibiometric system (feature + score)	0.1	86.27%
12	FFV + frank T-norm [4]	Multilevel multibiometric system (feature + score)	0.1	91.76%
13	fractional firefly (FFF) optimization + SVM [5]	Multilevel multibiometric system (feature + score)	0.05	95%
14	Sum + OR [7]	Multilevel multibiometric system (score + decision)	0.01	90%
15	LDA + LWSR [8]	Multilevel multibiometric system (score + score)	0.05	91%

12.5 CONCLUSION

This chapter presents a multibiometric multilevel framework which integrates complementary information from four score modalities of face and fingerprints. The proposed framework is developed using T-norm score-level fusion and weighted majority voting scheme. The weight assignment strategy depends on the performance metrics of the score fused systems. The multibiometric system proposed proves that the performance is significantly improved as compared to the unimodal biometric systems as well as single-level fusion systems. The performance of the proposed system improves as it takes the advantages of both score and decision-level fusion techniques. The proposed system achieves GAR of 92.16% at FAR of 0.0001. In future, the proposed method can be extended to develop the different objective functions to find the optimal weight score.

12.6 ACKNOWLEDGMENT

This chapter is being published under the minor research project titled "New Era of Securing Manifold Biometrics: Research on Forensic and Cyber Security Augmentation," supported by the grant from GUJCOST, Government of India. (Grant No. GUJCOST/MRP/2015–16/2640).

REFERENCES

[1] Jain, A., A. Ross, and K. Nandakumar. *Introduction to Biometrics*. 1st Edition. Springer Science and Business Media, LLC, 2011.

[2] Ross, A., K. Nandakumar, and A. K. Jain. *Handbook of Multibiometrics*. Springer, 2006.

[3] Ross, Arun, and Anil Jain. "Information fusion in biometrics." *Pattern Recognition Letters, Elsevier* 24, no. 13 (September 2003): 2115–2125.

[4] Chaudhary, G., S. Srivastava, and S. Bhardwaj. "Multi-level fusion of palmprint and dorsal hand vein." Book chapter In Satapathy, S., Mandal, J., Udgata, S., and Bhateja, V. (eds.). *Information Systems Design and Intelligent Applications, Advances in Intelligent Systems and Computing*. Vol. 433, pp. 321–330. Springer, 2016.

[5] Veluchamy, S., and L. R. Karlmarx. "System for multimodal biometric recognition based on finger knuckle and finger vein using feature-level fusion and k-support vector machine classifier." *IET Journals* 6, no. 3 (2017): 232–242, IET Biometrics.

[6] Grover, Jyotsana, and Madasu Hanmandlu. "Hybrid fusion of score level and adaptive fuzzy decision level fusions for the finger-knuckle-print based authentication." In *Applied Soft Computing*. Vol. 31, pp. 1–13. Elsevier, 2015.

[7] Tao, Q., and R. Veldhuis. "Hybrid fusion for biometrics: Combining score-level and decision-level fusion." In *IEEE Computer Society Conference on Computer Vision and Pattern Recognition*, pp. 1–6. IEEE, 2008.

[8] Razzak, Muhammad Imran, Rubiyah Yusof, and Marzuki Khalid. "Multimodal face and finger veins biometric authentication." *Scientific Research and Essays* 5, no. 17 (2010): 2529–2534. Academic Journals.

[9] Kittler, J. "On Combining Classifiers." *IEEE Transactions on Pattern Analysis and Machine Intelligence, (TPAMI)* 20, no. 3 (March 1998): 226–239.

[10] Jain, A. K., and A. Ross. "Multi biometric systems." *Communication of the ACM* 47, no. 1 (2004): 34–40, ACM Journals.

[11] Fahmy, M. S., A. F. Atyia, and R. S. Elfouly. "Biometric fusion using enhanced SVM classification." In *Fourth International Conference on Intelligent Information Hiding and Multimedia Signal Processing*, pp. 1043–1048. IEEE, 2008.

[12] Kumar, A., V. Kanhangad, and D. Zhang. "A new framework for adaptive multimodal biometrics management." *IEEE Transaction on Information Forensics Security* 5, no. 1 (2010): 92–102.

[13] Hanmandlu, Madasu, Jyotsana Grover, Ankit Gureja, and Hari Mohan Gupta. "Score level fusion of multimodal biometrics using triangular norms." *Pattern Recognition Letters*, 32, no. 14 (2011): 1843–1850. Elsevier.

[14] Mahmoud, S., and M. T. Melegy. "Evaluation of diversity measures for multiple classifiers fusion by majority voting." In *International Conference on Electrical, Electronic and Computer Engineering*, pp. 169–172. IEEE, 2004.

[15] Xu, L., A. Krzyzak, and C. Y. Suen. "Methods for combining multiple classifiers and their applications to handwriting recognition." In *IEEE Transactions on Systems, Man, and Cybernetics*. Vol. 22, pp. 418–435. IEEE, 1992.

[16] Ani, A., and M. Deriche. "A new technique for combining multiple classifiers using the Dempster—Shafer theory of evidence." *Journal of Artificial Intelligence Research* 1 (2002): 333–351.

[17] Tao, Q., and R. Veldhuis. "Threshold-optimized decision-level fusion and its application to biometrics." *Pattern Recognition* 42 (2009): 823–836.

[18] "Biometric score database." www.nist.gov/itl/iad/ig/biometricscores.cfm.

Blockchain

13

A Security Component for Data Security and Privacy—Current Trends in the Automotive Industry

Sruti C R, S Umamaheswari

Contents

13.1 INTRODUCTION

Blockchain technologies are said to have successfully replaced monetary dealing activities in different organizations, but have the ability for restructuring diverse marketing strategies in a multitude of sectors. While this ensures a firmly open platform to promote intelligence gathering, communication, and collaboration among all consumers and private entities, it is critical for researchers and policy makers to thoroughly study blockchain quality across various companies and market applications. Blockchain should be used as long as it is applicable and improves protection with higher satisfaction for extra income, and it also helps to reduce the cost for business modules. The large amount of blockchain quality has been frozen within its distinguishing features, suburbanized technology, and community nature. Blockchain has several advantages, including decentralization, tenacity, confidentiality, and perceptibility. Blockchain technologies include Bitcoin, investment banking, financial reporting, the Internet of Things (IoT), and a variety of other services. Because of their various advantages, blockchain technologies have been quickly became a dominant challenge for the latest century of net information captured, especially sensible agreements, government infrastructure, and the IoT, call structures, and spy agencies. We have a tendency to commit to determining various themes/dimensions that conjointly outline this same research field of integrity and confidentiality via blockchain in our current project analysis. Also, alongside discussion of security policy through all the blockchain becoming a rising researcher framework with an ineluctable extra stringent scientific subject, one would anticipate that prior literature would square predicated mostly, more or less, on a selected theme set upon by rival researchers. This literature review establishes the unifying theme known as blockchain information security and privacy, and at intervals which the primary class will vary subject topics like blockchain (safety) apps and blockchain (security) algorithms, besides various study classes which are said to be area zone and also unit equipped.

This is said to be the same auto sector which is given among a very few technically sophisticated industry sectors, with advancements varying to modified, internal combustion, and conscience-sensible vehicles to economic net with aspects (IoT device) convergence with the help of Internet of Things vehicles. Under the Business 4.0 paradigm, which represents a resulting stage in the world's digital technology, this same auto sector is dealing with operational problems as well as privacy concerns, which result in computer hackers, extra fatalities, occurrences, failures, expenses, and costs besides elements, as well as facilities. When the controlled systems have these types of cars or automobile-related systems, national security is jeopardized, so strong cybersecurity became a critical requirement. We have a tendency to believe that, when considering the prospects of the automotive system, blockchain technologies could provide a streamlined sparely populated framework wherever information concerning healthcare coverage, evidence given for ownership, copyrights, renovations, repairs, and real wealth can be firmly recorded, tracked, and managed. In contrast to the report linked citations, the whole research promotes a comprehensive method with blockchain for the auto industry which has thought the essentials besides planning blockchain-basic elaborated analysis mostly with thanks to the deployment and optimization of blockchain technologies for the automotive business, as well as the method by which the blockchain will radically rework the automotive sector.

13.1.1 Blockchain Basics for Security

- As previously mentioned, blockchain is claimed to be a distributed ledger which is said to be supported by a series of joined blocks that permit sharing of data.
- It offers multiple security edges such as confidentiality, access control, user access, relevant data and information protection, and so on.

13.1.2 Privacy

Blockchain has made use of wider government encryption to offer safety and confidentiality. These days, there is said to be one important business cryptographic suite for transmission control protocol (TCP): Rivest–Shamir–Adleman (RSA), which is mainly based on cryptographic features which additionally build usage and is said to be useful for cryptography because of a symmetric encryption neural network. This was indeed worth noting, as each of the clients who deals with blockchain is said to be known mostly by their IP address itself and hashing. Though government cryptokeys square measure is said to be free of a user's identity to protect privacy, it has potential to see bound identifications and evaluation of the executed transfers, though such associate assessments will be given and hence it will be made more difficult by victimization multichain. Furthermore, nil information evidences will give usage with encryption, which allows showing ownership of bound data while not revealing it. One example of a blockchain-basic architecture has been used in intelligent vehicles. Interlinked solutions in intelligent vehicles provide subtle advantages with any and any or all involved parties; however, such tools which are available at higher levels, used as one's development to a variety of data and protection of several critical attacks, are known as destination pursuit or ability to capture including its automotive for blockchain. Note that it is an issue to understand the potential consequences of the blockchain's suburbanized design. Here, we ought to examine whether or not the resulting privacy gains, i.e., which are resulted from suburbanized coordination control (as more important). Note that data protection comes with huge prices which are obtained and protected through modern tools, methods and techniques, but on another side, there is a chance of leaking privacy or personal information by such tools.

13.1.3 Identity Management

Identity management is outlined because the security programs and procedures designed to find identity are said to be concerned with managing the flow and value, form, and selectable information with characteristics which are given through identifications besides the particular framework. As a result, its identification supplier is in charge of the authorization including its various organizations. Several approaches will be considered. The purchaser of a centralized strategy may be the singular organization which regulates a framework. It should be mentioned that their concept and use typically extend well beyond centralized authority (e.g. the central state given national identification proof which is given validation for various frameworks).

Integrated strategies: Data that was officially launched with each cyberenvironment can be used to access a further database (e.g., the framework given for authentication).

Client strategies: One end-user owns and controls the identity (e.g., network authentication). Suburbanized client strategies, for example, now have also evolved rapidly.

A review of the various initiatives reveals the latest opportunities and needs for implementing e-wallets with access control.

13.1.4 Access Management

Access management denotes the laws, procedures, and techniques that are used to recognize and maintain licensed permissions to the management, as well as the framework.

13.1.5 Data and Information Security

To be considered secure, three major properties of the changed data must be preserved.

User authentication of vital data should not be permitted, which is known as confidentiality. As a result, the private information of knowledge purchases should be safeguarded. To maintain a user's confidential information, their personal code should have been safeguarded, as this secret is what is required in addition to the user's digital signature for imitating one's authentication.

This helps to restrict knowledge. Adjustments opposed to unauthorized users are called integrity; furthermore, it allows licensed users to change convalescent data in the event of bound harm. Blockchains are square measures intended for storing knowledge so that it can be kept once. To address this issue, some authors proposed a web structure for networks that uses blockchain to ensure the data protection.

The ability to access system knowledge when needed is called accessibility. By distributing knowledge among peers, a blockchain ensures accessibility. However, in some cases, accessibility will be jeopardized due to attacks.

Cloud knowledge security seems to be data which registers a background of a data center knowledge entity's development and processes; as a consequence, safe knowledge security seems to be critical besides knowledge responsibility, data analysis, and confidentiality. Blockchain technology has improved the effectiveness of Bitcoin knowledge services that provide interface documents, preserving knowledge traceability and responsibility and within data centers, and aiding in confidentiality and accessibility with secure knowledge.

13.2 REVIEW OF LITERATURE

However, we should have shown that the five net detectors can remove anonymity for cryptocurrency consumers. We usually provide dual similar but different threats. Fifth detectors can obtain information about customer orders on most search pages for marketing and analytical purposes (Goldfeder et al., 2018). We prove when the customer spends a token, detectors normally have enough information about the purchase which will unambiguously establish the transactions on the blockchain, which is said to be connected to the recipient's address, and more is said to be aforementioned in order to be linked to the recipient's address, as well as the recipient's real identification. Their secondary strike demonstrates that when any hunter links two payments made by the same consumer on their blockchain in such a manner, it would create the recipient's phase synthesis with identities and payments onto that blockchain, even if the consumer uses blockchain namelessness strategies such as Coin-Join. In general, the attacks which are static in nature or passive, require more effort i.e., more manpower/history of past transactions to protect against any malicious activity/attack.

Blockchain has been said to possess various advantages like decentralization, doggedness, anonymity, and privacy. There is a wide range of blockchain technologies available, including cryptocurrencies, financial systems, risk management, the IoT, and personal and government resources. Despite the fact that many articles have focused on the exploitation of blockchain technologies in a wide range for technology areas, there is no systematic analysis of blockchain technologies from both a technical and a software program standpoint. To bridge that difference, we performed a thorough study of blockchain technologies. The study, in particular, will include a blockchain typology, which is capable of introducing the standard blockchain agreement algorithms, reviewing blockchain implementations, and discussing technological problems, as well as latest developments in meeting the obstacles. Furthermore, it identifies the long-term trends in blockchain technologies (Zheng et al., 2018).

The rising sensible contract systems that are said to be overlocalized cryptocurrencies can permit the reciprocally distrustful parties to interact safely while not relying on the trust of third parties. It is said that this situation happens when a written agreement breaches or aborts; it is aforementioned that the localized blockchain can ensure that the honest parties can acquire the coterminous restitution. Current systems, nevertheless, neglect transaction-based anonymity. Both purchases and the supply of funds among the aliases, and hence that number paid back, are revealed in that blockchain. We also bestowed the Hawk technique, which is believed to be a localized sensible contractual scheme which doesn't hold money transfers in their transparent purchases which is given upon in blockchain, while retaining transaction-based secrecy from the population's read. The scientists may build the personal sensible system with the acceptance of Associate in Nursing which is given in an intuitive manner which do not require implementation of cryptography techniques. The Associate in Nursing who is our compiler can mechanically generate an economical cryptanalytic protocol wherever the parties UN agency have written agreement which can be mentioned to possess an interaction with the blockchain, by victimization cryptanalytic primitives like Evidences with nil information. They will get a propensity of being those people who can codify that blockchain paradigm for cryptographic, so explicitly outline and purpose surrounding for its safety and also for their tokens. Structured design which is something that we become involved in as a software developer. They will advise that team by using the correct framework when software upgrades till the latest version for regional blockchains (Kosba et al., 2016).

Bitcoin blockchain is the technology behind the decentralized banking wallet for stock trading. This incorporates a number of interconnected innovations, including the blockchain as its own public database for image retrieval; this Bitcoin has the distributed ledger technology which is used for determining if the substitution component is a valid, machine-controlled sensible agreement, and hence the structure connected for every block. We have projected the decentralized database for intellectual thought, but it has been said to be tied to monetary compensation sponsored by a blockchain which constitutes and democratizes academic prestige on their far side of the tutorial community. With Ethereum, which is attempting preliminary tests with blockchain, i.e., either preserving instructional data or other personal data, built additionally from their prior research, i.e., via given name/ control of applying the various standards (Sharples and Domingue, 2016).

Chris Noyes (2016) presents the architecture and implementation of BitAV, a completely unique anti-malware environment. It enables the decentralization of the software system's upgrade and repair mechanisms, which were previously handled by a single host, and employs a staggered screening process to boost efficiency. That community system management system reduced the speed of quality upgrade dissemination by 0.05 seconds and is much less vulnerable to coordinated ignorance threats. By transforming the file matching process into economical inquiries that run throughout provably regular frequency, the feedback control screening method significantly enhanced the earlier part efficiency of the malware matching scheme, to the tune of a distributed file system rise.

Blockchain is one of the latest trends that have attracted people's attention, and is now almost used in many applications, such as transportation, agriculture, logistics, and finance. It specifically maintains protection by authenticating coworkers who exchange digital currency, encrypt data, and generate hashes. According to the world currency business, the demand of safety cryptocurrency is expected to expand to about $20 million in the upcoming year (Park and Park, 2017). Besides, blockchain is often applied on the far side of the IoT environment; its implementations are designed to continue. Because of its potency and availability, virtual hosting has been widely embraced with IoT environments. Throughout this research, they have a propensity to explore the concept of blockchain technologies, which have been stated to be one of the hits inside the analysis trends. Furthermore, we will thoroughly investigate how to apply blockchain encryption to data storage and its technology solutions.

Blockchain, as well as the inspiration of Bitcoin, have been given in-depth attention lately. The blockchain is said to be an immutable ledger that will enable transactions to be wanted in an area exceeding the localized manner. Blockchain-based applications are arising, covering various fields together with money services, name systems, and therefore the IoT and so forth. There are some barriers to blockchain technologies, such as measurability, and therefore protection problems that must be solved. This research will provide a concise overview of blockchain technologies. First, we include an overview of blockchain architecture, and then we compare several common agreement protocols found by several blockchains. Furthermore, technological problems and recent developments are summarized. We really want to sketch out possible blockchain future trends (Zheng et al., 2017).

Interconnected smart vehicles provide a variety of subtle services that profit vehicle homeowners, transport authorities, automotive makers, and alternative service suppliers. This undoubtedly opens smart vehicles to a range of protection and data challenges, such as tracking devices or remote control sabotaging. Throughout this text, we suggest that blockchain, a troubled system which has seen a variety of uses ranging from cryptocurrency to sensible agreements, might also be a possible solution for certain challenges. To protect users' confidentiality and to strengthen the conveyance scheme's security, we typically suggest a blockchain-based architecture. Universal wireless app upgrades and other rising utilities, such as variable car compensation rates, are used to demonstrate the feasibility of the planned system implementation (Dorri et al., 2017a).

The data that documents the background for a development and operations conducted on a cloud knowledge entity is said to be the data knowledge source. Safe knowledge root was said to be critical to considerations such as knowledge accountability, toxicology, and confidentiality. Throughout this research, we designed a decentralized and trustworthy database intelligent root design that is completed using blockchain technologies. Blockchain-basic knowledge root will give us leak documents, will alter the integrity for software responsibleness at intervals which is stored in the database, and will facilitate the bolstering of the anonymity and availability for their root knowledge. They make use of their Google data situation and choose their database folder for the digital signal to discover understanding of the customer for aggregation root awareness. We created and implemented this concept. Prov-Chain is a blockchain-basic design that gathers and verifies database information through inserting its core knowledge through blockchain payments. Prov-Chain is said to operate in three stages: root knowledge selection, root knowledge space, and root knowledge verification. The findings of the progress report show that Prov-Chain offers safety measures, leak root, user safety, and dependability with limited competition from Google data apps (Liang et al., 2017).

IoT protection and confidentiality continue to be major concerns, owing to the large size and fragmented existence of wireless communication. Blockchain-based strategies can provide decentralized protection or confidentiality, but also require significant resources, latency, and process complexity, which is not incompatible with many energy networks. Earlier studies have provided the lightweight representation for the technology that is greatly tailored for being utilized all through smart devices through removing its evidence for labor (proof of work) and thus the construction for tokens. Our strategy was demonstrated in a smart home environment but comprised of three major tiers: Google drive, layer, and house automation; throughout this research, we will dive in depth and describe some various key components and roles for each sensible household stage. Any smart building is said to be a token, an elevated computer known as the "miner," which is in charge of managing all contact inside and outside the building. That worker also keeps the confidential or personal technology, which is used for controlling and monitoring emails. They demonstrate the security of our proposed blockchain-basic sensible residential system by properly analyzing its safety in relation to their essential policy goals for secrecy, honesty, and availability. Eventually, they tend to have simulation results to highlight that the overheads (in terms of traffic, measurement, or electricity generation) generated through the approach are negligible compared with its safety and data benefits (Dorri et al., 2017b).

This research investigates how IoT and blockchain technologies can benefit communication ecosystem implementation. The primary goal for this study was to understand how blockchain is typically used to build decentralized aged care funding features which encourage individuals to legitimize, safely, certain activities throughout order and generate extra income. While well-known social platform apps like Alibaba and Amazon are listed, there are many alternate ways for collaboration in the global marketplace. Through its latest development in the IoT and blockchain, the possibility will occur that it could be used to build a plethora of networking technologies such as community automated digital currencies, distribution networks, online privacy protection, and traditional heritage protection, to name a few. Although various kinds of sharing economy circumstances are proliferating, few of them have so far used the IoT and blockchain as innovations for building application software. The whole thesis would look at how we can make use of the IoT and blockchains to build strongly economic globalization access to lots (Huckle et al., 2016).

Equity investing via the Internet might also be a substitute platform for entrepreneurs to raise capital. It has smaller environmental footprint, cheap prices, and fast throughput, which promotes creativity. Over the last few days, several developments of creating a shared platform of Beijing have emerged. Even so, several questions remain unresolved in the following. Blockchain is a decentralized and smart contracts system that can be used to build knowledge authentication, accountability, and credibility. This invention was thought to provide huge upside throughout that financial sector since this could indeed be an interference. Our research thesis investigates existing problems throughout their context for creating shared platforms for 'Beijing'/ useful developments for raising capital in 'Beijing'. Blockchain technologies are believed to be a safe, reliable, and low-cost solution for the registration of shares and bonds for the company funded; blockchain technologies will alter the transactions or moreover the movement of cryptocurrency equity markets, thus facilitating the distribution. Blockchain technologies enable monitoring for payments among shareholders and stockholders, as well as the resolution of regulatory enforcement and investment management privacy concerns. Blockchain technology is sometimes accustomed to development for legal software of crowdinvesting which may lead us to be concerned with the company administration. It aims to safeguard the interests of small investors. Blockchain technologies aids policy makers in understanding trading dynamics and aids with regulatory practices such as monitoring stakeholders or fighting concealment (Zhu and Zhou, 2016).

According to Akins et al. (2014), with the rapid advancement in technical growth, blockchain also quickly has become one of the most well-liked Internet innovations in recent years. Since it is claimed to be the decentralized and centralized knowledge storage solution, blockchain also defined confidence through integrated cryptographic and an agreement process, thus offering authentication, transparency, and content honesty without any requirement of any third party. However, there are definite technological difficulties or drawbacks with blockchain. This research conducted a comprehensive analysis for established blockchain implementations in cryptography. To unravel the protection problems, the study examines the benefits that blockchain have brought in cryptography and summarizes recent research and implementation for blockchain to digital safety fields. The report which was given was the scope and overview for a current area of research; the research work will analyze different dimensions for problems and perform additional knowing the outcome for drawbacks. It suggests an improved access control approach using that essential element encoding technique.

Blockchain can solve many advanced issues in that area unit pertaining to ensuring credibility and truthfulness for fast, localized, advanced power exchanges and information transfers, moving for network stability commoditizing the relationship via permission-driven machine sensible agreements for contradicted enforceable representative democratic agreements supported by predefined suppliers which are disturbed energy and clients. Blockchain-based smart contracts additionally take away the need for interaction with private entities that facilitate their implementation or substantiation with variable renewable transfers and trades, including both energy flows and financial units. It will help reduce the level of the atmosphere costs as well as improve the protection and property of decentralized electricity source (DES) adoption, while urging the removal of barriers to the more decentralized more efficient electricity network. The research looks into how blockchain and smart contracts will be used to improve smart grid cyber-resilience and safe level of the atmosphere implementations.

The computer crimes platform (CCP) also achieved significant progress in a highly distributed process system. Through these schemes, detector instruments accumulate information that can be distributed to any or other which is involving cooperating individuals through the real universe in a really reliable way. Even so, the incredibly untrustworthy environment of Hertz, as well as the variety for vulnerabilities with current system middlewares, allow stable and efficient information which can be the cause of shipping networks as a difficult problem. Zhao et al. (2016) propose another substitution architecture known as a standard setting body (SSB) without middleware; this indicated that SSB is blockchain-basic honest transaction for name, which is given in this review. Publishing companies post another subject onto their blockchain in SSB, then consumers define a remarkable notification through creating the transaction for access to that category. That reader then communicates its cryptographic information for its matter with that blockchain when their importance communication fits that content, so that consumers can decode the cypher text and urge that material to label their reader as their name. Eventually, that editor will also been charged by their client. That latest legislation can give transparency as well as data dependability, consumer anonymity, or compensation equity among distributors and viewers. Unlike traditional standard setting body services, our framework does not rely on a shared database, owing to blockchain technologies. The defense for that scheduled SSB is also examined. The completion with that specification for reasonable transactions in Litecoin can begin to demonstrate the validity of StaysBASE Protocol.

13.3 OBJECTIVE

1. To examine blockchain technologies using data security

13.4 RESEARCH METHODOLOGY

13.4.1 Rivest–Shamir–Adleman (RSA) Algorithm

The RSA rule is an irregular cryptography rule. Irregular implies that it will work on two distinct keys, namely the larger population key and the personal key; the name implies that the general public secret is shared with everyone but also that the personal secret is kept unbroken. There are some discussions which take place about the confidentiality of messages between two users. It entails the creation of a public key, as well as the information key. Everyone is familiar with the basic IP address which is required for symmetric encryption. Signal processing technique using the final digital signature can only been decoded using the specific key. It is said that the personal secret is to be not known to the public; it's solely known to the receiver so that it will rewrite the encrypted message. These public keys and personal keys for the RSA rule area unit generated will exploit some mathematical operations. The principal goal is that the process of planning of any cryptography rule should be secured against unauthorized attacks. In the last decade, there has been a large increase among the buildup and communication of laptop knowledge in each personal and public sector.

13.4.2 Steps to be Followed When Using the RSA Algorithm

First, let us take two distinct prime numbers, p and q, which have to be compelled in order to be generated between the variants 3–11. The explanation for choosing prime numbers between these variants is:

1. Each prime has to be compelled to be of comparable bit-length.
2. Since these primes area unit are said to regenerate into binary—whereas when we do coding of the message, and so on, some of the general operations area unit will perform on these binary numbers—choice of the big variant of prime number wasn't done, as a result of their binary conversions which could get out of the variant, and therefore, this could produce some issues when we are doing more calculations.

After this, variety n is computed that is up to p × q (n = pq). This n issue that is given is used as the material properties of all their regular cryptographic secrets.

1. Then I computed phi(n) = (p–1)(q–1). We are able to select the associate for the whole number public exponent e such that $1 \le e \le$ phi(n) and strongest consistent element with (E, Phi[N]) ≤ 1; which is E and Phi(N) area unit professional and nonpublic exponent. We tend to use here some functions like gcd (int, int) to come exponent e and gcd2 (int, int) to seek out gcd of two numbers (gcd[] and gcd2[] which are area unit the functions employed in the first program code of the algorithmic rule; the code is created for the algorithm which has been asked).

2. Now, in addition to the preceding four steps, we've calculated the plain text, m, of the message to be encrypted, i.e. the whole number worth of the encoded kind of a statement. This statement has been interpreted to the folder by the program. As a result, developers will use the primary instance of correspondence within the algorithmic rule here.

3. Next, I apply another instance of correspondence within the algorithmic rule find private key and cipher text.

4. The calculation of private key is finished victimization operate priv(int, int) within the program. Whereas shrewd cipher text c(say), it involves operate $c = m^e(\text{mod } n)$; m raised to power e, then I take a remainder once dividing by n (which is up to pq, from step 2). In these threads, there are a unit many steps like calculation of m raised to power e, i.e. m^e. I have used here standard mathematical operation methodology and have applied the proper to a left binary methodology to calculate the worth of m (a two-digit variety in our program) raised to power e (single or two-digit whole number in our program). During this calculation of m^e, since it would be an outsized calculation, I have enforced some threads within this sub-thread, too, as explained following.

5. At the moment, we are able to merely verify d as the reciprocal of e mod phi(n).

6. The recipient then receives the encryption method and is using each method $m = c \times d \ (\text{mod } n)$ (where c seems to be the encryption method and d is the private key exponent) to decode the encrypted message, allowing them to scan the first message.

13.5 RESULTS ANALYSIS

13.5.1 RSA Algorithm for Encryption in Cryptography

```c
// C program for RSA asymmetric cryptographic
// algorithm. For demonstration values are
// relatively small compared to practical
// application
#include<stdio.h>
#include<math.h>
// Returns gcd of a and b
int gcd(int a, int h)
{
  int temp;
  while (1)
  {
    temp = a%h;
    if (temp == 0)
    return h;
    a = h;
    h = temp;
  }
}
// Code to demonstrate RSA algorithm
int main()
{
  // Two random prime numbers
  double p = 5;
  double q = 11;
  // First part of public key:
  double n = p*q;
```

```
// Finding other part of public key.
// e stands for encrypt
double e = 3;
double phi = (p-1)*(q-1);
while (e < phi)
{
  // e must be co-prime to phi and
  // smaller than phi.
  if (gcd(e, phi)==1)
    break;
  else
      e++;
}
// Private key (d stands for decrypt)
// choosing d such that it satisfies
// d*e = 1 + k * totient
int k = 3; // A constant value
double d = (1 + (k*phi))/e;
// Message to be encrypted
double msg = 30;
printf("Message data = %lf", msg);
// Encryption c = (msg ^ e) % n
double c = pow(msg, e);
c = fmod(c, n);
printf("\nEncrypted data = %lf", c);
// Decryption m = (c ^ d) % n
double m = pow(c, d);
m = fmod(m, n);
printf("\nOriginal Message Sent = %lf", m);
return 0;
}
```

13.5.2 Output

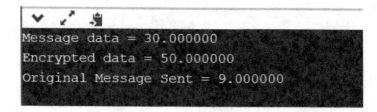

```
Message data = 30.000000
Encrypted data = 50.000000
Original Message Sent = 9.000000
```

13.6 LIMITATIONS

- Hence, we have shown that blockchain is said to be not scalable because of the counterpart centralized system. It means that a lot of individuals or nodes are said to be a part of the network, such that the possibilities that the network will weigh down will be a lot, as the network doesn't have scalability.
- It is said to have terribly high energy consumption, which is said to be a given about blockchain.
- Data immutableness has invariably been among the largest limitations of the blockchain. Once the information has been written, it cannot be removed.

- There are plenty of inefficiencies inside the vehicle system which uses blockchain technologies for providing secure communication/services.
- Storage within the blockchain is claimed to grow terribly massive over time.
- If at least half of the computers operating as nodes during a blockchain network validate one thing, then that is thought to be true. Through research, we reach to decision that if the value 0.5 of the node throughout a network tell a lie, then the lie square measure planning to be thought-as-true by the total blockchain network. Note that 51% attack in blockchain network and its applications considered as serious problems/ limitations among all the blockchain limitations.

13.7 CONCLUSION

In this ever-more-advanced scheme, the use of blockchain will provide the automotive sector with a platform ready to distribute trustworthy and non-collaborative structures: blockchain as an assessment technique for scoping and categorizing one's research across the blockchain cybersecurity analysis environment. A study identified five overlapping themes: confidentiality, access control, key management, cybersecurity, and knowledge safety.

REFERENCES

Benjamin W. Akins, Jennifer L. Chapman, Jason M. Gordon . "A whole new world: Income tax considerations of the Bitcoin economy." *Pittsburgh Tax Review* 12 (2014): 25.
Christian Cachin. "Architecture of the hyperledger blockchain fabric." Workshop on Distributed Cryptocurrencies and Consensus Ledgers, 2016.
Miguel Castro and Barbara Liskov . "Practical Byzantine fault tolerance." *OSDI* (1999): 173–186.
David Lee Kuo Chuen. Handbook of Digital Currency: Bitcoin, Innovation, Financial Instruments, and Big Data. Academic Press, 2015.
Dorri, A., S. S. Kanhere, R. Jurdak, and P. Gauravaram. "Blockchain for IoT security and privacy: The case study of a smart home." *2017 IEEE International Conference on Pervasive Computing and Communications Workshops (PerCom Workshops)* (2017a): 618–623.
Dorri, A., M. Steger, S. S. Kanhere, and R. Jurdak. "Blockchain: A distributed solution to automotive security and privacy." *IEEE Communications Magazine* 55 (2017b): 119–125.
Goldfeder, S., H. Kalodner, D. Reisman, and A. Narayanan. "When the cookie meets the blockchain: Privacy risks of web payments via cryptocurrencies." *Proceedings on Privacy Enhancing Technologies* 2018 (2018): 179–199.
Huckle S., R. Bhattacharya, M. White, and N. Beloff. "Internet of things, blockchain and shared economy applications." *Procedia Computer Science* 98 (2016): 461–466.
Kosba, Miller A., E. Shi, Z. Wen, and C. Papamanthou. "Hawk: The blockchain model of cryptography and privacy-preserving smart contracts." In *2016 IEEE Symposium on Security and Privacy (SP)* 2016 (2016): 839–858.
Liang, X., S. Shetty, D. Tosh, C. Kamhoua, K. Kwiat, and L. Njilla. "Provchain: A blockchain-based data provenance architecture in cloud environment with enhanced privacy and availability." *Proceedings of the 17th IEEE/ACM International Symposium on Cluster, Cloud and Grid Computing* (2017): 468–477.
Noyes, C. "Bitav: Fast anti-malware by distributed blockchain consensus and feedforward scanning." *arXiv preprint arXiv: 1601.01405* (2016).
Park, J. H., and J. H. Park. "Blockchain security in cloud computing: Use cases, challenges, and solutions." *Symmetry* 9 (2017): 164.
Sharples, M., and J. Domingue. "The blockchain and kudos: A distributed system for educational record, reputation and reward." *European Conference on Technology Enhanced Learning*, pp. 490–496, 2016.

Zheng, Z., S. Xie, H. Dai, X. Chen, and H. Wang. "An overview of blockchain technology: Architecture, consensus, and future trends." *2017 IEEE International Congress on Big Data (BigData Congress)* (2017): 557–564.

Zheng, Z., S. Xie, H.-N. Dai, X. Chen, and H. Wang. "Blockchain challenges and opportunities: A survey." *International Journal of Web and Grid Services* 14 (2018): 352–375.

Zhu, H., and Z. Z. Zhou. "Analysis and outlook of applications of blockchain technology to equity crowdfunding in China." *Financial Innovation* 2 (2016): 29.

TRACK 4

Blockchain with Other Computing Environments

The Future of Edge Computing with Blockchain Technology: Possibility of Threats, Opportunities, and Challenges

14

Aswathy S. U., Amit Kumar Tyagi and Shabnam Kumari

Contents

14.1 INTRODUCTION

In conventional cloud computing, all information produced by Internet of Things (IoT) gadgets should be shipped off, and incorporated workers and cloud workers should give stockpiling and registering administrations and then send results back to IoT gadgets. Distributed computing, paying little heed to where and when clients send solicitations to the cloud, will furnish clients with the limitless capacity of processing and capacity accessible on the Internet. Meanwhile, most clients have no clue about where their information or application writing computer programs is put away or run by cloud workers. With the quick extension of the quantity of IoT gadgets, a huge volume of information created by heterogeneous IoT gadgets is communicated to the cloud for processing and capacity administration, requiring high cloud stage effectiveness and an appeal for network transfer speeds and possibly unified danger. In this way, with procedures and IoT gadgets getting more engaged with human existence, the unified distributed computing model can scarcely handle recent concerns, such as concentrated cloud assurance, constant information conveyance and preparing, upholding availability, and so forth.

As a developing design that coordinates distributed computing and IoT, conveyed between focal cloud workers and IoT gadgets to take care of these issues, edge computing is presented. Edge computing will move the limit from the incorporated cloud to the edge workers of the organization for system applications, information stockpiling, and constant information handling and investigation, which will hold the center points of interest of distributed computing and move ongoing control and basic information stockpiling to the edge workers. In any case, insurance and protection concerns—for example, verification, interruption discovery, access control, and so on—in the edge processing engineering can scarcely be settled [1], since different programming and applications are installed in heterogeneous edge workers and powerless tools are incorporated to assist edge workers. Edge computing, matched with blockchain innovation, is turning into a proficient method to take care of the previously mentioned issues as blockchain advancements occur [2]. In 2008, Nakamoto previously proposed blockchain as a basic advanced cryptographic money innovation and dispatched it for Bitcoin in 2009 [3]. Blockchain can be characterized by many peer-to-peer (P2P) network clients as a circulated, decentralized, alternative safe public record that can be kept up, traded, reproduced, and synchronized. It can advance the improvement of a protected, trusted, and decentralized smart framework for the goal of security and protection issues in edge computing [4]. Therefore, blockchain-incorporated edge computing on circulated edge workers and cloud workers, just as brisk inquiry on IoT gadgets, will give sensitive information covering up and securing network access and control.

The key motivation for this chapter is to incorporate edge computing and blockchain technologies that could theoretically assist and bring out different aspects, such as healthcare, agriculture, the military, etc. This often brings challenges when implementing them into real-life circumstances. Mostly, the chapter aims to enlighten their futuristic minds to bring out new and groundbreaking future approaches that could theoretically assist in the respective fields.

The rest of the chapter following this introductory Section 14.1 is as follows. Section 14.2 depicts the background of edge and blockchain technology. Edge computing and its related network application are depicted in Section 14.3. Section 14.4 comes up with various smart applications using blockchain advancements. Applications while integrating IoT with blockchain are depicted in Section 14.5. Section 14.6 deals with edge-enabled IoT/blockchain advancements. Section 14.7 comes with the threat that can potentially arise with the integration of edge-enabled IoT/blockchain. Section 14.8 gives a view of how machine learning can empower edge-enabled IoT/blockchain advancements. Section 14.9 brings another view of how AI can empower edge-enabled IoT/blockchain advancements. Section 14.10 presents several critical challenges and opportunities for the future of edge computing and blockchain technology. Finally, this work is concluded (in brief) in section 14.11 with a summarized author's view on edge computing and blockchain technology.

The scope of the chapter is to bring out the various aspects of edge computing and blockchain, which gives so many opportunities for research specialists and many others who can develop and produce various angles of a system that can potentially be helpful for humanity.

14.2 BACKGROUND

Starting with cloud computing, the parent and the foundation, evolution, and advancements scientifically and technically has put forward fog computing in one of its best forms. The interplay and participation of emerging technologies have been producing drastic changes and alterations to its maturity. Fog computing and edge computing have no major differences between them. This difference is dependent on the location of computational power and intelligence. Generally, in fog computing, the power is vested in the local area network (LAN), while in edge computing, the majority of the processing occurs in the device itself which is then connected with gateway devices or proximity sensors. Hence, detailed information about each term—cloud, fog, and edge computing—follows.

- Cloud storage: Cloud computing is the mechanism by which data and other programs are saved, modified, stored, and accessed through the Internet instead of the hard drive of your computer. Storing/accessing data from the hard drive ensures that all we need is stored physically in the device we use, which means that it is simple and convenient to access any data from the hard drive, for the machine that the user uses, whereas other computers over the local network are not reliable [5]. It also provides users with many advantages, such as:
- Flexibility: It helps to expand and contract the computing power when required and enables computing power bursts to be used when needed, thereby making it optimal.
- Scalability: It allows users to rapidly scale up their work and resources, which can be provided at the user's desired speed.
- Mobility: It allows the user to connect from any remote location.

Fog computing is an architecture that extends services to edge devices provided by the cloud. Fog is seen as a new cloud, and when more IoT comes into being, it is assumed that it will replace the cloud by 2025. Basically, fog helps users to carry out distributed-level storage communication and application services. The IoT and cloud combination is known as fog. The need for fog over standard cloud is a result of problems which occur such as: Internet dependence causing latency, restricted bandwidth causing delays, security problems due to failure of data protection mechanism, and the requirement of Internet access. In such instances, fog has the upper hand because it does not run on a cloud; it operates on a network edge, so it is quicker. It brings IoT to life by providing distributed goods and computing capabilities and allowing an intermediate layer between things and the cloud to be created. During the recent era, IoT has been incorporated into our lives and will expand exponentially, meaning that there will be vast quantities of data that need to be diversified, and edge computing is proceeding to the future of Big Data. fog supports IoT applications that require real-time response, supports lower bandwidth mobility, is quicker and more reliable, and adds hacker protection to the cloud. Edge devices are devices such as routers, switches, MAN, LAN, etc.—in other words, devices that serve as a network gate or entry point. It helps devices to process some of their own data that would have depended on the cloud. Security cameras capture video from a remote location and share it over the cloud, consuming more bandwidth, thus reducing latency. However, latency is enhanced with the aid of edge computing or the time taken to produce a response from a data input, as well as to minimize the cost and necessity for mass data transmission [3]. Companies such as Amazon, Google, IBM, and Microsoft have merged AI and could computing to provide face recognition services that can receive a still image or video and return a cognitive response to find a difference between a product or feature type and quality.

The advantages of edge computing are bandwidth savings, latency reduction, protection and privacy enhancements. As for the difference between Edge and fog computing, both are effectively the same. Both are concerned with using the computing resources of a local network closer to the devices of the user to perform computing tasks that the cloud would usually perform. Both help companies minimize their reliance on cloud-based systems to analyze data, which often leads to problems with latency, rather than being able to make quicker data-driven choices. Where the processing of the data takes place is the key distinction between edge computing and fog computing. Edge computing typically takes place directly on the computers connected to the sensors or on a gateway computer that is physically near to the sensors. Fog computing transfers the operations of edge computing to processors linked to the LAN so that they can be physically more distant from the sensors and actuators. The data is then processed within an IoT gateway in fog computing, which is located within the LAN, and the data is processed on the computer or sensor itself in edge computing without being moved anywhere [6][7].

On another side, blockchain is a decentralized disseminated record in a shared (P2P) organization, whereby each client keeps a duplicate of the carefully marked and encoded exchanges annex just records. With Bitcoin, an overall electronic installment framework that began in 2009, blockchain has picked up enormous conspicuousness [8], in spite of the fact that it comes from early advances. As people are steadily developing their comprehension of blockchain, their innovation extension and executions are broadened.

14.2.1 Layers

The disintegration of the blockchain system into isolated layers is actualized based on the analysis in [9–11] to pick up a more profound and more clear comprehension of what mechanical commitments and execution enhancements have been created, which are subtleties, organizations, agreements, records of geography, impetus, agreements and bases of the top application. The information layer epitomizes the information created from various applications through exchanges and squares. Exchanges between two gatherings are investigated and pressed once again into a square with an "anchored" block header to the past block, bringing about an arranged block rundown. The block header indicates the metadata, including the hash of the past block, the hash of the current block, the timestamp for block creation, the nonce pertinent to the opposition for upper-layer mining, and the Merkle root coming about because of all the block body exchanges' hash tree. The organization layer in Figure 14.1 characterizes the sort of systems administration utilized in a blockchain.

The point of this layer is to scatter information delivered from the data layer. It is ordinarily conceivable to demonstrate the network, where companions are individuals, as a P2P organization. It will be circulated to the neighbors utilizing the systems administration framework before an exchange is made, and just the true exchanges will be sent. The agreement layer comprises an agreement calculation in decentralized frameworks to discover agreement among the dishonest hubs. In current frameworks, there are three key agreement components: proof of work (PoW) [8], proof of stake (PoS) [12–14], and practical Byzantine fault of tolerance (PBFT) [15][16].

Various explicit applications, a few other agreement systems, are additionally planned, for example, proof of service [17], proof of storage [18], proof of contribution (PoC) [19][20], and so forth. The record geography layer depicts the record geography for putting away the confirmed information made by the consensus layer. It incorporates the chain of blocks that store the record of the framework and furthermore some different states made by agreement. Early, in a customary supply chain (primary chain) structure, as appeared in Figure 14.2, we give uncommon consideration to some new chain geographies set up in versatility upgrade endeavors. For instance, as an order of lower-level "agreement" cases, sidechains first proposed [21] might have a lower level of decentralization than the high-level chain, and permit assets to be moved between chains through exchanges. Off-chain encourages the nonappearance of blockchain tasks. For instance, for sending exchanges whose worth is moved from the blockchain, the lightning network offers miniature installment channels. To amplify minimal effort profitability and net-settlement of

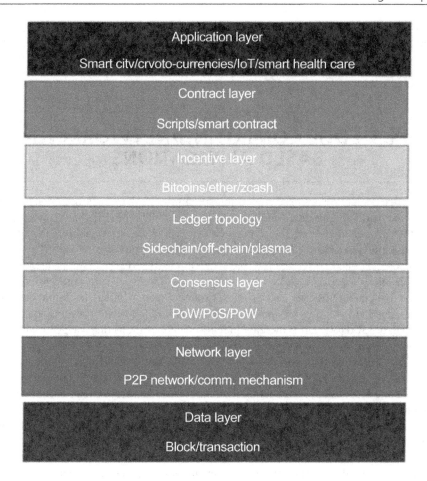

FIGURE 14.1   Several layers of blockchain.

exchanges, the marbleized proof is utilized by plasma chains formed in a tree pecking order to incorporate kid chains [22–24]. In blockchain, advancements—for example, digital money, the Internet of Things (IoT), shrewd urban areas, and so on—are the most noteworthy layer, which will revolutionize numerous fields, such as banking, assembling, etc. Blockchain, notwithstanding, is as yet in its early stages, and the scholarly world and industry are endeavoring to extend the innovation to help these high-level applications, especially from a data and correspondence innovation point of view.

14.2.2 Characterization

Blockchain innovation is as yet being worked to broaden its degree and usage. However, it is conceivable to describe the focal capacity as follows.

- Decentralized and transparent: A blockchain network without a concentrated authority furnishes numerous approving friend hubs with admittance to data. Thus, exchanges (records) are straightforward and detectable.
- Synchronized by agreement: The agreement convention guarantees that the majority of hubs agree on the new squares of exchanges that are methodically affixed to the shared record, whose copies are synchronized by the members.

- Protected and immutable: The shared, sealed, repeated record ensures its unchanging nature, and no renouncement is possible through the single direction cryptographic hash capacities. It is amazingly hard for adversaries to alter such a record in the event that they own the majority of the excavators.

14.3 EDGE COMPUTING/NETWORKING-BASED APPLICATIONS

The principle of edge computing has been responsible for improving the way information is treated, stored, and delivered in the world of devices. In addition, the Internet of Things (IoT) has grown exponentially in the number of Internet-connected devices, along with the emergence of groundbreaking applications that use real-time computing resources, leading to an increase in edge computing systems. The advent of faster networking technologies, such as 5G wireless, has made it possible to accelerate the creation and support of real-time applications through edge computing systems, supporting video processing and analytics, self-driving cars, artificial intelligence, and robotics, to name a few. Although the initial objectives of edge computing were aimed at resolving the expense of bandwidth due to data traveling long distances as a result of the growth of IoT data [5], this increase in real-time applications that use processing at the edge is one of the major factors responsible for pushing the technology forward. Edge computing solves the problem of storing data as it brings both computing and collecting data storage closer to the users, depending on a central location thousands of miles away at the basic level. This process is done in order to curb the latency issues that are responsible for affecting the output of an application that is bound to occur while dealing with data, especially real-time data. In addition, the additional advantage is that enterprises have the ability to save money as the processing is carried out locally as the volume of data to be processed in the case of a centralized or cloud-based location is reduced [25]. Think about the issues that occur with devices such as those that track factory floor production equipment or a remote office video camera that sends live footage through the Internet. While the transmission of data through a network is simple in the case of a single computer, the key issue is when the number of devices responsible for transmitting data increases. For instance, alter that by saying hundreds or thousands of cameras, instead of a single camera transmitting live footage. As a consequence, because of latency, the output will decrease, but bandwidth costs will increase tremendously. Because of the availability of a local source of processing and storage for large chunks of these systems [6], the previously mentioned problems are solved by edge computing services and hardware.

The edge computing gateway is called an edge gateway that can process data gathered from an edge computer, after which it then sends back only the necessary data via the cloud, resulting in bandwidth requirements being reduced. Otherwise, when the need for real-time implementation occurs, it is able to send back the data to the edge computer. Edge devices include different items, such as an IoT sensor, someone's laptop or new smartphone, or a security camera or even an Internet-connected microwave in someone's home. Also, within the infrastructure specified in edge computing, the edge gateways are themselves considered edge devices.

For a corporation, a key driver for introducing an edge-computing architecture can be cost savings. Companies that have embraced cloud computing for their various applications may have found that the cost of bandwidth is higher than they anticipated. Increasingly, however, one of edge computing's most important benefits is its ability to process and store data faster, creating more effective real-time applications that are essential to businesses. Usually, a smartphone that scans the face of a person to use it for facial recognition will run the facial recognition algorithm before edge computing, using a cloud-based service that definitely takes time to process. However, as smartphones have become more efficient with time, we can run the algorithm locally on either an edge server/gateway or even on a smartphone, using edge computing. Fast processing and response time are needed for applications such as virtual and augmented reality, self-driving cars, and smart cities and building automation systems. Companies such as the graphics card giant NVIDIA have now recognized the advantages and the need to increase processing at the edge, as a result of which we can see the rise in the number of new device modules that use the capability of artificial intelligence that has been built into them. Because of its small size, which is less than a credit card, the new Jetson Xavier NX module from NVIDIA was accepted by people in the tech community and can also be used in various smaller devices, including drones, robots, and medical devices. Since AI algorithms need to use enormous quantities of computing power, they often use cloud-based resources to operate their activities. This has resulted in the need for AI chipsets to be built that would be able to handle processing at the edge, allowing for better real-time responses using instant computing in applications [26][25].

Nevertheless, as is the case for all things in the universe, addressing one issue always results in the development of many others. The key challenge in the case of edge computing is from a security point of view; storing data at the edge can lead to issues, as the model uses multiple devices that can often not be so reliable, as opposed to a centralized/cloud-based system. As the number of Internet-connected devices grows, it is clear that IT has recognized the numerous possible security problems surrounding these devices, with the need to keep these systems secure. The measures to do this include ensuring that the data is encrypted, as well as implementing the proper methods of access control and also using the virtual private network (VPN) tunneling process. In addition, the various system requirements for power, electricity, and network communication processing will influence the reliability of any edge device. As a consequence, redundancy and failover management is needed for such devices to ensure that even when a single node goes down at the edge, the data has been delivered and processed correctly.

14.4 BLOCKCHAIN-BASED SMART APPLICATIONS

Without verification or review instruments, the issue of trust in data frameworks is mind-boggling, particularly when touchy data—for example, monetary exchanges with virtual monetary standards—must be tended to. Blockchain is the system for exchanges to be checked by a network of uncertain entertainers. It gives an appropriated, limited, straightforward, secure, and auditable record. The blockchain can be counseled transparently and broadly, giving admittance to all exchanges that have happened since the primary exchange of the framework, and can be checked on and examined whenever by any individual. Some applications are mentioned in what follows.

1. Supply chain management: For supply chain management, blockchain creates a trust layer. The protocol involves the transparency of the stage at which the order is placed with the manufacturer/producer of the product, followed by the transport and distribution of the product to the end user [27]. Blockchain issues include record keeping and inventory monitoring. Trading on provenance is difficult to keep track of all documents when a large number of items are managed by the machine. This leads to a lack of accountability and problems with prices. With the use of blockchain, embedded sensors and tags are used to access product data. Thus, it is possible to track goods from the manufacturing stage to the end stage, and to use them to detect any fraudulent activities [28]. In the supply chain, blockchain lowers the cost of shipping products. Elimination in the supply chain of third-party intermediaries and intermediaries saves risk of counterfeit and duplicate goods. It offers a single view and source of the facts about the purchase order's lifecycle. In the form of cryptocurrencies, transfers are made between the client and the supplier. Shadow ledger with a web-based user interface that offers handed visibility is seen in Figure 14.1 to collect buyer, seller, and carrier data to the blockchain. An unusual consideration is the chance of misplacement. It is able to connect the ledger and data points, preserving the integrity of the data [29]. Figure 14.2 depicts the supply chain using blockchain.

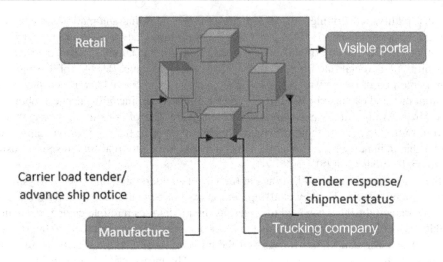

FIGURE 14.2   Supply chain management using blockchain.

2. Healthcare: The rules and regulations are cumbersome and lengthy bureaucratic procedures to improve the quality level of patient health management. Viability is thus not reached. The challenge is bridging the divide between suppliers of services and payers. The reliance on third parties makes it even worse. For example, the dispersed information in different departments and systems must be linked urgently to the vital patient information in order to quickly get the data. This will not provide us with the smooth running of jobs, information handling, and sharing. The lack or misuse of data, which is a major challenge to patient care and healthcare organizations, is challenging. With its high market strategies, blockchain is one of the leading innovations shaping the world. Modification cannot be achieved until the information is applied to the distributed ledger [30]. The strength is the highly increased defense. If any modifications are made, all subsequent blocks must also be changed. This offers safe and secure digital contact. The participant will be responsible for their own handling of reports when the blockchain is used in healthcare, and the user has all access rights to monitor the data. The standard of patient treatment has also been improvised by lower maintenance costs, and multiple level authentications have been dropped. It mainly facilitates the development and dissemination of a centralized health information database and convenient access to all the entities in the system. Higher protection and openness are permitted and the extra care and consideration shown by the doctor to patients for their treatment is shown in Figure 14.2. The approved blockchain allows the participants to exchange data and is intended for use within the organization, so the transaction is safely carried out. That will be the permanent record until the transaction is made by consensus and it is attached to the new block of the current one. The stored information is centralized without blockchain, and it is hard to fetch it. Patient data is isolated here. Once the scarce datasets are decentralized, smooth data flow takes place. Participants are enrolled in health studies and monetize data in the form of tokens. With evolving datasets, it will be possible to incorporate new technology such as machine learning and artificial intelligence in order to uncover health risks and risk factors. The total data falls into the wrong hands with regard to danger if hackers compromise the device. Blockchain may be used to prevent an entity from providing an internal infrastructure. The various participants have different levels of access to the blockchain ledger with the encryption embedded in the blocks that prevent the attack from external sources, so problems such as data theft or hardware failure can be avoided if properly implemented as can be seen in Figure 14.3.

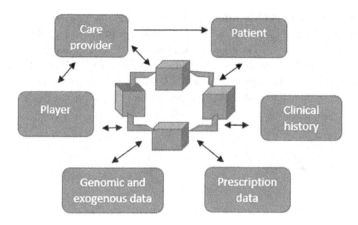

FIGURE 14.3   Healthcare using blockchain.

3. Smart contracts: Savvy contracts are a sort of course of action or agreement that triggers the execution of the arranged system code that is self-executing. It has three main components: a rate of recurrence to test conditions, a set of conditions, and an action that these conditions trigger. On an open and auditable public ledger, smart contracts become immutable, self-executing components of the program meeting. When smart contracts are programmed, central authority power is not taken over. This allows us to swap shares, properties, and resources by eliminating third-party operations. Via the use of smart contracts, we pay into the ledger in the form of Bitcoins, and the share or property concerned is exchanged [31]. The smart contract operation involves an optional contract between the parties, which is written into the public ledger in the form of code, which also includes the expiry date, strike price, etc. Regulators protect the privacy of the individual actor and the receipt of the transaction is kept in the form of a virtual contract and payment in the form of cryptocurrencies.

4. Blockchain-based noting (B-voting): The incorporation of blockchain into the voting system is implemented in order to minimize the vulnerabilities and thus improve the accuracy of valid votes cast and to verify that the qualified candidates are the voters and thus allow them to login and vote from any workstation. The distributed ledger [32] is used to issue the voting tokens to a polling station that in turn issues tokens separately to voters, and thus holds a record of voting in the sidechain at the end of the sidechain all together to form the main voting blockchain; it will be enforced under Ethereum and the vote is carried out using the smart contracts shown in Figure 14.4. Multi-signature is added by the polling station at the end of the vote to the latest vote of the electorate, and intelligent contracts will be passed to the ballot or candidate. Having the ability to hold the votes of the blockchain and the votes being validated using the smart contract, i.e. multi-signature feature, in order to preserve confidentiality poll station means that before the release of blockchain, both polling station and voter need to sign. We can create an open, verifiable, and anonymous voting system through the segregation of cryptographic hashes.

5. Insurance: It is possible to eliminate blockchain insurance fraud by using blockchain to increase the efficiencies of claiming the operational expenses of insurers that need to mitigate fraud. It can be stored using smart contracts. In order to know the policy information, the participants seeking to claim the insurance could access forms and documents using the distributed ledger. The datasets added to the distributed ledger are the insurance proof, claim form, and support claims evidence. Blockchain technology will affect the following procedures: reduce paperwork (frameworks can say that the insurance value chain can be checked and managed easily), decrease fraud, and increase data quality and performance. The distributed ledger uses cryptographic methods to prevent data from being added, changed, or deleted.

6. Smart land registry: The land information is stored, documented, and handled by the property rights in the decentralized public ledger. It allows the safe and fast instant transfer of land property when certain conditions are met from the perspective of the buyer and seller. Blockchain-based land registries remove the registration void, and simultaneously update the ledger automatically. It also offers automatic confirmation about the ownership of the land, enabling the user to view and understand the details about the property, as shown in Figure 14.5.

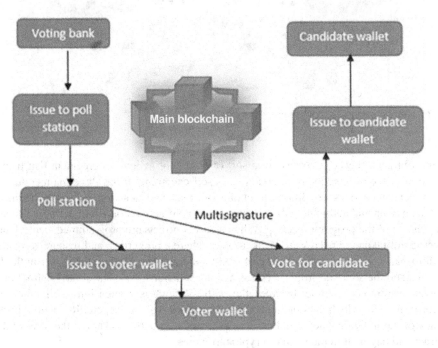

FIGURE 14.4   B-voting using blockchain.

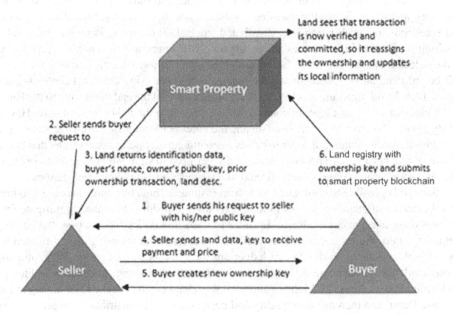

FIGURE 14.5   Smart land registry using blockchain.

14.5 INTERNET OF THINGS/BLOCKCHAIN INTEGRATED APPLICATIONS

The IoT is changing and enhancing manual cycles to make them some portion of the advanced age, gathering amounts of information that supply data at incredible levels. This mindfulness advances the improvement of brilliant innovation; for example, the upgrade of individuals' administration and personal satisfaction through the digitization of metropolitan administrations. Throughout the most recent couple of years, distributed computing advancements have added to giving the IoT the vital ability to examine and deal with data and to change over it into constant activity and information [33]. This remarkable development in IoT has opened up additional opportunities for the general public, for example, in terms of information access and sharing components. In these projects, the lead is the open information model. Be that as it may, perhaps the most basic weaknesses of these frameworks, as has been the situation in numerous situations, is the absence of certainty. Unified structures have contributed essentially to IoT improvement; for example, the one utilized in distributed computing. Be that as it may, concerning information protection, they go about as secret elements, and organization clients don't have an away from where and how the information they create will be utilized. Coordination of promising advancements, for example, IoT and distributed computing have ended up being important. We likewise comprehend the blockchain's huge capacity to upset the IoT. Blockchain will enhance the IoT by offering a confided in sharing support, where data is exact and can be recognizable. Information sources might be arranged whenever and information stays lasting over the long haul, accordingly expanding its security [34].

In situations where IoT data could be securely divided between numerous members, this coordination will speak to a key insurgency. For instance, the comprehensive recognizability of numerous food items is a vital segment of guaranteeing sanitation. Food discernibility could involve the association of numerous partners: fabricating, taking care of, treatment, dispersion, and so on [35]. An information break in any piece of the chain may prompt extortion in case of a foodborne flare-up and hinder contamination search techniques that can significantly affect individuals' lives and trigger significant monetary expenses for organizations, businesses, and nations. Improved checking in these zones will build sanitation [36], upgrade member information trade, and diminish search time on account of a foodborne episode that could save human lives. Also, the sharing of exact information in different territories—for example, keen urban communities and brilliant vehicles—could advance the incorporation of new individuals from the environment and add to the creation and reception of their administrations. Blockchain can likewise be utilized to supplement the IoT with exact and safe subtleties. In the IoT model, where blockchain innovation is known as the way to tackle issues of adaptability, security, and dependability [37], this has begun to be perceived. All the more correctly, changes that can be made by this joining include:

- Decentralization and adaptability: It will help forestall conditions where the preparing and capacity of countless individuals' information is constrained by a modest bunch of ground-breaking partnerships. Different advantages that accompany the decentralization of the engineering are a lift in adaptation to internal failure and framework adaptability. It will decrease IoT storehouses and further improve IoT adaptability [38].
- Personality: Using a typical member in the blockchain structure, each gadget can be distinguished. Furthermore, blockchain can give dependable conveyed confirmation and gadget approval for IoT applications. This will speak to an adjustment in the IoT field and its members.
- Self-rule: blockchain innovation enables cutting-edge application portability, permitting the advancement of savvy independent resources and equipment as a help. With blockchain, gadgets can speak with one another without the mediation of any workers. IoT applications can profit by this element to give gadgets skeptical and decoupled applications [39].

TABLE 14.1   Application of Blockchain/Internet of Things

APPLICATION	CLASSIFICATION	PLATFORM
LO3 Energy	Energy microgrid	Ethereum
ADEPT	Smart contracts involving IoT devices	Ethereum
Slock.it	Renting, selling, and sharing smart objects	Ethereum
Aigang	Insurance network for IoT assets	Ethereum
MyBit	Investment in IoT devices	Ethereum
AeroToken	Sharing airspace market for drone navigation	Ethereum
Chain of things	Identity, security, and interoperability	Ethereum
Chronicled	Identity, data provenance, and automation	Multiplatform
Modum	Data integrity for the supply chain	Multiplatform
Riddle and Code	Sharing and machine economy	Multiplatform
Blockchain of thing	Secure connectivity between IoT devices	Multiplatform

- Unwavering quality: IoT information will stay lasting and dispersed over the long haul in the blockchain. Members in the process can check the information's legitimacy and are sure that they have not been controlled. Moreover, the innovation makes sensor information detectability and straightforwardness conceivable. The essential element of the IoT to be actualized into the blockchain is dependability.
- Security: Data and interchanges can be made sure about in the event that they are put away as blockchain exchanges. Blockchain can treat framework message trades as exchanges, approved by keen agreements, to make sure about interchanges between gadgets. Current secure standard conventions utilized in IoT can be rearranged with the execution of the blockchain [40].

While the utilization of blockchain in the IoT is moderately later, this innovation is as of now being utilized by an enormous number of activities in various manners to create existing IoT innovation. A rundown of a portion of these thoughts is given in Table 14.1 [41–48].

14.6 INTERNET OF THINGS/BLOCKCHAIN AND EDGE COMPUTING-BASED INTEGRATED NETWORKS FOR THE FUTURE

Inside the design, each IoT framework is associated with an edge worker and speaks with the edge worker [49]. Each edge worker, alongside IoT gadgets associated with it, makes a neighborhood organization. Each edge worker is a nearby network control supervisor for the IoT gadgets. The IoT gadgets are enrolled with the confirmation authority by the edge worker. Any pair of organization gadgets which are helped by edge workers cooperate with one another [50]. In the network, fundamental simple correspondence can be viewed as an exchange between IoT gadgets, or IoT gadgets to the edge worker, or between workers for the trading of data. The edge worker is the blockchain director who deals with the blockchain, including the creation, check, and capacity of individual exchanges and squares of exchanges [51]. With blockchain rewards, blockchain put away on cloud workers, which is a proficient mix of blockchain and capacity framework, can shape a decentralized stockpiling framework. Contrasted with existing unified distributed computing, the appropriated blockchain cloud has the accompanying favorable circumstances: higher proficiency, more prominent assistance accessibility [52], and higher capacity to bear blame and lower costs. Since IoT gadgets have a place with various nearby organizations, correspondence between IoT gadgets can be split into two gatherings: device-to-device (D2D) correspondence within a single neighborhood organization and D2D correspondence between different neighborhood organizations. The source exchange demand is sent to its head in the first occasion, where it is confirmed [53], and they are then dispersed to the entire organization over the Internet. In the subsequent case, their individual chief verifies the exchange between any two gadgets across a nearby organization as the gadgets are not enlisted with a similar administrator [54].

IoT gadgets produce a mass of information in the organization that is required for handling and examination transmission to edge workers [55]. With high ongoing solicitations, the edge workers measure the information rapidly and store the touchy blockchain information, where the solicitations can be handled as exchanges kept in the blockchain by edge workers. At that point, it advances the pre-handled encoded information to the cloud workers with low constant and security for additional preparing and capacity. With the blockchain in the disseminated cloud workers, the information is then prepared. Subsequently, based on the diverse handling power, extra room, and source of the executive's abilities for the gadgets in the various layers, three kinds of blockchain can be implicit the organization: light blockchain, edge blockchain, and cloud blockchain [56]. In edge computing-based IoT organizations, the accompanying models would represent the use of blockchain advances: smart city, smart vehicle, modern IoT, smart home and smart matrix [57–67].

1. Smart cities: Smart urban communities have become an anticipated method to fix metropolitan arranging issues later on with the presentation of blockchain, IoT, and other cutting-edge innovations [68]. It will improve the adequacy of metropolitan administration and activities, and encourage the city's manageable and jump forward advancement by seeing data in a thorough and straightforward way; sending data rapidly, securely, and smartly; and beneficially preparing data. The advanced metropolitan arranging model permits the city to consequently decipher, settle on choices successfully, and sway them. Sharma P K et al. [45] described a blockchain-based appropriated cloud engineering with software-defined networking (SDN) with blockchain advances, comprising of three layers [57]—IoT PCs, edge workers, and cloud workers—and equipped for tackling a large number of the customary issues of distributed computing; for example, ongoing information transmission, adaptability, security and high accessibility. Rahman M A et al. [46] utilized blockchain and edge registering advancements to make a biological system that met the security and protection necessities of brilliant agreements in huge savvy urban communities. Geo-labeled sight and sound exchanges were performed by edge workers, and key data was extricated by AI innovation [58]. The preparing results were then saved in blockchain and disseminated distributed storage to empower shared-economy administrations.

2. Smart transportation: Developing smart transportation frame work plays a crucial problem in the area of the planet's vehicle innovative work industry by joining blockchain and edge computing. It joins clients and providers to make a steady, productive, and successful ongoing vehicle the executives' framework that can assume a part in a wide reach and all-around way. Li et al. [52] proposed a proficient carpooling plan that secures/ provides personal protection by consolidating the figured vehicle to advance restrictive protection, one-to-numerous nearness coordinating, objective coordinating, and information auditability. In Liu et al. [53], in the electric vehicle cloud and edge computing (EVCE) separately, blockchain-motivated information coins and energy coins were proposed based on the circulated agreement convention that utilized the recurrence of the information commitment and the measure of the energy commitment to make proof of work. Nguyen et al. [54] recommended blockchain-based mobility as a service (MaaS) to improve straightforwardness and trust between suppliers by disposing of the transitional layer used to control and track the connection between transport suppliers and passengers [61]. In the proposed blockchain-based MaaS, savvy contracts are executed on

anxious workers, which can associate voyagers straightforwardly to suppliers all the more successfully and accomplish numerous focal points, including approval, affirmation, and preparing. In Zhou et al. [55], a solid and high productivity vehicle-to-grid (V2G) energy exchanging framework was presented by considering blockchain innovation, contract hypothesis, and edge computing, which is called consortium blockchain-based secure energy exchanging. A motivator structure was then proposed, considering the conditions of data lop-sidedness. Therefore, to improve the yield probability of block creation, an edge computing-based assignment offloading approach was presented and an ideal evaluating procedure for edge computing administration was proposed.

3. Industrial Internet of Things (IIoT): A strong and updated stage for modern distributed storage, information handling, and access control is given by the blend of edge computing and blockchain, empowering the fast conveyance of edge worker registering administrations, which extraordinarily energizes the advancement of mechanical IoTs. Solid computational capacities are needed for blockchain mining errands, and it is exorbitant to introduce gear that meets this registering capacity. Accordingly, offload mining errands to the edge workers to permit the most extreme utilization of confined computing. The intensity of IIoT for mining will be a promising arrangement. To tackle the information handling and mining assignments in IIoT acknowledged by the blockchain, a multibounce communitarian dispersed registering offloading calculation was proposed by Chen et al [56]. To limit the expense of the IIoT gear, they set the offloading issue as a game issue, and the IIoT hardware would choose to get the most extreme worth independently. To accomplish the Nash harmony of low unpredictability, they have utilized message trade between IIoT gadgets to propose a proficient appropriated calculation. In [68], the creators proposed an IIoT design zeroed in anxious insight and blockchain approval to incorporate versatile and secure edge administration the board. To diminish the expense of edge administrations and lift administration abilities, they built up a cross-area common edge asset planning system and a credit differential edge exchange endorsement component. To address the issue of edge computing security in IIoT, the creators utilized self-confirmed cryptography innovation to accomplish the enlistment and confirmation of organization substances and planned a blockchain-based character board and access control framework. They proposed a convention dependent on self-affirmed public keys for a lightweight key agreement [57] that gives verification, auditability, and classification to IIoT. Another design has been created by Gai et al. [58] to join edge registering, blockchain, and IIoT, called the blockchain-based Internet of edge (BIoE) model. This model utilizes the advantages of edge computing and blockchain for adaptable and controllable IoT frameworks to propose a security structure for protection. The creators in [59] proposed the idea of the IIoT bazaar. This is an interest for decentralized mechanical edge applications that give all partners straightforwardness by means of blockchain innovation. It might coordinate observing applications that depend tense gadgets. In the IIoT bazaar biological system, fog figuring will incorporate edge gadgets with restricted processing assets. Clients can undoubtedly associate through augmented reality (AR) with edge gadgets. Few other variants of IoT are the Internet of medical things (IoMT), Internet of nano things (IoNT), etc. [60].

4. Smart homes: Scientists in the literature have proposed another security structure, which builds uprightness, secrecy, and availability by incorporating blockchain innovation into the smart home. Tantidham and Aung [61] utilized Ethereum blockchain innovation to plan a smart home crisis administration framework. Some untrusted frameworks can be decentralized through this structure; for example, access control administrations between home service providers (HSPs) and smart home IoT devices [62]. Their SHS incorporates: (i) Raspberry Pi (RPi) smart home sensor manager to gather ecological-related information as an edge IoT entrance, (ii) HSP excavators sending Meteor and Ethereum stages, and (iii) home clients and HSP laborers' electronic systems. The creators built up another engineering dependent on blockchain innovation [63]. To expand information transmission effectiveness and mistaken information ID, they

presented edge computing and another algorithm. In [64], the creators constructed a structure dependent on blockchain innovation. This plan causes clinical foundations to acquire some personal satisfaction data from the home climate through smart and share some data on security with other groups [65]. Specifically, by approving sensors equipped for following the personal satisfaction—for example, physiological attributes and the nature of the climate—this gadget accumulates information that is helpful for treatment and stores it in secure and devoted edge services [66].

5. Smart grid: In [67], the creators executed an allowed edge blockchain model in which blockchain and edge processing procedures were utilized to take care of two key issues: protection assurance and energy security for smart lattices. Zhou et al. [55] utilized edge figuring to propose a blockchain by means of shared confirmation and the principle smart network arrangement convention. The upside of this convention was that it was conceivable to accomplish restrictive namelessness and key administration without other complex cryptographic natives [69]. This technique additionally accomplishes P2P information dividing among confined smart toys and other edge gadgets in IoT frameworks. In [70], the creators proposed a system called SURVIVOR to accomplish energy exchanges in the V2G situation. Electric vehicles closer to the hubs at the edge take choices on energy exchanges. To guarantee the straightforwardness of exchanges including assets, the blockchain is utilized. It chose the endorsement hub from all the current hubs and was liable for confirming the exchange dependent on the utility element.

14.7 THREAT ANALYSIS IN IOT/BLOCKCHAIN AND EDGE COMPUTING NETWORKS

It is difficult to join blockchain innovation with IoT. Blockchain was created to work on internet-based activities and which in turn turn out to be an incredible system, and this is a long way from the IoT reality. The joining of the blockchain into the IoT is troublesome [71].

1. Capacity limit and versatility: Blockchain stockpiling limit and adaptability are as yet under discussion, as expressed; however, with regards to IoT applications, the innate limit and versatility impediments make these difficulties a lot more noteworthy. In this sense, blockchain may appear to be unseemly to IoT applications, yet there are manners by which it is conceivable to completely mitigate or get away from these limitations. This limitation is a significant obstruction to its fuse into the IoT blockchain, where gadgets can create constant gigabytes (GBs) of information. It is realized that some current blockchain usage can deal with only a couple of exchanges every second, so this might be a potential IoT bottleneck [72]. As a general rule, blockchain isn't proposed to store a lot of information such as those created in the IoT. By consolidating these advances, these worries can be managed. As of now, a great deal of IoT information is put away and just a little part is helpful for separating data and creating activity. Diverse IoT information sifting, standardization, and pressure strategies have been proposed in the literature to limit them. Implanted systems, correspondences, and target administrations (blockchain, cloud) are remembered for the IoT; countless layers can profit by investment funds in the measure of information produced by the IoT. The high volume of IoT information created by transmission, preparing errands, and capacity can be facilitated by information pressure. Ordinary activities for the most part do not need extra, basic data, in contrast to bizarre information [73].

2. Security: IoT frameworks need to determine security issues at various stages, however, with extra multifaceted nature because of absence of execution and raised heterogeneity of the stage.

Likewise, the IoT situation involves a bunch of properties that influence wellbeing; for example, portability, remote correspondence, or size. An exhaustive IoT security investigation is past the extent of this chapter, but thorough studies can be found. The expanding number of IoT network assaults, and their extraordinary effects, make the improvement of a more modern IoT insurance significantly more fundamental. To give the truly necessary IoT security updates, blockchain is seen by numerous specialists as a key innovation. Nonetheless, one of the vital difficulties in incorporating the IoT with the blockchain is the dependability of information created by the IoT [74]. Blockchain can guarantee the information is lasting in the chain and can distinguish their changes; however, when information shows up as of now undermined in the blockchain, they stay bad. Degenerate IoT information may emerge from numerous conditions aside from pernicious ones. The prosperity of the IoT design is influenced by a few elements; for example, the climate, members, defacing, and the disappointment of the structures. Now and then, the machines themselves and their sensors and actuators battle to work appropriately from the beginning. This condition will not be known until the gadget being referred to has been checked or it frequently works appropriately for some time and changes its conduct for reasons unknown (cut off, modified age, etc.). Notwithstanding these circumstances, there are different dangers that may influence the IoT; for example, snooping or forswearing of administration or control [75]. Thus, IoT gadgets should be altogether tried preceding their incorporation with blockchain, and they should be set and typified in the perfect spot to stay away from actual harm, notwithstanding giving methods to distinguish framework disappointments when they happen [76][77].

3. Anonymity and privacy of data: The issue of information security and anonymity—for example, in the e-health situation—is significant for some IoT applications to manage sensitive information; for example, when the gadget is connected to an individual. Blockchain is viewed as the ideal answer for tending IoT personality, in any case, likewise with Bitcoin [78], there may be executions where protection must be guaranteed. This is the situation of a wearable with the capacity to cover the character of the individual while sending individual subtleties or smart vehicles that ensure the protection of clients. The issue of information security in open and public blockchains has just been handled alongside the absolute most recent arrangements. Notwithstanding, greater intricacy is engaged with the issue of information security in IoT gadgets, as it begins with information assortment and proceeds to the correspondence and application levels. Ensuring the framework so that information is safely ensured and not compromised by individuals without authorization is an undertaking, as it includes the reconciliation of cryptographic security programming into the gadget. These progressions should consider the limitations on machine assets and restrictions on monetary reasonability. To make sure about correspondences utilizing encryption, numerous innovations (IPsec, SSL/TLS, DTLS) [79] have been utilized. To uphold these security components, for example in entryways, limitations on IoT gadgets regularly make it conceivable to utilize fewer confined gadgets. Utilizing cryptographic equipment could accelerate cryptographic exercises and forestall the over-burdening of convoluted ensured programming conventions. Information assurance and security are key worries for the IoT, and utilizing blockchain innovation will moderate the issue of character executives in the IoT. Another principal work of IoT is a certainty. Trust in IoT frameworks is depicted as one of the essential objectives to guarantee their adequacy [80]. Another strategy for guaranteeing information access while forestalling blockchain overburdened with the tremendous measure of IoT-produced information is information uprightness procedures. This can bring about open administrations; however, with compelling and confined admittance controls. MuR-DPA conveys dynamic information alarms and productive confirmation through open review check. The creators ensure information quality through another security safeguarding public examining system [81]. Table 14.2 provides how blockchain tackles/ or solves a few IoT issues.

TABLE 14.2 Blockchain Solving Internet of Things Issues

IOT ISSUES/ BLOCKCHAIN CHARACTERISTIC	DECENTRALIZATION	PERSISTENCY	ANONYMITY	SCALABILITY	RESILIENT BACKEND	HIGH EFFICIENCY	TRANSPARENCY	SMART CONTRACT
Data privacy	*		*					*
Data integrity	*	*						*
Third party	*				*	*		
Trusted data origin	*	*					*	
Access control	*					*	*	*
Single point of failure						*	*	
Scalability				*				
Privacy breach	*							

*Yes, Blank Spaces: Can not say yes/ no

14.8　MACHINE LEARNING–BASED BLOCKCHAIN TECHNOLOGY FOR INTERNET OF THINGS–BASED CLOUD/EDGE COMPUTING

Blockchain technology can be extended to machine learning because the learning capabilities can be used to make blockchain apps smarter. Two related technologies are artificial intelligence and machine learning; AI is the capacity of the machine to perform challenging tasks, while ML refers to an automated process machine to recognize data patterns (data analysis). In data processing, the integration of blockchain technology and machine learning would improve productivity. Complementing each other the two technologies mask their respective shortcomings. ML has problems with confidence, thorough description, and privacy, while blockchain suffers from stability, scalability, and efficiency problems [82–86]. With greater accuracy, the device can now process vast volumes of data safely and effectively. By designing better sharing paths, machine learning is used to make the system more time-efficient. In order to obtain a better model for using the blockchain technology decentralization property, ML uses data analysis. In blockchain technology–based applications, machine learning is embraced. Data and information from different sources, such as smartphones and IoT devices, are obtained by the application. As part of the application, these data are processed. The blockchain is a critical element here in this application. Machine learning is then used for analytics and real-time processing of data analysis. The ML is applied to the data and the datasets used by the ML are stored on the blockchain network as errors such as missing data values, noise, and repetition. As the blockchain is responsible for the data, the common problems about the ML's data are eliminated. The ML, however, can also be applied instead of the entire dataset to some segments in the blockchain. The advantages of applying machine learning are:

1. The efficiency of the machine learning model is enhanced by the knowledge received from the blockchain that helps to apply and contribute data efficiently.
2. User authentication and verification for requesting/performing transactions is performed on a blockchain network.
3. High standards of safety and trust are developed.
4. The blockchain incorporates the public machine learning model to shape contracts and restraints for terms and conditions.
5. Real-time payment processing is carried out in the BT environment.

Blockchain software means that it will never be inaccessible to clients. The first cryptocurrency and first blockchain forum was Bitcoin. Bitcoin is a computerized money that encourages exchanges between clients using cash the board decentralization. The security factor of utilizing a Bitcoin during exchanges is validation with a blockchain. If the data are shown publicly in the cloud computing environment, confidential data from the consumer may have detrimental consequences. Thus, for privacy and data integrity, the emphasis is on the protection of recording and transmitting data. Blockchain is an anonymity enforcement technology and the system can be used with improved security and stability when combined with cloud computing. Without fear of their details being disclosed, the user's data can now securely be saved in the cloud storage environment. In order to install a digital wallet, we use blockchain technology. There is an issue with this that if the e-wallet is wrongly removed, it will leave remnant user data behind. We have to safely install and uninstall the wallet in order to solve this problem.

With blockchain technology, there are other problems: false production of knowledge and double transactions. With a safe wallet, this can be solved. Protection of mobile devices also needs to be ensured. It must be built to create a truly secure digital wallet by minimizing and verifying the issues that occur after every step of the procedure. This process comprises: planning, review of specifications, execution, quality control and maintenance. In a cloud computing environment, we can use a form of blockchain-based digital wallet. On the client's system, the product important to utilize Bitcoin is downloaded and the state's public key is shipped off the advanced wallet when establishment is full. The e-wallet at that point presents the archive to check the wallet's e-legitimacy, then the stage and wallet trade the way in to claim the shared key. So, when an exchange utilizing a Bitcoin is mentioned, at that point, the record information that contains the timestamp data is encoded and sent with the previously mentioned shared key. The affirmation message is sent on the off chance that a client needs to discard the e-wallet; at that point, the client record that was available at establishment is recognized and taken out from the computerized wallet, and upon complete cancellation. To ensure that no leftover information is left, all connected records are likewise erased. This methodology ensures classification, genuineness, anonymity, security of protection, and insurance of remaining information. Classification checks if the data is spilled to unapproved peers, while respectability checks if during transmission or capacity, the information utilized in exchanges is changed or adulterated without punishment. Secrecy should ensure that it is not recognizable to the companion engaged with an exchange. The insurance of security shields the individual data of companions engaged with the exchange, while the assurance of lingering data administers the protected expulsion of client information at the hour of end of the exchange and evacuation of the product. To perform examination and produce conjectures of digital currency costs, AI can likewise be presented.

14.9 ARTIFICIAL INTELLIGENCE–BASED BLOCKCHAIN TECHNOLOGY SOLUTIONS FOR INTERNET OF THINGS–BASED EDGE COMPUTING

A combined architecture of blockchain and the Internet of things that incorporates AI algorithms at the edge (edge AI) is used for the effective management and protection of privacy in healthcare. Figure 14.6 depicts AI-blockchain–based edge computing.

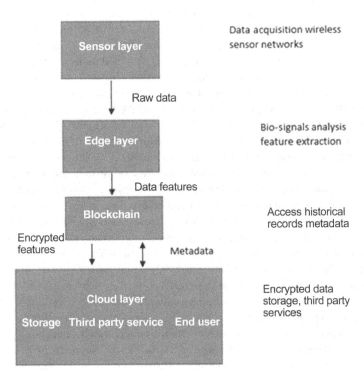

FIGURE 14.6 Artificial intelligence-blockchain–based edge computing.

With a distributed network based on the blockchain, the proposed architecture secures IoT data integrity using edge AI for computational unloading at the edge and fog layers. Integrating edge and fog computing provides new possibilities for improved security and allowed access for peer-peer networks [87]. It is also recommended that patients have the capability to access their own data in the healthcare IoT domain. Nevertheless, the data should be consistent, safeguarded, and unaltered by some third party or even the patients themselves over time. In addition to providing an integrity check that ensures immutability of data, it is also important to provide a high standard of security methods to ensure that the data transmitted over a network is safe and available to approved parties. Many attempts have been made to propose blockchain-based methods to boost healthcare transaction speed, protection, and fraud control [88].

The blockchain is a conveyed registering and capacity model with a scope of existing advancements. The appropriated agreement calculation communicates information between hubs through a shared organization to create and refresh information and keeps up the put-away information forever through a dispersed record. It additionally utilizes a computerized content code or savvy agreements to add upper-layer application logic [89]. So, blockchain offers another approach to safe stockpiling and movement of assault or bug information and gives a respectable climate. The blockchain procedure for the most dire security issues in IoT administrations is remembered for Area 1, whereas area 2 tends to the sharing of information assets starting with one mechanical gadget then onto the next mechanical gadget and gives some correspondence offices. Fixated on the IoT organizations, Area 3 incorporates improving ecological proficiency.

1. Administration security: To construct an IoT network that can be utilized, enormous terminal machines will be set up and each gadget in the IoT organization will get information from the whole IoT organization. As a result of the quantity of frameworks, a solitary framework's weakness cannot be kept away from. In the event that the gadget is hacked into, huge information in IoT administrations will be spilled out, which can have calamitous outcomes [89]. In this manner, the need to improve the security of IoT administrations is unavoidable. Associating these IoT gadgets is not protected because of the number of gadgets. Thus, it is simple for poorly arranged individuals to take the information which is divided among gadgets. Information security is as yet restricted, despite the fact that there are a few different ways to defeat the shortcoming; for example, CAPTCHAs. Blockchain innovation and AI innovation are accordingly utilized for addressing them. Two components will be added underneath: (i) access control and confirmation by the executives, and (ii) information security and reliability [90].

2. Information sharing: Data are the spine of an IoT network, more information can be gotten to, and the aftereffects of the audit and improvement of the system are more exact. In numerous fields—for example, agribusiness and healthcare—IoT information is right now gathered in a wide range of ways. This recommends that the sensors that gather distinctive information types are heterogeneous and that various firms, associations, or governments direct the database [91]. Information confinement costs a lot of energy and time because of the preparation of repetitive information. Trading data from the IoT assets of the information base would likewise better allocate the asset and diminish the cost that can be avoided. In any case, tremendous information, heterogeneous gadgets, absence of trust, security issues, and some different issues are hindrances to safe information sharing. For building an organization that can share information securely, blockchain is a decent alternative. We can make a conveyed network with trust without focal help from blockchain innovation [92]. An engineering called the Chain of Microthings was proposed by Zheng et al. [83]. In this design, they proposed an EC blockchain-based organization, and each point's information is wild and discernible. By making a proof of edge computing node dependent on proof of authority, information can be shared similarly [93].

3. Administration performance: The IoT blockchain application will successfully guarantee information security from IoT administrations, yet with the development of IoT administrations, the interest for processing sources will quickly surpass the assets that the Internet can give that influence the exhibition of IoT administrations. On the off chance that such a circumstance

occurs, it can bring about information floods, administration delays, etc. [94]. For the present, nonetheless, tending to the essential issue by just improving the handling limit of IoT gadgets is unrealistic. We are introducing some exploration examines that help increment the adequacy of IoT administrations from different angles underneath. Khanji et al. [95] examine the harmony between reserve limit and computational capacity to improve the presentation of the whole framework. They needed a system for mathematical programming that joins IoT networks with every information highlight trade data that can scatter a solitary system While tending to the issue of edge IoT offloading, Xu et al. [87] are building up a calculation that screens EC gadget assets through blockchain records and allots registering assets through non-ruled genetic calculation IIII arranging (NSGA-III).

14.10 CRITICAL CHALLENGES AND OPPORTUNITIES IN THE FUTURE

This section will provide the challenges and opportunities required in the future to be cleared and look forward in various advancements like edge computing and blockchain.

14.10.1 Critical Challenges and Opportunities of Edge Computing

1. General purpose processing: Technically, on a few hubs, including passageways, base stations, entryways, traffic conglomeration focuses, switches, switches, and so forth, edge computing can be encouraged between the edge framework and the cloud. Base stations, for instance, join digital signal processors (DSPs) custom-made for the outstanding burdens they handle. Base stations may not be proper by and by to deal with logical outstanding tasks at hand basically in light of the fact that DSPs for general reasons for existing are not intended for computing [96]. Also, it is difficult to know whether these hubs will perform estimations notwithstanding their present remaining burdens. The initial step has been taken by various business providers to coordinate edge processing utilizing programming arrangements. Nokia's Mobile Edge Computing (MEC) programming arrangement, for instance, intends to empower base station destinations to perform edge computing. Additionally, an execution climate is given by Cisco's 10×16 to its incorporated assistance switches. These arrangements are equipment explicit and may not, accordingly, be appropriate in a heterogeneous climate. One test in the tech room will be planning arrangements that are versatile across various conditions. There is examination to improve the abilities of edge hubs to encourage broadly useful processing. For example, a remote home switch can be moved up to help extra remaining burdens [97]. Intel's Smart Cell Platform utilizes virtualization to oblige extra outstanding burdens. By supplanting particular DSPs with tantamount universally useful CPUs, an elective arrangement is offered, yet this requires a colossal speculation.
2. Finding edge hubs: Discovering assets and administrations is a region which is very much investigated in a conveyed figuring climate. Various methodologies that are incorporated into checking tools [98–101] and administration brokerages [102–105] in intently and approximately related conditions advance this. Strategies—for example, benchmarking support—must be dynamic to plan tasks into the most remarkable instruments for improving outcomes. In any case, disclosure systems are expected to discover suitable hubs that can be utilized in a

decentralized cloud set up to exploit the edge of the organization. These instruments won't really be manual, because of the sheer volume of gadgets that will be open at this layer. Likewise, it will be essential to adjust to heterogeneous gadgets from different ages and current remaining burdens; for example, enormous scope AI errands, which have not been truly considered. To make the accessibility and limit of assets known, strategies for benchmarking should be impressively snappy. These structures should permit the consistent joining (and expulsion) of hubs in the computational work process at various progressive levels without raising latencies or trading off the client experience. It is advantageous to proficiently and proactively manage issues on the hub and autonomically recuperate from them. For discovering edge hubs, existing techniques utilized in the cloud will not be achievable in this specific situation.

3. Assigning and offloading undertakings: The approach of conveyed processing conditions has prompted the formation of various procedures to encourage the parceling of errands that can be performed at different geo-graphical areas [106][107]. For instance, for execution at discrete areas [97][108], work processes are apportioned. Errand parceling is normally communicated straightforwardly in a language or the executive framework. Notwithstanding, the utilization of edge hubs to release calculations represents the test of not just parceling computational errands adequately, but doing as such in an automatic way without fundamentally requiring expressly characterizing the abilities or area of edge hubs. The client of a language that can control edge hubs can anticipate that adaptability all together should make a calculation pipeline—progressively in arrangement (first at the server farm, at that point at the edge hubs or first at the edge hub and afterward at the server farm)—or potentially over various edge hubs at the same time. The need to construct schedulers that send parceled errands tense hubs is essentially vital.

4. Quality of service (QoS) and quality of experience (QoE): The quality given by the edge hubs can be caught by QoS and QoE conveys quality to the client. One rule that should be sought after in edge registering is not to flood hubs with system concentrated outstanding burdens [109]. The test here is to guarantee that the hubs accomplish superiority and are steady to deal with their normal remaining burdens, while giving extra outstanding tasks at hand from a server farm or edge gadgets. Whether or not an edge hub is mishandled, the client of an edge framework or server farm should give a base degree of administration. For example, if a base station is over-burdened, it can influence the administration giving to the edge gadgets that are connected to the base station. With the goal for errands to be deftly apportioned and planned, a careful comprehension of the pinnacle long stretches of edge hub utilization is required. The part of an administration framework is helpful, yet it raises issues identified with foundation, gadget, and application control, planning, and re-booking levels.

14.10.1.1 Opportunities for the Future/'Smart' Era

A few opportunities for blockchain technology or integration of blockchain with other technologies are listed in what follows.

1. Principles and benchmarks: Edge computing can be applied, practically speaking, and made freely accessible if the positions, connections, and dangers of all partners are enunciated. The National Institutes of Standards and Technology (NIST) 2021, the IEEE Standards Association, the International Standards Organization's Cloud Standards Customer Council (CSCC), and the International Telecommunication Union (ITU). There are various endeavors to make an assortment of cloud norms. In any case, to recognize the social, legitimate, and moral ramifications of the utilization of edge hubs, new partners—for example, public and private substances that own edge hubs—will currently have to re-evaluate such models. This is positively not straightforward work and needs devotion and speculation from public and private associations and scholastic establishments. Norms can be executed just when the productivity of edge hubs can

be precisely benchmarked against notable measurements. Among the benchmarking activities for the cloud is the Regular Performance Evaluation Company (RPEC) and distinctive scholarly researchers [110] [111]. In a loud climate—for example, the cloud—benchmarking presents significant difficulties. The current situation with craftsmanship is not yet experienced, and broad examination is required to give vigorous benchmarking suites that can gather measurements dependably. Subsequently, it will be harder to benchmark edge hubs; yet it would open up new roads for investigation. The utilization of edge hubs is an engaging possibility when capacities, connections, and dangers are framed. Like a cloud commercial center, an edge figuring commercial center that offers an assortment of edge hubs on the premise of paying more only as costs arise is possible. An examination into characterizing service level-agreement for edge hubs and estimating models will be expected to make such a commercial center.

2. Structures and dialects: There are numerous opportunities for application execution in the cloud worldview. Notwithstanding well-known programming dialects, there is a wide assortment of administrations to send applications on the cloud. For instance, when assets outside the cloud are utilized, a work process is normally used to run a bioinformatics outstanding task at hand on the public cloud, where input information is obtained from a private information base. Programming structures and toolboxes for programming huge work processes in a disseminated climate are a grounded road of research. In any case, with the expansion of edge hubs that will empower broadly useful registering, there will be the need to build structures and toolboxes. Instances of the utilization of edge investigation are probably going to contrast from existing work processes habitually concentrated in logical fields; for example, bioinformatics, or stargazing. Since edge examination may characterize its utilization cases in client-driven applications, sending an edge investigation work process may not be adequate for existing systems. The programming model that plans to abuse edge hubs should execute outstanding burdens on numerous progressive equipment levels simultaneously to help errand- and information-level parallelism. The language that underpins the programming model should consider the heterogeneity of equipment and the capacity of the instruments in the work process. In the event that edge hubs are more uncommon to the supplier, the systems that permit the work process cloud should represent them. This is harder than existing models that make the cloud accessible.

3. Lightweight libraries and algorithms: Due to equipment constraints, heavyweight programming is not upheld or normal for enormous worker edge hubs. For instance, the little cell base station of Intel's T3K Concurrent Dual-Mode System-on-Chip (SoC) has a four-center ARM-based processor and restricted memory, which is not sufficient to run complex information preparing devices—for example, Apache Spark—that need at any rate eight CPU centers and 8 GB of memory for good execution. For edge computing, lightweight calculations that can do discerning AI or information preparing assignments are needed. For instance, Apache Quarks is a lightweight library that can be utilized on small impression edge gadgets—for example, PDAs—to permit constant information examination. All things considered, Quarks underpins the preparation of essential information, for example, separating and windowing totals that are not suitable for cutting-edge insightful exercises, for example, setting mindful suggestions. AI libraries that utilization less memory and circle use can profit by information insightful instruments for edge hubs. TensorFlow is another model structure that upholds profound learning calculations and supports heterogeneous conveyed frameworks; however, it is still to be investigated for its edge examination potential.

4. Miniature operating systems and virtualization: The issues identified with the execution of heterogeneous edge hub applications can be rectified by using the working of miniature frameworks or miniature piece studies. As these hubs don't have monstrous assets—for example, in a worker—the universally useful processing climate that is encouraged on the edge should deplete fewer assets. It is alluring to have the advantages of fast organization, decreased boot-up speeds, and asset separation. Fundamental examination shows that, through multiplexing machine equipment through various virtual gadgets, versatile holders can give equivalent

execution to local equipment. Compartment advances—for example, Docker—are developing and making it conceivable to send applications rapidly on a heterogeneous stage. Further exploration is expected to execute compartments as an effective instrument for conveying applications nervous hubs.

5. Industry–academic collaborations: Edge computing presents a novel open door for the scholarly world to comprehensively re-center its exploration exercises around applied conveyed registering, particularly in cloud and portable processing. It is difficult for scholarly examination to zero in on scale without making suppositions that may not generally compare to the real world.

14.10.2 Critical Challenges and Opportunities of Blockchain

1. Versatility: With the number of exchanges developing step by step, the size of the blockchain is high and increasing. The blockchain of Bitcoin has arrived at 100 GB of capacity now. All exchanges should be put away for affirmation of the exchange. Besides, because of the first square size constraint and the time span used to develop another block, the Bitcoin blockchain can just handle around seven exchanges each second, which cannot fulfill the prerequisite to deal with a large number of exchanges continuously. Then, as the block limit is extremely low, as miners favor high-charge exchanges, numerous little exchanges can be deferred. Nonetheless, enormous block sizes can hinder the speed of dispersal and lead to divisions of blockchains. The subject of adaptability is consequently exceptionally troublesome. There is an assortment of recommended endeavors to address the adaptability issue of the blockchain, which could be parted into two sorts.

2. Blockchain streamlining capacity: To address the massive blockchain issue, a novel digital currency framework was proposed by Bruce et al. [98]. Old exchange records are eliminated in the new plan by the organization and an information base called an account tree is utilized to keep all non-void locations altogether. Thus, hubs do not have to store all the exchanges to check if an exchange is valid. This issue can likewise be tackled, aside from lightweight clients.

3. Protection leakage: The blockchain is viewed as secure as clients just make exchanges with produced addresses as opposed to real characters. Clients can likewise assemble various locations on account of data spillage. Notwithstanding, it is appeared in Meiklejohn et al. [99] and Kosba et al. [101] that blockchain doesn't ensure value-based privacy, since every open key is freely available for the estimations, all things considered, and balances. Also, a technique for connecting client *nom de plumes* IP addresses was presented by Biryukov et al. [102], regardless of whether clients are behind the interpretation of organization address (NAT) or firewalls. In Biryukov et al. [102], a bunch of hubs to which it associates will distinguish every customer extraordinarily. Nonetheless, to find the foundation of an exchange, this set can be explored and utilized. A few strategies have been acquainted with improved blockchain transparency, which could be inexactly isolated into two kinds: blending and anonymous.

4. Egotistical mining: In any case, ongoing exploration shows that even hubs with less than 51% control stay hazardous. Specifically, Eyal and Sirer [99] have indicated that the organization is defenseless, despite the fact that only a little bit of the hashing power is utilized to swindle. In the narrow-minded mining methodology, selfish excavators keep up their mined squares without broadcasting, and the private branch may be uncovered to people in general after specific conditions have been met. The two excavators will have it acknowledged since the private branch is longer than the current public chain. Preceding the private blockchain distribution, legitimate diggers were squandering their cash on a silly branch, while covetous excavators were mining their private chain without contenders. Hence, apparently covetous miners get more cash. Discerning excavators would be pulled in to join the pool of selfishness and the narrow-minded would have the option to arrive at 51% control without any problem. Numerous

different assaults have been recommended to demonstrate that, in light of egotistical mining, blockchain is not so steady. In difficult mining, miners could intensify their benefits [103] by non-inconsequentially creating mining assaults with overshadowing assaults at the network level. Trail-tenacity is one of the obstinate techniques that excavators actually mine the squares regardless of whether the private chain is abandoned. However, in specific cases, it can bring about 13% compared with a non–trail-difficult partner. Sapirshtein et al. [104] show that there are egotistical mining strategies that bring in more money and are gainful for more modest miners contrasted with basic selfish mining. However, there are relatively few advantages. Also, it shows that with less than 25% of system assets, assailants can at a present profit by mining. To help the egotistical mining issue, Heilman Billah et al. [105] recommended a novel answer for respectable excavators to choose the branch to join. With arbitrary guides and timestamps, genuine excavators can choose all the newer blocks. Billah et al. [105], nonetheless, are powerless against timestamps that can be fashioned. Zero Block Solat and Potop-Butucaru [106] expand on an essential framework: each block must be made and acknowledged by the organization within the timeframe. Eager excavators inside Zero Block cannot accomplish more than their ideal prize.

14.10.2.1 Opportunities for the Future/'Smart' Era

1. Blockchain testing: Various kinds of blockchains have as of late showed up, and CoinDesk has recorded more than 700 cryptographic forms of money up until now 2017). Notwithstanding, a few designers could adulterate their blockchain execution to draw speculators pulled in by the tremendous preferred position. Moreover, when clients decide to join blockchain into business, they need to know which blockchain accommodates their necessities. In this manner, a blockchain testing framework should be set up to test diverse blockchains. Blockchain testing might be part into two stages: the normalization cycle and the testing cycle. In the normalization cycle, all standards should be indicated and settled upon. In the event that the blockchain functions admirably when a blockchain is conceived, as designers guarantee, it very well may be tried with the concurred necessities to approve it. Concerning the testing stage with different boundaries, blockchain testing should be finished. For instance, a client who is responsible for the online retail organization deals with the presentation of the blockchain, so the assessment needs to test the normal time a client sends an exchange to the exchange being bundled into the blockchain, the capacity to hinder a blockchain, and so forth.
2. Stop the pattern: As a decentralized centralization framework, blockchain is planned. There is a pattern, in any case, that excavators are incorporated in the mining pool. Together, the best five mining pools—all things considered—have over 51% of the complete hash intensity of the Bitcoin organization (Bitcoin around the world).
3. Big Data analytics: Blockchain and enormous information could be joined well. The blend here has been inexactly arranged into two structures: the board information and the investigation of information. Blockchain can be utilized for information stockpiling, as it is disseminated and secure to store critical information. The innovation of the information can likewise be guaranteed by blockchain. For instance, if blockchain is utilized to store tolerant wellbeing records, it is preposterous to expect to mess with the data, and private data is hard to take. With regards to information analysis, blockchain exchanges could be utilized for large information examinations. For instance, clients exchanging examples may be extricated. Clients may utilize the analysis to anticipate their potential accomplices' exchanging propensities.
4. Savvy contracts: A smart agreement is a mechanized arrangement convention that actualizes the provisions of an agreement in Szabo et al. [107]. It has been proposed for quite a while, and this idea would now be able to be executed with the blockchain. A coding part that miners can execute naturally is the brilliant agreement in the blockchain. Stages are at present growing an ever-increasing number of savvy agreements, and keen agreements will accomplish

increasingly more usefulness. The blockchain might be utilized in numerous areas, for example, IoT in Christidis and Devetsikiotis et al. [108] and banking administrations in Peters and Panayi [109]. We order smart agreement contracts into two kinds: advancement and assessment. The advancement could be a smart agreement improvement or savvy contract stage improvement. Assessment implies code understanding and resulting assessment. Savvy contract bugs could prompt calamitous harm. For instance, because of the recursive call bug-the DAO, more than $60 million was taken from a smart agreement Jentzsch et.al. [110]. In this manner, keen agreement assault investigation is significant. Then again, savvy contract unwavering quality is likewise of basic significance to keen agreements. Increasingly more astute agreement-based applications will be placed into utilization with the dramatic development of blockchain innovation. The achievement of the program should be considered by organizations.

5. AI consciousness: The most recent improvements in blockchain innovation in Omohundro et al. [111] are arising additional opportunities for AI applications. In the blockchain, AI advances could help address numerous issues. There is frequently a prophet, for example, answerable for deciding whether the provisions of the agreement are met. Regularly, this prophet is a dependable outsider. The AI approach will help produce a smart prophet. It is not represented by any clustering; from an external perspective, it essentially learns and prepares itself. The smart arrangement would not contend thusly, and the shrewd agreement will get more intelligent. Decentralized Communication is presently entering into our lives to build trust among human being. Blockchain and a keen agreement could help keep AI items from causing offense. For instance, laws written in a savvy agreement can help limit bad behavior by driverless vehicles.

Further, several opportunities toward future technologies with and without blockchain technologies in various computing environments can be found in [112–118]. We request our readers to go through articles [112–118] to know more about various serious issues, challenges, and opportunities in various technologies for finding research gaps or important information for their research work [119–130].

14.11 CONCLUSION

This chapter offers an enormously creative and futuristic direction for researchers to build and also study new and groundbreaking aspects of the convergence of blockchain and edge computing. When combined with these technologies, it generates even more futuristic results with the aid of the latest and advanced technologies that are current and upcoming. We addressed the aspects of both edge computing and blockchain in this chapter, and how they can be merged, and how emerging technologies such as the Internet of Things (IoT), artificial intelligence (AI), and machine learning (ML) can be applied to the convergence of blockchain/edge computing. The problems and potential possibilities are therefore tackled and future researchers will then analyze and carry out even more new possibilities.

14.12 AUTHOR'S CONTRIBUTIONS

Aswathy S U and Shabnam Kumari has written this manuscript. Amit Kumar Tyagi has analyzed and approved this manuscript for final publication.

14.13 CONFLICT OF INTEREST

The authors have declared that there is no conflict with respect to publication of this chapter.

REFERENCES

[1] Yang, R., F. R. Yu, P. Si, Z. Yang, and Y. Zhang. "Integrated blockchain and edge computing systems: A survey, some research issues and challenges." *IEEE Communications Surveys & Tutorials* 21, no. 2, 2019.

[2] Croman, K., et al. "On scaling decentralized blockchains." In Clark, J., Meiklejohn, S., Ryan, P., Wallach, D., Brenner, M., and Rohloff, K. (eds.). *Financial Cryptography and Data Security. FC 2016. Lecture Notes in Computer Science*. Vol. 9604. Springer. https://doi.org/10.1007/978-3-662-53357-4_8.

[3] Nakamoto, S. "Bitcoin: A peer-to-peer electronic cash system." 2009.

[4] Li, C., and L.-J. Zhang. "A blockchain based new secure multi-layer network model for internet of things." *2017 IEEE International Congress on Internet of Things (ICIOT)*, 2017, pp. 33–41. https://doi.org/10.1109/IEEE.ICIOT.2017.34.

[5] Yu, W., et al. "A survey on the edge computing for the internet of things." *IEEE Access* 6 (2018): 6900–6919. https://doi.org/10.1109/ACCESS.2017.2778504.

[6] Garcia Lopez, P., et al. "Edge-centric computing: Vision and challenges." *ACM SIGCOMM Computer Communication Review* 45, no. 5 (October 2015): 37–42.

[7] Herrera-Joancomarti, Jordi. "Research and challenges on bitcoin anonimity." *The Proceedings of the 9th International Workshop on Data Privacy Management*. Springer, 2014. LNCS 8872, pp. 1–14.

[8] Lin, J., Y. Wei, N. Zhang, X. Yang, H. Zhang, and W. Zhao. "A survey on internet of things: Architecture, enabling technologies, security and privacy, and applications." *IEEE Internet of Things Journal* 4, no. 5 (October 2017): 1125–1142. https://doi.org/10.1109/JIOT.2017.2683200.

[9] Yu, F. R., J. Liu, Y. He, P. Si, and Y. Zhang. "Virtualization for distributed ledger technology (vdlt)." *IEEE Access* 6 (2018): 25019–25028. https://doi.org/10.1109/ACCESS.2018.2829141.

[10] Yu, F. R. "A service-oriented blockchain system with virtualization." *Transactions On Blockchain Technology and Applications* 1, no. 1 (First Quarter 2019).

[11] Buterin, V. "A next generation smart contract and decentralized application platform." *White Paper* 3, no. 37 (2014): 2233.

[12] Seijas, P. L., S. Thompson, and D. McAdams. "Scripting smart contracts for distributed ledger technology." Technical Report, International Association for Cryptologic Research, 2016.

[13] Cachin, C. "Architecture of the hyper ledger blockchain Fabri." 2016.

[14] King, S., and S. Nadal. "Ppcoin: Peer-to-peer crypto-currency with proof-of-stake." Report, 2012.

[15] Fernandez-Caram´es, T. M., and P. Fraga-Lamas. "A review on the use ´ of blockchain for the internet of things." *IEEE Access* 6 (2018): 32979–33001. https://doi.org/10.1109/ACCESS.2018.2842685.

[16] Sharma, P. K., M.-Y. Chen, and J. H. Park. "A software defined fog node based distributed blockchain cloud architecture for IoT." *IEEE Access* 6 (2018): 115–124. https://doi.org/10.1109/ACCESS.2017.2757955.

[17] Protocol-Labs. *File coin: A Decentralized Storage Network*. Protocol Labs, 2017.

[18] http://iex.ec/wp-content/uploads/2017/04/iExec-WPv2.0-English.pdf.

[19] Back, A., M. Corallo, L. Dashjr, M. Friedenbach, G. Maxwell, et al. *Enabling Blockchain Innovations with Pegged Sidechains*. Vol. 72, 2014. Retrieved from http://www. opensciencereview. com/papers/123/enablingblockchain-innovations-with-pegged-sidechains.

[20] Poon, J., and T. Dryja. "The bitcoin lightning network: Scalable off-chain instant payments." 2016.

[21] Poon, J., and V. Buterin. "Plasma: Scalable autonomous smart contracts." *White Paper* (2017): 1–47.

[22] Buterin, V. *On Sharding Blockchains*. Sharding FAQ, 2017.

[23] Garcia Lopez, P., A. Montresor, D. Epema, A. Datta, T. Higashino, A. Iamnitchi, M. Barcellos, P. Felber, and E. Riviere. "Edge-centric computing: Vision and challenges." *SIGCOMM Computer Communication Review* 45, no. 5 (October 2015): 37–42. https://doi.org/10.1145/2831347.2831354.

[24] Mukherjee, M., R. Matam, L. Shu, L. Maglaras, M. A. Ferrag, N. Choudhury, and V. Kumar. "Security and privacy in fog computing: Challenges." *IEEE Access* 5 (2017): 19293–19304. https://doi.org/10.1109/ACCESS.2017.2749422.

[25] www.pwc.in/assets/pdfs/publications/2018/block chain-the-next-innovation-to-make-our-citiessmarter.pdf.

[26] https://nvlpubs.nist.gov/nistpubs/ir/2018.

[27] Bashir, Imran. *Mastering Blockchain, Distributed Ledgers, Decentralization and Smart Contracts Explained.* Packt Publishing Ltd., 2018.

[28] Hinckeldeyn, Johannes, and Kreutzfeldt Jochen. "Developing a smart storage container for a blockchain-based supply chain application." *2018 Crypto Valley Conference on Blockchain Technology (CVCBT)*, 2018, pp. 97–100. https://doi.org/10.1109/CVCBT.2018.00017.

[29] Nayak, Arpita, and Kaustubh Dutta. "Blockchain: The perfect data protection tool." *2017 International Conference on Intelligent Computing and Control (I2C2)*, 2017, pp. 1–3. https://doi.org/10.1109/I2C2.2017.8321932.

[30] Kshetri, Nir, and Jeffrey Voas. "Blockchain-enabled evoting." *IEEE Software* 35, no. 4 (July–August 2018): 95–99. https://doi.org/10.1109/MS.2018.2801546.

[31] Díaz, M., C. Martín, and B. Rubio. "State-of-the-art, challenges, and open issues in the integration of internet of things and cloud computing." *Journal of Network and Computer Applications* 67 (2016): 99–117. https://doi.org/10.1016/j.jnca.2016.01.010.

[32] Buzby, J. C., and T. Roberts. "The economics of enteric infections: Human foodborne disease costs." *Gastroenterology* 136, no. 6 (1862): 1851–1862. https://doi.org/10.1053/j.gastro.2009.01.074.

[33] Malviya, H. "How blockchain will defend IoT." SSRN 2883711, 2016.

[34] Veena, P., S. Panikkar, S. Nair, and P. Brody. "Empowering the edge-practical insights on a decentralized internet of things empowering the edge-practical insights on a decentralized internet of things." *IBM Institute for Business Value* 17 (2015).

[35] Gan, S. *An IoT Simulator in NS3 and a Key-Based Authentication Architecture for IoT Devices Using Blockchain.* Indian Institute of Technology Kanpur, 2017.

[36] www.blockchainofthings.com/, https://filament.com/, https://modum.io/.

[37] Prisco, G. Slock. "IoT to introduce smart locks linked to smart Ethereum contracts, decentralize the sharing economy." *Bitcoin Magazine* (2016).

[38] Khan, M. A., and K. Salah. "IoT security: Review, blockchain solutions, and open challenges." *Future Generation Computer Systems* 82 (2017): 395–411.

[39] https://lo3energy.com/.

[40] Samaniego, M., and R. Deters. "Hosting virtual IoT resources on edge-hosts with blockchain." *2016 IEEE International Conference on Computer and Information Technology (CIT)*, 2016, pp. 116–119. https://doi.org/10.1109/CIT.2016.71.

[41] Aazam, M., and E. Huh. "Fog computing and smart gateway based communication for cloud of things." *2014 International Conference on Future Internet of Things and Cloud*, 2014, pp. 464–470. https://doi.org/10.1109/FiCloud.2014.83.

[42] http://ethraspbian.com/, https://chronicled.com, www.riddleandcode.com.

[43] Gaur, A., B. Scotney, G. Parr, and S. McClean. "Smart city architecture and its applications based on IoT." *Procedia Computer Science* 52 (2015): 1089–1094. https://doi.org/10.1016/j.procs.2015.05.122.

[44] Tang, B., Z. Chen, G. Hefferman, T. Wei, H. He, and Q. Yang. "A hierarchical dis-tributed fog computing architecture for big data analysis in smart cities." 2015.

[45] Sharma, P. K., and J. H. Park. "Blockchain based hybrid network architecture for the smart city." *Future Generation Computer Systems* 86 (2018): 650–655. https://doi.org/10.1016/j.future.2018.04.060.

[46] Rahman, M. A., M. M. Rashid, M. S. Hossain, E. Hassanain, M. F. Alhamid, and M. Guizani. "Blockchain and IoT-based cognitive edge framework for sharing economy services in a smart city." *IEEE Access* 7 (2019): 18611–18621. https://doi.org/10.1109/ACCESS.2019.2896065.

[47] Khan, Z., A. G. Abbasi, and Z. Pervez. "Blockchain and edge computing-based architecture for participatory smart city applications." *Concurrency and Computation: Practice and Experience* 32, no. 12 (2020). https://doi.org/10.1002/cpe.5566.

[48] Damianou, A., C. M. Angelopoulos, and V. Katos. "An architecture for blockchain over edge-enabled IoT for smart circular cities." *2019 15th International Conference on Distributed Computing in Sensor Systems (DCOSS)*, 2019, pp. 465–472. https://doi.org/10.1109/DCOSS.2019.00092.

[49] Xu, R., S. Y. Nikouei, Y. Chen, E. Blasch, and A. Aved. "BlendMAS: A blockchain-enabled decentralized microservices architecture for smart public safety." *2019 IEEE International Conference on Blockchain (Blockchain)*, 2019, pp. 564–571. https://doi.org/10.1109/Blockchain.2019.00082.

[50] Wang, R., W.-T. Tsai, J. He, C. Liu, Q. Li, and E. Deng. "A video surveillance system based on permissioned blockchains and edge computing." *2019 IEEE International Conference on Big Data and Smart Computing (BigComp)*, 2019, pp. 1–6. https://doi.org/10.1109/BIGCOMP.2019.8679354.

[51] Kotobi, K., and M. Sartipi. "Efficient and secure communications in smart cities using edge, caching, and blockchain." *2018 IEEE International Smart Cities Conference (ISC2)*, 2018, pp. 1–6. https://doi.org/10.1109/ISC2.2018.8656946.

[52] Sharma, P. K., S. Y. Moon, and J. H. Park. "Block-VN: A distributed blockchain based vehicular network architecture in smart city." *Journal of Information Processing Systems* 13, no. 1 (February 2017): 184–195.

[53] Sherly, J., and D. Somasundareswari. "Internet of things based smart transportation systems." *International Research Journal of Engineering and Technology* 2, no. 7 (2015): 1207–1210.

[54] Li, M., L. Zhu, and X. Lin. "Efficient and privacy-preserving carpooling using blockchain-assisted vehicular fog computing. *IEEE Internet of Things Journal* 6, no. 3 (June 2019): 4573–4584. https://doi.org/10.1109/JIOT.2018.2868076.

[55] Liu, H., Y. Zhang, and T. Yang. "Blockchain-enabled security in electric vehicles cloud and edge computing. *IEEE Network* 32, no. 3 (May–June 2018): 78–83. https://doi.org/10.1109/MNET.2018.1700344.

[56] Nguyen, T. H., J. Partala, and S. Pirttikangas. "Blockchain-based mobility-as-a-service." *28th International Conference on Computer Communication and Networks (ICCCN)*, 2019, pp. 1–6. https://doi.org/10.1109/ICCCN.2019.8847027.

[57] Zhou, Z., B. Wang, M. Dong, and K. Ota. "Secure and efficient vehicle-to-grid energy trading in cyber physical systems: Integration of blockchain and edge computing. *IEEE Transactions on Systems, Man, and Cybernetics: Systems* 50, no. 1 (January 2020): 43–57. https://doi.org/10.1109/TSMC.2019.2896323.

[58] Chen, W., et al. "Cooperative and distributed computation offloading for blockchain-empowered industrial internet of things. *IEEE Internet of Things Journal* 6, no. 5 (October 2019): 8433–8446. https://doi.org/10.1109/JIOT.2019.2918296.

[59] Zhang, K., Y. Zhu, S. Maharjan, and Y. Zhang. "Edge intelligence and blockchain empowered 5G beyond for the industrial internet of things." *IEEE Network* 33, no. 5 (September–October 2019): 12–19. https://doi.org/10.1109/MNET.001.1800526.

[60] Ren, Y., F. Zhu, J. Qi, J. Wang, and A. K. Sangaiah. "Identity management and access control based on blockchain under edge computing for the industrial internet of things." *Applied Sciences* 9, no. 10 (2019).

[61] Gai, K., Y. Wu, L. Zhu, Z. Zhang, and M. Qiu. "Differential privacy-based blockchain for industrial internet-of-things." *IEEE Transactions on Industrial Informatics* 16, no. 6 (June 2020): 4156–4165. https://doi.org/10.1109/TII.2019.2948094.

[62] Seitz, A., D. Henze, D. Miehle, B. Bruegge, J. Nickles, and M. Sauer. "Fog computing as enabler for blockchain-based IIoT app marketplaces - a case study." *2018 Fifth International Conference on Internet of Things: Systems, Management and Security*, 2018, pp. 182–188. https://doi.org/10.1109/IoTSMS.2018.8554484.

[63] Dorri, A., S. S. Kanhere, R. Jurdak, and P. Gauravaram. "Blockchain for IoT security and privacy: The case study of a smart home." *2017 IEEE International Conference on Pervasive Computing and Communications Workshops (PerCom Workshops)*, 2017, pp. 618–623. https://doi.org/10.1109/PERCOMW.2017.7917634.

[64] Tantidham, T., and Y. N. Aung. "Emergency service for smart home system using ethereum blockchain: System and architecture." *2019 IEEE International Conference on Pervasive Computing and Communications Workshops (PerCom Workshops)*, 2019, pp. 888–893. https://doi.org/10.1109/PERCOMW.2019.8730816.

[65] Casado-Vara, R., F. de la Prieta, J. Prieto, and J. M. Corchado. "Blockchain framework for IoT data quality via edge computing." *Proceedings of the 1st Workshop on Blockchain-enabled Networked Sensor Systems*, 2018, pp. 19–24.

[66] Rahman, M. A., M. Rashid, S. Barnes, M. S. Hossain, E. Hassanain, and M. Guizani. "An IoT and blockchain-based multi-sensory in-home quality of life framework for cancer patients." *2019 15th International Wireless Communications & Mobile Computing Conference (IWCMC)*, 2019, pp. 2116–2121. https://doi.org/10.1109/IWCMC.2019.8766496.

[67] Gai, K., Y. Wu, L. Zhu, L. Xu, and Y. Zhang. "Permissioned blockchain and edge computing empowered privacy-preserving smart grid networks. *IEEE Internet of Things Journal* 6, no. 5 (October 2019): 7992–8004. https://doi.org/10.1109/JIOT.2019.2904303.

[68] Wang, J., L. Wu, K. R. Choo, and D. He. "Blockchain-based anonymous authentication with key management for smart grid edge computing infrastructure." *IEEE Transactions on Industrial Informatics* 16, no. 3 (March 2020): 1984–1992. https://doi.org/10.1109/TII.2019.2936278.

[69] Yang, J., L. Zhihui, and W. Jie. "Smart-toy-edge-computing-oriented data exchange based on blockchain." *Journal of Systems Architecture* 87 (2018): 36–48.

[70] Eyal, I., A. E. Gencer, E. G. Sirer, and R. Van Renesse. "Bitcoin-NG: A scalable blockchain protocol 13th USENIX symposium on networked systems design and implementation." *13th {USENIX} Symposium on Networked Systems Design and Implementation ({NSDI} 16)*, 2016, pp. 45–59.

[71] Stathakopoulou, C., C. Decker, and R. Wattenhofer. "A faster bitcoin network." Technical report, ETH, Zurich, Semester Thesis, 2015.

[72] Li, X., P. Jiang, T. Chen, X. Luo, and Q. Wen. "A survey on the security of blockchain systems in future generation." *Computer and System* (2017): 1–25.

[73] Eyal, I., and E. G. Sirer. "Majority is not enough: Bitcoin mining is vulnerable." *Financial Cryptography and Data Security* (2014): 436–454.

[74] Bonneau, J., E. W. Felten, S. Goldfeder, J. A. Kroll, and A. Narayanan. "Why buy when you can rent? Bribery attacks on bitcoin." *Financial Cryptography and Data Security*, 2016: 9–26.

[75] https://bitcointalk.org/index.php?topic=3441.msg48384.

[76] Heilman, E., A. Kendler, A. Zohar, and S. Goldberg. "Eclipse attacks on bitcoin's peer-to-peer network." *24th {USENIX} Security Symposium ({USENIX} Security 15)*, 2015, pp. 19–26.

[77] Sasson, E. B., A. Chiesa, C. Garman, M. Green, I. Miers, and Tromer, M. "Zero cash: Decentralized anonymous payments from bitcoin Security and Privacy (SP)." *2014 IEEE Symposium on Security and Privacy*, 2014, pp. 459–474. https://doi.org/10.1109/SP.2014.36.

[78] Bonneau, J., A. Narayanan, A. Miller, J. Clark, J. A. Kroll, and E. W. Felten. "Mixcoin: Anonymity for bitcoin with accountable mixes." *Financial Cryptography and Data Security*, 2014, pp. 486–504.

[79] Maxwell, G. *Coin Swap: Transaction Graph Disjoint Trust-Less Trading.* CoinSwap: Transactiongraph disjointtrustlesstrading, 2013.

[80] Tanwar, S., Q. Bhatia, P. Patel, A. Kumari, P. K. Singh, and W. Hong. "Machine learning adoption in blockchain-based smart applications: The challenges, and a way forward." *IEEE Access* 8 (2020): 474–488. https://doi.org/10.1109/ACCESS.2019.2961372.

[81] Ourad, Z., B. Belgacem, and K. Salah. "Using blockchain for IoT access control and authentication management." *Internet of Things – ICIOT*, 2018, pp. 150–164.

[82] Cheng, Y., M. Lei, S. Chen, Z. Fang, and S. Yang. "IoT security access authentication method based on blockchain." *International Conference on Advanced Hybrid Information Processing*, 2019, pp. 229–238.

[83] Rui, H., L. Huan, H. Yang, and Z. YunHao. "Research on secure transmission and storage of energy IoT Information based on blockchain." *Peer-to-Peer Networking and Applications* 13, no. 4 (2019): 1225–1235.

[84] Xu, X., Q. Liu, X. Zhang, J. Zhang, L. Qi, and W. Dou. "A blockchain-powered crowdsourcing method with privacy preservation in mobile environment." *IEEE Transactions on Computational Social Systems* 6, no. 6 (December 2019): 1407–1419. https://doi.org/10.1109/TCSS.2019.2909137.

[85] Zheng, J., X. Dong, T. Zhang, J. Chen, W. Tong, and X. Yang. "MicrothingsChain: Edge computing and decentralized IoT architecture based on blockchain for cross-domain data shareing." *2018 International Conference on Networking and Network Applications (NaNA)*, 2018, pp. 350–355. https://doi.org/10.1109/NANA.2018.8648780.

[86] Truong, H. T. T., M. Almeida, G. Karame, and C. Soriente. "Towards secure and decentralized sharing of IoT data." *2019 IEEE International Conference on Blockchain (Blockchain)*, 2019, pp. 176–183. https://doi.org/10.1109/Blockchain.2019.00031.

[87] Liu, C. H., Q. Lin, and S. Wen. "Blockchain-enabled data collection and sharing for industrial IoT with deep reinforcement learning." *IEEE Transactions on Industrial Informatics* 15, no. 6 (June 2019): 3516–3526. https://doi.org/10.1109/TII.2018.2890203.

[88] Lin, X., J. Li, J. Wu, H. Liang, and W. Yang. "Making knowledge tradable in edge-AI enabled IoT: A consortium blockchain-based efficient and incentive approach." *IEEE Transactions on Industrial Informatics* 15, no. 12 (December 2019): 6367–6378. https://doi.org/10.1109/TII.2019.2917307.

[89] Khanji, S., F. Iqbal, Z. Maamar, and H. Hacid. "Boosting IoT efficiency and security through blockchain: Blockchain-based car insurance process - a case study." *2019 4th International Conference on System Reliability and Safety (ICSRS)*, 2019, pp. 86–93. https://doi.org/10.1109/ICSRS48664.2019.8987641.

[90] Xu, Zhanyang, Wentao Liu, Jingwang Huang, Chenyi Yang, Jiawei Lu, and Haozhe Tan. "Artificial intelligence for securing IoT Services in edge computing: A survey." *Security and Communication Networks* 2020: 2020. https://doi.org/10.1155/2020/8872586.

[91] Tan, X., and B. Ai. "The issues of cloud computing security in high-speed railway." *Proceedings of 2011 International Conference on Electronic & Mechanical Engineering and Information Technology*, 2011, pp. 4358–4363. https://doi.org/10.1109/EMEIT.2011.6023923.

[92] Randles, M., D. Lamb, and A. Taleb-Bendiab. "A comparative study into distributed load balancing algorithms for cloud computing." *2010 IEEE 24th International Conference on Advanced Information Networking and Applications Workshops*, 2010, pp. 551–556. https://doi.org/10.1109/WAINA.2010.85.

[93] Nuaimi, K. A., N. Mohamed, M. A. Nuaimi, and J. Al-Jaroodi. "A survey of load balancing in cloud computing: Challenges and algorithms." *2012 Second Symposium on Network Cloud Computing and Applications*, 2012, pp. 137–142. https://doi.org/10.1109/NCCA.2012.29.

[94] Fehling, C., F. Leymann, R. Retter, W. Schupeck, and P. Arbitter. "Chapter 2: Cloud computing fundamentals." *Cloud Computing Patterns* (2014): 21–78.

[95] Nicho, M., and M. Hendy. "Dimensions of security threats in cloud computing: A case study." *Review of Business Information Systems (RBIS)* 17, no. 4 (2013): 159–170. https://doi.org/10.19030/rbis.v17i4.8238.

[96] Varghese, B., N. Wang, S. Barbhuiya, P. Kilpatrick, and D. S. Nikolopoulos. "Challenges and opportunities in edge computing." 2016. https://doi.org/10.1109/SmartCloud.2016.18.

[97] Povedano-Molina, J., J. M. Lopez-Vega, J. M. Lopez-Soler, A. Corradi, and L. Foschini. "DARGOS: A highly adaptable and scalable monitoring architecture for multi-tenant clouds." *Future Generation Computer Systems* 29, no. 8 (2013): 2041–2056. https://doi.org/10.1016/j.future.2013.04.022.

[98] Ward, J. S., and A. Barker. "Varanus: In situ monitoring for large scale cloud systems." *2013 IEEE 5th International Conference on Cloud Computing Technology and Science*, 2013, pp. 341–344. https://doi.org/10.1109/CloudCom.2013.164.

[99] Beck, M. T., and M. Maier. "Mobile edge computing: Challenges for future virtual network embedding algorithms." *Proceedings of the Eighth International Conference on Advanced Engineering Computing and Applications in Sciences (ADVCOMP 2014)* 1, no. 2 (2014): 3.

[100] Varghese, B., O. Akgun, I. Miguel, L. Thai, and A. Barker. "Cloud benchmarking for performance." *2014 IEEE 6th International Conference on Cloud Computing Technology and Science*, 2014, pp. 535–540. https://doi.org/10.1109/CloudCom.2014.28.

[101] Barker, A., B. Varghese, J. S. Ward, and I. Sommerville. "Academic cloud computing research: Five pitfalls and five opportunities." *6th USENIX Workshop on Hot Topics in Cloud Computing (HotCloud 14)*, 2014.

[102] Bruce, J. "The mini-blockchain scheme." *White Paper*, 2014.

[103] Eyal, I., and E. G. Sirer. "Majority is not enough: Bitcoin mining is vulnerable." *Financial Cryptography and Data Security* (2014): 436–454.

[104] Meiklejohn, S., M. Pomarole, G. Jordan, K. Levchenko, D. McCoy, G. M. Voelker, and S. Savage. "A fistful of bitcoins: Characterizing payments among men with no names." *Proceedings of the 2013 Conference on Internet Measurement Conference*, 2013, pp. 127–140. https://doi.org/10.1145/2504730.2504747.

[105] Kosba, A., A. Miller, E. Shi, Z. Wen, and C. Papamanthou. "Hawk: The blockchain model of cryptography and privacy-preserving smart contracts." *2016 IEEE Symposium on Security and Privacy (SP)*, 2016, pp. 839–858. https://doi.org/10.1109/SP.2016.55.

[106] Biryukov, A., D. Khovratovich, and I. Pustogarov. "Deanonymisation of clients in bitcoin p2p network." *Proceedings of the 2014 ACM SIGSAC Conference on Computer and Communications Security*, 2014, pp. 15–29. https://doi.org/10.1145/2660267.2660379.

[107] Nayak, K., S. Kumar, A. Miller, and E. Shi. "Stubborn mining: Generalizing selfish mining and combining with an eclipse attack." *2016 IEEE European Symposium on Security and Privacy (EuroS&P)*, 2016, pp. 305–320. https://doi.org/10.1109/EuroSP.2016.32.

[108] Sapirshtein, Ayelet, Yonatan Sompolinsky, and Aviv Zohar. "Optimal selfish mining strategies in bitcoin." *Financial Cryptography and Data Security* (2016): 515–532.

[109] Billah, S. "One weird trick to stop selfish miners: Fresh bitcoins, a solution for the honest miner." 2015.

[110] Solat, S., and M. Potop-Butucaru. "Zero block: Timestamp-free prevention of block-with holding attack in Bitcoin." arXiv preprint arXiv:1605.02435, 2016.

[111] Szabo, N. "Bitcoin and beyond: A technical survey on decentralized digital currencies." *White Paper*, 1997.

[112] Christidis, K., and M. Devetsikiotis. "Blockchains and smart contracts for the internet of things." *IEEE Access* 4 (2016): 2292–2303. https://doi.org/10.1109/ACCESS.2016.2566339.

[113] Peters, Gareth, Efstathios Panayi, and Ariane Chapelle. "Trends in cryptocurrencies and blockchain technologies: A monetary theory and regulation perspective (November 7, 2015)." *Journal of Financial Perspectives* 3, no. 3 (2015). SSRN: https://ssrn.com/abstract=3084011

[114] Jentzsch, C. "The history of the DAO and lessons learned." *Slock It Blog* 24 (2016).

[115] Omohundro, S. "Cryptocurrencies, smart contracts, and artificial intelligence." *AI Matters* 1, no. 2 (2014): 19–21. https://doi.org/10.1145/2685328.2685334.

[116] Sawal, N., A. Yadav, A. K. Tyagi, N. Sreenath, and G. Rekha. "Necessity of blockchain for building trust in today's applications: An useful explanation from user's perspective (May 15, 2019)." Available at SSRN: https://ssrn.com/abstract=3388558 or http://dx.doi.org/10.2139/ssrn.3388558.

[117] Tyagi, Amit Kumar, S. U. Aswathy, and Ajith Abraham. "Integrating blockchain technology and artificial intelligence: Synergies, perspectives, challenges and research directions." *Journal of Information Assurance and Security* 15, no. 5 (2020): 1554–1010.

[118] Tyagi, A. K., S. Kumari, T. F. Fernandez, and C. Aravindan. "P3 block: Privacy preserved, trusted smart parking allotment for future vehicles of tomorrow." In Gervasi, O., et al. (eds.). *Computational Science and Its Applications—ICCSA 2020. ICCSA 2020. Lecture Notes in Computer Science*. Vol. 12254. Springer, 2020. https://doi.org/10.1007/978-3-030-58817-5_56.

[119] Tyagi, A. K., T. F. Fernandez, and S. U. Aswathy. "Blockchain and Aadhaar based electronic voting system." *2020 4th International Conference on Electronics, Communication and Aerospace Technology (ICECA)*, pp. 498–504, Coimbatore, 2020. https://doi.org/10.1109/ICECA49313.2020.9297655.

[120] Tyagi, Amit Kumar, Meghna Manoj Nair, Sreenath Niladhuri, and Ajith Abraham. "Security, privacy research issues in various computing platforms: A survey and the Road Ahead." *Journal of Information Assurance & Security* 15, no. 1 (2020): 1–16.

[121] Tyagi, Amit Kumar, and Meghna Manoj Nair. "Internet of everything (IoE) and internet of things (IoTs): Threat analyses." *Possible Opportunities for Future* 15, no. 4 (2020).

[122] Nair, Siddharth M., Varsha Ramesh, and Amit Kumar Tyagi. "Issues and challenges (privacy, security, and trust) in blockchain-based applications." *Book: Opportunities and Challenges for Blockchain Technology in Autonomous Vehicles* (2021): 14. https://doi.org/10.4018/978-1-7998-3295-9.ch012.

[123] Rekha, G., S. Malik, A. K. Tyagi, and M. M. Nair. "Intrusion detection in cyber security: Role of machine learning and data mining in cyber security." *Advances in Science, Technology and Engineering Systems Journal* 5, no. 3 (2020): 72–81.

[124] Tyagi, Amit Kumar. "Cyber physical systems (CPSs)—opportunities and challenges for improving cyber security." *International Journal of Computer Applications* 137, no. 14 (March 2016): 19–27. Published by Foundation of Computer Science (FCS), NY, USA.

[125] Tyagi, A. K., T. F. Fernandez, S. Mishra, and S. Kumari. "Intelligent automation systems at the core of industry 4.0." In Abraham, A., Piuri, V., Gandhi, N., Siarry, P., Kaklauskas, A., Madureira A. (eds.). *Intelligent Systems Design and Applications. ISDA 2020. Advances in Intelligent Systems and Computing.* Vol. 1351. Springer, 2021. https://doi.org/10.1007/978-3-030-71187-0_1

[126] Kumari, S., V. Vani, S. Malik, A. K. Tyagi, and S. Reddy. "Analysis of text mining tools in disease prediction." In Abraham, A., Hanne, T., Castillo, O., Gandhi, N., Nogueira Rios, T., and Hong, T. P. (eds.). *Hybrid Intelligent Systems. HIS 2020. Advances in Intelligent Systems and Computing.* Vol. 1375. Springer, 2021. https://doi.org/10.1007/978-3-030-73050-5_55

[127] Varsha, R., S. M. Nair, A. K. Tyagi, S. U. Aswathy, and R. RadhaKrishnan. "The future with advanced analytics: A sequential analysis of the disruptive technology's scope." In Abraham, A., Hanne, T., Castillo, O., Gandhi, N., Nogueira Rios, T., and Hong, T. P. (eds.). *Hybrid Intelligent Systems. HIS 2020. Advances in Intelligent Systems and Computing.* Vol. 1375. Springer, 2021. https://doi.org/10.1007/978-3-030-73050-5_56

[128] Nair, M. M., S. Kumari, and A. K. Tyagi. "Internet of things, cyber physical system, and data analytics: Open questions, future perspectives, and research areas." In Goyal, D., Gupta, A. K., Piuri, V., Ganzha, M., and Paprzycki, M. (eds.). *Proceedings of the Second International Conference on Information Management and Machine Intelligence. Lecture Notes in Networks and Systems.* Vol. 166. Springer, 2021. https://doi.org/10.1007/978-981-15-9689-6_36.

[129] Mishra, Shasvi, and Amit Kumar Tyagi. "The role of machine learning techniques in internet of things based cloud applications." In *AI-IoT Book.* Springer, 2021.

[130] Shreyas Madhav, A. V., and Amit Kumar Tyagi. *The World with Future Technologies (Post COVID 19): Open Issues, Challenges and the Road Ahead, Book: IIMSHA 2021.* Springer, 2021.

CryptoCert

A Blockchain-Based Academic Credential System

15

Varun Wahi, Aswani Kumar Cherukuri,
Kathiravan Srinivasan, and Annapurna Jonnalagadda

Contents

15.1 INTRODUCTION

Blockchain is a distributed technology that works along with smart contracts to create immutable ledgers in different application domains. Extensive research is still ongoing on how to utilize blockchain in industries such as healthcare, education, and finance, just to name a few. This chapter proposes blockchain-based academic credential verification. Replacing current verification systems in educational institutions with those based on blockchain proves to benefit all the stakeholders. This chapter evaluates this proposal and presents a system, CryptoCert, as a proof of concept. By removing the need for a third party for verification, a lot of time and money will be saved for the stakeholders. More importantly, blockchain's immutability provides a unique and efficient way to curb the widespread fraud and falsification of academic credentials in matters such as degrees, transcripts, and learning achievement certificates.

Blockchain was first implemented as the core idea behind Satoshi Nakamoto's white paper introducing Bitcoin [1]. Although the original intention of the paper was to introduce decentralized cryptocurrencies, the benefits of blockchain can be applied to a variety of fields today, including education [2], healthcare [3, 4], and land records management [5]. It is even being used to disrupt traditional computer science domains such as the cloud [6] and preservation of privacy [7].

The main benefits that implementing a blockchain bring to the table are disintermediation (removing the need for third parties), decentralization, security (immutability), permanence, and computational trust. All the industries previously mentioned can benefit immensely by harnessing these advantages. In particular, by implementing disintermediation, a huge amount of time and money in the form of administrative overhead can be saved, and used instead for more important actions.

Academic credentials play a very important role in a student's career. They stand as a proof of achievement for all the work the student has done. These include degrees, transcripts, and learning achievement certificates. However, presently there is a lot of fraud and malpractice in this field. The issuance of fake degrees and certificates is especially prevalent in a developing country like India, which is where we reside. A fake degree that can fool even the most rigorous inspection can be bought for as low as Rs. 2,000 (around $30) [8]. According to the University Grants Commission (UGC) of India, the capital New Delhi itself has 66 colleges issuing degrees without their permission [9]. India is also infamous for "diploma mills," which are basically fake universities that grant degrees for a fee, without providing any educational training [10].

Many efforts have been made to make this process more secure. In the case of physical certificates, efforts have been made to add watermarks or barcodes to them to make them tamper-proof and detect any attempt of alteration [11, 12, 13, 14]. However, the problems that exist with general paper certificates are still there, such as issuing multiple certificates for multiple verifiers, and being dependent on the issuer every time you want to issue a new certificate.

Significant strides have also been made in the case of digitizing certificates. However, most of the solutions depend on digital signatures. This means that the student is again dependent on the central public key infrastructure authority [15], and if something were to happen to it, their certificates would be lost forever.

Using blockchain instead of these described systems will remove the risk of fraud and malpractice. Moreover, the student will never have to worry about the issuing institution closing down or being destroyed. The lifelong achievement record of the student will be permanently and securely stored in the blockchain [2]. The benefits of using blockchain for this purpose are explained in more detail in Section 15.2.3.

This chapter focuses on the possibilities of integrating blockchain technologies into the domain of education, more specifically in academic credential verification. It begins by presenting all the background and concepts of blockchain and how it benefits education. Then, it reviews the existing literature, after which it presents a system, CryptoCert, that tests and validates all the claims made throughout the chapter. It summarizes all relevant information relating to the particular problem of academic credential verification, including the blockchain technologies we used. It ends with results and discussions, along with the scope of future work.

15.2 BACKGROUND

15.2.1 Blockchain

A blockchain is essentially a distributed ledger containing information. The main advantages of this ledger over traditional databases are its immutability and integrity. Once data is stored in a blockchain, it cannot be removed or changed. Its integrity is preserved by the fact that anyone can view the entire history of this ledger, unedited. Furthermore, this ledger is decentralized. This means that any stakeholder has their own copy of the ledger and can view and verify it at any point of time. This removes a single point of failure. The only way to completely destroy a blockchain, and in turn, lose all the data, would be to destroy each node that is participating in the blockchain protocol. In the current scenario, this would entail destroying millions of computers.

Another key feature of a blockchain is that it is very secure. The only known way to introduce fraudulent records or transactions into the blockchain is the 51% attack. This attack is only possible if more than half of all the nodes in the blockchain come under the control of a malicious organization. This is almost impossible, given the sheer amount of nodes in every popular blockchain these days.

Finally, the most important feature of a blockchain is that it removes the need for a central authority of trust. Trust is instead maintained through computational power. Participants trust the nodes that have expended the most computational power. This is explained in detail in the next section.

15.2.2 Functionality of a Blockchain

Although the core technical details of how a blockchain works are quite complex, the gist of it can be explained in a lucid manner. A blockchain, in its simplest terms, can be thought of as a distributed ledger, with a copy of the ledger being in the possession of all the stakeholders, at all times. How can we ensure that each participant (hereby referred to as a node) would have the same copy of the ledger, and be confident that whatever transactions are stored in it can be trusted? This is achieved through what is known as a consensus protocol.

First, whenever a node wants to add a new record to the blockchain, they broadcast a digitally signed transaction to the network. Signing the transaction proves that the message is indeed coming from the sender, preventing repudiation. Next, special nodes known as miners listen to multiple such transactions, and collect them into a block. After this, each of these miners immediately engages in solving a cryptographic puzzle that is based on the block. It is a sort of miniature lottery, which utilizes computing power to solve. This lottery is known as proof of work (PoW) [1].

Whoever wins this lottery is said to have mined the block, and is allowed to broadcast this to all the nodes. A block is only accepted by a node if it has been mined. This can be easily verified by a node, by checking the solution to the cryptographic puzzle. The block is then added to all the previously mined blocks; hence the name blockchain.

All the blocks are temporally linked to each other, by including the hash of the current block in the header of the next one. This ensures a block's immutability, as changing even a single character in any one of the blocks will change its hash, which won't match with the hash in the next block's header, thereby invalidating the blockchain.

Miners who win these lotteries are rewarded for their efforts by receiving some cryptocurrency as compensation for the electricity and computational time spent.

Putting all this together, in order to fool the blockchain, the malicious nodes will have to keep winning this lottery every time. As long as they don't have control of more than 51% of the nodes in the network, doing so is probabilistically impossible. Therefore, as long as more than 51% of the nodes are operated by honest people, it is impossible to introduce a new record into the blockchain without consensus. Even if a malicious node is able to mine a fraudulent block once or twice, the nodes always accept the longest chain. Thus, eventually, the honest nodes will overpower the malicious ones.

This is how a blockchain removes the need for a central authority to verify each transaction. Trust is instead shifted to computational power and cryptography. In other words, implementing blockchain leads to a trustless system.

15.2.3 Blockchain in Education

The qualities of the blockchain just described can be effectively harnessed to improve on the current education system, especially in the domain of verifying and issuing academic credentials. Presently, there is widespread fraud in this area. Recent literature indicates potential applications of blockchain in education sector [16, 17, 18, 19]. Blockchain can solve this problem by providing a decentralized way for stakeholders to verify a document holder's credentials. Moreover, the verifier can trust that the credentials stored in the blockchain have not been tampered with (due to its immutability). Additionally, because of its permanence, data once stored in the blockchain can never by removed or edited, thereby keeping all its transactions public and open.

Most importantly, blockchain removes the need for the verifier to contact the issuer in order to validate the credentials. The verifier can directly query the blockchain, and if the data in the blockchain is to their satisfaction, they can rest assure that the certificate is indeed valid, from the claimed issuer, and not been tampered with since it was uploaded to the chain. The three main stakeholders involved are:

1. The issuer: This can be the university that wishes to issue certificates, diplomas, degrees, or transcripts to the blockchain. It can also be massive online course organizations such as Coursera, Udemy, and edX, which wish to certify student achievements directly to the blockchain. It can also be extended to include organizations such as Open Badges (https://openbadges.org/), which wish to issue informal learning achievements of students to the blockchain.
2. The verifier: This includes the employer, who wishes to verify an employee's academic credentials. It can also include banks, which wish to verify academic credentials for the purposes of extending loans. Moreover, it can also include higher education universities themselves, which wish to verify the credentials of a student applying for higher studies.
3. The student or recipient: These are the recipients of the academic credentials uploaded to the blockchain.

15.2.4 Problems with Traditional Systems

The current system of physical academic credentials is very susceptible to potential frauds and malpractice. It also leads to a lot of administrative overhead, wasting huge amounts of time and money.

More importantly, physical certificates are almost completely dependent on the issuer. If the issuing authority somehow closes down, goes bankrupt, or is unfortunately destroyed in a natural disaster, proof of the student's achievement is lost forever.

Some of the major obstacles faced by using physical certificates are:

- Every time the student has to send his transcripts to a verifier, he has to contact the university's concerned department, pay them money, wait a few days, and then go and collect it.
- Sending the credential to the verifier is completely dependent on the courier service.

- For the issuer, lot of time, money, and materials such as paper are wasted printing and authorizing the same credential.
- For an employers, to verify the credential, they have to contact the concerned issuer for each academic credential sent by the potential employee, and repeat this process for thousands of potential employees, wasting a ton of time and labor.
- Students who are refugees, and fleeing to other countries, have no way to prove their existing academic credentials.

15.2.5 Problems with Existing Digital Certificates

Digital certificates eliminate a lot of the problems just listed, mainly those of storage and transportation. However, many problems still remain:

1. A digital certificate's integrity relies on digital signatures. These signatures, although definitely an upgrade over physically printed credentials, still need to be stored and issued by a central key repository. This means trusting a central authority, which in turn leads to another single point of failure.
2. If somehow the key infrastructure is destroyed or lost, the certificates become unverifiable forever.
3. The employer will still have to contact the issuing authority for their public key, in order to confirm their identity. This leads to even more time wasted.

Overall, we can clearly see how much time, money, labor, and material is unnecessarily wasted in the current system of academic credential verification. As we will discuss in the next few sections, implementing a blockchain-based system will eliminate the need for a lot of overhead, and will allow for these resources to be allocated to much more important and urgent tasks instead.

15.3 RELATED WORK

There have been many attempts at building blockchain-based systems that issue degrees, documents, and learning certificates to the blockchain. Most of these attempts have some limitations, which we will explain in Section 15.6. There are mainly two types of implementations, some which are software implementations, and others which are research-based discussions. We will discuss them both in this section.

Sony Global Education [20, 21] has decided to use Hyperledger Fabric to create a custom blockchain and to host that system using IBM's cloud, which will provide the network infrastructure for issuing and verifying educational records. It will also track student learning progress throughout their educations. It will provide a transparent and validated record of all student achievements. SAP [22] is developing a set of command line libraries that use the Ethereum public blockchain to issue records of academic achievement, which they are piloting for a specific class on the OpenSAP MOOC (massively open online course).

Learning Machine and MIT [23] launched a system for issuing blockchain-based verifiable records to students (www.blockcerts.org/). It is the only fully developed and open source implementation currently available. First, the issuer invites the student to receive a blockchain credential. Once the student accepts the request, the issuer sends the student a blockchain and address, and then proceeds to store a hash of the document on the blockchain, then sends the credential back to the student. When a verifier wants to verify the student's credential, the student sends them their blockchain credential. The verifier in turn looks up the same credential on the blockchain. If both the credentials match, the verifier accepts the document. Educhain (https://educhain.io/) is a company based in Dubai [24] that enables instant issuance and authentication of digital records for institutions, corporations, and governments using blockchain. It provides a digital wallet, in which all of the student's achievements can be stored, and later verified by any potential employer or university.

Calicut University in India plans to use blockchain technology [25] for digital certification and validation of academic certificates and mark lists. University of Nicosia in Cyprus was the first university to issue a student's credential to the Bitcoin blockchain for its own MOOC [26].

Now we will review the research literature published related to the topic. Sharples and Domingue [27] analyzed the use of blockchain in academics. First, they discuss how the blockchain can be used to develop a system of consolidated academic records for a student, such as their transcripts, certificates, and achievements, then they proposed a distributed system for recording intellectual effort and ideas. They also proposed an intellectual currency called KUDOS, which could be used to establish a reputation based system for all academic institutions. It can then be used as the sort of cryptocurrency for the blockchain, and traded between the institutions and students, to issue or verify certificates.

Gräther et al. [2] proposed and evaluated a blockchain-based system for issuing and verifying certificates. They listed the benefits for the three main stakeholders: students, employers, and institutions. Finally, they described in detail a conceptual architecture which could implement the discussed features. They also discussed a system of the implementation they built and how it performed on an evaluation with the stakeholders.

Gresch et al. [28] discussed the implementation of a blockchain-based system in the University of Zurich (UZH) in Switzerland for the issuance and verification of diplomas. Their aim was not to build a universal system, but a system to specifically help UZH to issue student diplomas to the Ethereum blockchain. They discussed the requirements of the records issuance and IT offices of the university. They then proceeded to build a prototype on the Ethereum blockchain using smart contracts. Finally, they discussed how their specific prototype satisfies all their desired requirements.

They implemented a basic system, in which first the hash of a PDF file of the diploma is uploaded to the blockchain. It included a frontend which communicated directly with the Ethereum blockchain. Whenever a verifier wished to verify a diploma, they used the frontend to get the hash of the student's document, and compare it with the hash stored on the blockchain, thereby validating the diploma without ever contacting UZH.

Palma et al. [29] implemented a prototype for storing Brazilian higher education degrees to the Ethereum blockchain. They worked alongside the government and relevant authorities to implement an integrated degree issuing system for higher educational institutes in Brazil. They used the Brazilian Public Key Infrastructure for the purpose of digital signing. Their implementation made use of several smart contracts which ensured that only valid institutes can issue these degrees.

Further, they proposed a unique concept using smart contracts. They suggested that smart contracts could be used to keep track of a student's entire credit and course history. Then, when all the requirements were objectively complete, the contract could automatically issue a new degree for the student to the blockchain. This completely automated process can save a lot of time and money for the issuers, verifiers, as well as the students.

Blockchain in Education by Grech et al. [15] is a comprehensive overview of the use of blockchain technologies to improve on current educational systems. It was published by the Joint Research Centre (JRC), the European Commission's science and knowledge center. Its main aim was make European policy makers aware of this new and potentially disruptive domain. After discussing in great detail all the facets of this technology, they finally concluded with a set of recommendations to the European policy makers to help them in implementing, monitoring, and making laws for this domain. Following are the main conclusions:

- Blockchain technology will accelerate the end of a paper-based system for certificates.
- Blockchain technology allows for users to be able to automatically verify the validity of certificates directly against the blockchain, without the need to contact the organization that originally issued them.

- The ability of blockchain technologies to create data management structures where users have increased ownership and control over their own data could significantly reduce educational organizations' data management costs.
- Blockchain-based cryptocurrencies are likely to be used to facilitate payments within some institutions.

We will compare all these existing implementations with each other, as well as with the one we propose in Section 15.6.

15.4 THE PROPOSED SYSTEM

Almost all the implementations and literature evaluated in Section 15.3 proposed to only store the document hash in the blockchain. Then, the student had to send the document to the verifier, who hashed it again to compare it against the hash stored in the blockchain. Only [29] proposed something different, by suggesting the storage of all student credits, as well as course histories, in the blockchain, in order to automatically issue diplomas later. What we propose is more unique, robust, and secure. We propose to upload the entire credential, i.e. the entire degree, transcript, or learning certificate, to the blockchain. This is better than the existing systems in two areas, namely efficiency and robustness. In the case of efficiency, it removes the need to compute the document hash at two separate ends. In the case of robustness, it is much more secure and permanent to store the entire credential to the blockchain. The hash of a document is very sensitive, and even a small inadvertent change could lead to a big misunderstanding between the stakeholders. On the other hand, storing the entire credential is much more secure, robust, and fault tolerant. A minute mistake in uploading the certificate won't impact the core details of the credential a lot. Moreover, seeing the entire credential being stored in the blockchain will give the verifier much more confidence that the document is original and has not been tampered with.

Another difference in our implementation is the use of a central issuing authority that will grant the institutes the power to issue credentials. This will help the government to continue monitoring the issuance of major credentials such as diplomas, and will also prevent fake, malicious, or unknown institutes from issuing credentials to the students.

15.4.1 Choice of Blockchain

There are mainly three different types of blockchain architectures: public, private, and consortium [3]. For our proposal, the public blockchain architecture ticks all the boxes, for the following reasons:

1. A private blockchain is controlled by some authority, who decides which nodes can make transactions, and who can verify them. This destroys the whole purpose of a free and open blockchain, which created the decentralized paradigm in the first place. It leaves a bit too much control in the hand of a few special nodes. Therefore, the verifier cannot completely trust the credential.
2. A large public blockchain provides a ready to use place to develop applications on top of it. It saves a lot of developer time which would have been used to develop a completely new and customized blockchain.
3. Finally, a large popular blockchain already has a known factor of trust, as it is already being used for important transactions such as financial ones. Moreover, they already have millions of nodes in the network, which makes them even more secure, robust, trustworthy, and efficient to use.

15.4.2 Architecture and Design

Our proposed system is divided into three parts: the proposed architecture, the issuing of a new credential, and finally the verification process. But first, we present the overall workflow in Figure 15.1.

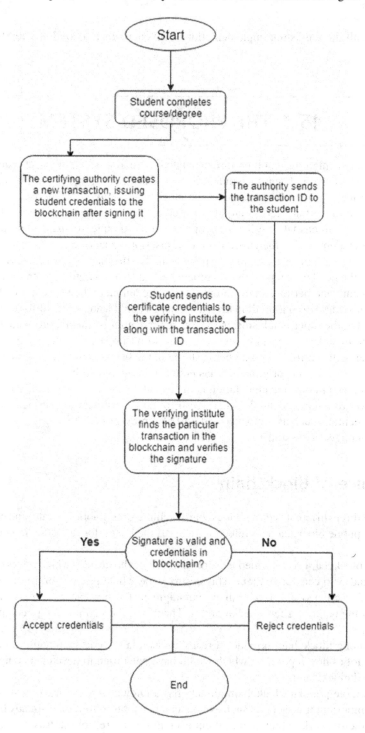

FIGURE 15.1   The overall workflow.

Next, the proposed central architecture of our proposal is given in Figure 15.2.

Now, we present the design for the issue module. It will be used to upload the academic records (transcripts, certificates, skills etc.) to the blockchain after approval from the institution. We have designed an easy six-step process, as presented in Figure 15.3.

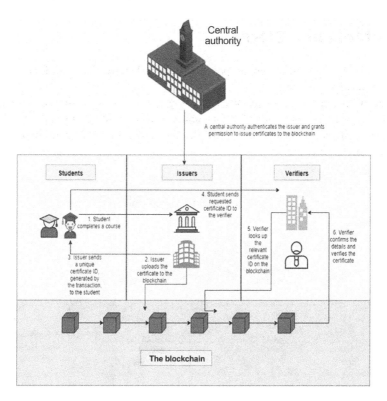

FIGURE 15.2   The proposed architecture.

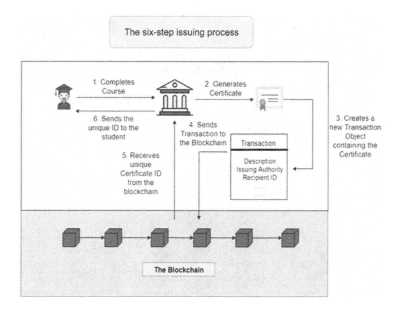

FIGURE 15.3   The six-step issuing process.

Now, we present the design for the verification module. It will be used by institutions such as universities, employers, and banks to verify a person's records on the blockchain, without the need to involve the original institution. It is designed as a 5five-step process, as presented in Figure 15.4.

The exact details, workings, and implementation of these architectures are presented in Section 15.5.

15.4.3   Contents of a Block

A single block in the blockchain of our proposed system will have a series of transactions, with each transaction storing a single credential.

As discussed in this section, our proposal is going to upload the entire credential, instead of just its hash. Therefore, we need some sort of JSON schema which will fit our certificate model. We have designed a unique certificate structure, which will be uploaded to the blockchain in the final implementation. It is given in Figure 15.5.

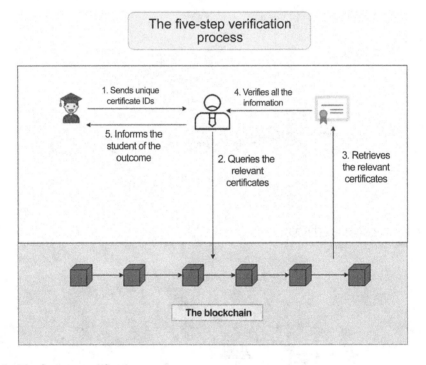

FIGURE 15.4   The five-step verification process.

```
{
    "id": "9489314001520539691260236535645428859783163161 6407868931102
    234519522628457978",
    "description": "Solidity Tutorial",
    "issuingAuthority": "VIT University",
    "recipientID": "15BIT0102",
    "issuingDate": "Friday, April 5th, 2019, 3:15:10 PM",
    "typeOfCertificate": "Course Completion",
    "details": "Good performance!"
}
```

FIGURE 15.5   The certificate JSON.

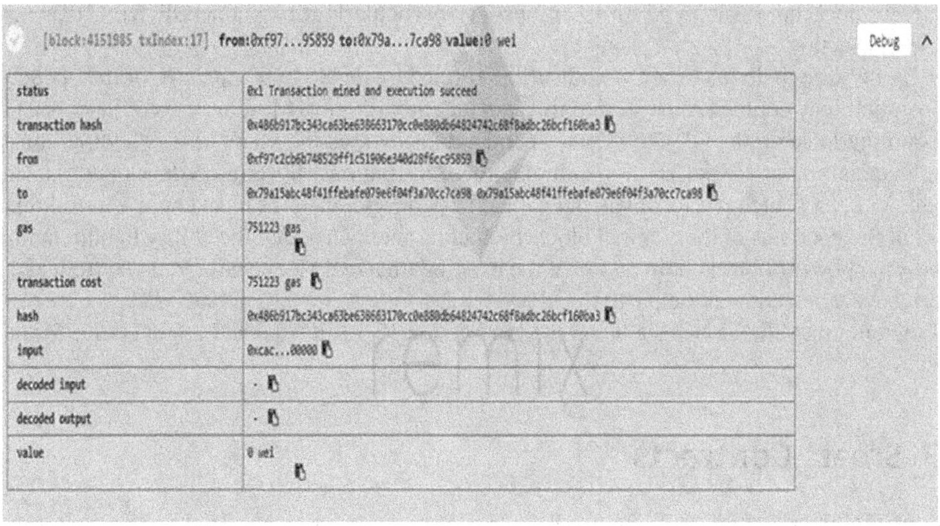

FIGURE 15.6   A transaction.

Each transaction in a particular block will store a unique credential in the form of the proposed structure. All transactions are then hashed and stored to a block, which is ultimately mined to the blockchain. Figure 15.6 presents the format of a transaction in our proposed system.

15.5 IMPLEMENTATION

15.5.1 Implementation Details

To demonstrate the proof of concept for our proposal, an Ethereum DApp (a distributed app deployed to the Ethereum blockchain) was built and deployed. It was then compared to our initial proposal and requirements, providing satisfactory results. Although there is a lot of scope for improvement (as discussed in Section 15.7.2), the main purpose of this app was not to build a complete product, but to demonstrate the viability of our proposal, and to provide a valid proof of concept.

The DApp was built using the Solidity programming language and deployed to the Ethereum blockchain. It made use of the core concept behind Ethereum: self-controlled accounts known as smart contracts. All these technologies are explained in detail in the next few sections.

15.5.2 Ethereum

Ethereum is an open source blockchain infrastructure, introduced by a young computer scientist by the name of Vitalik Buterin in late 2013 [30]. He found the original Bitcoin implementation of the blockchain to be quite limiting and constricting. He envisioned that the idea of a blockchain could be expanded. Virtually any field involving digital storage could benefit from the decentralized, immutable, and secure blockchain.

Buterin found that to build applications on top of Bitcoin's already existing financial blockchain is really complex and limiting. In particular, the only way to store data other than financial transactions in the Bitcoin blockchain was to add it to an opcode (particularly the opcode OP_RETURN) of a new blockchain transaction.

Even if one were to do that, they would still be limited by the 80 byte max size of the opcode, which would mean that they could at most store only a document hash in it. Moreover, there have been talks of Bitcoin planning to scrap the OP_RETURN opcode altogether, as they believe it is adding unnecessary clutter to financial transactions [29]. To overcome these limitations, Buterin co-developed the Ethereum blockchain, an open source platform which enabled easy development of blockchain apps on top of it. It contained all the good bits of the original blockchain idea, and then added the ability to build unique apps that harness the power of blockchain on top of the existing financial blockchain. It also introduced its own cryptocurrency, called ether, to help run the blockchain.

As Ethereum met all our criteria mentioned in Section 15.4.1, it was the perfect choice for our proof of concept.

15.5.3 Smart Contracts

The most well-known feature of Ethereum it is its use of smart contracts. In the simplest terms, smart contracts can be thought of as computer controlled nodes running on the Ethereum network. They have their own address and ether balance. The main difference between a smart contract and a normal account is that smart contracts are completely autonomous agents.

In technical terms, deploying a smart contract to the network is just like adding any other transaction to the chain, the only difference being that the smart contract creation transaction will not have a "to" address, because it is not sending money to anyone. Once deployed to the network, they have to follow exactly the instructions that were coded into them before being deployed. Since the particular instructions (code) are deployed to the blockchain along with the contract, they cannot be changed and are present on every node in the network. Due to these qualities, a smart contract can be used as an intermediary between, say two businesses which do not trust each other, and can be used to mediate transactions between them.

For example, business A wants to only send money to business B when it completes a certain amount of work. This logic can be coded into a smart contract and then deployed to the Ethereum blockchain. Once it has been done, no one can alter the conditions, and when the conditions are met, it is guaranteed that the smart contract will automatically run, and perform the required transactions. In the case of our system, we do not particularly use the autonomous feature of smart contracts. Instead, we use a complementary feature that allows us to store data in the form of *structs* directly to the Ethereum blockchain. Once the data is stored in the blockchain using the smart contract, we can write code into it that will later help us retrieve that data at any given point in time.

15.5.4 Solidity Programming Language

Solidity is the language written by the Ethereum blockchain developers that is used to code smart contracts. It is a Turing-complete language based on JavaScript. It is a strongly-typed language.

Smart contracts are executed on the blockchain using the Ethereum Virtual Machine (EVM) that is running in the Ethereum blockchain. The main function of the EVM is to convert the high-level solidity code into machine readable byte opcodes. These opcodes are the core assembly-level language instructions that actually run and carry out the contract instructions stored on the blockchain.

15.5.5 Building the Frontend

The frontend of our system, CryptoCert, was built using the React JavaScript framework. This choice was made looking at two main reasons. First, the entire business logic while making a DApp is run on the frontend. There is no server to which we can connect to retrieve information from the blockchain. We have to, instead, make use of the node running a full copy of the blockchain on the client side to retrieve information from it. Developing this logic using just plain, vanilla JavaScript would lead to really complex and long code. To avoid this, we decided to use React, which provides a fully developed JavaScript frontend library, that handles much of the dirty work for us.

Second, using React enables us to run our web server using NodeJS. This makes it much easier in the long run to host our website onto the real world, and also to use the plethora of amazing node packages available through the Node Package Manager (NPM), which make developing much easier.

Finally, we have also used a sub-library of React, called Next.js, to seamlessly create a multipage dynamic frontend for our DApp. Next.js also provides server side optimizations which help the web page to load quicker.

15.5.6 Connecting the Blockchain to our Frontend

In order to connect to the Ethereum blockchain to store and retrieve data via our frontend, we used the Web3.js library. It is the missing piece that allows JavaScript in the browser (frontend) to understand the solidity code stored in the blockchain, and execute commands on it by directly connecting to the blockchain through the client's node. Figure 15.7 explains this process.

When the solidity compiler complies our smart contract, it throws out two main pieces of information (Figure 15.8) for each compiled contract: the bytecode, which is sent to the transaction which initializes the smart contract in the blockchain; and the ABI (application binary interface), which is a JSON file that tells JavaScript exactly how to communicate with the blockchain through the smart contract. The ABI is what is given as an input to Web3, and tells it how to interact with the blockchain.

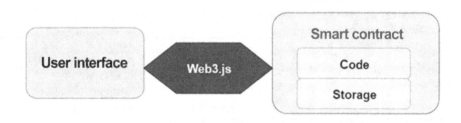

FIGURE 15.7   The need for Web3.js.

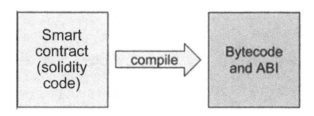

FIGURE 15.8   The solidity compiler overview.

15.5.7 The Smart Contracts

As explained in Section 15.1, smart contracts are the core elements behind our implementation, and are the ones that communicate with the Ethereum blockchain to store and retrieve academic credentials. We are only going to discuss these smart contracts, as the rest of the code is out of the scope of this chapter.

Our implementation made use of two smart contracts. The first one initializes the central issuing authority. The central issuing authority is the only entity (Ethereum account) that can add new credential issuers. This was done to prevent any random institute from impersonating another and start issuing certificates. It also ensures that only well-known and established institutes would have the power to issue academic credentials to students. This authority could, for example, be the education department of the government, which already has records of all the bona fide institutions, and can also be flexible enough to accommodate recognized online course organizations such as Coursera and Udacity. Note that this contract is only run once, in the beginning of the implementation. It is presented in Figure 15.9.

The second smart contract is the brains of our implementation. It is the one which initializes the issuer, and gives it the power to add new credentials, as well as retrieve previous ones. It also has some helper functions. Note that this contract ensures that only the issuer's address (Ethereum account) can be used to add new credentials, in order to prevent misuse. It is presented in Figure 15.10.

Another unique thing we've implemented in the second contract is the use of the *keccak256* function. It is basically the same as the SHA3 hashing function [31], implemented for use in the Ethereum world. We have used this function to generate a unique certificate ID for each certificate. This ID is generated by hashing the certificate description, the name of the issuing authority, and the current time. It is given to the student, who keeps it with them. Whenever the student wants to get a certificate verified, they send that unique ID to the verifier, who then compares it with the ID stored in the blockchain. As the ID in the blockchain is secure and immutable, if both the IDs match, then the certificate is valid. The verifier can then move on to check all the other displayed details of the certificate.

```
contract IssuerFactory {
    address[] public issuers;
    address public centralAuthority;

    modifier authorized() {
        require(msg.sender == centralAuthority);
        _;
    }

    function IssuerFactory() public {
        centralAuthority = msg.sender;
    }

    function createNewIssuer(string name, address creator) public
authorized {
        address newIssuer = new Issuer(creator, name);
        issuers.push(newIssuer);
    }

    function getIssuers() public view returns (address[]) {
        return issuers;
    }
}
```

FIGURE 15.9 The central authority contract.

```
contract Issuer {
    struct Certificate {
        uint id;
        string description;
        string issuingAuthority;
        string recipientID;
        uint issuingDate;
        string typeOfCertificate;
        string details;
    }

    address public issuer;
    string public issuerName;
    Certificate[] public certificates;

    modifier restricted() {
        require(msg.sender == issuer);
        _;
    }

    function Issuer(address creator, string name) public {
        issuer = creator;
        issuerName = name;
    }

    function generateID(string recipientID, string issuingAuthority)
private view returns (uint) {
        return uint(keccak256(recipientID, issuingAuthority, now));
    }

    function issueCertificate(string description, string issuingAuthority,
string recipientID,
        string typeOfCertificate, string details) public restricted {
        Certificate memory newCertificate = Certificate({
            id: generateID(recipientID, issuingAuthority),
            description: description,
            issuingAuthority: issuingAuthority,
            recipientID: recipientID,
            issuingDate: now,
            typeOfCertificate: typeOfCertificate,
            details: details
        });

        certificates.push(newCertificate);
    }

    function getNumberOfCertificates() public view returns (uint) {
        return certificates.length;
    }
}
```

FIGURE 15.10   The issuer contract.

Notice how the employer did not need to contact the university even once during this entire process, and can trust that what is being viewed is a genuine and untampered version of the student's credential.

The final system, CryptoCert, was hosted on https://edu-blockchain.herokuapp.com, and all the code can be found at https://github.com/varun27wahi/educhain. It satisfied all our major requirements. It will be compared with the other implementations in the next section. We end this section by showcasing a few screenshots of the system in Figure 15.11, Figure 15.12, and Figure 15.3.

FIGURE 15.11   The home page.

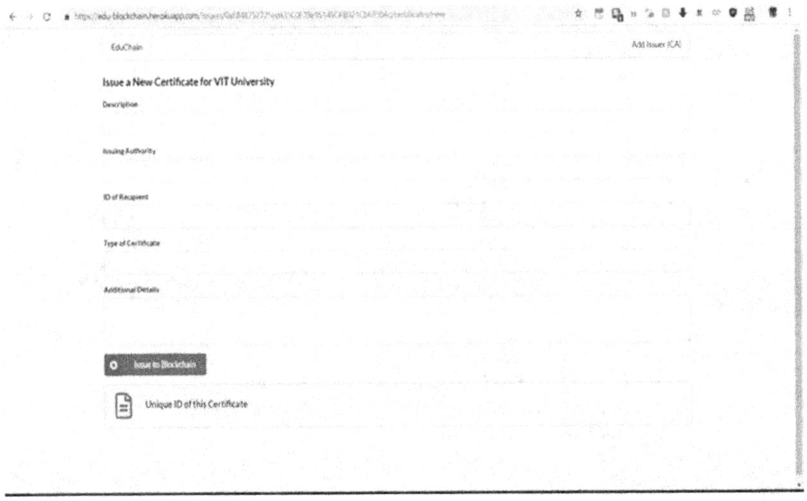

FIGURE 15.12   Issue a new certificate.

FIGURE 15.13   Verifying a certificate.

15.6 RESULTS

In this section, we compare how our system, CryptoCert, stacks up against the other implementations. We will also discuss about the monetary charges for implementing this system on the Ethereum blockchain.

15.6.1 Comparison with Other Implementations

We decided to compare the major implementations based on five different parameters in Table 15.1.

- Integrity and proof of existence: These are the two major features guaranteed by the use of blockchain, which make the entire idea possible. They ensure that the certificate exists, and that it has not been tampered with.
- Universal: This parameter looks at whether the current implementation can be extended to all the issuers or to different documents (such as transcripts or degrees).
- Approving authority: This parameter compares if the implementation has a central issuing authority which will approve issuers before they can start issuing credentials to the students.
- Hash or credential? (H/C): This parameter compares if the entire credential is being uploaded to the blockchain, or only the hash of the document.

The implementations [28] and [29] did not satisfy the "Universal" parameter, as the [28] system was implemented just for that particular university, with only its employees eligible to use the system; and [29] is again fully dependent on the Brazilian Public Key Infrastructure, and therefore mostly useful for Brazilian HEIs. The implementations [27] and [2] do not mention the use of a central issuing authority in their proposals. Blockcerts [23] does not have a central issuing authority, but does allow for the student to confirm the issuer's identity before getting the credential issued. The implementation [27] is unique in the sense that is does not give any concrete implementation. The main aim of the paper is to propose the idea of the intellectual currency, KUDOS, as discussed in Section 15.3. Apart from our implementation, only [29] have planned to upload something other than the hash of the document to the blockchain. In particular, in the diploma smart contract of their proposal, a *diploma struct* with core details about the diploma is being uploaded to the blockchain. We can conclude from the comparison that our implementation is the only one that satisfies all our elicited requirements completely.

TABLE 15.1   A Comparison between the Different Implementations

	INTEGRITY	PROOF OF EXISTENCE	UNIVERSAL	APPROVING AUTHORITY	HASH OR CREDENTIAL? (H/C)
Blockcerts [23]	✓	✓	✓	✓*	H
University of Zurich [28]	✓	✓	-	✓	H
Brazil HEIs [29]	✓	✓	-	✓	C
KUDOS [27]	✓	✓	✓	-	-
Lifelong Learning Passport [2]	✓	✓	✓	-	H
CryptoCert	✓	✓	✓	✓	C

partially met the requirement

15.6.2 Cost Analysis

In this section, we are going to explain the concept of gas in Ethereum. In Section 15.2, we have already seen how processing every new transaction to the blockchain takes a decent amount of time and money in the form of electricity, which is used to solve the complex cryptographic puzzle in order to mine the block (and make the transaction valid in the process).

Consequently, malicious users could easily overpower and spam the network by creating or using smart contracts that contain code which require a lot of computational power to run and execute. In doing so, they will waste a miner's precious resources which should instead have been used for mining genuine transactions that are essential for the functioning of a blockchain.

To preclude such a scenario, the developers of Ethereum introduced the idea of gas. Each trivial operation that is being executed by a smart contract (in the form of an opcode), be it simple addition and subtraction, all the way up to finally broadcasting a transaction, costs an amount of gas to the user. An example of the exact amount of gas charged by the EVM to carry out certain operations is presented in Table 15.2.

Therefore, each transaction issued by the user toward the smart contract costs a certain amount of gas. This total amount of gas is multiplied by another variable, known as the "gas price," to get the final cost in ether that the user has to pay in order to successfully complete the transaction. Gas price is the price per unit gas that the user is ready to pay in order to add the transaction to a block. The higher this price, the quicker and surer the block containing the transaction is mined to the blockchain. The gas price is normally specified in Gwei, which is approximately 10^{-9} ether.

The total costs for running each of the functions in our particular smart contracts were calculated, and the results are summarized in Table 15.3. As we can see, the costs are very minimal, and will not affect the current functioning of things in anyway. Most importantly, the issuer will not have to charge students extra to avail this facility. When we consider all the time and money that will be saved by replacing current systems with the proposed one, the issuer stands to instead make a large profit, and can sanction the extra money to more pertinent issues. Note that a user usually pays a gas price of 2 Gwei to balance between the need to get the block mined quickly and the expense of this being done.

TABLE 15.2   Gas Costs for Some Trivial Operations

VALUE	MNEMONIC	GAS USED	SUBSET	REMOVED FROM STACK	ADDED TO STACK	NOTES
0x00	STOP	0	zero	0	0	Halts execution
0x01	ADD	3	very low	2	1	Addition operation
0x02	MUL	5	low	2	1	Multiplication operation
0x03	SUB	3	very low	2	1	Subtraction operation
0x04	DIV	5	low	2	1	Integer division operation

TABLE 15.3   Cost for Each Operation ($)

OPERATION	COST	
	AT GAS PRICE OF 1 GWEI	AT GAS PRICE OF 2 GWEI
Creating the central authority	22 cents	45 cents
Adding a new issuer	19 cents	40 cents
Issuing a new certificate	5 cents	10 cents

15.7 DISCUSSION AND FUTURE WORK

15.7.1 Discussion

CryptoCert satisfied all our requirements, as discussed in Section 15.6.1. Most importantly, we were able to achieve academic credential verification without involving any third party (e.g. the issuer, or a notary). This is a major improvement over the traditional system of issuing and verifying academic credentials.

If implemented, our proposed system would bring about the following benefits for our stakeholders.

- For the student, getting credentials issued to the blockchain would save a lot of time and money. Students will not need to contact the university repeatedly to get transcripts sent to a potential university or employer. They also would not have to pay for multiple copies. They will also have control over their achievements, and lifelong indestructible records/proof of work.
- For the issuer, using the blockchain will save thousands of dollars in printing and administrative costs. Each document needs to be generated only once. Moreover, they will not have to deal with hundreds of queries each day from verifiers, asking them to confirm a student's degree or transcript. This will save them tons of money and overhead.
- For the verifier, hours of time spent verifying each detail of hundreds of employees will be saved. There will also be no need to contact the original issuer to verify academic credentials.

15.7.2 Future Work

The next logical step to our proposal would be to develop, for each student, a lifelong learning passport as proposed by Gräther et al [2]. The main idea behind this is to have a single document of sorts for each student, that keeps a track of all the student's achievements to date. This includes not just formal degrees or transcripts, but also MOOC certificates, informal skill endorsements, badges, approval ratings, and so on.

By doing so, students will have a permanent record of all their lifelong achievements. Also, they will not have to depend on the original issuer to get these records validated for a verifier, since they will be stored on the blockchain. Because of this, even if the original issuer is destroyed or goes bankrupt, or the student moves to another country, students will never have to worry again about losing these important credentials. They will act as his proof of achievement all over the world. Finally, our system, CryptoCert, could be improved in numerous ways. For example, we could add a search bar that the verifier can use to find a particular certificate, instead of manually going through the list of certificates in the table of a particular issuer. However, as mentioned before, this system was just built as a proof of concept, and was not the main goal of this chapter. These issues can be improved before deploying a production-ready solution.

15.8 CONCLUSION

In conclusion, we proposed and tested a new system, CryptoCert, for the issuing and verification of academic credentials. In doing so, we discussed in detail exactly how using blockchain technologies in any domain today can revolutionize all sectors and industries. In particular, we demonstrated how all the unique qualities of blockchain can be successfully harnessed to revolutionize the education sector. The system we proposed has innumerable benefits over the traditional paper-based system for issuing important academic documents. Not only that, we also discussed how our blockchain-based solution beats even the more modern digital certificates system in terms of, but not limited to, security, efficiency, and disintermediation. This is explained in much more detail in Section 15.2.4 and Section 15.2.5. Finally, we have successfully demonstrated how using blockchain to remove the need of a third party for the purpose of verification leads to a tremendous amount of time and money saved, which can be used instead in improving other major flaws in the current education system. Our study has described all the details of a proposed system, so that it can be used as a platform to disrupt traditional issuing systems.

15.9 ACKNOWLEDGMENTS

Aswani Kumar Cherukuri sincerely acknowledges the financial support from the Ministry of Human Resource Development (MHRD), Govt. of India, under the research grant: SPARC/2018–2019/P616/ SL under the SPARC scheme. Also, he acknowledges the financial support from Vellore Institute of Technology under the VIT SEED Grant.

REFERENCES

[1] "India to stamp out degree fraud with blockchain technology." *NewsBTC*, January 1, 2018. Retrieved May 17, 2019, from www.newsbtc.com/2018/02/06/india-stamp-degree-fraud-blockchain-technology/.

[2] Pandey, N. "Students, beware: 23 Universities, 279 technical institutes in India fake." *Hindustan Times*, March 21, 2017. Retrieved May 17, 2019, from www.hindustantimes.com/education/23-universities-279-technical-institutes-are-fake-delhi-tops-list/story-EqeyFblUDKphKvT2tdrvjI.html.

[3] Børresen, L. J., and S. A. Skjerven. "Detecting fake university degrees in a digital world." *University World News*, September 14, 2018. Retrieved May 17, 2019, from www.universityworldnews.com/post.php?story=20180911120249317.

[4] Mthethwa, S., N. Dlamini, and G. Barbour. "Proposing a blockchain-based solution to verify the integrity of hardcopy documents." 2018. Retrieved May 17, 2019, from 10.1109/iconic.2018.8601200.

[5] Husain, A., M. Bakhtiari, and A. Zainal. *Printed Document Integrity Verification Using Barcode* 70, no. 1 (n.d.). Retrieved May 17, 2019, from 10.11113/jt.v70.2857.

[6] Zaiane, O., M. Nascimento, and S. Oliveira. "Digital watermarking: Status, limitations and prospects, 02–01." *University of Alberta*, 2002. Retrieved May 17, 2019, from https://web.archive.org.

[7] Eldefrawy, M. H., K. Alghathbar, and M. K. Khan. "Hardcopy document authentication based on public key encryption and 2D barcodes." *International Symposium on Biometrics and Security Technologies* (2012): 77–81. Retrieved May 17, 2019, from 10.1109/isbast.2012.16.

[8] Grech, A., and A. F. Camilleri. "Blockchain in education." *Publications Office of the European Union*, 2017. Retrieved May 17, 2019, from http://publications.jrc.ec.europa.eu/repository/handle/JRC108255.

[9] Gräther, W., S. Kolvenbach, R. Ruland, J. Schütte, C. Torres, and F. Wendland. "Blockchain for education: Lifelong learning passport." *European Society for Socially Embedded Technologies (EUSSET)* 2, no. 10 (2018). Retrieved May 17, 2019, from https://dl.eusset.eu/handle/20.500.12015/3163.

[10] Nakamoto, S. *Bitcoin: A Peer-to-Peer Electronic Cash System*. Bitcoin, 2008. Retrieved May 17, 2019, from https://bitcoin.org/bitcoin.pdf.

[11] "Sony global education develops technology using blockchain for open sharing of academic proficiency and progress records." *Sony*, January 1, 2016. Retrieved May 18, 2019, from www.sony.net/SonyInfo/News/Press/201602/16-0222E/index.html.

[12] Zhang, Z. US Patent (US20170346637). 2017. Retrieved May 18, 2019, from www.freepatentsonline.com/20170346637.pdf.

[13] Boeser, B. "Meet TrueRec by SAP: Trusted digital credentials powered by blockchain." *SAP News Center. SAP*, July 24, 2017. Retrieved May 18, 2019, from https://news.sap.com/2017/07/meet-truerec-by-sap-trusted-digital-credentials-powered-by-blockchain/.

[14] Durant, E., and A. Trachy. "Digital diploma debuts at MIT." *MIT*, October 1, 2017. Retrieved May 18, 2019, from https://news.mit.edu/2017/mit-debuts-secure-digital-diploma-using-bitcoin-blockchain-technology-1017.

[15] "University blockchain experiment aims for top marks." *CNN*, January 1, 2019. Retrieved May 18, 2019, from https://edition.cnn.com/videos/tv/2018/06/28/blockhain-university-dubai-global-gateway.cnn/video/playlists/global-gateway/.

[16] Turkanovic, M., M. Holbl, K. Kosic, M. Hericko, and A. Kamisalic. "EduCTX: A blockchain-based higher education credit platform." *IEEE Access* 6 (2018): 5112–5127. Retrieved May 18, 2019, from 10.1109/ACCESS.2018.2789929.

[17] Chen, G., B. Xu, M. Lu, and N.-S. Chen. "Exploring blockchain technology and its potential applications for education." *Smart Learning Environments* 5, no. 1 (2018). Retrieved May 18, 2019, from 10.1186/s40561-017-0050-x.

[18] Dimitrov, D. V. "Blockchain applications for healthcare data management." *Healthcare Informatics Research* 25, no. 1 (2019): 51. Retrieved May 18, 2019, from 10.4258/hir.2019.25.1.51.

[19] Yakovenko, I., L. Kulumbetova, I. Subbotina, G. Zhanibekova, and K. Bizhanova. "The blockchain technology as a catalyst for digital transformation of education." *International Journal of Mechanical Engineering and Technology* (2019): 886–897. Retrieved May 18, 2019, from www.iaeme.com/ijmet/issues.asp?JType=IJMET&VType=10&IType=01.

[20] "Calicut university plans to utilize block chain tech for academic records." *The Times of India*, September 21, 2018. Retrieved May 18, 2019, from https://timesofindia.indiatimes.com/city/kozhikode/cu-plans-to-utilize-block-chain-tech-for-academic-records/articleshow/65892634.cms.

[21] "DFIN 511: Introduction to digital currencies." *University of Nicosia*, January 1, 2017. Retrieved May 18, 2019, from www.unic.ac.cy/blockchain/free-mooc/.

[22] Sharples, M., and J. Domingue. "The blockchain and kudos: A distributed system for educational record." *Reputation and Reward* (2016): 490–496. Retrieved May 18, 2019, from 10.1007/978-3-319-45153-4_48.

[23] Gresch, J., B. Rodrigues, E. Scheid, S. S. Kanhere, and B. Stiller. *The Proposal of a Blockchain-Based Architecture for Transparent Certificate Handling* (2019): 185–196. Retrieved May 18, 2019, from 10.1007/978-3-030-04849-5_16.

[24] Palma, L. M., M. A. G. Vigil, F. L. Pereira, and J. E. Martina. "Blockchain and smart contracts for higher education registry in Brazil." *The International Journal of Network Management* (n.d.): e2061. Retrieved May 18, 2019, from 10.1002/nem.2061.

[25] Hölbl, M., M. Kompara, A. Kamišalić, and L. Nemec Zlatolas. "A systematic review of the use of blockchain in healthcare." *Symmetry* 10, no. 10 (n.d.): 470. Retrieved May 18, 2019, from 10.3390/sym10100470.

[26] Zhu, L., Y. Wu, K. Gai, and K.-K. R. Choo. "Controllable and trustworthy blockchain-based cloud data management." *Future Generation Computer Systems* 91 (2019): 527–535. Retrieved May 18, 2019, from 10.1016/j.future.2018.09.019.

[27] Yang, M., T. Zhu, K. Liang, W. Zhou, and R. H. Deng. "A blockchain-based location privacy-preserving crowd-sensing system." *Future Generation Computer Systems* 94 (2019): 408–418. Retrieved May 18, 2019, from 10.1016/j.future.2018.11.046.

[28] Anand, A., M. McKibbin, and F. Pichel. "Colored coins: Bitcoin, blockchain, and land administration." *Cadasta*, May 2, 2017. Retrieved May 18, 2019, from https://cadasta.org/resources/white-papers/bitcoin-blockchain-land/.

[29] Buterin, Vitalik. "Ethereum: A next-generation smart contract and decentralized application platform." 2014. Retrieved May 18, 2019, from https://github.com/ethereum/wiki/wiki/White-Paper.

[30] "ethereum/eth-hash." *Ethereum*, January 1, 2018. Retrieved May 18, 2019, from https://github.com/ethereum/eth-hash.

[31] Bartolomé Pina, A. R., C. Bellver Torlà, L. Castañeda Quintero, and J. Adell Segura. "Blockchain en Educación: introducción y crítica al estado de la cuestión." *Edutec-e*, no. 61 (n.d.): 363. Retrieved May 18, 2019, from 10.21556/edutec.2017.61.915 (English version).

A Comprehensive Transformative Effect of IoT, Machine Learning, and Blockchain in Computing Technology

16

Deepshikha Agarwal, Khushboo Tripathi, and Kumar Krishen

Contents

16.1 INTRODUCTION

The world has witnessed the use of three well-known technologies: the Internet of Things (IoT), artificial intelligence (AI) and blockchain. Blockchain is a security-based mechanism which provides the services of greater trust, transparency, security, and privacy in business processes. This technology is based on the storing of a ledger in distributed locations, and hence, a greater level of security is ensured. The Internet of Things is also known as The Internet of Devices which consists of interconnected autonomous devices. The devices are connected always and are accessible at any point of time. Such a network serves the purpose of remote accessing, monitoring, and management of resources in a controlled way. It is a visionary technology which will connect everything on the fly. Machines which can act intelligently and make decisions independently without human intervention are equipped with AI. Until now, research was done independently in each of the three technologies. But actually, IoT cannot be realized in its full capacity until it is combined with blockchain to ensure security of communication and data and AI to make autonomous intelligent decisions by identifying patterns and optimizing resources [1]. These innovations combined together have the potential to change the future by improving business processes, creating new business models, and providing connectivity everywhere and all the time. In IoT networks, large amounts of data are produced. These data can be stored and managed efficiently using blockchain technology in combination with AI. This convergence will bring transformation in the way business models are incorporated; for example, autonomous agents like wireless sensors, automatic vehicles, and intelligent cameras will be capable of making decisions autonomously without human help. People will be able to use them for high-security money transactions using blockchain and will help in sustaining IoT networks with advanced features. Therefore, the convergence will help in improving management of data, security of data, and remote automation [2]. The following sections will present a detailed discussion of the three technologies and their effective convergence.

16.1.2 Data Management

As shown in Figure 16.1, The major services that are covered are: data management, authentication, and automation. These services help in improving standardization, privacy, security, and scalability of data [3]. IoT devices are varied in their capabilities and features. Depending on the type of application, the IoT devices can be anything ranging from smart meters, smart appliances, smart lighting, wireless sensors, relay machines, smart grids, etc. All these devices work continuously to generate huge amounts of data for interpretation and control. This data is stored on servers which work in a centralized manner. The data format may also be different because different companies manage those servers.

Blockchain can help in standardizing the format by creating a stable digital platform for such networks in the future. This is possible due to the usage of hash functions for creating blocks. This also helps in optimizing management of data by allowing interoperability.

16.1.2 Authentication

Securing the communication or transactions is of utmost importance in any application network because of the constant danger of eavesdropping by outside access. Hence, it needs to be taken care of using a strong security mechanism. There are several mechanisms defining protocols to deal with this problem, like symmetric and asymmetric encryption methods and use of hash functions. However, none of these are capable of dealing with large amounts of spontaneous data. Blockchain technology is the future of secure IoT systems. By using blockchain, trust on the devices is increased, and identity of every IoT device can be management separately and independently. It allows fast transactions with low costs. It is practically impossible to forge the immutable record of an identity. This is helpful because in the future, billions of devices will be connected to the Internet and will be acting as beacons in money transactions. This will require a centralized database for storing the separate identities of every transacting authority which will have to be maintained and managed. Consequently, identity management on a blockchain will play a key role.

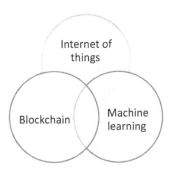

FIGURE 16.1 Services provided by convergence of IoT, ML and blockchain.

16.1.3 Automation

The need for remote monitoring and management of devices has always been the need of humans. This requires automatic functioning of devices without human intervention. It also necessitates fast and easy remote access. The joint convergence of these three technologies will leverage the automation process in any application. Automation heavily relies on intelligence and decision-making capabilities which are realized using machine learning models implemented for AI. It requires the use of smart contracts which specify a digital protocol to execute harmonious working of these technologies. These are similar to simple if/then rules which define a specific outcome based on the inputs given. It will enable extensive use of digital currency which was previously not used due to low security features.

16.1.4 Data Management

Securing the communication or transactions is of utmost importance in any application network because of the constant danger of eavesdropping by outside access. Hence, it needs to be taken care of using a strong security mechanism. There are several mechanisms defining protocols to deal with this problem like symmetric and asymmetric encryption methods and use of hash functions. However, none of these are capable of dealing with large amount of spontaneous data. Blockchain technology is the future of secure IoT systems. By using Blockchain, trust on the devices is increased, identity of every IoT device can be management separately and independently. It allows fast transactions with low costs. It is practically impossible to forge the immutable record of an identity. This is helpful because in future, billions of devices will be connected to the internet and will be acting as beacons in money transactions. This will require a centralized database for storing the separate identities of every transacting authority will have to be maintained and managed. Consequently, identity management on a blockchain will play a key role.

16.2 CONCEPT OF IOT

The Internet of Things has been be defined as "An interconnection of several autonomous devices of variable capabilities and capacities which can wirelessly or through wired connection, send and receive sensed parameters in the form of information to and from the remote observer" [4]. Each of these devices is equipped with some necessary components to enable Internet working among them. The IoT is a huge network of such devices which can sense, transmit, make decisions, and act in physical reality. The number of devices or types of devices is not fixed in any IoT network. This number merely depends on the type of application which is being realized by the IoT. Some examples of full scale applications are: smart grids, smart homes, smart surveillance, smart traffic monitoring, structural health monitoring [5][6], etc., to name a few. Each of these applications involve the use of different types of devices to work in conjugation to realize complete automation. For example, smart home application will enable mechanical and digital machines working together. Of course, to make them IoT-enabled devices, they need to be equipped with several sensors, antenna, and small microprocessors to make it an intelligent device. The major benefits of an IoT system are first, access to information anywhere and everywhere and at all times [7][8]; and second, fast transfer of data, low cost of packet transmission, and automation of the highest level. The next section will discuss the components of an IoT system.

16.2.1 Components of IoT

The complete implementation of an IoT system requires a combined effort of several fundamental components [9] together as shown in Figure 16.2, with the seven following components:

1. Sensors.
2. Networks.
3. Cloud.
4. Intelligent Analysis.
5. Actuators.
6. User interface.
7. Data.

16.2.1.1 Sensors

These are small transducer devices capable of sensing a parameter. Wireless sensors can also communicate this parameter to a nearby device through wireless communication by taking multihops. These sensors can sense parameters like pressure, humidity, temperature, heat, velocity, strain, salinity, and light as physical values which are converted into electrical signals for transmission purposes. These sensors can be attached onboard the device and can sense continuously until the battery is exhausted. The batteries can be replaced later on. Advantages of sensors include small size, low cost, ease of deployment, and low power consumption [10]. However, they suffer with issues like small battery capacity, low coverage area, duplication of data, inefficient routing, etc.

Van Laerhoven [11] provided an overview of various types of sensors used for building smart applications. Some examples of sensors are accelerometer, thermocouple or thermistors, level sensors, photo resistor sensors, hygrometer sensors, strain gauge sensors, and anemometer sensors.

16.2.1.1.1 Mobile Phone Sensors

In today's world, mobile describes a ubiquitous device which contains a multiverse of several sensors embedded in a single device. It is also handy and user friendly with super data processing speed and capabilities. As the popularity of IoT applications have increased, researchers are finding the mobile phones as a convenient solution to building the IoT network. The sensors embedded in the mobile phones can sense many parameters like tilting, touch, sound, light, and movement with built-in cameras with high sensitivity.

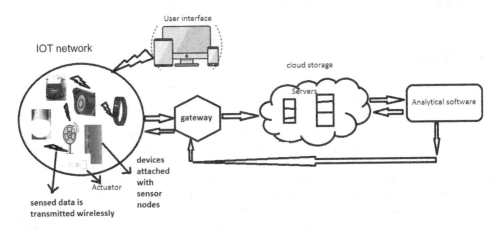

FIGURE 16.2   Components of IoT.

Nowadays, several smartphones are already equipped with inbuilt sensors for barometric pressure, temperature, and humidity. Smart mobile homes can collect data using these sensors which can be analyzed using machine learning algorithms to deduce significant information related to running, walking, cycling, etc. Another ubiquitous device is the medical sensor wristband which can sense heartbeat, temperature, calories, etc. This data is then analyzed to determine the fitness level of a person.

Wang et al. [12] have discussed mobile applications which can be completely compatible with smartphones. They have showed that it can be useful for a college student for assessing the health and performance. Another paper by McClernon and Choudhury [13] researched the detection of situations and cases when the user starts smoking. This has been done using context information; for example: number of smokers in the vicinity, location of the person, and other associated activities.

16.2.1.1.2 Wearable Sensors

This paper discusses sensors which can be worn on a human body[13]. Wearable sensor devices can play a major role in creating an IoT-enabled healthcare solutions. Wearable sensors are available as smart watches and smart patches. Big brand companies like Apple, Sony, and Samsung have floated smart watches with advanced features like connectivity with a smartphone for easy tracking and access. Also, sensors can be used to track brain activities by attaching them on the head of the patient. EEG signals catch brain waves and frequency changes to detect the neurological health of the patient. In the future, this can help to train the mind for increasing concentration, stress management, and overall wellbeing of the person.

16.2.1.1.3 Environmental Sensors

These sensors are used for sensing parameters of the physical environment to check toxicity levels, pollution, pressure, humidity, etc. They can be effectively used in weather forecasting. In the future, they will be able to be used for sensing presence of viruses in the vicinity for effective solutions and send alerts to the person on a mobile phone [14]. They can also be used to check food quality and agricultural products.

16.2.1.2 Networks

For the parameters to be communicated to the remote observer or the controlling machine, a suitable network should be setup with proper connectivity. In some applications, Internet connection is a necessary requirement. For others, local connections like Bluetooth connectivity and personal area networks can be useful. Efficient working requires a protocol suite and gateway to convert between the different protocol standards across different networks. As IoT is a collection of several different devices of variable capabilities and functions, the protocols followed are also different. A proper method of mixing them together to make the system working together is a very import feature of IoT.

16.2.1.3 Cloud

The huge amount of data generated due to continuous sensing and transmission has to be stored and managed effectively. The cloud is the place which provides storage of the data on the fly. There are also several software and other applications available which can be accessed using the cloud by the ubiquitous device to process the data and produce analytical results. The cloud can allow fast access and retrieval of stored data, which is a necessary requirement of any IoT network. The cloud is pool of vast resources which have huge computing power, huge storage capabilities, options for networking, analytical software, and other service components which make it an attractive resource for the consumers. Another related term which is being coined is fog computing. This term is used for a facility which can provide very high performance of computation and offers scalability with a decreased cost of operation. Similarly, edge computing is a preferred technology when the requirement is for bulk of data for processing and storage.

16.2.1.4 Intelligent Analysis

This term is related to use of algorithms to carry out analysis of the collected data parameters to find meaning in the data and make suitable predictions. Intelligent analysis provides undisputable one-point decisions, e.g. whether room temperature should be lowered, or when to apply brakes in a fast-moving car. This can be achieved using machine learning methods for productive analysis. Deep learning models can be a great help in this arena and can suggest plans for making useful business decisions [15].

16.2.1.5 Actuators

These devices are electromechanical relays which can carry out physical actions based on the analysis of the data; for example: closing a switch, putting on a hose pipe, or unlocking a door. There are several actuators, which can induce movement. They are categorized into the following categories: electrical, hydraulic, and pneumatic actuators. The selection of the appropriate actuators solely depends on the operation. For example, mechanical motion is produced by hydraulics using fluid or hydraulic power.

16.2.1.6 User Interface

This part involves a user-friendly interactive model which can be easily understood and controlled by the IoT user. This interface provides the actual human-to-machine communication. It hides all the complex details of the underlying protocols and the working procedures of the network ad makes it handy for any user to work in the IoT application. Interface can be realized in the form of a software or hardware. Some examples include: Amazon's Alexa, Apple's Siri, and Google's voice assistance. The design is a major feature of the interface which defines the ease of use with the multifunctional capability for controlling the IoT environment. This can be achieved using touch interfaces, use of colors, font, or voice.

16.2.1.7 Data

This is one of the most important entities of any IoT network. The actual information which is generated by the sensors attached to devices is communicated to the cloud for storage and processing for analytics. The data is voluminous in any IoT application, due to the continuous working. The IoT network is never on sleep mode. Significant amounts of duplicate information has to be removed, and only necessary data has to be communicated to reduce the excess load on the network. Data has to be communicated using packets of small size to avoid packet delay, data loss, etc.

16.2.2 Architecture of IoT

Several different architectures have been proposed by researchers for IoT [16]. We discuss them in detail in what follows.

16.2.2.1 Three-Layer Architecture

This is the most basic architecture for an IoT network which was introduced when IoT was perceived as a network. In this architecture, there are three layers: perception layer, network layer, and application layer. The function of each of these layers is explained in what follows.

Perception layer: This layer is the lowermost layer, which acts as the physical layer of the open system interconnection (OSI) reference model. It is concerned with sensor devices which sense and gather information about the environment. It is concerned with physical measurement and functioning of the sensors, bit transmission, etc.

Network layer: This layer is similar to the network layer of the OSI model, which is responsible for actual connection with other smart devices in the network. Other functions involve processing and transmission of data collected by the sensors.

Application layer: This layer provides user interface which is application-specific to the user e.g., smart homes, smart health monitoring, smart transportation.

This architecture is purely a primitive one which provides the basic dead of how the IoT is going to function. However, it ignores security aspects of the data, multiprotocol communication, multinetwork issues, and reliability of communication. Hence, it is necessary to include more layers to deal with this aspect.

16.2.2.2 Five-Layer Architecture

This architecture is the most prevalent one as it covers most of the aspects which were not taken care of in the three-layer architecture. The five layers are: transport layer, processing layer, business layers, perception layer, and application layers. The perception and application layers have the same function as in the three-layer architecture. The functions of the remaining three layers are explained in what follows.

Transport layer: This layer is used to transfer the data collected by the sensors to the processing layer and vice versa. It is done by networks: wireless, 3G, LAN, Bluetooth, RFID, and NFC.

Processing layer: This layer is also called the middleware layer. The major functions of this layer are storing, analysis, and processing of the vast quantity of data. This layer manages and provides a services to the lower layers by employing databases, cloud computing, and Big Data processing modules.

Business layer: This layer manages the entire IoT system, which includes applications, business and profit models. It also deals with providing security and privacy to users. Figure 16.3 shows the architectures of IoT.

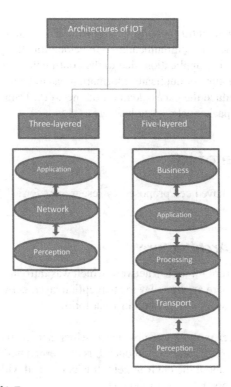

FIGURE 16.3 Architectures of IoT.

16.2.2.3 Brain–IoT Architecture

One other architecture which was proposed by Ning and Wang [7] is a tree-level framework much similar to the functioning of a human brain. The first level is like the human brain, which has the ability to memorize, store, react, and make decisions. The second level is the spinal cord of the network, which constitutes the distributed network to support all the devices in communication. Third layer is made of a network of nerves which correspond to actual physical devices like sensors and other physical components.

16.2.2.4 Cloud- and Fog-Based Architectures

The previously described architectures are protocol-based and define different steps for completing IoT communication [17]. However, there can be other architectures which can be system-based instead of protocol-based. Examples of system-based architectures are cloud architecture and fog architecture. In some applications, cloud is a very important entity which can store huge amounts of data and allow processing functions by providing access to software applications. The cloud is a central storage resource. It has the advantages of flexibility and scalability.

In a fog-based system architecture, sensors and gateways carry out the functions of data processing and analytics. The architecture has layered framework for monitoring, preprocessing, storage, and providing security considerations. The next layer functions to monitor the power, resources, responses, and services. The preprocessing layer deals with the functions pertaining to filtration, processing, and analytics of data from sensors. Another layer called the temporary storage layer executes the functionalities for storage, data replication, and distribution. Finally, encryption and decryption, data integrity, and privacy of data is ensured by the security layer. In the end, monitoring and preprocessing functions are carried out at the edge of the network before the data is sent to the cloud.

16.2.2.5 Social IoT Architecture

The Social IoT or SIoT network explores the relationship between the objects and the human. This type of network allows easy navigation to all the connected devices through a single device using social networks. The social relationship is based on trustworthiness of the connected devices. The basic components of this network are bots, which are actually both devices and services. These bots are responsible for creating a network of devices based on trust relations, which helps in seamless operation between different devices for completing a complex task. Some other required components are a unique ID for every device, met information, security control, a service directory, and relationship management.

The architecture proposed for the SIoT has a server-side architecture. The server manages and connects all the devices and aggregates the services. It acts as a single point of service to the users, and hence eliminates the inconvenience of additional messages and components. It has three layers. The *base* layer contains the database for storing the details of all the devices, attributes, meta information, and their relationships. The second layer is the *component* layer, which contains the code to interact with the devices, query their status, and use a subset of them to effect a service. The uppermost layer is the *application* layer, which provides services to the users. Similarly, the device side has two layers. The first is the *object* layer, which enables a device to connect to other devices and allows communication between them using standard protocols and exchanges of information. The second layer, the *social* layer, manages the execution of applications, queries, and interaction with the application layer on the server.

16.2.4 Design Issues of IoT

The IoT network suffers from some major drawbacks, which can be envisioned as greater security threat, scalability issues, failures and significant downtimes, design of small sensors, and no standard set of rules [18–20], as shown in Figure 16.4.

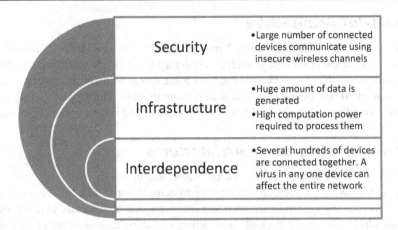

FIGURE 16.4   Issues in IoT networks.

IoT devices have to be equipped with one or more small sensor nodes which have a full capability of sensing parameters and transmitting them wirelessly to the nodes in the vicinity. The design of such small sensors with large ranges of transmission, processing and networking power, and low power consumption is a challenging problem for realization of IoT. Another important consideration is the power backup; the working of sensor node should be such that it is able to sustain and provide services for a long time. Suitable methods, i.e. sleep/awake sensing, should be done to save the battery from being quickly depleted. Some of the sensors might get charged by the device to which they are connected and need no battery replacement. We also need to choose a suitable wireless networking protocol; for example, Zigbee, Sigfox or LoraWAN.

These connected devices produce huge amounts of data which have to be stored, managed, and analyzed. The storage and time delay issues are important considerations. If there is a bug in any one device, it might affect all the other connected devices, as well, so a failure of any one device can lead to the failure of the entire network. This requires strict security measures to be taken to protect all the devices in the network by applying multilevel firewalls.

The IoT is characterized by huge collection of different devices or things. Every device requires a new unique ID which is either locally or globally unique for communicating. Currently, we use Internet-based communication using IPv4 or IPV6 with billions of devices connected together. But once IoT is realized in its full potential, we will need to think of another ID system to allow such large number of devices to connect together. Another major problem will be dealing with the huge congestion, delays, and data packet failures in the network.

Middleware suffers with limited support for IoT devices. It should be designed in a way to help to interoperate with different varieties of communication protocols and devices, but this is not always possible, so there a requirement for strict compatibility with different devices and protocols for communication for which a proprietary solution is the better choice.

16.3 MACHINE LEARNING

Machine learning (ML) is the method to achieve artificial intelligence (AI) in a machine. Artificial intelligence is a technology which enables a machine to simulate human behavior [21]. As the name suggests, ML involves procedures and algorithms to make the machine learn from experience and develop its own thinking and decision making capabilities. This requires training using some known cases and later testing the machine's understanding of finding a solution to a problem based on the training given to it. The training allows machine to develop its own model which acts as a black box for the machine's CPU to produce a favorable output, given some input. This allows automation to happen, and at times, the machine's deciding ability provides a fair judgment of the situations. If a machine achieves high levels of training, it can make decisions and manage the surrounding automatically without requiring any human intervention. Today, several researchers have developed and proposed machine learning–based applications which can also be applied in IoT.

16.3.1 Background

ML is comparable with traditional programming methods in which the data and is output is fed as an input to the computer which develops a computer program or a model. This program or model can then be used to generate independent results, given any input. Machine learning can be envisioned as seeds to a bigger tree. Today, we can find several applications which are already working with machine learning to create an AI environment [22]. Examples include Google's search engine, drug identification, medical imagining, e-commerce, Facebook, space exploration, and robotics, to name a few. Figure 16.5 shows the general working of a machine learning model.

There are several algorithms existing to realize ML. However, all algorithms have the three following basic components.

- Knowledge representation using decision trees, sets of rules, instances, graphical models, neural networks, support vector machines, model ensembles, and others.
- Evaluation of candidate programs or hypotheses using accuracy, prediction, and recall, squared error, likelihood, posterior probability, cost, margin, entropy k-L divergence, and others.
- Optimization of candidate programs using combinatorial optimization, convex optimization, and constrained optimization.

There are four types of machine learning:

- Supervised learning or inductive learning, where training data is labeled.
- Unsupervised learning, in which training data does not include desired outputs or labels. An example is clustering. It is hard to tell what is good learning and what is not.
- In semi-supervised learning, few outputs are available in the training data.
- Reinforcement learning provides rewards for the deciding capability of the machine. Based on the positive or negative rewards, the machine develops an understanding. It requires a good choice of parameters to decide reward framework.

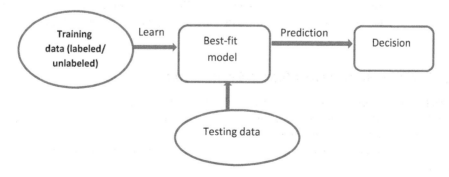

FIGURE 16.5 Process of machine learning.

TABLE 16.1   Comparison of Supervised, Unsupervised and Re-Enforced Learning

TYPES\CRITERION	SUPERVISED	UNSUPERVISED	REINFORCEMENT
Type of data	Labeled	Unlabeled	Not predefined
Type of problems	Regression, classification	Association, clustering	Reward-based
Training	Supervised externally	Not supervised	Not supervised
Approach	Mapping inputs with labels to known outputs	Identification of patterns in unlabeled input	Maps input to an output and gets points; tries to collect more positive points to reduce error

Currently, the most mature and most well-understood machine learning approach is that of supervised learning. Several applications have been already developed in which supervised learning model has provided easy learning. Table 16.1 shows the comparison of these methods in a concise form.

16.3.2 Algorithms

Supervised learning involves building of a regression model such that the output is continuous value, e.g. stock prediction. The algorithms used are linear regression, decision tree, random forest, and neural network. Classification is done when the output is discrete and can fall under a specific category due to higher similarity index, e.g. corona or not corona. It involves the use of algorithms: logistic regression, support vector machine, naïve Bayes, decision tree, random forest, neural network [23].

Unsupervised learning is done on unlabeled data such that the output is grouping of data known as clustering of data points. This can be achieved using k-means, hierarchical, mean-shift, density based dimensionality reduction-process of reducing the dimension of the feature set called as principal component analysis. These algorithms are detailed in what follows.

16.3.2.1 Linear Regression

- Find best-fit line for establishing a function between the labeled inputs x and y. X and Y are called independent and dependent variables.
- Function is used to estimate accurate values. Example: price of used car.
- Line is known as regression line and is represented by the well-known linear equation

$$y = m \times x + c \qquad (16.1)$$

- where y is dependent variable, m is slope, x is independent variable, and c is the intercept
- Two types are simple linear regression and multiple linear regression. Simple linear regression has one independent variable, whereas multiple linear regression has more than one independent variable.

16.3.2.2 Logistic Regression (Logit Regression)

- Classification algorithm which can estimate discrete values 0 or 1.
- Used to predict the probability of occurrence of any event.
- Fits the unlabeled data to a category.
- An example can be identifying the best area of interest for a student to decide their course stream.

16.3.2.3 Decision Tree

- Classification algorithm used for creating categories and also for continuous dependent variables.
- Data is divided into several homogeneous sets based on attributes which are most significant.
- An example to understand this algorithm is the Jezzball game from Microsoft.

16.3.2.4 Support Vector Machine

- Classification technique whereby every data item is plotted as a single point in the n-dimensional space.
- 'n' is number of features whereby the value of each feature is the coordinate in space.
- So if there are only two features, then every data point will be plotted on the graph with X and Y coordinates defined by the two features, e.g. age and salary. Afterwards, the best-fit line is found to estimate the relation between the coordinates.

16.3.2.5 Naïve Bayes

- Classification algorithm works with the assumption that if a dataset has the presence of any feature, it is not related to any known category.
- Example: an object like a fruit can be categorized as apple if the color is red or green, it is round in shape, and the diameter is about 3 inches.
- Easy and simple to build, and very useful when the dataset is huge.
- Outperforms other methods in most cases.
- Bayes theorem is used to calculate the posterior probability $P(a|x)$ from $P(a)$, $P(x)$ and $P(x|c)$ as:

$$\Pr(a|x) = \Pr(x|a)\ \Pr(a)/\Pr(x) \tag{16.2}$$

- Where $\Pr(a|x)$ is the posterior probability of *class* (a, *target*) given *predictor* (x, *attributes*), $\Pr(a)$ is the prior probability of *class*, and $\Pr(x|a)$ is the is the posterior probability of *class* (x).

16.3.2.6 k-Nearest Neighbors

- Useful for classification and regression.
- Stores the available cases and later uses them for classifying new cases using the vote of k-nearest neighbors.
- Distance functions can be Euclidean, Manhattan, Minkowski, or Hamming distance.
- Out of these, the Euclidean, Manhattan, and Minkowski are used for continuous function, and Hamming distance is used for categorical variables.
- Choosing appropriate values of "K" turns out to be a difficult task. However, some drawbacks of KNN are: computationally expensive, higher-range variables can cause bias in predictions.

16.3.2.7 k-Means

- This algorithm is used for unsupervised algorithm to "k" cluster the unlabeled data according to their characteristics.
- The points inside a cluster are of homogeneous characteristics, whereas they are heterogeneous to other clusters.
- Clusters are formed by picking "k" centroids and contain points with similar centroids.

16.3.2.8 Random Forest

- This technique refers to the collection of decision trees.
- It is used for classification whereby for every new object, the attributes are matched with the best fit and the tree votes for the class which is most similar to it.
- The planting and nurturing of the tree is done in the following manner:
- Suppose, there are "N" number of cases in the training data, then "N" number of samples are taken randomly but with replacement. The significance of these samples is for growing the tree.
- Suppose, for "M" number of input variables, there is another number "m" which is lesser than "M." This smaller number is specified at each vertex of the tree where, out of "M" variables, "m" is chosen randomly to carry out the best split. Value of "m" is constant while the forest is growing.
- Pruning is avoided. The tree is allowed to grow to its fullest.

16.3.2.9 Dimensionality Reduction Algorithms

- It is used in unsupervised learning models to reduce the number of dimensions or features of a dataset.
- The need for doing the reduction is that ML performance becomes poor when there is a large number of features associated to particular data.
- This reduction offers several advantages like improved accuracy, faster result generation, less storage requirements, and less complexity.

16.3.3 Case Studies on ML Applications

16.3.3.1 Facebook

Facebook is a well-known social media platform for forming social relationships with different people and groups. It also allows chatting conversations, photo sharing, tagging functionality, and detection of inappropriate posts, pictures, and videos. This is achieved using moderation and flagging by machine learning algorithms to detect them. Those messages or content which are labeled as inappropriate are straightway blocked from viewing automatically by the ML model. Facebook also uses ML to make the latest posts to be shown first on the page to the user. This needs identification of the time it was posted and to synchronize with the current time to identify as a latest post. In the future, Facebook aims at creating an amalgam of several ML algorithms for sorting queues and prioritizing posts based on number of times its shared, their severity, and the likelihood that users are breaking the rules.

Facebook uses an ML model named WPIE, which stands for "whole post integrity embeddings," for assessing the posts and other content. The algorithms judge the type of content based on several points together by taking as input, posts, caption, image, or video. This means that the algorithms judge various elements in any given post in concert, trying to work out what the image, caption, poster, etc., reveal together. The use of certain words in the caption (like "potent") might tip the judgment one way or the other. Figure 16.6 shows the prioritizing procedure used by Facebook.

16.3.3.2 Google Maps

Google Maps is a great utility application for people who are travelers. It provides features like fastest route, alternate routes, voice navigation, and congestion on the road. It is said to employ ML models for prediction. Google has partnered with DeepMind, an Alphabet AI research lab, to improve the accuracy of its traffic prediction capabilities. Google Maps uses memory to store the historic traffic patterns for roads over time and then analyzes it to deduce important results for estimating the best route between a

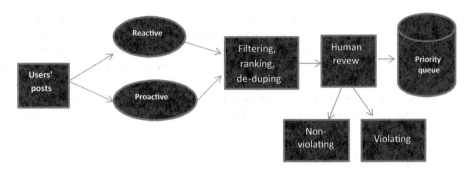

FIGURE 16.6 Prioritizing procedure used by Facebook.

pair of locations. This is done by looking at the traffic pattern at different times of the day, along with the average speed of the traffic. The algorithms combine this historical data with live traffic conditions to suggest the best route and estimated time of arrival (ETA) to reach the destination. It also accepts feedback—recommendations from users and local government guidelines—to create a near-perfect solution. Incident reports from drivers over the Google feedback mechanism allows to quickly generate alerts and modify the navigation for alternate routes due to lane blockages, road damage, accidents, etc. As a result, Google Maps automatically reroutes to help in avoiding any traffic jams and getting to the destination on time.

16.3.4 Issues in ML

Machine learning works best on a suitable dataset of large size [23][24]. The better we can train the model, the better its decision making abilities will be. However, it is very difficult to achieve such ideal data. Normally, the data available is not labeled properly or the size of data is too small. Moreover, the parameters used to define the input/output relationship might not be very clear in the data due to tolerance errors. This might cause a different best-fit line, and the perceived function definition for the data points will be incorrect.

   Like any other software system which is capable of a security breach, the ML algorithms–based systems are low on security and can be hacked by an outsider, destroying the entire system. The database can be modified and the training data can be altered to generate incorrect functions. ML puts more focus on algorithms which can be easily implemented and understood. In this effort, it may compromise the performance and complexity improvements that are typically studied in mathematical programming. Optimization is at the heart of all ML algorithms. But, for proper realization, ML needs proper resources like storage facilities of test and training data, better models, and application-dependent methods to achieve better and more refined results. Currently, ML models are very rigid and use the same well-known standards across all kinds of data and applications to which ML is applied. This does not guarantee customized optimization, and may lack some special features defined by the testing data; this may hamper the accuracy percentage of correct decisions by the machine.

16.4 BLOCKCHAIN TECHNOLOGY

As the name suggests, blockchain is a shared and immutable ledger which helps in the process of recording, storing, processing, and tracking of assets in any business network. An asset is any tangible or intangible quality or information, such as patents, property, copyrights, houses, cars, cash, gold, etc. [25]. As the name suggests, it is made of blocks of data stored in a distributed manner which forms a chain network. Blockchain facilitates the trading of virtually any asset with the least security risk and low cost. It is a very important because all businesses run on information. There is a heavy requirement of fast and accurate transactions. Blockchain provides sharing and storage of information on immutable ledgers which can be accessed and read or written only by members who are given permission. It is suitable for tracking orders, payments, accounts, and production. It allows transparency of order details, and hence helps in building grater trust and confidence on the system. It was invented in 2008 by a group of people for creating a public system for transactions. It was inspired by Bitcoin, which was the first cryptocurrency to solve the problem of a convenient method of online business. It offers the advantages of greater trust, security, and efficiency.

16.4.1 Background

In the beginning, the first generation of blockchain technology was intended to be used by the public with cryptocurrency as its only application. It was governed by a centralized entity. Later, the concept changed to allow distributed storage and process of the blocks. Of course, it is more difficult to manage the distributed resources, but still it saves from a single point of failure to happen. However, due to low scalability, the time consumed to calculate mathematical formulas was a drawback [26]. Mostly, the public blockchain technology is useful for only specific kinds of organizations or businesses. This was so because if every aspect of their business goes public, competitors may take advantage and increase their business by using it. Due to this reason, a second type of blockchain was introduced called as a private blockchain. It is private because the organization using it can decide whom to allow access to their information. Now there are four major types of blockchains: public, private, hybrid and consortium.

In public blockchain, the transactions can be verified using either of two consensus methods: proof of work (PoW) or proof of stake (PoS). If there are no peer participating groups for solving transactions, then it will become non-functional. Some advantages of such a technology are easy access, no need for intermediate parties, and transparency among the groups. The private blockchain offers the same set of features as a public blockchain, but it is in a restricted environment of permissioned groups. Examples of this type are MultiChain, Hyperledger Fabric, Hyperledger Sawtooth, and Corda. It offers the following advantages: fast operation and scalability. Disadvantages include not being purely distributed and a less secure environment. The consortium or federation type of blockchain allows use as both public and private features. Some aspects are made public, and the rest remain private. This chain is maintained by several organizations together. Hence, there is no single centralized authority for controlling the transactions. There is also a validator node which validates the transactions and also initiates or receive transactions. Examples of consortium blockchain are Energy Web Foundation and IBM Food Trust. Advantages offered by this type are customizability and control over resources, more security, better scalability, efficiency and a well-defined structure. The disadvantages include less transparency and less anonymity compared to other types of blockchain. The fourth type is called hybrid blockchain, which is similar to the consortium type. It deploys the best of both private and public types. Examples are Dragonchain and XinFin's hybrid blockchain. The advantages envisioned by this type are that there is no need to make everything public, customizable rules, more immunity to security attacks, high scalability. However, it is not completely transparent, and updating is difficult.

16.4.2 Architecture

Blockchain is a peer-to-peer network based on Internet Protocol (IP) [27]. The general architecture for blockchain contains major components of node, transactions, block, miners, and consensus. Figure 16.7 shows the architectural components in a P2P network.

1. Node: Nodes are every entity or participating device which is capable of processing and verifying the transaction. Every node has a replica of the entire database. The nodes are responsible for carrying out algorithms on any new transaction. If all nodes give the same consensus, it is considered as a valid transaction and accepted into the ledger.

2. Transactions: Transactions are used to hold data, sender's address, and recipient's address. The transactions get distributed, verified, and processed by every node in the chain network for entry into the blockchain (Figure 16.8).

3. Block: Blocks bundle several transactions together and distribute them among each node of the network. Blocks are created by the miners and consist of metadata stored in the header of the block. This is useful in verifying the data inside the block. Metadata contains fields—previous header hash, root hash, timestamp, "n" bits, number once used.

4. Miners: Miners are special nodes which are used to add hash function value to the block. Due to the use of hash functions, metadata are secure and cannot be altered. The miners also check the difficulty level of the block.

5. Consensus: The processing and validation of the blocks is called consensus. It contains a set of rules which are followed by the nodes for validating a transaction. If the network becomes scalable, the consensus also grows stronger to control the security aspects.

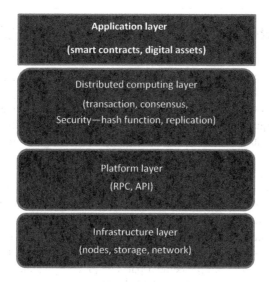

FIGURE 16.7 Architecture of blockchain.

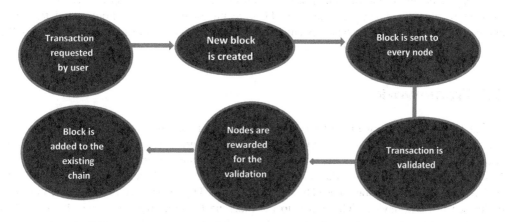

FIGURE 16.8 New block added into the chain.

16.4.3 Issues in Blockchain

Blockchain technology suffers with speed issues and the transactions become extremely slow for large number of transactions [28]. The system is not yet adept at becoming scalable. A second issue is interoperability between different peer networks and protocols. Various projects have been launched to deal with this problem; for example, Smartbridge architecture can allow communication between different hosts [29]. Every transaction requires some amount of computation to solve complex mathematics to process, verify and provide security to the network. To remove this problem, PoW mechanism is changed into PoS. There are still very few people who have the knowledge and training to maintain this network. Adoption of blockchain completely into a network is dependent on the professionals managing it. There is an acute shortage of blockchain experts to deal with other problems. Another important issue is the lack of standardization. This leads to interoperability issues, increased costs of computation, complex mechanisms, and low scalability [30][31]. Security and privacy are also of prime importance.

16.5 CONVERGENCE OF IOT, ML, AND BLOCKCHAIN

Discussions on the preceding topics have led to the fact that blockchain, IoT, and ML are going to be the key technologies which will drive the next wave of the digital universe [32]. Imagine a smart home IoT network which consists of all tube lights, bulbs, fans, and TVs connected to each other. Let each of these devices have their own unique identity and work using blockchain. Blockchain identity means that the device is working on its own and is autonomous. Hence, by using smart contracts, mini payments can be made to the device to enable its working. In this way, any user can make payments to the device, which will work according to the tariff charged. All these devices are connected in a peer-to-peer blockchain network, and so they will also store data pertaining to their use, their performance, and their failures. Here, ML can be used efficiently to increase and optimize the working of all the devices in the IoT network [33]. ML algorithms inside the device can use the data stored in the devices to determine if any failure has happened and immediately suggest or take appropriate action to reduce the downtime. This would also allow real-time monitoring and maintenance of the IoT devices [34]. Additionally ML can also improve the processing of ordering of replacement parts by precisely calculating the statistics. This kind of system can be realized for a commercially available building or rooms where investors can invest in the building and maintenance of these devices, and they can earn their share on the profit of individual device.

This kind of convergence will benefit business models, commercial products, and their services. This will largely be applicable on vehicles, industrial machines, CCTV cameras, etc. This will aid in development of value-aided services to the user. These technologies also revolutionize analytics, storage, and maintenance of Big Data database systems and their performance improvement [35]. This will also provide convenience and use-on-demand services.

16.5.1 Framework

Figure 16.9 displays the framework for the combined working of these three technologies. As can be seen, the framework can be defined to be working in a three-level hierarchy. The first tier is the lowest level, which comprises the devices which are attached with sensor nodes capable of sensing and transmitting wirelessly. They can send or receive data packets. The user can access these devices through a user interface which is mostly mobile phone–based browsing or access. The second tier, or the middle tier, consists of intelligence in these devices. This refers to the machine learning algorithms which can be locally installed in these devices, or there can be a central controller running the ML algorithms [36]. It can also

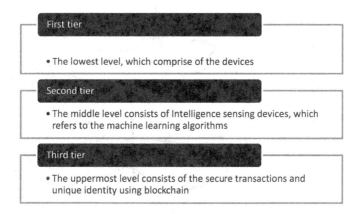

FIGURE 16.9   Framework of levels of working concept of IoT devices, ML and blockchain.

be implemented using cloud infrastructure. These algorithms collect the data and analyze it for making predictions. For example, breakage in the refrigerator door lock or food items stored in the fridge getting stale. These predictions can be used to call for immediate corrective actions by putting off the refrigerator using a small attached electromechanical relay. The uppermost tier, or the third tier, consists of the secure transactions and unique identity using blockchain. Every device connected in the IoT network can become its own profit center by working autonomously. Any client can access these devices for personal use and profit. The blockchain necessitates a smart contract binding these devices and the consumers [37]. Whenever a consumer wants to access the devices, he has to make a micro payment to the device to get the services. Once this transaction is validated, its added to the ledger and due to its transparent process, each of the members are aware of the transaction and the details. Figure 16.9 refers the framework concepts of computing technologies.

16.5.2 Future Applications for Combined Computing Technology

The convergence of these technologies is going to build a revolution far beyond what the human mind can encompass. A few sectors which will highly benefit from this convergence are healthcare, transportation, education, banking, etc. The two latest applications among them are discussed next. Figure 16.10 shows the convergence of the three computing technologies.

16.5.3 Issues in Combined Computing Technologies

This convergence has the ability to create a future digital transformation which will change the look of the world. However, the realization of such a network holds some necessary points to ponder upon. The network should have all the necessary and sufficient infrastructure to support the Big Data which will be generated by IoT and blockchain technologies [38]. Blockchain technology is still in its infant stage and suffers from scalability and computation delay issues. To make the network fast, administrators must ensure high-speed connectivity to transmit large amounts of data, and hardware and protocol changes in devices to cooperate together. Lots of funding is required by stakeholders to allow research for realizing the convergence and for the development of this network. Moreover, all the three technologies are currently working separately for different applications [39]. Their convergence will require heavy changes in the protocol suites to allow compatibility between the flow of payload. Serious security concerns are also

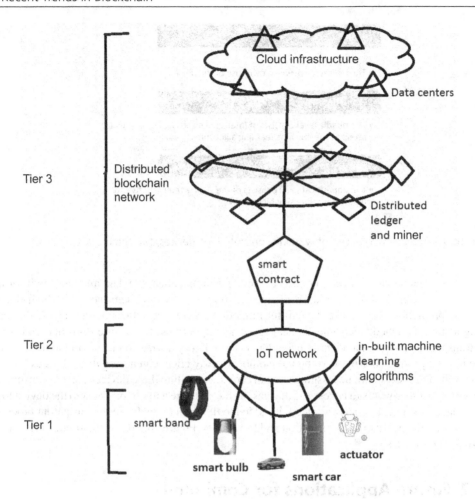

FIGURE 16.10 Framework of convergence of the three technologies.

present in ML modeling, input data and vulnerability of IoT devices. Security breaches can cause complete failure of the system, as everything is connected together and dependent for its operation. Another very important aspect is that due to its vastness, any failure in the system is going to lead to heavy downtime and loss of revenue for the stakeholders. A single point of control and monitoring is dangerous for the automated system. This will also involve legal issues, as several groups of people will access the network and share the services. Legal contracts [40] can be self-executing smart contracts which may be using AI for its automatic control and infrastructure. However, a smart contract is not alterable or stoppable once its executed. This could cause as recoverable damage in case of a bug or virus which gets inside the network. The larger convergent systems become, and the more autonomous they are, the more likely we are to be faced with deciding difficult questions. Figure 16.11 displays the issues occurring due to the convergence. On the basis of this discussion, the key issues can be listed as follows.

- Interoperability.
- Infrastructure.
- Legal regulations.
- Funding.
- Governance.
- Lack of expertise.

- Scalability.
- Latency, computation power.

To deal with these hurdles, several steps can be taken. First, adequate and targeted funding should be achieved, as all technological research and development requires funding. Governments should design the rules for conglomeration of these different technologies. Second, responsible ownership should be granted. For seamless operation across different platforms, private and public partnerships should be invited. Finally, there are severe ethical issues and protection and regulation requirements [41]. The regulations should be designed to cover the application and the way the emerging technology is used, rather than the technology itself.

16.6 FUTURE RESULTS FOR COMBINED COMPUTING TECHNOLOGIES

16.6.1 Conceptual Impact of IoT, ML, and Blockchain in Intelligent Transportation Systems

Road transportation is another important area which requires automated, intelligent, and secure operation including traffic monitoring and accident alerts [42]. Consider a case where a car is moving at a fast speed on a national highway in an area which is very sparsely populated. There are very rarely police vans or ambulances along the entire stretch of the highway. If the car suffers an accident on the highway, it will be a long time before anybody will be able to find out about the situation, and help may only arrive after a long delay. To deal with any such situation, all the people traveling inside the car will be equipped with medical sensing devices. Even the vehicle will be attached with sensors to sense stress and strain on the vehicle. Once the vehicle suffers an accident, the sensors attached to the body will generate abnormal data which will be stored in the blockchain ledger using unique identity. The results will be analyzed by the ML software using sensing IoT devices on the cloud to assess the situation, the degree of damage, and vital statistics of the people traveling inside the vehicle. In the case that the situation is beyond control and people need immediate medical help, an alert will be generated by the software to the nearby police and ambulances to reach to the crash site and look at the parameters from the ledger. In this way, fast identification can save lives in real time. A flowchart is shown in Figure 16.11.

Following proposed algorithm demonstrates the use of blockchain [43] on Unsupervised learning model of Machine Learning:

```
// CREATE BLOCKCHAIN STRUCTURE OF NEWLY RECEIVED DATA FROM PATIENT
determine hash value for adding digital fingerprints in blocks
store data in the blockchain

   {//Build the starting block of the chain
      Hash value of starting block =0

//add new blocks into the chain

// Consensus algorithm (Proof of work) for mining the block
     Calculate new hash value
       Is proof True?
       If false, Create new proof = proof +1

// Mining a new block using previous block and proof
```

```
//Check validity of blockchain
// APPLYING UNSUPERVISED MACHINE LEARNING MODEL OF LOGISTIC REGRESSION
Get Block (values of X and Y)
Intialize X and Y values
store the error values
initializing learning rate alpha = 0.01
e = 2.71828
  //Training
for all values of X, Y and number of epocs
  Accessing index after every epoch
// Make prediction
double p = -(b0 + b1 * x1[idx]+ b2* x2[idx])
//calculate the final prediction by applying sigmoid
  double pred = 1/(1+ pow(e,p));
//Calculate error
err = y[idx]-pred;
// Update the values
  b0 = b0—alpha * err*pred *(1-pred)* 1.0
  b1 = b1 + alpha * err * pred*(1-pred) *x1[idx]
  b2 = b2 + alpha * err * pred*(1-pred) * x2[idx]
  Print all the values b1, b2, b0 after every step
  error.push_back(err);}
// sort based on absolute error difference //Testing result
double pred=b0+b1*test1+b2*test2; //make prediction
if(pred>0.5)
pred=1;
else pred=0;
  }
```

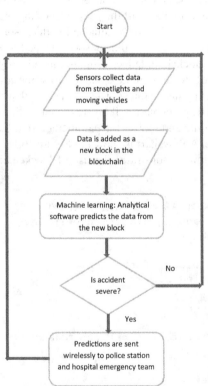

FIGURE 16.11   Flowchart of intelligent transportation system with computing technology.

16.6.2 Conceptual Impact of IoT, ML, and Blockchain in Intelligent Healthcare Systems

Healthcare is one of those fields which will always be needed to sustain healthy life and wellbeing of people. Nowadays, people are very much aware of their health and want to stay fit and in fine shape. Medical services and techniques have also evolved and advanced to a premium state. The healthcare sector covers medical illness, medicines, accidents, and insurance [44]. There are also mobile-based applications which can access the monitoring devices attached to a person's body to measure real-time values for temperature, heartbeat, blood pressure, etc. Sometimes these devices are embedded inside the skin or they may be wearable in the form of a smart wristband. The attached sensors can relay the parameters to the mobile phone which is connected 24/7. These devices have unique blockchain ID, and any new information which may indicate any abnormal difference in the reading of the patient will be stored in the ledger of the blockchain in a secure way. The ledger can be read by the ML software to carry out analytics and carefully identify the present condition of the patient. Based on the records, the ML software can immediately start a procedure to call the doctor or nearby ambulance in case any disorder is found. The doctor can access the ledger and see the reports and previous history to take measures. This method will allow fast identification and accurate prediction, and will reduce the risk to the patient. It is typically suitable for elderly citizens and also critically ill patients. A flowchart is shown in Figure 16.12.

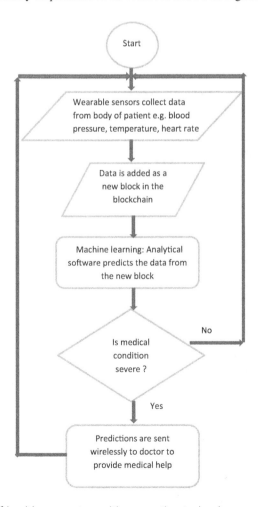

FIGURE 16.12 Flowchart of healthcare system with computing technology.

Expected outcome in both the application areas will be highly dependent on the machine algorithms used and implemented for further decisions using blockchain technology. With the rapid growth in blockchain technology in different areas of applications, the results are being reported in various research papers and articles [45–47].

The concept of applying blockchain with supervised machine learning algorithm is shown in the following algorithm:

```
// CREATE BLOCKCHAIN STRUCTURE OF NEWLY RECEIVED DATA FROM PATIENT
determine hash value for adding digital fingerprints in blocks
store data in the blockchain

{//Build the starting block of the chain
    Hash value of starting block =0
        first.chain = []
        first.create_block(pf=1, prev_hash='0')

   //add new blocks into the chain
            New_block ={ index_len(first.chain) + 1, 'new_block_timestamp':
str(datetime.datetime.now()), 'new_block_proof': proof, 'prev_hash': prev_hash}
        first.chain.append(block)
        return New_block

    // Consensus algorithm (Proof of work) for mining the block
        new_prf = 1
        check_new_prf = False

      do while (check_new_prf == False)
            {hash_value1 = hashlib.sha256(str(new_prf**2 -prev_prf**2).encode()).
hexdigest()
            if (hash_operation[:4] == '00000')
                then check_new_prf = True}
            else
                new_prf = new_prf + 1

       return (new_prf)

    def hash(first, blk):
        coded_blk1 = json.dumps(blk, sort_keys=True).encode()
        return hashlib.sha256(coded_blk1).hexdigest()

    def blkchain_valid(first, blkchain):
        prev_block = blkchain[0]
        blk_index = 1

      do  while (blk_index < len(blkchain))
            blk = blkchain[blk_index]
            if (blk['prev_hash'] != first.hash(prev_block))
                then return False

            prev_prf = prev_block['proof']
            prf = blk['proof']
            hash_op = hashlib.sha256(str(prf**2 - prev_prf**2).encode()).hexdigest()
            if (hash_op[:4] != '00000')
                then return False
                else prev_blk = blk
```

```
            blk_index = blk_index + 1

        return True

// Mining a new block
    prev_blk = blockchain.print_prev_blk()
    prev_prf = prev_blk['proof']
    prf = blockchain.pof(prev_prf)
    prev_hash = blkchain.hash(prev_blk)
    blk = blockchain.create_block(prf, prev_hash)

    generating_response = block['index':'timestamp':'proof': 'prev_hash']

    return (generating_response)

//Check validity of blockchain
    Is_valid = blockchain.chain_is_valid(blkchain.chain)
Is_valid = blockchain.chain_is_valid(blkchain.chain)

// APPLYING MACHINE LEARNING SUPERVISED MODEL OF LINEAR REGRESSION TO DETECT
THE DISEASE
Get Block (x,y,size of (x or y))
Input the values of x in array a
Input the values of y in array b
Input the size of x and y =num
Average of x= all values of x/num
Average of y= all values of y/num
Find the deviation of a and b
For (every value of num = i)
 {
  div[i] = a[i]—mean_xy;
  txy= div[i] * div[i];
  sum_x_y = sum_x_y + txy;
 }
 Sum_x_y = sum_x_y/num;
 *s = sqrt(sum_x_y);
For every value 'i' of X and Y
{
 s_xy = s_xy + divx[i] * divy[i];
 cor_coeff = s_xy/(num * sx1 * sy1);
//regression coefficient is 'x over y' or 'y over x'
 type_coeff
{if (strcmp(type_ceoff, "x over y") == 1)
    then reg_coeff_x_y = corr_coeff * (sx1 / sy1);
   lin_reg_coeff = reg_coeff_x_y

   else reg_coeff_y_x = corr_coeff * (sy1 / sx1);
   lin_reg_coeff= reg_coeff_y_x
 } else
  Input new reg_coeff
}
```

The results for these applications will be more exciting in terms of collecting good number of identified parameters. Thus, in the future, these algorithms can be applied for the combined technologies in different applications. The metrics can be calculated in integrated software for real-time simulations. These metrics can be privacy, security, transferable and non-transferable identities, mobility, text/voice data, positive and negative responses, etc.

16.7 CONCLUSION

This chapter aimed to cover the major aspects of three recent technologies: the Internet of Things, machine learning, and blockchain. This work presents a comprehensive analysis of the existing research in computing technologies and a transformative impact on different applications like in healthcare and intelligent transport systems by using IoT, ML, and blockchain technologies together for accessing useful information. The convergence of blockchain, Machine Learning, and IoT will provide scalable, secure, high-level intellectual functioning that will be the new paradigm of digital information systems. This convergence will bring transformation to the services and applications provided for complete automation. Several issues are envisioned—like data mining, data analytics, scalability, infrastructure development, funding issues, security threats—which are the challenging research areas in combined computing technology. However, with proper use of machine learning algorithms, IoT devices, and blockchain technologies, together with regulations and partnerships of private and public authorities, challenging issues can be addressed in the near future.

REFERENCES

[1] Balasubramanian, T. A. "The convergence of IoT, AI and blockchain technologies." *IEEE India Info* 14, no. 1 (January–March 2019): 58–62.

[2] Daniels, J., S. Sargolzaei, A. Sargolzaei, T. Ahram, P. A. Laplante, and B. Amaba. "The internet of things, artificial intelligence, blockchain, and professionalism." *IT Professional* 20, no. 6 (November–December 1, 2018): 15–19.

[3] Rejeb, Abderahman, John G. Keogh, and Horst Treiblmaier. "Leveraging the internet of things and blockchain technology in supply chain management." *Future Internet* 11, no. 161 (2019): 1–22.

[4] Al-Fuqaha, A., and M. Guizani. "Internet of things: A survey on enabling technologies, protocols, and applications." *IEEE Communications Surveys & Tutorials* 17 (2015): 2347–2376.

[5] Zanella, A., and C. Angelo. "Internet of things for smart cities." *International Journal of Internet of Things* 1 (2014): 22–32.

[6] Chen, S., and H. Xui. "A vision of IoT." *International Journal of Internet of Things* 1 (2014): 349–359.

[7] Stankovic, J. A. "Research directions for the Internet of Things." *IEEE Internet of Things Journal* 1 (2014): 3–9.

[8] Liu, T. "The application and development of IoT." *Proceedings 2012 International Symposium on Information Technologies in Medicine and Education (ITME)* 2 (2012): 991–994.

[9] Zanella, A. "Internet of Things for smart cities." *IEEE Internet of Things Journal* 1 (2014): 22–32.

[10] Yang, J. "Broadcasting with prediction and selective forwarding in vehicular networks." *International Journal of Distributed Sensor Networks* (2013): 1–9.

[11] Dachyar, M. "Knowledge growth and development: IoT research." *ScienceDirect Heliyon* 5 (2019): 1–14.

[12] Widyantara, M. O. "IoT for Intelligent traffic monitoring system." *International Journal of Computer Trends and Technology* 30 (2015): 169–173.

[13] Laerhoven, K. V. "Making sensors, making sense, making Stimuli: The state of the art in Wearables research." *IEEE Pervasive Computing* (2020): 87–91.

[14] Wang, H., and C. Liao. "What affects mobile application use? The roles of consumption values." *International Journal of Marketing Studies* 5 (May 2013).

[15] McClernon, F. J., and R. R. Choudhary. "I am your smartphone, and I know you are about to smoke: The application of mobile sensing and computing approaches to smoking research and treatment." *Nicotine and Tobacco Research* 15, no. 10 (October 2013): 1651–1654.

[16] Hammi, B. "IoT technologies for smart cities." *IET Journals* (2017): 1–14.

[17] Margeret, V. "A survey on transport system using internet of things." *IOSR Journal of Computer Engineering* 20 (2018): 1–3.

[18] Kadam, S. G. "Internet of Things (IOT)." *IOSR Journal of Computer Engineering* (2018): 69–74.

[19] Bajaj, R. K. "Internet of things (IoT) in the smart automotive sector: A review." *IOSR Journal of Computer Engineering* (2018): 36–44.

[20] Agarwal, Deepshikha. "Study of IoT and proposed accident detection system using IoT." *IOSR Journal of Computer Engineering* 22, no. 1 (2020): 27–30.

[21] Angra, S., and S. Ahuja. "Machine learning and its applications: A review." In *2017 International Conference on Big Data Analytics and Computational Intelligence (ICBDAC)*, pp. 57–60. Chirala, 2017.

[22] Ray, S. "A quick review of machine learning algorithms." In *2019 International Conference on Machine Learning, Big Data, Cloud and Parallel Computing (COMITCon)*, pp. 35–39, 2019.

[23] Obulesu, O., M. Mahendra, and M. ThrilokReddy. "Machine learning techniques and tools: A survey." *2018 International Conference on Inventive Research in Computing Applications (ICIRCA)*, pp. 605–611, 2018.

[24] Zantalis, F., and G. Koulouras. "A review of machine learning and IoT in smart transportation." *Future Internet* 11 (2019): 94–100.

[25] Dorri, A., and S. S. Kanhere. "Blockchain for IoT security and privacy: The case study of a smart home." *Proceedings of the 2017 IEEE International Conference on Pervasive Computing and Communications Workshops* (PerCom Workshops), pp. 13–17, 2017.

[26] Rauchs, M., A. Glidden, and B. Gordon. *Distributed Ledger Technology Systems: A Conceptual Framework.* Cambridge Center for Alternative Finance: Judge Business School, 2018.

[27] Pilkington, M. "Blockchain technology: Principles and applications." In *Research Handbook on Digital Transformations*, pp. 1–39. Edward Elgar, 2016.

[28] Dodd, N. "The social life of Bitcoin." *Theory, Culture & Society* 35 (2018): 35–56.

[29] Makhdoom, I., and M. Abolhasan. "Blockchain for IoT: The challenges and a way forward." *Proceedings of the 15th International Joint Conference on e-Business and Telecommunications.* Vol. 2, July 26–28, 2019.

[30] Adiono, T., B. A. Manangkalangi, R. Muttaqin, S. Harimurti, and W. Adijarto. "Intelligent and secured software application for IoT based smart home." *Proceedings of the IEEE 6th Global Conference on Consumer Electronics (GCCE)*, pp. 1–2, October 2017.

[31] Kshetri, N. "Can blockchain strengthen the internet of things?" *IT Professional* 19, no. 4 (2017): 68–72.

[32] Keertikumar, M., and M. Shubham. "Evolution of IoT in smart vehicles: An overview." *Proceedings of the 2015 International Conference on Green Computing and Internet of Things (ICGCIoT)*, pp. 804–809, October 2015.

[33] Cam-Winget, N., and Y. Jin. "Can IoT be secured: Emerging challenges in connecting the unconnected." *Proceedings of the 53rd Annual Design Automation Conference (DAC'16)*, June 2016.

[34] Louridas, P., and C. Ebert. "Machine learning." *IEEE Software* 33, no. 5 (September–October 2016): 110–115.

[35] Fabiano, N. "Internet of things and blockchain: Legal issues and privacy. The challenge for a privacy standard." *Proceedings of the 2017 IEEE International Conference on Internet of Things (iThings) and IEEE Green Computing and Communications (GreenCom) and IEEE Cyber, Physical and Social Computing (CPSCom) and IEEE Smart Data (SmartData)*, pp. 727–734, June 21–23, 2017.

[36] Atlam, H. F., and G. B. Wills. "Intersections between IoT and distributed ledger." *Advances in Computers* (2019): 1–41.

[37] Hossain, M. M., M. Fotouhi, and R. Hasan. "Towards an analysis of security issues, challenges, and open problems in the internet of things." In *Proceedings of the IEEE World Congress on Services*, pp. 21–28. IEEE, June 2015.

[38] Atlam, H. F., and A. Alenezi. "Blockchain with internet of things: Benefits, challenges, and future directions." *International Journal of Intelligent Systems and Applications* 10 (2018): 40–48.

[39] Strugar, D., R. Hussain, and M. Mazzara. "An architecture for distributed ledger-based M2M auditing for electric autonomous vehicles." *Proceedings of the Workshops of the International Conference on Advanced Information Networking and Applications*, pp. 116–128, March 2019.

[40] Christidis, K., and M. Devetsikiotis. "Blockchains and smart contracts for the internet of things." *IEEE Access* 4 (2016): 2292–2303.

[41] Hussain, F., R. Hussain, S. A. Hassan, and E. Hossain. "Machine learning in IoT Security: Current solutions and future challenges." *IEEE Communications Surveys & Tutorials* 22, no. 3 (April 2020): 1686–1721.

[42] Liang, F., W. G. Hatcher, W. Liao, W. Gao, and W. Yu. "Machine learning for security and the internet of things: The good, the bad, and the ugly." *IEEE Access* 7 (2019): 158126–158147.

[43] Retrieved December 12, 2020, from www.geeksforgeeks.org/create-simple-blockchain-using-python/?ref=rp.

[44] Tahsien, S. M., H. Karimipour, and P. Spachos. "Machine learning based solutions for security of internet of things (IoT): A survey." *Journal of Network and Computer Applications* 161 (2020).

[45] Astarita, V., V. P. Giofre, G. Mirabelli, and V. Solina. "A review of blockchain based system in transportation." *MDPI, Information 2020* (December 2019): 1–24.

[46] Du, X., Y. Gao, C. H. Wu, R. Wang, and D. Bi. "Blockchain-based intelligent transportation: A sustainable GCU application system." *Journal of Advanced Transportation* (2020): 1–14. Wiley, Hindawi.

[47] Roehrs, A., C. A. Costa, R. R. Righi, V. F. D. Silva, J. R. Goldim, and D. C. Schmidt. "Analyzing the performance of a blockchain-based personal health record implementation." *Elsevier, Journal of Bioinformatics* 92 (2019): 103–140.

Index